ANNUAL EDITIONS

The Family 10/11

Thirty-Sixth Edition

EDITOR

Kathleen R. Gilbert
Indiana University

Kathleen Gilbert is an associate professor in the Department of Applied Health Science at Indiana University. She received a BA in Sociology and an MS in Marriage and Family Relations from Northern Illinois University. Her PhD in Family Studies is from Purdue University. Dr. Gilbert's primary areas of interest are loss and grief in a family context, trauma and the family, family process, and family diversity. She has published several books and articles in these areas.

McGraw Hill **Higher Education**

Boston   Burr Ridge, IL   Dubuque, IA   New York   San Francisco   St. Louis
Bangkok   Bogotá   Caracas   Kuala Lumpur   Lisbon   London   Madrid   Mexico City
Milan   Montreal · New Delhi   Santiago   Seoul   Singapore   Sydney   Taipei   Toronto

Higher Education

ANNUAL EDITIONS: THE FAMILY, THIRTY-SIXTH EDITION

1 2 3 4 5 6 7 8 9 0 QWD/QWD 0 9

ISBN 978–0–07–813588–0
MHID 0–07–813588–5
ISSN 1092–4876

Managing Editor: *Larry Loeppke*
Senior Managing Editor: *Faye Schilling*
Developmental Editor: *Dave Welsh*
Editorial Coordinator: *Mary Foust*
Editorial Assistant: *Cindy Hedley*
Production Service Assistant: *Rita Hingtgen*
Permissions Coordinator: *DeAnna Dausener*
Senior Marketing Manager: *Julie Keck*
Marketing Communications Specialist: *Mary Klein*
Marketing Coordinator: *Alice Link*
Project Manager: *Joyce Watters*
Design Specialist: *Tara McDermott*
Senior Production Supervisor: *Laura Fuller*
Cover Graphics: *Kristine Jubeck*

Compositor: Laserwords Private Limited
Cover Image: © Banana Stock/agefotostock/RF (inset); © Corbin/RF, © Dynamic Graphics/Jupiter Images (background)

Library in Congress Cataloging-in-Publication Data
Main entry under title: Annual Editions: The Family. 2009/2010.
 1. The Family—Periodicals. I. Gilbert, Kathleen R., *comp.* II. Title: The Family.
658'.05

www.mhhe.com

Editors/Academic Advisory Board

Members of the Academic Advisory Board are instrumental in the final selection of articles for each edition of ANNUAL EDITIONS. Their review of articles for content, level, and appropriateness provides critical direction to the editors and staff. We think that you will find their careful consideration well reflected in this volume.

ANNUAL EDITIONS: The Family 10/11
26th Edition

EDITOR

Kathleen R. Gilbert
Indiana University

ACADEMIC ADVISORY BOARD MEMBERS

Preface

In publishing ANNUAL EDITIONS we recognize the enormous role played by the magazines, newspapers, and journals of the public press in providing current, first-rate educational information in a broad spectrum of interest areas. Many of these articles are appropriate for students, researchers, and professionals seeking accurate, current material to help bridge the gap between principles and theories and the real world. These articles, however, become more useful for study when those of lasting value are carefully collected, organized, indexed, and reproduced in a low-cost format that provides easy and permanent access when the material is needed. That is the role played by ANNUAL EDITIONS.

The purpose of *Annual Editions: The Family 10/11* is to bring to the reader the latest thoughts and trends in our understanding of the family, to identify current concerns as well as problems and potential solutions, and to present alternative views of family processes. The intent of this anthology is to explore intimate relationships as they are played out within the family and, in doing this, to reflect the family's evolving function and importance.

The articles in this volume are taken from professional journals as well as other professionally oriented publications and popular lay publications aimed at both special populations and a general readership. The selections are carefully reviewed for their currency and accuracy. In some cases, contrasting viewpoints are presented; in others, articles are paired in such a way as to personalize more impersonal scholarly information. In the current edition, a number of new articles have been added to reflect reviewers' comments on the previous edition. As the reader, you will note the tremendous range in tone and focus of these articles, from first-person accounts to reports of scientific discoveries as well as philosophical and theoretical writings. Some are more practical and applications-oriented, while others are more conceptual and research-oriented.

This anthology is organized to address many of the important aspects of family and family relationships. The first unit takes an overview perspective and looks at varied perspectives on the family. The second unit examines the beginning steps of relationship building as individuals go through the process of exploring and establishing connections. In the third unit, means of finding and maintaining a relationship balance, romantic as well as for other intimate relationships, are examined. Unit 4 is concerned with crises and ways in which these can act as challenges and opportunities for families and their members. Finally, the fifth unit takes an affirming tone as it looks at family strengths and ways of empowering families.

Annual Editions: The Family 10/11 is intended to be used as a supplemental text for lower-level, introductory marriage and family or sociology of the family classes, particularly when they tie the content of the readings to essential information on marriages and families, however they are defined. As a supplement, this book can also be used to update or emphasize certain aspects of standard marriage and family textbooks. Because of the provocative nature of many of the essays in this anthology, it works well as a basis for class discussion about various aspects of marriages and family relationships.

This edition of *Annual Editions: The Family* contains websites that can be used to further explore topics addressed in the articles. These sites are cross-referenced by number in the *topic guide*.

I would like to thank everyone involved in the development of this volume. My appreciation goes to those who sent in article rating forms and comments on the previous edition as well as those who suggested articles to consider for inclusion in this edition. To all of the students in my Marriage and Family Interaction class who have contributed critiques of articles, I would like to say thanks.

Anyone interested in providing input for future editions of *Annual Editions: The Family* should complete and return the postage-paid *article rating form* at the end of this book. Your suggestions are much appreciated and contribute to the continuing quality of this anthology.

Kathleen R. Gilbert

Kathleen R. Gilbert
Editor

Contents

UNIT 1
Evolving Perspectives on the Family

UNIT 2
Exploring and Establishing Relationships

The concepts in bold italics are developed in the article. For further expansion, please refer to the Topic Guide.

UNIT 3
Family Relationships

The concepts in bold italics are developed in the article. For further expansion, please refer to the Topic Guide.

The concepts in bold italics are developed in the article. For further expansion, please refer to the Topic Guide.

UNIT 4
Challenges and Opportunities

The concepts in bold italics are developed in the article. For further expansion, please refer to the Topic Guide.

The concepts in bold italics are developed in the article. For further expansion, please refer to the Topic Guide.

UNIT 5
Families, Now and into the Future

The concepts in bold italics are developed in the article. For further expansion, please refer to the Topic Guide.

The concepts in bold italics are developed in the article. For further expansion, please refer to the Topic Guide.

Correlation Guide

The *Annual Editions* series provides students with convenient, inexpensive access to current, carefully selected articles from the public press. **Annual Editions: The Family 10/11** is an easy-to-use reader that presents articles on important topics such as *family composition, love and sex, family stressors,* and many more. For more information on *Annual Editions* and other *McGraw-Hill Contemporary Learning Series* titles, visit www.mhcls.com.

This convenient guide matches the units in **Annual Editions: The Family 10/11** with the corresponding chapters in two of our best-selling McGraw-Hill Family textbooks by Newman and DeGenova/Rice.

Annual Editions: The Family 10/11	Families: A Sociological Perspective by Newman	Intimate Relationships, Marriages, and Families, 8/e by DeGenova/Rice
Unit 1: Evolving Perspectives on the Family	**Chapter 1:** Defining Families **Chapter 2:** Declining Families/Enduring Families **Chapter 4:** Gendered Families **Chapter 5:** Diverse Families/Similar Families **Chapter 6:** Unequal Families **Chapter 8:** Marriage and Cohabitation **Chapter 15:** Change, Stability, and Future Families	**Chapter 1:** Intimate Relationships, Marriages, and Families in the Twenty-First Century **Chapter 2:** Family Backgrounds and How They Influence Us **Chapter 9:** Work, Family Roles, and Material Resources
Unit 2: Exploring and Establishing Relationships	**Chapter 7:** Love, Sexuality, and Relationship Formation **Chapter 8:** Marriage and Cohabitation **Chapter 14:** Divorce and Remarriage	**Chapter 1:** Intimate Relationships, Marriages, and Families in the Twenty-First Century **Chapter 5:** Attraction and Dating **Chapter 6:** Love and Mate Selection **Chapter 7:** Qualities of a Successful Marriage
Unit 3: Family Relationships	**Chapter 7:** Love, Sexuality, and Relationship Formation **Chapter 8:** Marriage and Cohabitation **Chapter 9:** Work and Family	**Chapter 1:** Intimate Relationships, Marriages, and Families in the Twenty-First Century **Chapter 2:** Family Backgrounds and How They Influence Us **Chapter 9:** Work, Family Roles, and Material Resources **Chapter 10:** Power, Decision Making, and Communication **Chapter 13:** Parent-Child Relationships **Chapter 14:** Parents and Extended Family Relationships
Unit 4: Challenges and Opportunities	**Chapter 2:** Declining Families/Enduring Families **Chapter 6:** Unequal Families **Chapter 9:** Work and Family **Chapter 13:** Intimate Violence **Chapter 14:** Divorce and Remarriage	**Chapter 10:** Power, Decision Making, and Communication **Chapter 13:** Parent-Child Relationships **Chapter 14:** Parents and Extended Family Relationships **Chapter 15:** Conflict, Family Crises, and Crisis Management **Chapter 16:** The Family and Divorce **Chapter 17:** Coming Together: Remarriage and Stepparenting
Unit 5: Families, Now and into the Future	**Chapter 1:** Defining Families **Chapter 2:** Declining Families/Enduring Families **Chapter 15:** Change, Stability, and Future Families	**Chapter 1:** Intimate Relationships, Marriages, and Families in the Twenty-First Century **Chapter 2:** Family Backgrounds and How They Influence Us

Topic Guide

This topic guide suggests how the selections in this book relate to the subjects covered in your course. You may want to use the topics listed on these pages to search the Web more easily.

On the following pages a number of websites have been gathered specifically for this book. They are arranged to reflect the units of this Annual Editions reader. You can link to these sites by going to *http://www.mhcls.com.*

All the articles that relate to each topic are listed below the bold-faced term.

Abuse
19. Prickly Père
24. Recognizing Domestic Partner Abuse
25. Domestic Abuse Myths

Adoption
12. Adopting a New American Family

Affiliative families
22. Aunties and Uncles

Aging
23. Roles of American Indian Grandparents in Times of Cultural Crisis
35. Navigating Practical Dilemmas in Terminal Care

Bereavement
36. Bereavement after Caregiving
37. Love, Loss—and Love

Biology
5. This Thing Called Love
9. Fats, Carbs and the Science of Conception
10. Starting the Good Life in the Womb
11. Not Always 'the Happiest Time'
26. Children of Alcoholics

Caregiving
33. Partners Face Cancer Together
34. Dealing *Day-to-Day* with Diabetes
35. Navigating Practical Dilemmas in Terminal Care
36. Bereavement after Caregiving

Childcare
3. Children as a Public Good

Children
2. Interracial Families
3. Children as a Public Good
4. Family Partnerships
12. Adopting a New American Family
18. Children of Lesbian and Gay Parents
20. The Forgotten Siblingss
21. Being a Sibling
26. Children of Alcoholics
27. Impact of Family Recovery and Pre-Teens and Adolescents
39. Children of the Wars
45. Sustaining Resilient Families for Children in Primary Grades

Communication
6. Pillow Talk
8. On-Again, Off-Again
29. Love but Don't Touch
33. Partners Face Cancer Together
43. Get a Closer Look
44. The Joy of Rituals
47. Sparking Interest in Nature—Family Style

Dating
8. On-Again, Off-Again
13. Free as a Bird and Loving It

Divorce
1. Marriage and Family in the Scandinavian Experience
40. A Divided House
41. Civil Wars
42. Stepfamily Success Depends on Ingredients

Emotions
6. Pillow Talk
17. Do We Need a Law to Prohibit Spanking?
36. Bereavement after Caregiving
44. The Joy of Rituals

Family and marriage
1. Marriage and Family in the Scandinavian Experience
2. Interracial Families
3. Children as a Public Good
14. Gay Marriage Lite
15. Two Mommies and a Daddy
22. Aunties and Uncles
42. Stepfamily Success Depends on Ingredients

Family interaction
17. Do We Need a Law to Prohibit Spanking?
19. Prickly Père
21. Being a Sibling
34. Dealing *Day-to-Day* with Diabetes
40. A Divided House
42. Stepfamily Success Depends on Ingredients
43. Get a Closer Look
44. The Joy of Rituals
45. Sustaining Resilient Families for Children in Primary Grades
47. Sparking Interest in Nature—Family Style

Finances, family
1. Marriage and Family in the Scandinavian Experience
31. The Opt-Out Myth
32. Making Time for Family Time
42. Stepfamily Success Depends on Ingredients
46. The Consumer Crunch

Gay marriage
1. Marriage and Family in the Scandinavian Experience
14. Gay Marriage Lite
18. Children of Lesbian and Gay Parents

Gender roles
1. Marriage and Family in the Scandinavian Experience
33. Partners Face Cancer Together

Government roles
1. Marriage and Family in the Scandinavian Experience
3. Children as a Public Good
14. Gay Marriage Lite
15. Two Mommies and a Daddy
38. Stressors Afflicting Families during Military Deployment
47. Sparking Interest in Nature—Family Style

Internet References

The following Internet sites have been selected to support the articles found in this reader. These sites were available at the time of publication. However, because websites often change their structure and content, the information listed may no longer be available. We invite you to visit *http://www.mhcls.com* for easy access to these sites.

Annual Editions: The Family 10/11

General Sources

AARP (American Association of Retired Persons)
http://www.aarp.org

This major advocacy group for older people includes among its many resources suggested readings and Internet links to organizations that deal with social issues that may affect people and their families as they age.

Encyclopedia Britannica
http://www.britannica.com

This huge "Britannica Internet Guide" leads to a cornucopia of informational sites and reference sources on such topics as family structure, the family cycle, forms of family organization, and other social issues.

Planned Parenthood
http://www.plannedparenthood.org

Visit this well-known organization's home page for links to information on the various kinds of contraceptives (including outercourse and abstinence) and to discussions of other topics related to sexual and reproductive health.

Social Science Information Gateway
http://sosig.esrc.bris.ac.uk/

This is an online catalog of Internet resources relevant to social science education and research. Sites are selected and described by a librarian or subject specialist.

Sympatico: HealthyWay: Health Links
http://www1.sympatico.ca/Contents/health/

This Canadian site, which is meant for consumers, will lead you to many links that are related to sexual orientation. *Sympatico* also addresses aspects of human sexuality as well as reproductive health over the life span.

UNIT 1: Evolving Perspectives on the Family

American Studies Web
http://www1.georgetown.edu/departments/american_studies/

This site provides links to a wealth of resources on the Internet related to American studies, from gender to race and ethnicity to demography and population studies.

Anthropology Resources Page
http://www.usd.edu/anth/

Many cultural topics can be accessed from this site from the University of South Dakota. Click on the links to find comparisons of values and lifestyles among the world's peoples.

UNIT 2: Exploring and Establishing Relationships

Bonobo Sex and Society
http://songweaver.com/info/bonobos.html

This site, accessed through Carnegie Mellon University, contains an article explaining how a primate's behavior challenges

traditional assumptions about male supremacy in human evolution. This interesting site is guaranteed to generate much spirited debate.

Go Ask Alice!
http://www.goaskalice.columbia.edu/index.html

This interactive site of the Columbia University Health Services provides discussion and insight into a number of personal issues of interest to college-age people and those younger and older.

The Kinsey Institute for Research in Sex, Gender, and Reproduction
http://www.indiana.edu/~kinsey/

The purpose of this Kinsey Institute website is to support interdisciplinary research in the study of human sexuality.

Mysteries of Odor in Human Sexuality
http://www.pheromones.com

This is a commercial site with the goal of selling a book by James Kohl. Look here to find topics of interest to nonscientists about pheromones. Check out the diagram of "Mammalian Olfactory-Genetic-Neuronal-Hormonal-Behavioral Reciprocity and Human Sexuality" for a sense of the myriad biological influences that play a part in sexual behavior.

The Society for the Scientific Study of Sexuality
http://www.sexscience.org

The Society for the Scientific Study of Sexuality is an international organization dedicated to the advancement of knowledge about sexuality.

UNIT 3: Family Relationships

Child Welfare League of America
http://www.cwla.org

The CWLA is the largest U.S. organization devoted entirely to the well-being of vulnerable children and their families. This site provides links to information about such issues as teaching morality and values.

Coalition for Marriage, Family, and Couples Education
http://www.smartmarriages.com

CMFCE is dedicated to bringing information about and directories of skill-based marriage education courses to the public. It hopes to lower the rate of family breakdown through couple-empowering preventive education.

The National Academy for Child Development
http://www.nacd.org

The NACD, dedicated to helping children and adults reach their full potential, presents links to various programs, research, and resources into a variety of family topics.

National Council on Family Relations
http://www.ncfr.com

This NCFR home page leads to valuable links to articles, research, and other resources on issues in family relations, such as stepfamilies, couples, and children of divorce.

Internet References

Positive Parenting
http://www.positiveparenting.com

Positive Parenting is an organization dedicated to providing resources and information to make parenting rewarding, effective, and fun.

SocioSite
http://www.pscw.uva.nl/sociosite/TOPICS/Women.html

Open this site to gain insights into a number of issues that affect family relationships. It provides wide-ranging issues of women and men, of family and children, and more.

UNIT 4: Challenges and Opportunities

Alzheimer's Association
http://www.alz.org

The Alzheimer's Association, dedicated to the prevention, cure, and treatment of Alzheimer's and related disorders, provides support to afflicted patients and their families.

Caregiver's Handbook
http://www.acsu.buffalo.edu/~drstall/hndbk0.html

This site is an online handbook for caregivers. Topics include medical aspects and liabilities of caregiving.

National Crime Prevention Council
http://www.ncpc.org

NCPC's mission is to enable people to create safer and more caring communities by addressing the causes of crime and violence and reducing the opportunities for crime to occur.

Widow Net
http://www.widownet.org

Widow Net is an information and self-help resource for and by widows and widowers. The information is helpful to people of all ages, religious backgrounds, and sexual orientation who have experienced a loss.

UNIT 5: Families, Now and into the Future

National Institute on Aging
http://www.nih.gov/nia/

The NIA presents this home page that will take you to a variety of resources on health and lifestyle issues that are of interest to people as they grow older.

UNIT 1

Evolving Perspectives on the Family

Unit Selections

1. **Marriage and Family in the Scandinavian Experience,** David Popenoe
2. **Interracial Families,** Carol Mithers
3. **Children as a Public Good,** Myra H. Strober
4. **Family Partnerships,** JoBeth Allen

Key Points to Consider

- How do marriages and families compare in Sweden and the United States? Do you see trends they share in common?

- What are your views on the changing nature of the American family? What are your thoughts on interracial families?

- What are your expectations for the family as an institution? How do personally held views of family influence policy? What might be the effect of this?

- How can schools and families collaborate to support student learning?

Student Website
www.mhcls.com

Internet References

American Studies Web
   http://www1.georgetown.edu/departments/american_studies/
Anthropology Resources Page
   http://www.usd.edu/anth/

Digital Vision

Our image of what family is and what it should be is a powerful combination of personal experience, family forms we encounter or observe, and attitudes we hold. Once formed, this image informs decision making and interpersonal interaction throughout our lives and has far-reaching effects: On an intimate level, it influences individual and family development as well as relationships both inside and outside the family; on a broader level, it affects legislation as well as social policy and programming.

In many ways, this image can be positive. It can act to clarify our thinking and facilitate interaction with like-minded individuals. It can also be negative, because it can narrow our thinking and limit our ability to see that other ways of carrying out the functions of family have value. Their very differentness can make them seem "bad." In this case, interaction with others can be impeded because of contrasting views.

This unit is intended to meet several goals with regard to perspectives on the family: (1) to sensitize the reader to sources of beliefs about the "shoulds" of the family—what the family should be and the ways in which family roles should be carried out, (2) to show how different views of the family can influence attitudes toward community responsibility and family policy, and (3) to show how views that dominate one's culture can influence awareness of ways of structuring family life.

In the first reading, "Marriage and Family in the Scandinavian Experience," David Popenoe explores the differences and

© Digital Vision/PunchStock RF

similarities in marriage and family experiences in the United States and Sweden. These comparisons provide information that may surprise the reader. The nature of "Interracial Families" and children of these families is explored in the next reading. The level of responsibility a society should take for the care and well-being of children is explored in the next reading, "Children as a Public Good." Collaboration between families and the schools is the focus of the final reading in this unit, "Family Partnerships."

Marriage and Family in the Scandinavian Experience

DAVID POPENOE

Many Americans have long had a ready answer to America's family problems: We should become more like Scandinavia. Whether the issues are work-family, teen sex, child poverty, or marital break-up, a range of Scandinavian family and welfare policies is commonly put forth with the assertion that, if only these could be instituted in America, family life in our nation would be improved significantly. But what can we in the United States really learn from Scandinavia? The Scandinavian nations are so small and demographically homogeneous that the idea of simply transferring their social policies to this country must be viewed as problematic. Sweden, for example, the largest Scandinavian nation and the one featured in this essay, has only 9 million people compared to our population of nearly 300 million. And how well have these policies actually worked in Scandinavia? As this essay will make clear, some of the Scandinavian family policies have, indeed, been quite successful on their own home ground. Yet aside from the potential non-transferability of these policies, by focusing so much attention on them we may be overlooking some even more important aspects of the Scandinavian family experience.

Sweden and the United States

It is now well known that there has been a weakening of marriage and the nuclear family in advanced, industrialized societies, especially since the 1960s. What is not well known is the surprising fact that the two nations that lead in this weakening are Sweden and the United States—two nations that stand at almost opposite extremes in terms of their socioeconomic systems. Let us look at one telling statistical measure. Defining the nuclear family as a mother and father living together with their own biological children, a good measure of nuclear familism in a society is the percentage of children under the age of 18 who live with both biological parents. This percentage for the United States is 63, the lowest among Western industrialized nations. The second from lowest is Sweden, at 73!

How is this possible? At the one socioeconomic extreme, Sweden has the strongest public sector, the highest taxes, and is the most secular. At the other, the United States has the weakest public sector, the lowest taxes, and is the most religious. Could these fundamental factors be mostly irrelevant to family change? And if so, what key factors are involved? As we shall see, the answer to this intellectual puzzle is to be found largely in the realm of a postmodern trend shared by both nations. But first we need to consider other family differences between the two nations. Two key differences stand out: in the United States more people marry, but they also divorce in large numbers; in Sweden, fewer people marry, but the Swedish divorce rate is a little lower than in the United States.

Here is the recent statistical record, beginning with Sweden. The Swedish marriage rate by the late 1990s was *one of the lowest in the world;* indeed, one of the lowest marriage rates ever recorded and considerably lower than the rates of other Western European nations. (Number of marriages per 1000 unmarried women in 2002—Sweden: 17.5; U.S.: 43.4. Unless otherwise noted, all statistics in this essay were gathered or computed by the National Marriage Project from official statistical sources in each nation.) If this rate holds, only about 60 percent of Swedish women today will "ever marry," compared to over 85 percent in the United States. This is a quite recent development. Not so long ago the two nations were quite similar: For the generation marrying in the 1950s, the figure for Sweden was 91 percent and for the United States 95 percent.

Sweden's low marriage rate does not mean that Swedes are living alone; rather, they are living together outside of marriage—another area in which Sweden has been in the vanguard. In fact, Sweden leads the Western nations in the degree to which nonmarital cohabitation has replaced marriage. The United States, on the other hand, has a lower rate of nonmarital cohabitation than all but the Catholic nations of southern Europe. About 28 percent of all couples in Sweden are cohabiting, versus 8 percent of all American couples. In Sweden, virtually all couples live together before marriage, compared to around two-thirds of couples currently in America. Many couples in Sweden don't marry even when they have children. In a recent opinion poll, Swedish young adults were asked whether it was OK to cohabit even after having children; 89 percent of women and 86 percent of men answered "yes."

Why is the Swedish marriage rate so low relative to other nations? In brief, because religion there is weak, a left-wing political ideology has long been dominant, and almost all governmental incentives for marriage have been removed. First, the religious pressure for marriage in Sweden is all but gone (although of the marriages that do occur, many are for vague religious reasons). Any religious or cultural stigma in Sweden against cohabitation is no longer in evidence; it is regarded as irrelevant to question whether a couple is married or just living together. Second, the political left wing throughout Europe has generally been antagonistic to strong families, based on a combination of feminist concerns about patriarchy and oppression, an antipathy toward a bourgeois social institution with traditional ties to nobility and privilege, and the belief that families have been an impediment to full equality. Finally, unlike in the United States, all government benefits in Sweden are given to individuals irrespective of their intimate relationships or family form. There is no such thing, for example, as spousal benefits in health care. There is also no joint-income taxation for married couples; all income taxation is individual.

Turning to the United States, if Sweden stands out for having the lowest marriage rate, the United States is notable for having the world's highest divorce rate. Given the divorce rates of recent years, the risk of a marriage ending in divorce in the United States is close to 50 percent, compared to a little over 40 percent in Sweden. Why is the American divorce rate so high relative to other nations? Mainly because of our relatively high ethnic, racial and religious diversity, inequality of incomes with a large underclass, and extensive residential mobility, each of which is associated with high divorce rates. Revealingly, if one looks at the divorce rate of the relatively homogeneous and Scandinavian-settled state of Minnesota, it is only slightly higher than that of Sweden. (Number of divorces per 1000 married women in 2002—Sweden: 13.7; Minnesota: 14.7; United States: 18.4.)

Another big divorce risk factor in America is marrying at a young age; the average U.S. ages of first marriage today are 25 for women and 27 for men, versus 31 and 33 in Sweden. As a more consumer-oriented and economically dynamic society, in addition, there is probably something about this nation that promotes a more throw-away attitude toward life. And let us not overlook the dominant influence of Hollywood and pop culture in general, with their emphasis on feel good and forget the consequences.

Of course, if people don't marry, they can't divorce. And that is one reason why, by certain measures, Sweden has a lower divorce rate. But if couples just cohabit they certainly can break up, and that is what Swedish nonmarital couples do in large numbers. It is estimated that the risk of breakup for cohabiting couples in Sweden, even those with children, is several times higher than for married couples. By one indication, in the year 2000 there were two-and-one-half separations or divorces per 100 children among married parents, almost twice that number among unmarried cohabiting parents living with their own biological children, and three times that number among cohabiting couples living with children from a previous relationship. (A recent study found that 50 percent of children born to a cohabiting couple in the United States see their parents' union end by age five, compared to only 15 percent of children born to a married couple. [Wendy D. Manning, Pamela J. Smock, and Debamm Majumdar, "The Relative Stability of Cohabiting and Marital Unions for Children," *Population Research and Policy Review* 23 (2004): 135–159].)

Already one of the highest in Western Europe, the Swedish divorce rate has been growing in recent years, while the U.S. rate has been declining. If we consider this convergence of divorce rates, and count both cohabiting couples and married couples, *the total family breakup rate in the two nations today is actually quite similar.*

So why, in view of the similarity of overall family breakup rates, are more Swedish than American children living with their biological parents? This is especially surprising in view of the fact that the Swedish nonmarital birth percentage is much higher than that of the United States (56 percent in Sweden vs. 35 percent in the U.S.). The main reason is that far more nonmarital births in Sweden, about 90 percent, are actually to biological parents who are living together but have not married, compared to just 40 percent in the United States. The great majority of nonmarital births in the U.S., 60 percent, are to truly single, non-cohabiting mothers. This discrepancy reflects the far higher rate of births in the United States to teenagers, the stage of life at which the father is least likely to remain involved with the mother and child. (Births per 1000 girls ages 15–19 in 2002—United States: 43; Sweden: 5.) The relatively high U.S. teen birthrate, in turn, is commonly accounted for by more teen sexual activity combined with less use of contraceptives. There is also a discrepancy between the two countries in that the United States has about twice Sweden's rate of "unwanted" children.

Having sketched out these noteworthy differences in family structure between the United States and Sweden, together with some causal explanations for the differences, what are some reasonable conclusions that can be drawn from the Scandinavian family experience?

The Decline of Marriage

If a society deinstitutionalizes marriage, as Sweden has done through its tax and benefit policies and the secularization of its culture, marriage will weaken. In addition, because most adults still like to live as couples, human pair-bonding doesn't disappear when this happens. Rather, the institution of marriage is replaced by nonmarital cohabitation—marriage lite. Then, if one institutionalizes nonmarital cohabitation in the laws and government policies, as Sweden has also done, making it the virtual equivalent of marriage, marriage will decline still further.

In the modern world, people are reluctant to make strong commitments if they don't have to; it's easier to hang loose. The problem is that society ends up with adult intimate relationships that are much more fragile. It is, indeed, surprising that Sweden has such a high level of couple breakup, because it is the kind of society—stable, homogeneous, and egalitarian—where one would expect such breakups to be minimal. Yet the high breakup level is testimony to the fragility of modern marriage in which most of the institutional bonds have been stripped away—economic dependence, legal definitions, religious sentiments, and family pressures—leaving marriage and other pair-bonds held together solely by the thin and unstable reed of affection.

The losers in this social trend, of course, are the children. They are highly dependent for their development and success in life on the family in which they are born and raised, and a convincing mass of scientific evidence now exists pointing to the fact that not growing up in an intact nuclear family is one of the most deleterious events that can befall a child. In Sweden, just as in the United States, children from non-intact families—compared to those from intact families—have two to three times the number of serious problems in life. We can only speculate about the extent of psychological damage that future generations will suffer owing to today's family trends. That the very low marriage rate and high level of parental breakup are such non-issues in Sweden, something which few Swedes ever talk about, should be, in my opinion, a cause there for national soul searching.

All that said, however, there are other important conclusions one can draw from the Scandinavian family experience. What most Americans don't realize is that, in a strict comparison, Scandinavia is probably preferable to the United States today as a place to raise young children. In other writings I have suggested that the ideal family environment for raising young children has the following traits: an enduring two-biological parent family that engages regularly in activities together, has developed its own routines, traditions and stories, and provides a great deal of contact time between adults and children. Surrounded by a community that is child friendly and supportive of parents, the family is able to develop a vibrant family subculture that provides a rich legacy of meaning and values for children throughout their lives. Scandinavians certainly fall short on the enduring two-biological-parent part of this ideal (yet even there they are currently ahead of the United States), but on the key ingredients of structured and consistent contact time between parents and their children in a family-friendly environment, they are well ahead of us.

In America today, the achievement of this ideal family environment requires what many parents are coming to consider a Herculean countercultural effort, one that involves trying to work fewer hours and adopting the mantra of "voluntary simplicity" for those who can afford it; turning off the TV set and avoiding popular culture; seeking employment in firms that have family-friendly policies such as flexible working hours; and residing in areas that are better designed for children and where the cost of living is lower. Families in Scandinavia need not be so countercultural to achieve these goals because the traits of the ideal childrearing environment are to a larger degree already built into their societies.

The Scandinavian societies tend to be "soft" or low-key, with much more leisure time and not so much frantic consumerism and economic striving as in the United States. Perhaps one could even say that they practice "involuntary simplicity." The average American would probably find life in Scandinavia rather uncomfortable due to high taxes, strict government regulation, limited consumer choice, smaller dwelling units, social conformity, and a soft work ethic, not to mention possible boredom. There are also growing concerns about the quality of education in Scandinavia. Moreover, the Scandinavian system may ultimately prove to be so counterproductive for economic growth that it becomes unsustainable. At any one time more than 20 percent of working-age Swedes are either on sick leave, unemployed, or have taken early retirement, and the nation has recently sunk to one of the lowest per capita income levels in Western Europe! (Reported in Sweden's leading newspaper, *Dagen's Nyheter,* on August 23, 2004.) But in the meantime, and compared to other modern nations, the system seems particularly good for the rearing of young children.

The Scandinavian childrearing advantage is probably as much cultural as governmental, as much due to the way Scandinavians think about children as to specific welfare state policies (although the two are, of course, interrelated.) Scandinavian culture has always been more child centered than the more individualistic Anglo societies. The emphasis in Scandinavian culture on nature and the outdoor environment, conflict-aversion, and even social conformity happens to be especially child friendly. Children benefit from highly structured, stable, and low-conflict settings. There are in Scandinavia many statues of children and mothers in public parks (in place of war heroes!), and planned housing environments are heavily oriented to pedestrian access and children's play. Scandinavian children even have their own Ombudsmen who represent them officially in the government and monitor children's rights and interests. Interestingly, Minnesota—the most Scandinavian-settled U.S. state—was recently ranked the number one state in the nation for child well-being by the Kids Count Data Book. (Annie E. Casey Foundation, 2004, Baltimore, MD)

Scandinavian Family Policies

The Scandinavian concern for children, sometimes even smacking of "traditional family values," is expressed in some areas that should surprise those Americans who think only of "decadent welfare states." For example, all Swedish married couples with children aged 16 and younger, should they want a divorce, have a six-month waiting period before a divorce becomes final. Most American states make no distinction in their divorce laws between couples with children and those without. In vitro fertilization in Sweden can be performed only if the woman is married or cohabiting in a relationship resembling marriage, and completely anonymous sperm donations are not allowed, whereas the practice of "assisted reproduction" in America goes virtually unregulated. And no Swedish abortion can take place after the 18th week of pregnancy, except under special circumstances and only with permission from the National Board of Health. The laws permitting abortion are much more liberal in the United States. Some of these positions are made possible, of course, by the fact that the Scandinavian societies are more homogeneous, unified, and less rights-oriented than the United States.

Just as in the United States at least up until welfare reform, welfare policies in Scandinavia have not been drawn up with an eye toward encouraging marriage and limiting family breakup, a very serious problem as noted above. There are relatively few economic disincentives to becoming a single parent in Sweden, in fact probably fewer than in any other society in the world. Nevertheless, many Scandinavian welfare-state policies have brought significant benefits to children and to childrearing families. Scandinavian family leave policies, especially, seem highly desirable for young children. Almost all mothers in Sweden, for example, and far more than in the United States, are at home with their infants up until age one—which is the critical year for mother-child connection. They have one year off from their jobs at 80 percent or more of their salary (and an additional six months at reduced salary), with a guarantee of returning to their old jobs or an equivalent when they reenter the labor force. Recently, two months leave has been set aside solely for fathers to take; if they don't take it, the benefit is lost. Because of these family-leave policies very few Swedish infants under the age of one are in day care or other out-of-home child care arrangement, a quite different situation from the United States. In addition, to help defray the expenses of childrearing, all Swedish parents receive a non-means-tested child allowance and there is also a means-tested housing allowance.

Beyond these benefits, Scandinavian mothers and fathers have far more flex-time from their work to be home with children during the growing-up years, and most women with young children work just part time. There are certainly fewer full-time, non-working, stay-at-home mothers in Sweden than in the United States, in fact almost none because it is economically prohibitive. But in actual parenting time—although good comparative data are unavailable—Sweden may well be in the lead. The larger number of stay-at-home moms in the United States is off-set by the larger number of full-time working mothers, many of whom return to work during their child's first year. It is of interest to note that many fewer Swedish women have top positions in the private sector than is the case in the United States, and this has long been a bone of contention for American feminists when they look at Sweden. By one recent analysis, only 1.5 percent of senior management positions are filled by women in Sweden, compared to 11 percent in the United States. The amount of time that Swedish mothers devote to child care clearly has affected their ability to rise in the private sector hierarchy of jobs, although this is off-set in some degree by their much stronger status in the public sector where a high percentage of the jobs are located.

As a result of welfare state policies child poverty in Sweden is virtually nonexistent (for the 1990s, 1 percent compared to 15 percent in the United States) and all children are covered by health insurance. These and related factors are doubtless of importance in placing Sweden at the top of the list of the best places in the world to live, surpassed only by Norway according to the Human Development Index prepared by the United Nations Development Program (2004), and based on income, life expectancy and education. The United States ranks well down the list, in eighth place, no doubt due in part to the fact that we have a different population mix than other nations.

Again, the two societies are such polar opposites, at least among Western nations, as we have indicated, that it is a mistake to think that what works in Sweden could necessarily be transplanted to the United States. Up to now, at least, the Scandinavian nations have had that strong sense of "brotherhood" or "sisterhood" that is required for a strong welfare state. The common sentiment has been that the high taxes are going for a good cause, "my fellow Swede." Indeed, the lack of outcry against high taxation in Scandinavia comes as a shock to most visiting Americans. To suggest that this communal spirit and attitude toward government and taxation could ever exist in the United States, with all its diversity and individualism, is to enter the realm of utopian thinking. Thus, it is unclear how many of these family policies could be implemented in the United States, and what their actual effect would be if they were.

This leaves us with a final conclusion from the Scandinavian family experience, a more general one. The fact that family breakdown has occurred so prevalently in both the United States and Scandinavia, two almost opposite socioeconomic systems, suggests that the root cause lies beyond politics and economics and even national culture in an overarching trend of modernity that affects all advanced, industrial societies. Basic to this trend is the growth of a modern form of individualism, the single-minded pursuit of personal autonomy and self-interest, which takes place at the expense of established social institutions such as marriage. It shows up in low marriage and high cohabitation rates in the Scandinavian societies, even though they are relatively communitarian. And it is expressed in high divorce and high solo parenting rates in the United States, despite our nation's relatively religious character.

One paramount family goal for modern societies today, put forward by many experts, is to create the conditions whereby an increasing number of children are able to grow up with their own two married parents. If this is a worthy goal, both Scandinavia and the United States have failed badly, and millions of children have been hurt. If we are to take seriously the record of recent history in these nations, the market economy on its own, no matter how strong, is unlikely to be of much help in achieving this goal. The wealthier we become, the weaker the family. But neither helpful, apparently, are the many governmental policies of the welfare state. They may help to soften the impact of family breakup, but the state appears relatively powerless to contain family decline and often even contributes to it. What we must look for, are ways to curtail the growth of modern individualism. While in Scandinavia the main thrust of such efforts probably should focus on resisting the anti-marriage influences of political ideologies and social policies, in the United States the issue is to find better ways to insulate marriage and the family from the pernicious effects of a self-interested market economy that is tethered increasingly to a coarsening popular culture.

DAVID POPENOE is co-director of the National Marriage Project at Rutgers, The State University of New Jersey. He is author of *War Over the Family, Disturbing the Nest,* and *Private Pleasure, Public Plight* all available from Transaction.

From *Society,* 43(4), May/June 2006, pp. 68–72. Copyright © 2006 by Springer Science and Business Media. Reprinted by permission.

Interracial Families

Marriages between people of different races have mushroomed in the last three decades, and the children of these unions have a whole new point of view.

CAROL MITHERS

The growth of mixed-race marriage: According to the most recent Census figures, the percentage of couples who are interracial increased sevenfold from 1970 to 2000, and the number of children in interracial families quadrupled to 3.4 million. The most prevalent pairing is white men and Asian women. Among people under 30, interracial couples are at least 30 percent more common.

Changing attitudes: More than 300 years ago, Maryland was the first state to outlaw interracial marriage. In 1967 the Supreme Court ruled such laws unconstitutional but many states kept their statutes. Alabama didn't remove its law until 2000. Yet a 2003 poll showed that 86 percent of blacks, 79 percent of Latinos and 66 percent of whites would accept a child marrying someone of a different race.

Tracking the trend: In 2000 Americans could check more than one box for ethnicity and race, and about 7 million did. Estimates put the multiracial population even higher.

Representative family: Sandra and Steven Stites, of Kansas City, Missouri. Married 19 years, both are 46-year-old doctors with three children.

For the Stites children, an interracial life "is all they've ever known," says Sandra, and they are perfectly comfortable with it. Ailea says her friends have affectionately labeled her "halfrican." Her younger sister, Sierra, has dubbed herself a "wack," short for white-black.

Sandra and Steven became friends in 1982 when they were lab partners in an anatomy class at the University of Missouri-Columbia. "We met over a cadaver," Steven jokes. They didn't expect to marry. Steven had grown up in virtually all-white Independence, Missouri. Sandra's Kansas City neighborhood was black but she went to a mostly white private school and briefly dated a white boy. Still, after her first date with Steven, she told a friend, "He's perfect, except he's white."

Once you learn that people aren't as different as you think they are, the fear goes away.

The couple dated for four years. "It was important to me that we both loved the outdoors and musical theater," Steven says. "We had common ground, even if it didn't include race."

Sandra had concerns, however. "If we had kids, would they be accepted?" she remembers thinking at the time. "Would we be accepted?" They kept their relationship secret for two months. Once they went public, Sandra's fears were realized. Some classmates avoided them. Steven's father said that marrying Sandra would limit his career. Sandra's parents worried "because Steven was 'different.' "

By the time Sandra and Steven married, their parents had come around. "My father got to know Sandra," says Steven. "Most racism is based on a fear of difference. Once you learn that people aren't as different as you think, the fear goes away."

Sandra's family, too, discovered that Steven was less "different" than they'd thought. "His mother was from the South," says Sandra. "My grandfather would prepare food like collard greens and say, 'That boy won't eat this!' But this was food Steven knew."

When Ailea was born, in 1990, Steven and Sandra had already agreed they wanted their children to recognize their dual heritage. The children have contact with white culture in their neighborhood and school, and they are close to Sandra's parents, who live near the Stiteses' home, as well as her extended family in Dallas. "We want the kids to understand the struggles," says Sandra.

Not everyone is on board, though. Steven has an uncle who refuses to let the couple in his house. And while nobody looks twice at the Stites family in Kansas City, in the suburban malls, "we get what we call 'the triangle look,' " says Sandra. "Eyes go to Steven, then me, then the kids. And salespeople don't see us as a couple. Sometimes we pretend we're not together and then say, 'Your name is on my checkbook! How did that happen?' "

"What really rankles are the thoughtless remarks from strangers who see Sandra with her children. "They'll ask, 'Are you the nanny?' " Sandra says.

The Stiteses send their kids to a private school, though they picked one that is 17 percent nonwhite. When the children classified themselves on school forms, Ailea wrote "multiracial," Sierra picked "other," and James chose both African-American and white.

"Their generation doesn't see color the way it used to be seen," says Sandra. "When Ailea describes a guy she likes, she mentions the color of his eyes and skin and hair. She describes his looks, but it never occurs to her to mention his race at all."

Children as a Public Good

MYRA H. STROBER

Whose responsibility are children? In twenty-first-century America, the answer too often is "their parents." Although politicians and pundits frequently make pious pronouncements calling children "our best hope," "our future," and "our nation's most valuable resource," mouthing such sentiments is a far cry from taking collective responsibility. In the current election season, one listens in vain for concrete proposals from candidates to improve the lives of children. The United States lags behind all other western democracies in providing for their needs. We have to revise the national mindset, visible on the left as well as the right, that puts sole responsibility for children in the hands of individual families, many of whom are ill-equipped to give them the care and opportunities necessary to provide for the citizens, workers, and human beings we wish to develop. Further, instead of viewing parents with professional careers as irresponsible workaholics, we should appreciate the incredibly hard work that parents do when they are simultaneously holding jobs and raising children.

Certainly, parents have primary responsibility for meeting the needs of their children; the argument here is that meeting children's needs should be a collective responsibility as well. Although parents reap the rewards of well-reared children (emotional rather than economic rewards in this day and age), children whose needs have been met confer benefits as well on society as a whole. We need to make a reality of the rhetoric that sees children as our most valuable asset.

As an economist, I argue that children must be considered a public good whose welfare and education need to be addressed collectively. In other words, it really does take a village to raise a child. A public good is one whose provision confers externalities—benefits beyond those accruing to the direct beneficiaries. Public schooling confers such externalities; the public as well as individual students and parents benefit when its citizens are literate and numerate, and when they understand the benefits of democracy. This is how the state justifies taxing the public to provide for children's schooling.

The notion that children are a private good leads to the conclusion that their economic and emotional care is the sole responsibility of their parents. This philosophy was most clearly articulated by President Richard Nixon, when he vetoed the Child Development Act of 1971: "For the Federal Government to plunge headlong financially into supporting child development would commit the vast moral authority of the National Government to the side of communal approaches to child rearing over against [sic] the family-centered approach." There was no sense that parents and the federal government might engage in a partnership for child care, no sense that there were public benefits to be gained from federal involvement in improving the child care system. Or, consider the case of the city of Fremont, California, which defeated a 1989 measure asking taxpayers to approve a $12 per year property tax levied on all residential dwelling units to pay for childcare services. An exit poll found that 88 percent of the three-fourths of the electorate that had voted against the measure agreed with the statement, "Child care should be paid for by parents, not by the whole community."

If, instead, we thought of children as public goods, we would behave far differently toward their economic and emotional needs. And we would seek collective solutions for their care. I want to spell out several critical areas in which children's needs are not being met and argue for public investment to remedy that situation. This is not a new argument on the left, but it is one rarely articulated these days.

Freedom from Poverty

What are we doing about child poverty? What are we doing about the fact (published by our own government) that 12.9 million children under the age of eighteen—17.6 percent of all children—live in poverty, that they go hungry, have inadequate clothing and shelter, and are ill-equipped for the education they need? Among white children, 14.3 percent live in poverty, but among black children, an astounding 34.1 percent are poor. Although children under eighteen represent about one-quarter of the total population, they are more than one-third of those in poverty. Similarly, in 2000, families with children under eighteen accounted for 36 percent of Americans who were homeless.

Not only does poverty affect children's economic well-being, it is also associated with poorer performance in school, in part because children in poor neighborhoods go to schools with lower per-pupil expenditures. Data from the National Assessment of Educational Progress (NAEP) indicate that in tests of children in the fourth and eighth grades, those who live in poverty (as measured by being eligible for the National School

Lunch Program) score lower in several subjects as compared to better-off children. NAEP data for twelfth-grade students show that Title I Schools (those with the highest levels of poverty) have a much higher proportion of students who score below basic skill levels in reading, writing, and civics, and especially in math and science.

Let us compare children's poverty in the United States and other developed countries in the late 1990s and 2000. Data from the Luxembourg Income Study show that if we use 50 percent of median adjusted disposable income for all persons in a family as the measure of poverty, 22 percent of all U.S. children are in poverty, one of the highest percentages in the study. Among the 25 countries surveyed, the percentage of all children in poverty ranged from a low of 3 percent in Finland to a high of 24 percent in Russia. The only other country with a rate higher than 20 percent was Italy.

Living with a single mother increases children's chances of being in poverty in all the countries in the Luxembourg study. In some countries, the probabilities triple or quadruple. For example, in Finland, the probability of being in poverty in 2000 was 2 percent for children in two-parent families, but 8 percent for children with a single mother. In the United States, the probability of being in poverty in 2000 was 15 percent for children in two-parent families, but almost 50 percent for children in single-mother families.

Child Care

I won't focus here on the timeworn debate about whether mothers of young children should work outside the home. Others in this series will discuss the rhetoric and sentiments associated with the changing norms of motherhood and their intensive demands. It is enough to say that mothers are in the workforce by economic necessity and seek an income so that they can improve their lives and the lives of their families. For the vast majority of families, the division of emotional and housekeeping labor and income-producing labor between men and women is no longer an option. One could also argue that child care outside the home may offer benefits not to be found in the home—also the topic of another discussion.

But let us consider the pressing needs of families today for quality, affordable, collective child care. Depending on the ages of their children, between 55 percent and 80 percent of mothers are employed. According to the Bureau of Labor Statistics, in 1999, the labor-force participation rate of mothers with school-age children, six to seventeen, was 79 percent; among mothers with children ages three to five, it was 72 percent; among those with children under three, the rate was 61 percent. In 2000, among mothers with infants, the labor-force participation rate was 55 percent, down slightly from 59 percent two years earlier.

These figures represent a sea change from the situation in 1966, when the BLS first began publishing data on mothers' labor-force participation by age of child. In 1966, only about one-fifth of married mothers with a child under age three, and only about 40 percent of widowed and divorced mothers with children under three, were in the labor force.

The role of wives in providing for the money income needs of their families has become exceedingly important. In dual-earner families, wives provide about 40 percent of family income, and in about 25 percent of those families, wives earn more than their husbands. Moreover, in recent years, while men's average earnings have failed to grow (not even keeping up with a modest rate of inflation), women's average earnings have grown, so that the increases in average family income are attributable to women's earnings.

Because mothers now provide for their children's need for emotional and physical care *and* their need for money income (including, often, access to employer-sponsored health insurance), families face serious issues about how to meet these two sets of needs. Because children are considered a private good and child-rearing a private activity, they get little assistance from either employers or the government.

Mothers balance the needs of their children for care and income by using child-care services—either informal (unpaid) or formal (paid). A report by the Urban Institute, based on the 1999 Survey of America's Families, provides information about the primary child-care arrangements for children under the age of thirteen while the adults "most responsible for their care" (most often their mothers) were employed.

Among preschoolers, age zero to four, there were three equally prevalent types of care, which together accounted for slightly more than 80 percent of all the primary-care arrangements of preschoolers: center-based care, care by a parent, and care by a relative. Care by a parent means care by the parent who is not at the place of employment during the time of child care; in two-parent families, it generally means that the parents split shifts. In addition, 14 percent of preschoolers were cared for in family child care, and 4 percent were cared for primarily by a nanny or babysitter.

Among five-year-olds, 40 percent were cared for at centers, 19 percent by a parent, 19 percent by a relative, 11 percent in family child care, 8 percent in before- and after-school programs, and 3 percent by a nanny or babysitter. Among school-age children, ages six to twelve, 41 percent were cared for by a parent, 23 percent by a relative, 15 percent in before- and after-school programs, 10 percent by the child him or herself, 7 percent in family child care, and 4 percent by a nanny or babysitter.

A recent book by Suzanne Helburn and Barbara Bergmann underscores the problems with our current child-care system (or lack thereof). Child care in a center is expensive, and many families cannot afford it; it costs between $5,000 and $10,000 per year per child, depending on the age of the child (infant care costs more) and the geographic location. In some areas, it is even more expensive than $10,000 per year. Median household income in the United States in 2000 was $42,178; the median income for families with four persons was $62,228. Using either measure, child-care costs for two children represent a significant fraction of income.

The second (related) problem with child care is its quality. The Cost, Quality, and Childhood Outcomes Study (CQO) looked at a hundred randomly selected centers in 1993. Although it found that the majority of classrooms provided minimally adequate care, only about 25 percent of preschool care and less than 10 percent of toddler care was rated as "good" or "developmentally appropriate." The highest quality centers were run by public agencies, private schools and colleges, and employers.

Determining the quality of care in family-child-care homes is difficult, because so many are unlicensed. Studies of family-child-care homes find that their quality is more variable than that in centers. In some cases, these homes provided care on par with centers, but particularly in unlicensed homes, care was often found to be poor. Quality control, as currently practiced, has more to do with the child's physical safety than with the emotional or educational skills of the provider or the content of the program.

The search costs of finding good quality child care are high, particularly because parents are generally not well informed about what to look for when they interview potential providers. Parents report that their primary considerations when purchasing child care are location and convenience, the hours of service provided, their child's safety and well-being, and cost. Absent public subsidies, they may not be able to spend enough to assure the high quality of their children's child care.

Policies That Would Help

Helping children in poverty requires more than simply transferring resources to them, although that is certainly important. It requires helping their parents, and particularly their mothers, earn higher incomes. Much of the research on the effects of the recent Temporary Aid to Needy Families (aka "welfare reform") legislation indicates that women are not being trained for the higher paying jobs—that is, for jobs that traditionally have been filled by men only. Women who have been on welfare need training for those jobs if they are to keep their children out of poverty. At the same time, because most poor women will continue to do women's jobs, it is important to raise their wages. In recent years, there has been little progress on the matter of pay equity (paying women the same as men for jobs requiring the same education and experience). Mothers of children in poverty are in dire need of pay equity.

There needs to be national recognition of the service that parents are providing to the society as a whole—and some kind of reimbursement for their efforts. In other countries, most notably Japan, Spain, and Italy, people have reacted to the unwillingness of employers and the government to help parents combine work with child-rearing by not having children or by having only one. The birth rates in these countries are now below replacement. Although Americans have not (yet) taken that tack, government and employers should act now to enable us to meet the emotional, physical, and economic needs of future citizens and workers.

A change in the national mindset about the value of children would lead government, private businesses, and nonprofit organizations to develop policies to assist parents in meeting their child-rearing responsibilities. We might begin by providing partially paid leave to parents during the first year after the birth of their child. We are one of the few industrialized countries that do not provide such leave.

We could also stop discriminating against part-time workers, paying them less per hour than employees who do the same work full time, and often offering them no benefits. Working part time is one of the ways that mothers balance raising children and earning money. We should stop punishing them for working part time. Legislation prohibiting discrimination against part-time workers is long overdue. It would be easy to add a prohibition against discrimination in earnings and benefits for part-time workers to the Fair Labor Standards Act. This would be expensive for employers, and so it might result in less part-time work. On balance, however, the prohibition would be beneficial. The European Union has already begun to move in this direction.

Jerry Jacobs has suggested that we deal with the extraordinary demands for long work hours for highly educated professionals and managers in certain industries by amending the Fair Labor Standards Act so that currently exempted workers are covered. If that were done, employers who wanted their professional and managerial workers to put in more than forty hours a week would have to pay time and a half for overtime and double time for weekends. Jacobs suspects, as I do, that under those circumstances, employers would get the same work done by hiring more employees and helping current employees to work more efficiently. If such a penalty for long hours were enacted, children might well get to see more of their highly educated parents and, presumably, the public interest would be better served.

Lotte Bailyn has done research on firms that have changed their professional structures to allow parents (and others) to work on more reasonable schedules. She has found that such changes produce win-win situations. Not only do employees experience reduced stress, higher morale, and a greater ability to respond to their family's needs, but employers gain increased productivity.

Finally, we must mend our child-care system so that all children who need it get quality care. Helburn and Bergmann estimate (without even considering that child-care workers need higher wages), that the United States would have to spend an additional $26 billion a year on child care. We could afford it, if we didn't spend it elsewhere—or if we stopped reducing taxes. Having a good child-care system simply requires a collective will to spend tax revenues for that purpose.

How will these changes come about? Children are one of the few groups that have not yet created a social movement to improve their situation. Such a movement may one day emerge, but one problem with childhood as a basis for a social movement is that people grow out of it rather quickly. A second problem is that children don't vote. It needs to be adults who lead the way in a movement on children's behalf. There are of course several well-known child advocacy groups, but because they have not been successful in getting Americans to change the way in which we view children, they have not been successful in winning over policymakers. Most child advocates, coming from an equity perspective, argue that treating children well is the right thing to do. This argument has had little traction in our increasingly selfish world. I argue that treating children well is the right thing to do from a self-interest perspective. Collectively meeting the needs of children enhances the well-being of each of us. To get the change we need, children should be viewed as a public good.

Sources of Statistics Cited

Ed Source, "NAEP Results Consistently Show Achievement Gaps Nationally," 2003. http://www.edsource.org/sch_naep03.cfm

Luxembourg Income Study, "Poverty Rates for Children by Family Type," 2000. http://www.lisproject.org/keyfigures/childpovrates.htm

National Education Association, "America's Top Education Priority: Lifting Up Low-Performing Schools," February 2001. http://www.nea.org/lac/bluebook/priority/html

Freya L. Sonenstein, et al., "Primary Child Care Arrangements of Employed Parents: Findings from the 1999 National Survey of America's Families," Occasional Paper No. 59. Washington, D.C.: The Urban Institute, May 2002.

U.S. Bureau of Labor Statistics, "Report on the American Workforce," 1999.

U.S. Dept. of Labor, Bureau of Labor Statistics, "Current Population Survey," 2002. Washington, D.C., U.S. Government Printing Office, 2000. http://ferret.bls.census.gov/macro/032002/pov/new01_001.htm

U.S. Census Bureau, Census of Population, 2000. Washington, D.C.: U.S. Government Printing Office, 2000. http://www.census.gov/population/www/cen2000/phc-t9.html

U.S. Census Bureau, Income 2000 (Income of Households by State). http://www.census.gov/hhes/income/income00/statemhi.html

U.S. Census Bureau, Current Population Reports, pp. 60–226, "Income, Poverty, and Health Insurance Coverage in the United States, 2003," Washington, D.C.: U.S. Government Printing Office, 2004. http://www.census.gov/prod/2004pubs/p60-226

U.S. Census Bureau, Median Family Income for Families with Four Persons, http://www.census.gov/hhes/income/4person.html

U.S. Census Bureau, "Labor Force Participation for Mothers with Infants Declines for First Time," Census Bureau Reports, Press Release, October 18, 2001. http://www.census.gov/Press-Release/www/2001/cb01-170.html

U.S. Dept. of Labor, Bureau of Labor Statistics, "Working in the Twenty-First Century," 1999. http://www.bls.gov/0pub/working/home.html

---

MYRA H. STROBER is a labor economist and professor of education and business at Stanford University.

Family Partnerships That Count

**How can schools meaningfully engage families
in supporting student learning?**

JoBeth Allen

Uptown High School's Mardi Gras Carnival, organized by the 21-person Parent Advisory Council, is a fun family event that raises nearly $1,000 each year.

Midtown Elementary teachers reach their goal of 100 percent participation in parent-teacher conferences, in which they strive to convey all the important information about programs, test scores, and grades in only 15 minutes.

Downtown Middle School draws more than half of its families to Technology Night. Parents walk through impressive exhibits of student projects and then enjoy refreshments in the cafeteria, converted to a student-run Cyberspace Café.

Which of these endeavors to "involve parents" contribute to student learning?

To start a conversation about this question at your school, you might want to gather a group of educators, students, and family members to brain storm a list of everything the school does to involve families. If you're like most schools, it will be an impressive list. Next, put each item in one of three categories: Builds Deep Relationships; Supports Student Learning; or Does Neither (But We Keep Doing It Anyway). Finally, examine the activities in the first two columns and ask, Which families are benefiting? Which families are not?

Contrary to the prevailing myth, when parents or guardians walk into school, their children's learning does not automatically increase. Mattingly, Radmila, McKenzie, Rodriguez, and Kayzar (2002) analyzed 41 parent involvement programs. They concluded that some things we count as parental that Count involvement—being room parents, signing behavior reports, attending PTA meetings, and so on—don't improve student achievement. So what does?

Henderson and Mapp (2002) examined 80 studies on parental involvement, preschool through high school, throughout the United States. They concluded that family involvement was likely to increase student achievement when that involvement was connected to academic learning. Let's look at three important approaches they identified: building respectful relationships, engaging families in supporting learning at home, and addressing cultural differences.

Building Respectful Relationships
Family Funds of Knowledge

Horses. That was the common thread Kathy Amanti noticed from home visits with three families in her multiage bilingual classroom. She learned that Carlos's father was teaching his sons how to care for and ride the family's three horses; that Fernando rode and cared for horses each summer when he stayed with his grandparents in Mexico; and that the Rivera family had gathered to watch a videotape of a relative riding in a horse race in Sonoyta, Mexico.

Surveying the rest of her class, Amanti found a great deal of interest in and knowledge about horses. Together, she and her students designed an interdisciplinary unit on horses, which included taking a field trip to Carlos's home, observing a parent shoeing a horse, and viewing the Riveras' video. Families were resources on individual projects as well, helping students study Spanish explorers; the history of saddles; local horse ordinances; horse anatomy; measurement (converting hands to inches and feet); and horse gestation and evolution.

Amanti was one of a group of teachers and professors who worked with Mexican and Yaqui Indian families in Tucson, Arizona (Gonzáles, Moll, & Amanti, 2005). These educators challenged the deficit model and developed a powerful alternative: learning about and incorporating family *funds of knowledge* into the classroom. Teachers studied the history of their border community. They visited homes and entered into conversations—*not* scripted interviews—centering on family and work history (border crossings, extended families, religious traditions, work experiences); household activities (gardening, home and car repair, caring for children, recreation); and parents' views of their roles (raising children, languages spoken at home, schooling).

The home visits enabled teachers and families to build *confianza* (mutual trust) and to create *reciprocity* (a healthy partnership in which teachers and parents give in ways that support one another and support the student). The teachers learned that all families have important experiences, skills, and knowledge that teachers can tap into. The teachers also became more knowledgeable about how their students learned outside school. For example, in many Mexican and Yaqui families, children are active participants and ask questions that guide their own learning, skills not always encouraged at school.

Throughout the year, teachers met in study groups to discuss what they learned and to create thematic units that built on their community's funds of knowledge. They learned that families had a wealth of knowledge about ranching, farming, mining, and construction. In the area of business, they knew about appraising, renting and selling, labor laws, and building codes. Household management acumen included budgeting, child care, cooking, and repair. Many had knowledge of both contemporary and folk medicine for people and animals. Religious knowledge included rituals; texts (especially the Bible); and moral and ethical understandings.

We've seen how Kathy Amanti incorporated family funds of knowledge into meaningful learning that went beyond the classroom. Here's another example of the way learning with and from families can support student achievement.

Teacher-Parent Partnerships for Learning

Antonio was 13, had a broad vocabulary, and was fluent in oral Spanish and English. He had been homeless for five years, and his family frequently moved. He stopped reading specialist Paula Murphy in the hall one day, asking, "I need help in reading. Can I go to your class?"

Paula started making home visits to Antonio's family at the shelter, at a friend's apartment, and at other temporary housing. She learned that his mother and stepfather helped him with homework; his mother wrote short stories, provided emotional support, and encouraged him to do well in school. Paula designed a reading program that actively involved his parents. She engaged in regular communication with the family. She also intervened with the district so Antonio could stay in her school when the family moved. In one year, Antonio's reading and writing skills improved significantly. Paula reflected,

> As a Puerto Rican . . . I felt that sharing the culture and the language of my Latino students was enough to understand their world. . . . I learned I know nothing about growing up poor, homeless, and in an environment of violence. . . . I learned of my responsibility to understand not only my students' ethnic culture, but their community culture as well. (Murphy, 1994, p. 87)

Although there is no substitute for the personal relationships and deep understanding of family knowledge developed in home visits, it's not always possible for teachers to visit every student's home on a regular basis. But there's another way of learning about a student's life outside of school—hand her a camera!

Photographs of Local Knowledge Sources (PhOLKS)

I was part of a teacher study group in Georgia that used photography to learn about family funds of knowledge (Allen et al., 2002). The PhOLKS group served a culturally, linguistically, and economically diverse student population. Educators in our group were African American, Colombian, and European American; Christian and Jewish; originally from the Northeast, Midwest, and South; with childhoods from poor to privileged. This diversity was essential in mediating our understanding of cultural differences.

With a small grant, we paid for three 35mm cameras, film, and processing for each classroom. We invited students to photograph what was important to them in their homes and neighborhoods. Teachers prepared students by analyzing photographic essays, sharing photographs of their own lives outside school, and inviting parents who enjoyed photography to help students learn how to see through the camera's eye. English as a second language teacher Carmen Urdanivia-English read from her photo-illustrated memoir about growing up in Colombia and then invited a reporter from the local Spanish-language newspaper to show students ways to document family and community histories.

Students took cameras home on a rotating schedule, charged with capturing their out-of-school lives. Teachers invited students and family members to write or dictate stories about their photos. Parents and guardians contributed descriptions, memories, poetry, letters, and personal stories.

Cyndy, a white teacher, worried about Kenesha, a black student who often slept in class. Other teachers at the school said her mother was never involved and had been in special education when she attended the school. When Kenesha took her photo journal home with an invitation to write about the pictures, her mother wrote,

> My daughter name is Kenesha. . . . She is very sweet all the teacher and people love her because she is understanding and nice, polite, sweet, listen, smart. She have her good days & bad days but she is the sweetest child you like to spend time with. . . . Members of the church love to hear her sing she sings so good you love her. She like to read and talk a lot. She loves dogs. She like to play with dolls. She love her new baby brother. (Allen et al., 2002, p. 317)

Cyndy and Kenesha's mother began communicating frequently through notes and phone calls. Mom wanted to know how Kenesha was doing. She promised to make sure Kenesha got more sleep.

One photograph, one invitation, and one letter did not change Kenesha's life. The family still struggled, and so did Kenesha—but now there was a partnership working together to teach her.

Engaging Families in Supporting Learning at Home

The parental support that made a difference for Antonio and Kenesha did not involve parents coming into the classroom, yet the parent-teacher-student relationships affected not only the students' participation in the classroom community but also their learning. That was also the case for the students of two primary-grade teachers with whom I worked in Georgia.

School-Home Reading Journals

I learned about genuine family-school partnerships from Betty Shockley and Barbara Michalove, 1st and 2nd grade teachers (respectively) who invited parents and other family members to join them in teaching their children to read and write.

Betty, Barbara, and I are European American, middle-class, experienced educators who joined in partnership with families in a high-poverty, predominantly black school. To connect home and school literacy learning, Betty and Barbara designed family-school connections including, among other practices, school-home reading journals.

Teachers and families exchanged reading journals all year. Children took home these spiral-bound or sewn notebooks two or three times a week along with books from the classroom libraries. Parents or others in the family sustained a remarkable commitment to read with their children, talk about the books, and write together in the journals.

Betty and Barbara honored the families' investment of time by responding to every entry, as we see from these excerpts from the journal of Lakendra's mother, Janice:

Janice: In the story "I Can Fly" Lakendra did very good. Her reading was very good. And maybe she's ready to move on to . . . a book with a few more words. If you think so also. (9/30)

Betty: I agree. She can read more difficult books but like everybody, young readers enjoy reading things that are easy for them too. (10/1)

Janice: In the story of the Halloween Performance, Lakendra seem to have some problems with many of the words. Maybe she get a story with too many difficult words for her right now. But still I enjoyed her reading. Thank You. Janice (10/2)

Betty: When you get ready to read together each night, you might begin by asking Lakendra, Do you want to read your book to me or do you want me to read to you? Sometimes after you read even a more difficult book, she may ask to read it after you. Let her be the leader. One of the most important things about sharing books together is talking about them together. Thanks. (10/3)

Janice: Lakendra was very excited about the books she chose to read to me. So excited she read them over and over again. And I was so pleased. Maybe last night she did want me to read the story to her I don't know but I will ask her from now on. Because she was a little upset that she didn't know a lot of the words. And I don't ever want her to feel pressured. Thanks. Janice (10/3) (Shockley, Michalove, & Allen, 1995, pp. 42–43)

This kind of extended written communication, which did not involve enlisting parents to solve discipline problems or to sign reading logs, established deep relationships that supported emerging readers and writers at home as well as at school in ways neither teacher nor parent could have accomplished alone. Without ever entering the school, parents became members of the classroom community.

Addressing Cultural Differences

We are all cultural beings shaped by time and place, religion and race, language and gender, and a host of other ongoing influences. In my work with educators, we use a number of strategies as a springboard for conversations among parents and teachers of diverse cultural backgrounds.

For example, drawing maps of childhood neighborhoods, or *memory maps* (Frank, 2003), might take place during a home visit, or in a classroom, or during a whole-school event such as a family night. Each participant draws an annotated map of his or her childhood neighborhood(s). Next, in small groups that include both teachers and families, participants walk one another through their neighborhood maps. Participants at one school had had very different childhood experiences: One of us made daily trips to the corner grocery store in Philadelphia; one rarely left the farm until he was in high school; one moved from a small town in Mexico and learned English at the Boys and Girls Club. We were amazed at the differences as well as the similarities (for example, "Back then it was safe for a child to go to the store alone").

Neighborhood maps may lead to stories of schooling. Each teacher and parent writes down or draws two memories of schooling, one positive and one negative. The sharing of these stories is often quite intense. It's important for parents to know that teachers have both kinds of memories; many parents may believe that all teachers had only positive, successful school experiences. Conversely, teachers need to learn about parents' positive memories as well as the "ghosts at the table," Sara Lawrence-Lightfoot's (2003) expression for those memories from their own schooling that haunt parents and hover over the conference table when parents and teachers try to talk about a student.

A third and potentially deeper exploration of cultural understanding occurs through developing cultural memoirs. Family members—including students—and teachers can ask themselves, Who am I as a cultural being and what are the influences in my life that have made me who I am? These are some ways to approach this project with families:

- *Read and discuss cultural memoirs.* A great place to start is by reading and discussing memoirs deeply contextualized in time and place, such as *All Over But the Shoutin',* by Rick Bragg (Pantheon, 1997), or *The*

House on Mango Street, by Sandra Cisneros (Vintage, 1989). Busy parents and teachers may appreciate shorter memoirs from popular magazines, television biopics, or radio broadcasts such as National Public Radio's StoryCorps.

- *Gather photographs and other cultural artifacts.* Go through those boxes, albums, and digital files asking, What were my cultural influences in terms of race, social class, gender, ethnicity, geographic region, religion, nationality, language/dialect, sexual orientation, schooling, physical or mental health or ability, and family structure?

- *Share cultural memoirs.* Create a form to represent your multicultured self, such as a poem, scrapbook, telenovela, photo essay, iMovie, or picture book. Some teachers and parents create classroom coffee house atmospheres and invite families in during the school day, in the evening, or on Saturday to share memoirs. Find out from parents what works for them, and consider holding two or three events so everyone can participate. You might plan one meeting for adults only, but remember that students love hearing their parents' and teachers' stories, too.

Educators and family members begin to understand cultural differences when they share their lives and make connections that build a foundation of respect and trust. When we make culture central to creating family-school partnerships, we acknowledge differences with respect, marvel at similarities, and open up dialogue about how to support each student as a unique learner.

Educators and family members begin to understand cultural differences when they share their lives.

A Starting Point

We've examined funds of knowledge, home visits, photography, reading journals, and other ways teachers have engaged families in creating positive learning experiences for students at home and in the classroom. Any of these practices could be a starting point. But let me suggest another logical place to start. Go back to that list you made of your school's parent involvement activities: Builds Deep Relationships; Supports Student Learning; Does Neither (But We Keep Doing It Anyway).

What are you already doing that you can build on? What might you do with your equivalent of Uptown High School's Mardi Gras Carnival—that fun tradition that doesn't really build relationships or support student learning? In addition to

striving for high parent participation in conferences as Midtown Elementary does, what if you held student-led conferences, focusing only on student learning? How could you involve parents in the preparation for a Technology Night event? Perhaps students could interview their parents and grandparents about changes in technology in their lifetimes, how they use technology in their jobs, and the pros and cons of various aspects of technology. Parents might engage with students in studying the effects of technology on global warming by surveying their home, work, and community settings to assess how much energy is used to run computers, cell phones, and other technologies.

How will you create opportunities *with* families?

How will you create opportunities *with* families that really improve and deepen student learning?

References

Allen, J., Fabregas, V., Hankins, K., Hull, G., Labbo, L., Lawson, H., et al. (2002). PhOLKS lore: Learning from photographs, families, and children. *Language Arts, 79*(4), 312–322.

Frank, C. (2003). Mapping our stories: Teachers' reflections on themselves as writers. *Language Arts, 80*(3), 185–195.

Gonzáles, N., Moll, L., & Amanti, C. (Eds.). (2005). *Funds of knowledge: Theorizing practices in households, communities, and classrooms.* Mahwah, NJ: Erlbaum.

Henderson, A., & Mapp, K. (2002). *A new wave of evidence: The impact of school, family, and community connections on student achievement.* Austin, TX: Southwest Educational Development Laboratory.

Lawrence-Lightfoot, S. (2003). *The essential conversation: What parents and teachers can learn from each other.* New York: Random House.

Mattingly, D. J., Radmila, P., McKenzie, T. L., Rodriguez, J. L., & Kayzar, B. (2002). Evaluating evaluations: The case of parent involvement programs. *Review of Education Research, 72*(4), 549–576.

Murphy, P. (1994). Antonio: My student, my teacher. *Language Arts, 1*(2), 75–88.

Shockley, B., Michalove, B., & Allen, J. (1995). *Engaging families: Connecting home and school literacy communities.* Portsmouth, NH: Heinemann.

JoBeth Allen is Professor, Department of Language and Literacy Education, University of Georgia, Athens; jobethal@uga.edu. She is the author of *Creating Welcoming Schools: A Practical Guide to Home-School Partnerships with Diverse Families* (Teachers College Press, 2007).

UNIT 2

Exploring and Establishing Relationships

Unit Selections

Key Points to Consider

- What are key components to this thing we call "love"? How do we maintain a satisfying sexual relationship? What do you look for in a mate? Do you seem to struggle with lasting relationships? Why do you think this is so?

- Do you see children as a part of your life? Why or why not? At what age do you think one should stop considering having a child? What should be the determining factor? How would you respond if you learned you could not have children? Would you consider adoption?

Student Website

www.mhcls.com

Internet References

Bonobo Sex and Society
http://songweaver.com/info/bonobos.html

Go Ask Alice!
http://www.goaskalice.columbai.edu/index.html

The Kinsey Institute for Research in Sex, Gender, and Reproduction
http://www.indiana.edu/~kinsey/

Mysteries of Odor in Human Sexuality
http://www.pheromones.com

The Society for the Scientific Study of Sexuality
http://www.sexscience.org

By and large, we are social animals, and as such, we seek out meaningful connections with other humans. John Bowlby, Mary Ainsworth, and others have proposed that this drive toward deep connections is biologically based and is at the core of what it means to be human. However it plays out in childhood and adulthood, the need for connection, to love and be loved, is a powerful force moving us to establish and maintain close relationships.

As we explore various possibilities, we engage in the complex business of relationship building. In doing this, many processes occur simultaneously: Messages are sent and received; differences are negotiated; assumptions and expectations are or are not met. The ultimate goals are closeness and continuity.

How we feel about others and what we see as essential to these relationships play an important role in our establishing and maintaining relationships. In this unit, we look at factors that underlie the establishment of relationships as well as the beginning stages of relationships.

The first subsection takes a broad look at factors that influence the building of meaningful connections and at the beginning stages of adult relationships. The first essay, "This Thing Called Love" takes a cross-cultural perspective on the nature of romantic love. Among its interesting and controversial suggestions is that passionate love has a natural lifespan and shares characteristics with obsessive compulsive disorder. "Pillow Talk" documents a conversation with Stephen and Andrea Levine about love and lust, the nature of marriage, and of true intimacy. The next essay goes on to discuss "24 Things Love and Sex Experts Are Dying to Tell You"—key pieces of information for couples.

In the second subsection, an aspect of the choice of a mate is examined. "On-Again, Off-Again" examines a number of explanations for why some couples break up and make up, over and over again. Why does this happen and what can they do to break the cycle?

The third subsection looks at pregnancy and the next generation. "Fats, Carbs and the Science of Conception" explores new research on the role of diet, exercise, and weight control in fertility. "Starting the Good Life in the Womb" addresses important behaviors that pregnant women can engage in to improve their baby's chances of growing into healthy adults. The following article, "Not Always 'the Happiest Time'" looks at pregnancy and depression, long assumed to occur only after birth, if at all. This article addresses the potential that those at risk for depression are not protected and may, in fact, hide their depression out of shame. In "Adopting a New American Family," the evolving nature of adoption in the United States, with increasing use of international adoptions and open adoption, in which birth parents and adoptive parents maintain contact after the adoption, are chronicled.

This Thing Called Love

LAUREN SLATER

My husband and I got married at eight in the morning. It was winter, freezing, the trees encased in ice and a few lone blackbirds balancing on telephone wires. We were in our early 30s, considered ourselves hip and cynical, the types who decried the institution of marriage even as we sought its status. During our wedding brunch we put out a big suggestion box and asked people to slip us advice on how to avoid divorce; we thought it was a funny, clear-eyed, grounded sort of thing to do, although the suggestions were mostly foolish: Screw the toothpaste cap on tight. After the guests left, the house got quiet. There were flowers everywhere: puckered red roses and fragile ferns. "What can we do that's really romantic?" I asked my newly wed one. Benjamin suggested we take a bath. I didn't want a bath. He suggested a lunch of chilled white wine and salmon. I was sick of salmon.

What can we do that's really romantic? The wedding was over, the silence seemed suffocating, and I felt the familiar disappointment after a longed-for event has come and gone. We were married. Hip, hip, hooray. I decided to take a walk. I went into the center of town, pressed my nose against a bakery window, watched the man with flour on his hands, the dough as soft as skin, pushed and pulled and shaped at last into stars. I milled about in an antique store. At last I came to our town's tattoo parlor. Now I am not a tattoo type person, but for some reason, on that cold silent Sunday, I decided to walk in. "Can I help you?" a woman asked.

"Is there a kind of tattoo I can get that won't be permanent?" I asked.

"Henna tattoos," she said.

She explained that they lasted for six weeks, were used at Indian weddings, were stark and beautiful and all brown. She showed me pictures of Indian women with jewels in their noses, their arms scrolled and laced with the henna markings. Indeed they were beautiful, sharing none of the gaudy comic strip quality of the tattoos we see in the United States. These henna tattoos spoke of intricacy, of the webwork between two people, of ties that bind and how difficult it is to find their beginnings and their elms. And because I had just gotten married, and because I was feeling a post wedding letdown, and because I wanted something really romantic to sail me through the night, I decided to get one.

"Where?" she asked.

"Here," I said. I laid my hands over my breasts and belly.

She raised her eyebrows. "Sure," she said.

I am a modest person. But I took off my shirt, lay on the table, heard her in the back room mixing powders and paints. She came to me carrying a small black-bellied pot inside of which was a rich red mush, slightly glittering. She adorned me. She gave me vines and flowers. She turned my body into a stake supporting whole new gardens of growth, and then, low around my hips, she painted a delicate chain-linked chastity belt. An hour later, the paint dry, I put my clothes back on, went home to film my newly wed one. This, I knew, was my gift to him, the kind of present you offer only once in your lifetime. I let him undress me.

"Wow," he said, standing back.

I blushed, and we began.

We are no longer beginning, my husband and I. This does not surprise me. Even back then, wearing the decor of desire, the serpentining tattoos, I knew they would fade, their red-clay color bleaching out until they were gone. On my wedding day I didn't care.

I do now. Eight years later, pale as a pillowcase, here I sit, with all the extra pounds and baggage time brings. And the questions have only grown more insistent. Does passion necessarily diminish over time? How reliable is romantic love, really, as a means of choosing one's mate? Can a marriage be good when Eros is replaced with friendship, or even economic partnership, two people bound by bank accounts?

Let me be clear: I still love my husband. There is no man I desire more. But it's hard to sustain romance in the crumb-filled quotidian that has become our lives. The ties that bind have been frayed by money and mortgages and children, those little imps who somehow manage to tighten the knot while weakening its actual fibers. Benjamin and I have no time for chilled white wine and salmon. The baths in our house always include Big Bird.

If this all sounds miserable, it isn't. My marriage is like a piece of comfortable clothing; even the arguments have a feel of fuzziness to them, something so familiar it can only be called home. And yet . . .

In the Western world we have for centuries concocted poems and stories and plays about the cycles of love, the way it morphs and changes over time, the way passion grabs us by our flung-back throats and then leaves us for something saner.

If *Dracula*—the frail woman, the sensuality of submission—reflects how we understand the passion of early romance, the *Flintstones* reflects our experiences of long-term love: All is gravel and somewhat silly, the song so familiar you can't stop singing it, and when you do, the emptiness is almost unbearable.

We have relied on stories to explain the complexities of love, tales of jealous gods and arrows. Now, however, these stories—so much a part of every civilization—may be changing as science steps in to explain what we have always felt to be myth, to be magic. For the first time, new research has begun to illuminate where love lies in the brain, the particulars of its chemical components.

Anthropologist Helen Fisher may be the closest we've ever come to having a doyenne of desire. At 60 she exudes a sexy confidence, with corn-colored hair, soft as floss, and a willowy build. A professor at Rutgers University, she lives in New York City, her book-lined apartment near Central Park, with its green trees fluffed out in the summer season, its paths crowded with couples holding hands.

Fisher has devoted much of her career to studying the biochemical pathways of love in all its manifestations: lust, romance, attachment, the way they wax and wane. One leg casually crossed over the other, ice clinking in her glass, she speaks with appealing frankness, discussing the ups and downs of love the way most people talk about real estate. "A woman unconsciously uses orgasms as a way of deciding whether or not a man is good for her. If he's impatient and rough, and she doesn't have the orgasm, she may instinctively feel he's less likely to be a good husband and father. Scientists think the fickle female orgasm may have evolved to help women distinguish Mr. Right from Mr. Wrong."

One of Fisher's central pursuits in the past decade has been looking at love, quite literally, with the aid of an MRI machine. Fisher and her colleagues Arthur Aron and Lucy Brown recruited subjects who had been "madly in love" for an average of seven months. Once inside the MRI machine, subjects were shown two photographs, one neutral, the other of their loved one.

What Fisher saw fascinated her. When each subject looked at his or her loved one, the parts of the brain linked to reward and pleasure—the ventral tegmental area and the caudate nucleus—lit up. What excited Fisher most was not so much finding a location, an address, for love as tracing its specific chemical pathways. Love lights up the caudate nucleus because it is home to a dense spread of receptors for a neurotransmitter called dopamine, which Fisher came to think of as part of our own endogenous love potion. In the right proportions, dopamine creates intense energy, exhilaration, focused attention, and motivation to win rewards. It is why, when you are newly in love, you can stay up all night, watch the sun rise, run a race, ski fast down a slope ordinarily too steep for your skill. Love makes you bold, makes you bright, makes you run real risks, which you sometimes survive, and sometimes you don't.

I first fell in love when I was only 12, with a teacher. His name was Mr. McArthur, and he wore open-toed sandals and sported a beard. I had never had a male teacher before, and I thought it terribly exotic. Mr. McArthur did things no other teacher dared to do. He explained to us the physics of farting. He demonstrated how to make an egg explode. He smoked cigarettes at recess, leaning languidly against the side of the school building, the ash growing longer and longer until he casually tapped it off with his finger.

What unique constellation of needs led me to love a man who made an egg explode is interesting, perhaps, but not as interesting, for me, as my memory of love's sheer physical facts. I had never felt anything like it before. I could not get Mr. McArthur out of my mind. I was anxious; I gnawed at the lining of my cheek until I tasted the tang of blood. School became at once terrifying and exhilarating. Would I see him in the hallway? In the cafeteria? I hoped. But when my wishes were granted, and I got a glimpse of my man, it satisfied nothing; it only inflamed me all the more. Had he looked at me? Why had he not looked at me? When would I see him again? At home I looked him up in the phone book; I rang him, this in a time before caller ID. He answered.

"Hello?" Pain in my heart, ripped down the middle. Hang up.

Call back. "Hello?" I never said a thing.

Once I called him at night, late, and from the way he answered the phone it was clear, even to a prepubescent like me, that he was with a woman. His voice fuzzy, the tinkle of her laughter in the background. I didn't get out of bed for a whole day.

Sound familiar? Maybe you were 30 when it happened to you, or 8 or 80 or 25. Maybe you lived in Kathmandu or Kentucky; age and geography are irrelevant. Donatella Marazziti is a professor of psychiatry at the University of Pisa in Italy who has studied the biochemistry of lovesickness. Having been in love twice herself and felt its awful power, Marazziti became interested in exploring the similarities between love and obsessive-compulsive disorder.

She and her colleagues measured serotonin levels in the blood of 24 subjects who had fallen in love within the past six months and obsessed about this love object for at least four hours every day. Serotonin is, perhaps, our star neurotransmitter, altered by our star psychiatric medications: Prozac and Zoloft and Paxil, among others. Researchers have long hypothesized that people with obsessive-compulsive disorder (OCD) have a serotonin "imbalance." Drugs like Prozac seem to alleviate OCD by increasing the amount of this neurotransmitter available at the juncture between neurons.

Marazziti compared the lovers' serotonin levels with those of a group of people suffering from OCD and another group who were free from both passion and mental illness. Levels of serotonin in both the obsessives' blood and the lovers' blood were 40 percent lower than those in her normal subjects. Translation: Love and obsessive-compulsive disorder could have a similar chemical profile. Translation: Love and mental illness may be difficult to tell apart. Translation: Don't be a fool. Stay away.

Of course that's a mandate none of us can follow. We do fall in love, sometimes over and over again, subjecting ourselves, each time, to a very sick state of mind. There is hope, however, for those caught in the grip of runaway passion—Prozac. There's nothing like that bicolored bullet for damping down the sex drive and making you feel "blah" about the buffet. Helen

Fisher believes that the ingestion of drugs like Prozac jeopardizes one's ability to fall in love—and stay in love. By dulling the keen edge of love and its associated libido, relationships go stale. Says Fisher, "I know of one couple on the edge of divorce. The wife was on an antidepressant. Then she went off it, started having orgasms once more, felt the renewal of sexual attraction for her husband, and they're now in love all over again."

Psychoanalysts have concocted countless theories about why we fall in love with whom we do. Freud would have said your choice is influenced by the unrequited wish to bed your mother, if you're a boy, or your father, if you're a girl, Jung believed that passion is driven by some kind of collective unconscious. Today psychiatrists such as Thomas Lewis from the University of California at San Francisco's School of Medicine hypothesize that romantic love is rooted in our earliest infantile experiences with intimacy, how we felt at the breast, our mother's face, these things of pure unconflicted comfort that get engraved in our brain and that we ceaselessly try to recapture as adults. According to this theory we love whom we love not so much because of the future we hope to build but because of the past we hope to reclaim. Love is reactive, not proactive, it arches us backward, which may be why a certain person just "feels right." Or "feels familiar." He or she is familiar. He or she has a certain look or smell or sound or touch that activates buried memories.

Love and obsessive-compulsive disorder could have a similar chemical profile. Translation: Love and mental illness may be difficult to tell apart. Translation: Don't be a fool. Stay away.

When I first met my husband, I believed this psychological theory was more or less correct. My husband has red hair and a soft voice. A chemist, he is whimsical and odd. One day before we married he dunked a rose in liquid nitrogen so it froze, whereupon he flung it against the wall, spectacularly shattering it. That's when I fell in love with him. My father, too, has red hair, a soft voice, and many eccentricities. He was prone to bursting into song, prompted by something we never saw.

However, it turns out my theories about why I came to love my husband may be just so much hogwash. Evolutionary psychology has said good riddance to Freud and the Oedipal complex and all that other transcendent stuff and hello to simple survival skills. It hypothesizes that we tend to see as attractive, and thereby choose as mates, people who look healthy. And health, say these evolutionary psychologists, is manifested in a woman with a 70 percent waist-to-hip ratio and men with rugged features that suggest a strong supply of testosterone in their blood. Waist-to-hip ratio is important for the successful birth of a baby, and studies have shown this precise ratio signifies higher fertility. As for the rugged look, well, a man with a good dose of testosterone probably also has a strong immune system and so is more likely to give his partner healthy children.

Perhaps our choice of mates is a simple matter of following our noses. Claus Wedekind of the University of Lausanne in Switzerland did an interesting experiment with sweaty T-shirts. He asked 49 women to smell T-shirts previously worn by unidentified men with a variety of the genotypes that influence both body odor and immune systems. He then asked the women to rate which T-shirts smelled the best, which the worst. What Wedekind found was that women preferred the scent of a T-shirt worn by a man whose genotype was most different from hers, a genotype that, perhaps, is linked to an immune system that possesses something hers does not. In this way she increases the chance that her offspring will be robust.

It all seems too good to be true, that we are so hardwired and yet unconscious of the wiring. Because no one to my knowledge has ever said, "I married him because of his B.O." No. We say, "I married him (or her) because he's intelligent, she's beautiful, he's witty, she's compassionate." But we may just be as deluded about love as we are when we're *in* love. If it all comes down to a sniff test, then dogs definitely have the edge when it comes to choosing mates.

Why doesn't passionate love last? How is it possible to see a person as beautiful on Monday, and 364 days later, on another Monday, to see that beauty as bland? Surely the object of your affection could not have changed that much. She still has the same shaped eyes. Her voice has always had that husky sound, but now it grates on you—she sounds like she needs an antibiotic. Or maybe you're the one who needs an antibiotic, because the partner you once loved and cherished and saw as though saturated with starlight now feels more like a low-level infection, tiring you, sapping all your strength.

Studies around the world confirm that, indeed, passion usually ends. Its conclusion is as common as its initial flare. No wonder some cultures think selecting a lifelong mate based on something so fleeting is folly. Helen Fisher has suggested that relationships frequently break up after four years because that's about how long it takes to raise a child through infancy. Passion, that wild, prismatic insane feeling, turns out to be practical after all. We not only need to copulate; we also need enough passion to start breeding, and then feelings of attachment take over as the partners bond to raise a helpless human infant. Once a baby is no longer nursing, the child can be left with sister, aunts, friends. Each parent is now free to meet another mate and have more children.

Biologically speaking, the reasons romantic love fades may be found in the way our brains respond to the surge and pulse of dopamine that accompanies passion and makes us fly. Cocaine users describe the phenomenon of tolerance: The brain adapts to the excessive input of the drug. Perhaps the neurons become desensitized and need more and more to produce the high—to put out pixie dust, metaphorically speaking.

Maybe it's a good thing that romance fizzles. Would we have railroads, bridges, planes, faxes, vaccines, and television if we were all always besotted? In place of the ever evolving technology that has marked human culture from its earliest tool

20

use, we would have instead only bonbons, bouquets, and birth control. More seriously, if the chemically altered state induced by romantic love is akin to a mental illness or a drug-induced euphoria, exposing yourself for too long could result in psychological damage. A good sex life can be as strong as Gorilla Glue, but who wants that stuff on your skin?

Once upon a time, in India, a boy and a girl fell in love without their parents' permission. They were from different castes, their relationship radical and unsanctioned. Picture it: the sparkling sari, the boy in white linen, the clandestine meetings on tiled terraces with a fat, white moon floating overhead. Who could deny these lovers their pleasure, or condemn the force of their attraction?

Their parents could. In one recent incident a boy and girl from different castes were hanged at the hands of their parents as hundreds of villagers watched. A couple who eloped were stripped and beaten. Yet another couple committed suicide after their parents forbade them to marry.

Anthropologists used to think that romance was a Western construct, a bourgeois by-product of the Middle Ages. Romance was for the sophisticated, took place in cafés, with coffees and Cabernets, or on silk sheets, or in rooms with a flickering fire. It was assumed that non-Westerners, with their broad familial and social obligations, were spread too thin for particular passions. How could a collectivist culture celebrate or in any way sanction the obsession with one individual that defines new love? Could a lice-ridden peasant really feel passion?

Easily, as it turns out. Scientists now believe that romance is panhuman, embedded in our brains since Pleistocene times. In a study of 166 cultures, anthropologists William Jankowiak and Edward Fischer observed evidence of passionate love in 147 of them. In another study men and women from Europe, Japan, and the Philippines were asked to fill out a survey to measure their experiences of passionate love. All three groups professed feeling passion with the same searing intensity.

But though romantic love may be universal, its cultural expression is not. To the Fulbe tribe of northern Cameroon, poise matters more than passion. Men who spend too much time with their wives are taunted, and those who are weak-kneed are thought to have fallen under a dangerous spell. Love may be inevitable, but for the Fulbe its manifestations are shameful, equated with sickness and social impairment.

In India romantic love has traditionally been seen as dangerous, a threat to a well-crafted caste system in which marriages are arranged as a means of preserving lineage and bloodlines. Thus the gruesome tales, the warnings embedded in fables about what happens when one's wayward impulses take over.

Today love marriages appear to be on the rise in India, often in defiance of parents' wishes. The triumph of romantic love is celebrated in Bollywood films. Yet most Indians still believe arranged marriages are more likely to succeed than love marriages. In one survey of Indian college students, 76 percent said they'd marry someone with all the right qualities even if they weren't in love with the person (compared with only 14 percent of Americans). Marriage is considered too important a step to leave to chance.

Studies around the world confirm that, indeed, passion usually ends. No wonder some cultures think selecting a lifelong mate based on something so fleeting is folly.

Renu Dinakaran is a striking 45-year-old woman who lives in Bangalore, India. When I meet her, she is dressed in Western-style clothes—black leggings and a T-shirt. Renu lives in a well-appointed apartment in this thronging city, where cows sleep on the highways as tiny cars whiz around them, plumes of black smoke rising from their sooty pipes.

Renu was born into a traditional Indian family where an arranged marriage was expected. She was not an arranged kind of person, though, emerging from her earliest days as a fierce tennis player, too sweaty for saris, and smarter than many of the men around her. Nevertheless at the age of 17 she was married off to a first cousin, a man she barely knew, a man she wanted to learn to love, but couldn't. Renu considers many arranged marriages to be acts of "state-sanctioned rape."

Renu hoped to fall in love with her husband, but the more years that passed, the less love she felt, until, at the end, she was shrunken, bitter, hiding behind the curtains of her in-laws' bungalow, looking with longing at the couple on the balcony across from theirs. "It was so obvious to me that couple had married for love, and I envied them. I really did. It hurt me so much to see how they stood together, how they went shopping for bread and eggs."

Exhausted from being forced into confinement, from being swaddled in saris that made it difficult to move, from resisting the pressure to eat off her husband's plate, Renu did what traditional Indian culture forbids one to do. She left. By this time she had had two children. She took them with her. In her mind was an old movie she'd seen on TV, a movie so strange and enticing to her, so utterly confounding and comforting at the same time, that she couldn't get it out of her head. It was 1986. The movie was *Love Story*.

"Before I saw movies like *Love Story,* I didn't realize the power that love can have," she says.

Renu was lucky in the end. In Mumbai she met a man named Anil, and it was then, for the first time, that she felt passion. "When I first met Anil, it was like nothing I'd ever experienced. He was the first man I ever had an orgasm with. I was high, just high, all the time. And I knew it wouldn't last, couldn't last, and so that infused it with a sweet sense of longing, almost as though we were watching the end approach while we were also discovering each other."

When Renu speaks of the end, she does not, to be sure, mean the end of her relationship with Anil; she means the end of a certain stage. The two are still happily married, companionable, loving if not "in love," with a playful black dachshund they bought together. Their relationship, once so full of fire, now seems to simmer along at an even temperature, enough to keep them well fed and warm. They are grateful.

"Would I want all that passion back?" Renu asks. "Sometimes, yes. But to tell you the truth, it was exhausting."

From a physiological point of view, this couple has moved from the dopamine-drenched state of romantic love to the relative quiet of an oxytocin-induced attachment. Oxytocin is a hormone that promotes a feeling of connection, bonding. It is released when we hug our long-term spouses, or our children. It is released when a mother nurses her infant. Prairie voles, animals with high levels of oxytocin, mate for life. When scientists block oxytocin receptors in these rodents, the animals don't form monogamous bonds and tend to roam. Some researchers speculate that autism, a disorder marked by a profound inability to forge and maintain social connections, is linked to an oxytocin deficiency. Scientists have been experimenting by treating autistic people with oxytocin, which in some cases has helped alleviate their symptoms.

In long-term relationships that work—like Renu and Anil's—oxytocin is believed to be abundant in both partners. In long-term relationships that never get off the ground, like Renu and her first husband's, or that crumble once the high is gone, chances are the couple has not found a way to stimulate or sustain oxytocin production.

"But there are things you can do to help it along," says Helen Fisher. "Massage. Make love. These things trigger oxytocin and thus make you feel much closer to your partner."

Well, I suppose that's good advice, but it's based on the assumption that you still want to have sex with that boring windbag of a husband. Should you fake-it-till-you-make-it?

"Yes," says Fisher. "Assuming a fairly healthy relationship, if you have enough orgasms with your partner, you may become attached to him or her. You will stimulate oxytocin."

This may be true. But it sounds unpleasant. It's exactly what your mother always said about vegetables: "Keep eating your peas. They are an acquired taste. Eventually, you will come to like them."

But I have never been a peas person.

It's 90 degrees on the day my husband and I depart, from Boston for New York City, to attend a kissing school. With two kids, two cats, two dogs, a lopsided house, and a questionable school system, we may know how to kiss, but in the rough and tumble of our harried lives we have indeed forgotten how to *kiss*.

The sky is paved with clouds, the air as sticky as jam in our hands and on our necks. The Kissing School, run by Cherie Byrd, a therapist from Seattle, is being held on the 12th floor of a run-down building in Manhattan. Inside, the room is whitewashed; a tiled table holds bottles of banana and apricot nectar, a pot of green tea, breath mints, and Chapstick. The other Kissing School students—sometimes they come from as far away as Vietnam and Nigeria—are sprawled happily on the bare floor, pillows and blankets beneath them. The class will be seven hours long.

Byrd starts us off with foot rubs. "In order to be a good kisser," she says, "you need to learn how to do the foreplay before the kissing." Foreplay involves rubbing my husband's smelly feet, but that is not as bad as when he has to rub mine. Right before we left the house, I accidentally stepped on a diaper the dog had gotten into, and although I washed, I now wonder how well.

"Inhale," Byrd says, and shows us how to draw in air.

"Exhale," she says, and then she jabs my husband in the back. "Don't focus on the toes so much," she says. "Move on to the calf."

Byrd tells us other things about the art of kissing. She describes the movement of energy through various chakras, the manifestation of emotion in the lips; she describes the importance of embracing all your senses, how to make eye contact as a prelude, how to whisper just the right way. Many hours go by. My cell phone rings. It's our babysitter. Our one-year-old has a high fever. We must cut the long lesson short. We rush out. Later on, at home, I tell my friends what we learned at Kissing School: We don't have time to kiss.

A perfectly typical marriage. Love in the Western world.

Luckily I've learned of other options for restarting love. Arthur Aron, a psychologist at Stony Brook University in New York, conducted an experiment that illuminates some of the mechanisms by which people become and stay attracted. He recruited a group of men and women and put opposite sex pairs in rooms together, instructing each pair to perform a series of tasks, which included telling each other personal details about themselves. He then asked each couple to stare into each other's eyes for two minutes. After this encounter, Aron found most of the couples, previously strangers to each other, reported feelings of attraction. In fact, one couple went on to marry.

Novelty triggers dopamine in the brain, which can stimulate feelings of attraction. So riding a roller coaster on a first date is more likely to lead to second and third dates.

Fisher says this exercise works wonders for some couples. Aron and Fisher also suggest doing novel things together, because novelty triggers dopamine in the brain, which can stimulate feelings of attraction. In other words, if your heart flutters in his presence, you might decide it's not because you're anxious but because you love him. Carrying this a step further, Aron and others have found that even if you just jog in place and then meet someone, you're more likely to think they're attractive. So first dates that involve a nerve-racking activity, like riding a roller coaster, are more likely to lead to second and third dates. That's a strategy worthy of posting on Match.com. Play some squash. And in times of stress—natural disasters, blackouts, predators on the prowl—lock up tight and hold your partner.

In Somerville, Massachusetts, where I live with my husband, our predators are primarily mosquitoes. That needn't stop us from trying to enter the windows of each other's soul. When I propose this to Benjamin, he raises an eyebrow.

"Why don't we just go out for Cambodian food?" he says.

"Because that's not how the experiment happened."

As a scientist, my husband is always up for an experiment. But our lives are so busy that, in order to do this, we have to make a plan. We will meet next Wednesday at lunchtime and try the experiment in our car.

On the Tuesday night before our rendezvous, I have to make an unplanned trip to New York. My husband is more than happy to forget our date. I, however, am not. That night, from my hotel room, I call him.

"We can do it on the phone," I say.

"What am I supposed to stare into?" he asks. "The keypad?"

"There's a picture of me hanging in the hall. Look at that for two minutes. I'll look at a picture I have of you in my wallet."

"Come on," he says.

"Be a sport," I say. "It's better than nothing."

Maybe not. Two minutes seems like a long time to stare at someone's picture with a receiver pressed to your ear. My husband sneezes, and I try to imagine his picture sneezing right along with him, and this makes me laugh.

Another 15 seconds pass, slowly, each second stretched to its limit so I can almost hear time, feel time, its taffy-like texture, the pop it makes when it's done. Pop pop pop. I stare and stare at my husband's picture. It doesn't produce any sense of startling intimacy, and I feel defeated.

Still, I keep on. I can hear him breathing on the other end. The photograph before me was taken a year or so ago, cut to fit my wallet, his strawberry blond hair pulled back in a ponytail. I have never really studied it before. And I realize that in this picture my husband is not looking straight back at me, but his pale blue eyes are cast sideways, off to the left, looking at something I can't see. I touch his eyes. I peer close, and then still closer, at his averted face. Is there something sad in his expression, something sad in the way he gazes off?

I look toward the side of the photo, to find what it is he's looking at, and then I see it: a tiny turtle coming toward him. Now I remember how he caught it after the camera snapped, how he held it gently in his hands, showed it to our kids, stroked its shell, his forefinger moving over the scaly dome, how he held the animal out toward me, a love offering. I took it, and together we sent it back to the sea.

Pillow Talk

A conversation with Stephen and Ondrea Levine about lust, the meaning of marriage, and true intimacy.

NINA UTNE

What is a good long-term relationship? *When we asked the question around the office and among our friends, we heard a lot of fear and even more relief. Fear because asking questions inevitably rocks the boat of marriage and family. Relief because after we admit that there are few long-term relationships to emulate, we can begin an honest exploration of how to do it differently. Stephen and Ondrea Levine, with three marriages behind them, have made their marriage work for 26 years and have raised three children. They work as counselors and writers, with a focus on death and dying as well as relationship issues. Good relationships are entirely idiosyncratic, they say, but self-respect, clarity of intent, and commitment to growth are the key elements. Ondrea says each of us has to start by answering the question "What do you want out of this very short life?" But ultimately, Stephen says, it's about "when you get to just loving the ass off that person and you still don't know what love means."*

Nina: We hear a lot about how relationships begin, and plenty about how they end. But there's not a lot of honest talk about how to make them last—or, for that matter, why they should.

Ondrea: Once the lust of the first couple of years wears off, once the other person is off the pedestal, and you're off the pedestal, and you're facing each other and you see each other's craziness, frailties, vulnerabilities—that's when the work really starts. The initial intensity of the passion cools, and love comes to a middle way, a balance. You have to have something more than the fact that you're in love to keep it going and keep it growing.

Nina: And what is that something?

Stephen: I think relationships persevere because you're interested in what's going to happen the next day and your partner is an interesting person to share it with.

O: Also, the people with the best relationships often have some kind of practice. It can be religious practice, love practice, nature practice, whatever, but they have something that's so essentially helpful in their growth that it keeps the relationship going.

S: People who get into a relationship who don't already have something that's more important to them than themselves—generally spiritual practice and growth, or maybe service work—are less liable to stay with the process when the relationship doesn't give them exactly what their desire system wishes for.

N: Someone wrote that 35 percent of his relationship comes from the fact that he brings his wife a cup of coffee in bed every morning.

S: What a weak relationship! Boy, that's a miserable relationship. This guy better get himself another hobby!

O: I was just thinking how very thoughtful that is. Serving each other is exceptionally important.

S: Growth. Growth is also important.

O: Yes, various levels of growth, but certainly heart expansion. Everybody would define growth so differently, but love has to grow, your heart has to open more, you have to get clearer about your intentions, clearer about what you really want out of this very short life.

And it's so individual; it depends so much on life experience. Love and simple human kindness are of huge value to me, and I find that I'm drawn to people who are thoughtful and kind. I used to be drawn to people who were only wise.

N: It seems like the bottom line is the level of consciousness and openheartedness that we bring to a long-term relationship.

S: In a relationship, we're working on a mystical union. That's a term that came from the Christian tradition, but it's part of almost all devotional traditions. And it means uniting at a level way beyond our separation. After 26 years, the line between Ondrea and the Beloved is very, very blurred. In that context, you may ask what happens when two people's goals change. Well, if they're working on becoming whole human beings, they'll change in a whole way, whether it means being together or separate.

N: Growth and service and practice are important. But what happens if you have those intentions but there are kids and hectic lives and petty annoyances and betrayals? How does mystical union accommodate that?

S: But that's what everybody has to work with. I mean, if you can't get through that stuff, there is no mystical union. If only mystical union were so easy—if people could just lean into each other's soul space, as it were. In fact, people think they're doing that, and it's actually lust, generally. We say that love is as close as you get to God without really trying. When people live together, maybe they do feel each other's soul, maybe they do feel the Beloved, maybe they both enter the Beloved. But mind arises, preference arises, attitude arises, inclination arises.

O: We raised three kids, and we certainly had our share of times when our hearts were closed to each other and we felt separate, but our commitment was to work on that and to work with it by trying to stay open, trying to understand the other person's conditioning, because our conditionings were so different.

For instance, what you might think of as betrayal I might not think is betrayal, so all of that has to be defined in a relationship. How I might work with betrayal, you might not be willing to, and that's part of what you have to work out with your partner. Some levels of betrayal are workable, and some are not worth putting in the energy for some relationships. There's no right way other than your way.

S: And *betrayal* is a loaded word. A lot of people naturally feel resentment in a relationship because there are two people with two desire systems. Sometimes they're complementary and sometimes contradictory. And when someone doesn't get what he or she wants—it can be something so simple, like not enough gas in the car, little things—the feeling of betrayal may arise. Now, sexual betrayal, that's something else entirely.

N: What do you think about the possibility of open marriages?

S: Raging bullshit. Well, it's fine for young people who don't want a committed relationship. But you might as well kiss your relationship good-bye once you open it. I don't think there is such a thing. People who open their relationships open them at both ends. The relationship becomes something you're just passing through. There's no place for real trust. There's no place where you're concerned about the other person's well-being more than your own, which is what relationship is, which is what love is. I've never, ever seen it work, and we've known some extremely conscious people.

N: But when I look at the carnage in so many marriages, I think maybe we need to step back and look at the whole agreement. There are many, many different kinds of love, and maybe we're just being too narrow.

O: We've known a couple of people who have had multiple relationships within their marriage and it's worked out for them, but it takes a certain inner strength and a depth of self-trust. Part of why marriage has been set up is because of trust, and keeping track of lineage and money and paternity and all that stuff. I think it's all based on trust, and we don't seem to have the capacity to trust deeply unless it's just one other person.

S: Then again, for some, sexual betrayal is like an active catapult. It can throw them right into God. It can clarify their priorities.

N: So you're saying that an open arrangement undercuts intimacy?

O: So many people nowadays run to divorce court because it's easier than trying to work it through. And it's so exciting to go on to that next new relationship, where someone really loves you and doesn't know your frailties. I know many people who keep going from relationship to relationship because it's easier. Although they wouldn't say that. They wouldn't even think of the children. They would only think of themselves, and that's okay too, but I don't think you get as much growth.

S: That sex thing, that's way overrated. Way, way overrated. Because if two people love each other, the part that becomes most interesting in sex is the part that may be the least interesting in the beginning. It's the quality of taking another person internally. I don't think people realize, with our loose sexual energy, the enormity of letting someone inside your aura, so to speak. To let someone closer to you than a foot and a half, you are already doing something that is touching on universal wonders and terrors.

As the intimacy becomes more intimate, though the sex may not be as hot, the intimacy becomes much hotter. Much more fulfilling. Sexual relationships actually become more fulfilling the longer they go on if you start getting by all the hindrances to intimacy—all your fears, your doubts, your distrust. Sex has an exquisite quality to support a relationship, not because of the skin sensory level, but because of heart sensory level.

N: What significance is there in the formality of marriage? The contract?

O: That depends on your conditioning. For us, marriage meant that we were going to work as hard as we could. But we both said that if the other person wanted to go another way or had a major epiphany or wanted a change in life, we would honor that.

The contract gives you a sense of security that both people are willing to work as hard as they can. I certainly don't know that the marriage contract is for everyone, although I think it can be helpful with kids. Then again, I'm 60, and that's an old style of thinking. That's why I think nowadays maybe a six-month marriage contract might be more skillful. The most important thing is to be honest about how you see your relationship: Do you see it as 'til death do you part, do you see it as until you just can't stand each other, do you see it as until the kids are 18? Anything is workable.

N: **I'm thinking about children, this container we call family. For me, there's a certain mystical union in families. Sometimes "staying together for the sake of the children" is actually about honoring this idea of family.**

O: Of course we didn't stay together for the children, because we're both divorced and had children.

S: It's only my third marriage . . . I'm working at it!

O: I got married for the old reason that many women in my generation did. I was pregnant. I didn't really want to get married, but I would've been a *puta,* a prostitute—looked at as a lesser woman in those days.

I think that it mostly is an empty relationship when you're staying together for the kids, but we have known some people whose love for their kids was so great that they became more brotherly and sisterly, and it worked very well for them, but that's pretty rare.

S: And usually when people are in that kind of disarray, the children do not benefit from their staying together.

N: **Are there other options than the train wreck to divorce?**

S: Depends on the individuals. It depends on their spiritual practice. I think it has a lot to do with their toilet training.

O: Oh, we're screwed.

S: What I mean is that our earliest self-esteem and self-image comes into play. The most beautiful thing about love—and the most difficult—is that it makes us go back to our unfinished places and relationships and, maybe, finish them. Your partner is the person who helps you do that, not by serving you, but by serving as a mirror for you, by his or her own honesty. By observing our partners' struggle to be honest we learn to be honest ourselves.

N: **I just see so many people who are either rushing to divorce or living in dead marriages. They seem afraid to ask these deep kinds of questions and have these kinds of conversations.**

O: I have worked with thousands of people who are dying, and I have heard several common complaints on the deathbed. The first was: "I wish I had got a divorce." Mostly it was fear: They didn't want to start all over again with someone else. Oh, some people were happy. They said marriage was the most wonderful ride of their lives. But many were unhappy. They wished that they hadn't let fear get in the way. But, you know, to wait until you're on your deathbed to start reflecting on what your needs are—it's not too late, but it's awfully late.

N: **That's a lot of procrastination.**

To learn more about the ideas of counselors, teachers, and writers Stephen and Ondrea Levine, visit their website at www.warmrocktapes.com.

24 Things Love and Sex Experts Are Dying to Tell You

Ellise Pierce

At REDBOOK, we're dedicated to helping you get the most out of every part of your life—*especially* your love life. That's why we created the REDBOOK Love Network, a brain trust of today's top authorities on relationships, to provide you with the best, most current info on the ins and outs, and ups and downs, of sex and love. Here, our experts share the essential pieces of advice every couple needs.

1 Never Underestimate the Power of a Compliment

"Every day, tell your partner about one thing they did that you appreciate. Everybody is quick to let their partner know what they didn't do right, and what made you angry. Make sure you balance this with what they do that pleases you. From the small things to the big things, the more you say 'Thank you,' the more of what makes you happy will come your way."

—Jane Greer, PhD, couples therapist and author of *Gridlock: Finding the Courage to Move On in Love, Work, and Life*

2 Sex: Just Do It

"Have sex—even when you don't want to! Many times, arousal comes before desire. Once you get going, you'll probably find yourself enjoying it. And the more you experience sex, the more your body will condition itself to want it. You'll feel more sensual and energized, and your partner will pick up on this sexy change."

—Laura Berman, PhD, director of the Berman Center in Chicago and author of *The Passion Prescription*

3 Listen More, Talk less

"Communication is 85 percent listening and 15 percent talking. The more you listen, the more you'll enhance communication. Try getting out of the house, taking a long walk without your cell phones, and just looking into your partner's eyes and listening to him. It's an amazing thing in a relationship when you truly feel listened to!"

—Neil Clark Warren, PhD, founder of eHarmony.com and author of *Falling in Love for All the Right Reasons*

4 Sweep Your Problems (The Little Ones) Under the Rug

"It really is okay to drop certain subjects and not even come back to them. People think this means you're avoiding key issues. But for everyday little things, successful couples agree to ignore the small problems. It's not worth the aggravation to insist on winning everything."

—David Wexler, PhD, executive director of the Relationship Training Institute in San Diego and author of *When Good Men Behave Badly*

5 Treat Your Love Like a Cherished Friendship

"The happiest couples relate to each other with respect, affection, and empathy. They choose their words carefully, avoiding the most poisonous relationship behaviors— criticism, defensiveness, contempt, and stonewalling— and feel emotionally connected."

—John Gottman, PhD, cofounder of the Gottman Institute in Seattle and author of *10 Lessons to Transform Your Marriage*

6 To Change Your Relationship, Change Yourself

"In most relationships, we think, I'm right, you're wrong, and I'll try to convince you to change. The truth is, if one person changes, the relationship changes. People say, 'Why do I have to change?' But when I show them how to tip over the first domino, their only question is, "Why did I wait so long?"

—**Michele Weiner-Davis, couples therapist and author of *The Sex-Starved Marriage***

7 Watch out for Harsh Comments—They Hit Harder than You Think

"When you're tired or frustrated, it's easy to slip into being critical of your partner. But remember, negative expressions and comments and behaviors hold much more weight than positive interactions. Make sure that for every one negative interaction, you have five positive interactions to counteract it—a touch, a laugh, a kiss, an act of love, a compliment."

—**Scott Haltzman, MD, Psychiatrist and author of *The Secrets of Happily Married Men***

8 Don't Knock It Till You've Tried It . . . Twice

"Try being adventurous in bed. Even if you don't like something, give it at least two chances before you give up on it—it may grow on you!"

—**Laura Berman, PhD**

9 Be the First to Offer the Olive Branch

"Often when there's a problem, each person will wait for the other to take the initiative to work things out. But the longer you wait, the more frustrated you both get and the worse you feel. Try making the first move to break a stalemate. It doesn't mean that you're giving in. You're getting the ball rolling, rather than being stuck."

—**Norman Epstein, PhD, marriage researcher and family therapist at the University of Maryland**

10 How to Be a Couple and Still Be Free

Give the love you want to get. "Put out lots of love and appreciation and doing your share, and you're much more likely to get it back. Put out demands and complaining, and you'll get that back too."

—**Tina B. Tessina, PhD, couples therapist and author of *How to Be a Couple and Still Be Free***

11 Fight for Your Love

"I've never seen a decent marriage where there wasn't a lot of conflict. Conflict is always the result of uniqueness, the differences between two people rubbing up against each other. Lots of people try to shut themselves down in order to avoid conflict, but any two people living full and vibrant lives are going to clash at some point. If you manage it carefully and thoughtfully, conflict can actually give your marriage a shot of energy. You can have a broader, fuller, more interesting relationship."

—**Neil Clark Warren, PhD**

12 Sex Matters; Couple Time Matters Even More

"Often couples focus on scheduling sex and working very hard on their sex life, and they don't get anywhere. But when they focus instead on spending time together—going to the movies, working on a project together—then often a better sex life will grow out of that."

—**Ian Kerner, PhD, sex therapist and author of *She Comes First* and *He Comes Next***

13 Don't Get Caught up in Right or Wrong

"It's easy to fall into a power struggle of who's right and who's wrong, but that prevents you from actually solving the real problem. You're not going to be punished for being wrong, so don't worry about who's right—work together to solve the problem."

—**Tina B. Tessina, PhD**

14 Feed Your Relationship

"People often make their own needs a first priority, and then say they can't get what they want out of the relationship. It's like going to your garden and saying,

'Feed me,' and you haven't put any plants in the ground. Make your relationship your first priority. Maybe your relationship needs more time, more vacation. Maybe you need to put in more positive statements or more moments of connection. Become partners in taking care of this relationship. If you get couples engaged in a mutual project, which is their relationship, no matter what they come up with, it's good. It's the working together that does it."

—Harville Hendrix, PhD, founder/ director of Imago Relationship International and author of *Getting the Love You Want*

15 Words Are Like Food—Nurture Each Other with Good Ones

"Say things such as 'I love you,' 'I really appreciate that,' 'I'd love to hear your thoughts about. . . you name it.' And use more empathetic words, like, 'It seems like you're struggling with this.' You'll communicate genuineness and respect, and make your partner feel loved."

—Alan Hovestadt, EdD, president of the American Association for Marriage and Family Therapy

16 Never Mind Equality; Focus on Fairness

"Everything doesn't have to be 50/50. Having a sense that each person is doing what's fair—even if it's not always equal—is what really makes a happy marriage. That applies not just to housework, but to the relationship itself."

—Barbara Dafoe Whitehead, PhD, codirector of the National Marriage Project at Rutgers University

17 Remember That You Were Partners before You Were Parents

"If you have children, don't forget about your own connection and relationship and put everything into the children. Make relating to each other one-on-one—not just as parents, but as lovers a priority."

—Lou Paget, sex educator and author of *The Great Lover Playbook*

18 Learn How to Communicate without Saying a Word

"We are profoundly affected by touch, both physically and emotionally. Happy couples touch each other frequently. A caring touch offers a simple acknowledgment of your partner, saying, 'Way to go' or 'I know that was difficult for you,' without words."

—Alan Hovestadt, EdD

19 Pay Back Your Partner Using His or Her Currency

"Each of us wants our mate to pay us back for our contributions, to give us positive reinforcement. But this payment needs to be in currency that we recognize. A wife may say, 'The way I show I care is that I make his bed every day,' but if he doesn't even notice that, it's ineffective. Get to know what your partner is looking for and make sure you speak his language."

—Scott Haltzman, MD

20 Draw on Your Successes as a Couple

"One way to bring out the best in a relationship is to focus on what you've done right in the past. For example, if you're trying to break a habit of bickering a lot, think back to a time when you were bickering but ended it differently, with humor or by dropping it or in some other way. Every couple has a big hat of experiences when they handled things well, and it's important to draw on this catalog of successes. Rather than just focusing on the times when things ended negatively."

—David Wexler, PhD

21 Dream a Big Dream for Your Relationship

"When two people dream a great dream for their marriage, they typically see their relationship take a dramatic step in the direction of that dream. Start dreaming big— envision where you want your lives and your relationship to be in 10 years. Then let yourself be inspired by these dreams to make whatever changes are necessary to live these dreams out."

—Neil Clark Warren, PhD

22 See Things through Each Other's Eyes

"A lot of conflict comes from always putting a negative spin on what your partner does. Instead of telling yourself that your partner is being thoughtless or irritating, try to think about it from the other person's point of view—ask yourself, What is going on inside that would make him or her act that way? The behavior might still be a problem, but being aware of your partner's intention can change how you view the problem, and make it easier to communicate about it."

—David Wexler, PhD

23 Cultivate Trust to Grow Intimacy

"Trust issues are like sparks in a dry forest—you want to deal with them as fast as you can, whether it's something major, like an affair, or something smaller, like a wife sharing intimate things about her marriage with her best friend. You have to remove the masons for lack of trust so that you can both feel safe sharing yourselves deeply."

—Neil Clark Warren, PhD

24 Never Lose Sight of the Romance

It's important to keep setting aside time for romance. It doesn't always mean that you have to go out for dinner or take a trip. Be imaginative. In fact, I think it's better to have little romantic episodes more often than to have one romantic blowout a year. You want this romantic feeling to be threaded through all your days, so it becomes part of the lifeblood of the marriage."

—Barbara Dafoe Whitehead, PhD

On-Again, Off-Again

What drives couples to repeatedly break up and then make up?

ELIZABETH SVOBODA

For Laura, a 35-year-old corporate recruiter from New York City, dating had always felt like a Ferris wheel ride. When a relationship started to feel wrong, she'd leave to get a new vantage point on things, but as the pain of singleness set in, she retreated to her former partner for comfort, ending up back where she started. She'd repeat the cycle several times before breaking things off permanently. "It became this crazy pattern," she says. "They weren't good guys at all, but whenever something in my life was difficult, I would go back."

Laura's longtime boomeranging habit puts her in good company. The dynamic is quite common. University of Texas communications professor René Dailey found that 60 percent of adults have ended a romantic relationship and then gotten back together, and that three-quarters of those respondents had been through the breakup, makeup cycle at least twice. But embarking on this bumpy relational road takes an emotional toll: On-off couples have more relational stress than non-cyclical couples, she found.

Given the obvious costs, why do couples keep dancing the on-and-off tango? Many who seesaw from freeze-outs to fervent proclamations of love know deep down that the relationship probably isn't right, says psychologist Steven Stosny. But when couples are faced with the loneliness and low self-esteem that accompany a breakup, they continually fall back on the temporary relief of reconciliation.

It's often the fleeting high points of a fundamentally rocky relationship that convince embattled partners to keep coming back for more, spurring a tortuous dynamic with no end in sight. "Often there is something that works very well for you about this person," says Gail Saltz, a Manhattan-based psychiatrist and author of *Becoming Real*. But when your mate's dreamy qualities are accompanied by deal-breaker ones like dishonesty or irresponsibility, it can be difficult to make a clear-headed assessment of whether to stay or leave.

Many couples with a boomeranging habit know deep down that the relationship probably isn't right.

While problem behaviors may prompt a periodic hiatus, on-again, off-again couples continue to reunite out of a persistent hope that the moments of happiness and fulfillment they've known will someday constitute the entire relationship. "People say, 'I can fix this other part of my partner,'" Saltz says, even though efforts at "remodeling" a mate are typically useless. The self-deprecating internal monologues that serial on-off artists conduct after a breakup—"What was I thinking? I'll never meet

Breaking the Breakup Cycle

On-again, off-again couples often find themselves caught between their desire for freedom and their fear of regret. Here's how to decide whether to sign on for the long haul or get out for good.

- **Adopt a worst-case-scenario** mindset. Many perpetual boomerangers keep returning because they assume they can change their partner's worst habits. But that's wishful thinking, psychotherapist Toni Coleman says. "You have to assume that the behaviors you see will get *more* entrenched and worse over time. Ask yourself, 'If that turns out to be the case, would I still want to be in this relationship?'"
- **Seek advice from** a trusted third party. Therapists fill the bill nicely, but family and friends can be just as helpful. Because they don't have as much invested in your partner as you do, they can provide unbiased opinions as to whether smooth sailing is in your relationship's future.
- **Take a time-out.** In an on-again, off-again pairing, hiatuses are par for the course. But resolve to make this one different. Use the emotional distance to think clearly about what you want from a long-term relationship. Make a list if it helps you organize your thoughts. If your partner doesn't measure up, make the hiatus permanent.

someone as funny, smart, and attractive ever again!"—can also lead to repeated reconciliations.

While periodic estrangement is painful, some couples see a silver lining. By experiencing life without their significant others for a while, they come away with a deeper understanding of the value of their bond, even if the romance doesn't always have storybook qualities.

But this kind of "pruning" is no panacea. Virginia psychotherapist Toni Coleman warns couples to steer clear of the false epiphanies making up and breaking up can encourage. After an emotion-filled reunion, it's tempting to assume your partner has permanently changed for the better. But underlying conflicts that simmered before the breakup will resurface—just ask consummate on-off artists Pamela Anderson and Tommy Lee, who married and divorced twice before breaking up for good. "Things will change only if both people commit to working on the big issues," says Coleman.

Saltz recommends veterans of the breakup, makeup carousel take time to think about why they've been there so long in the first place. "The key is in recognizing that there is a pattern," she says. "You need to elucidate what the draw of this relationship really is for you." Some on-off cyclists, she explains, repeatedly return to partnerships with flaws that mirror those in their own parents' marriage, which they've unconsciously internalized as fundamental to any relationship. If your mother took her cheating partner back over and over again, you maybe inclined to do the same. "Just the awareness of that can help you step out: 'Oh, my gosh, this is really me being my mother, and I don't want to recapitulate her love story,'" says Saltz.

Another way to decide whether to fish or cut bait for good, Coleman says, is to take as long a view as possible. By forcing partners to consider the implications of "forever," so-called fast-forwarding scenarios may make them less likely to acquiesce to the temporary high of being "on" again with a problematic mate.

Since casting aside her most recent drama-ridden relationship, Laura has decided to steer clear of the dating world for a while. She sees her new freedom as a chance to step back and contemplate how to avoid the trap in the future. "The whole love industry makes you feel like you have to be in a relationship all the time, but right now I'm just taking some time to figure things out," she says. "I truly am happy on my own."

ELIZABETH SVOBODA is a freelance writer in San Jose, California.

Fats, Carbs and the Science of Conception

In a groundbreaking new book, Harvard researchers look at the role of diet, exercise and weight control in fertility. Guarantee: you will be surprised.

JORGE E. CHAVARRO, M.D., WALTER C. WILLETT, M.D., AND PATRICK J. SKERRETT

Every new life starts with two seemingly simple events. First, an active sperm burrows into a perfectly mature egg. Then the resulting fertilized egg nestles into the specially prepared lining of the uterus and begins to grow. The key phrase in that description is "seemingly simple." Dozens of steps influenced by a cascade of carefully timed hormones are needed to make and mature eggs and sperm. Their union is both a mad dash and a complex dance, choreographed by hormones, physiology and environmental cues.

A constellation of other factors can come into play. Many couples delay having a baby until they are financially ready or have established themselves in their professions. Waiting, though, decreases the odds of conceiving and increases the chances of having a miscarriage. Fewer than 10 percent of women in their early 20s have issues with infertility, compared with nearly 30 percent of those in their early 40s. Sexually transmitted diseases such as chlamydia and gonorrhea, which are on the upswing, can cause or contribute to infertility. The linked epidemics of obesity and diabetes sweeping the country have reproductive repercussions. Environmental contaminants known as endocrine disruptors, such as some pesticides and emissions from burning plastics, appear to affect fertility in women and men. Stress and anxiety, both in general and about fertility, can also interfere with getting pregnant. Add all these to the complexity of conception and it's no wonder that infertility is a common problem, besetting an estimated 6 million American couples.

It's almost become a cliché that diet, exercise and lifestyle choices affect how long you'll live, the health of your heart, the odds you'll develop cancer and a host of other health-related issues. Is fertility on this list? The answer to that question has long been a qualified "maybe," based on old wives' tales, conventional wisdom—and almost no science. Farmers, ranchers and animal scientists know more about how nutrition affects fertility in cows, pigs and other commercially important animals than fertility experts know about how it affects reproduction in humans. There are small hints scattered across medical journals, but few systematic studies of this crucial connection in people.

We set out to change this critical information gap with the help of more than 18,000 women taking part in the Nurses' Health Study, a long-term research project looking at the effects of diet and other factors on the development of chronic conditions such as heart disease, cancer and other diseases. Each of these women said she was trying to have a baby. Over eight years of follow-up, most of them did. About one in six women, though, had some trouble getting pregnant, including hundreds who experienced ovulatory infertility—a problem related to the maturation or release of a mature egg each month. When we compared their diets, exercise habits and other lifestyle choices with those of women who readily got pregnant, several key differences emerged. We have translated these differences into fertility-boosting strategies.

At least for now, these recommendations are aimed at preventing and reversing ovulatory infertility, which accounts for one quarter or more of all cases of infertility. They won't work for infertility due to physical impediments like blocked fallopian tubes. They may work for other types of infertility, but we don't yet have enough data to explore connections between nutrition and infertility due to other causes. And since the Nurses' Health Study doesn't include information on the participants' partners, we weren't able to explore how nutrition affects male infertility. From what we have gleaned from the limited research in this area, some of our strategies might improve fertility in men, too. The plan described in The Fertility Diet doesn't guarantee a pregnancy any more than do in vitro fertilization or other forms of assisted reproduction. But it's virtually free, available to everyone, has no side effects, sets the stage for a healthy pregnancy, and forms the foundation of a healthy eating strategy for motherhood and beyond. That's a winning combination no matter how you look at it.

Slow Carbs, Not No Carbs

Once upon a time, and not that long ago, carbohydrates were the go-to gang for taste, comfort, convenience and energy. Bread, pasta, rice, potatoes—these were the highly recommended, base-of-the-food-pyramid foods that supplied us with half or more of our calories. Then in rumbled the Atkins and South Beach diets. In a scene out of George Orwell's "1984," good became bad almost overnight as the two weight-loss juggernauts turned carbohydrates into dietary demons, vilifying them as the source of big bellies and jiggling thighs. Following the no-carb gospel, millions of Americans spurned carbohydrates in hopes of shedding pounds. Then, like all diet fads great and small, the no-carb craze lost its luster and faded from prominence.

It had a silver lining, though, and not just for those selling low-carb advice and products. All the attention made scientists and the rest of us more aware of carbohydrates and their role in a healthy diet. It spurred several solid head-to-head comparisons of low-carb and low-fat diets that have given us a better understanding of how carbohydrates affect weight and weight loss. The new work supports the growing realization that carbohydrate choices have a major impact—for better and for worse—on the risk for heart disease, stroke, type 2 diabetes and digestive health.

New research from the Nurses' Health Study shows that carbohydrate choices also influence fertility. Eating lots of easily digested carbohydrates (fast carbs), such as white bread, potatoes and sugared sodas, increases the odds that you'll find yourself struggling with ovulatory infertility. Choosing slowly digested carbohydrates that are rich in fiber can improve fertility. This lines up nicely with work showing that a diet rich in these slow carbs and fiber before pregnancy helps prevent gestational diabetes, a common and worrisome problem for pregnant women and their babies. What do carbohydrates have to do with ovulation and pregnancy?

More than any other nutrient, carbohydrates determine your blood-sugar and insulin levels. When these rise too high, as they do in millions of individuals with insulin resistance, they disrupt the finely tuned balance of hormones needed for reproduction. The ensuing hormonal changes throw ovulation off-kilter.

Knowing that diet can strongly influence blood sugar and insulin, we wondered if carbohydrate choices could influence fertility in average, relatively healthy women. The answer from the Nurses' Health Study was yes. We started by grouping the study participants from low daily carbohydrate intake to high. One of the first things we noticed was a connection between high carbohydrate intake and healthy lifestyles.

Women in the high-carb group, who got nearly 60 percent of their calories from carbs, ate less fat and animal protein, drank less alcohol and coffee, and consumed more plant protein and fiber than those in the low-carb group, who got 42 percent of calories from carbohydrates. Women in the top group also weighed less, weren't as likely to smoke and were more physically active. This is a good sign that carbohydrates can be just fine for health, especially if you choose good ones.

The *total* amount of carbohydrate in the diet wasn't connected with ovulatory infertility. Women in the low-carb and high-carb groups were equally likely to have had fertility problems. That wasn't a complete surprise. As we described earlier, different carbohydrate sources can have different effects on blood sugar, insulin and long-term health.

Evaluating total carbohydrate intake can hide some important differences. So we looked at something called the glycemic load. This relatively new measure conveys information about both the amount of carbohydrate in the diet and how quickly it is turned to blood sugar. The more fast carbs in the diet, the higher the glycemic load. (For more on glycemic load, go to health.harvard.edu/ newsweek.) Women in the highest glycemic-load category

were 92 percent more likely to have had ovulatory infertility than women in the lowest category, after accounting for age, smoking, how much animal and vegetable protein they ate, and other factors that can also influence fertility. In other words, eating a lot of easily digested carbohydrates increases the odds of ovulatory infertility, while eating more slow carbs decreases the odds.

Because the participants of the Nurses' Health Study complete reports every few years detailing their average daily diets, we were able to see if certain foods contributed to ovulatory infertility more than others. In general, cold breakfast cereals, white rice and potatoes were linked with a higher risk of ovulatory infertility. Slow carbs, such as brown rice, pasta and dark bread, were linked with greater success getting pregnant.

Computer models of the nurses' diets were also revealing. We electronically replaced different nutrients with carbohydrates. Most of these substitutions didn't make a difference. One, though, did. Adding more carbohydrates at the expense of naturally occurring fats predicted a decrease in fertility. This could very well mean that natural fats, especially unsaturated fats, improve ovulation when they replace easily digested carbohydrates.

In a nutshell, results from the Nurses' Health Study indicate that the *amount* of carbohydrates in the diet doesn't affect fertility, but the *quality* of those carbohydrates does. Eating a lot of rapidly digested carbohydrates that continually boost your blood-sugar and insulin levels higher can lower your chances of getting pregnant. This is especially true if you are eating carbohydrates in place of healthful unsaturated fats. On the other hand, eating whole grains, beans, vegetables and whole fruits—all of which are good sources of slowly digested carbohydrates—can improve ovulation and your chances of getting pregnant.

Eating whole grains, beans, vegetables and whole fruits—all sources of 'slow carbs'— can improve ovulation and chances of pregnancy.

Balancing Fats

In 2003, the government of Denmark made a bold decision that is helping protect its citizens from heart disease: it essentially banned trans fats in fast food, baked goods and other commercially prepared foods. That move may have an unexpected effect—more little Danes. Exciting findings from the Nurses' Health Study indicate that trans fats are a powerful deterrent to ovulation and conception. Eating less of this artificial fat can improve fertility, and simultaneously adding in healthful unsaturated fats whenever possible can boost it even further.

Women, their midwives and doctors, and fertility researchers have known for ages that body fat and energy stores affect reproduction. Women who don't have enough stored energy to sustain a pregnancy often have trouble ovulating or stop menstruating altogether. Women who have too much stored energy often have difficulty conceiving for other reasons, many of which affect ovulation. These include insensitivity to the hormone insulin, an excess of male sex hormones and overproduction of leptin, a hormone that helps the body keep tabs on body fat.

A related issue is whether *dietary* fats influence ovulation and reproduction. We were shocked to discover that this was largely uncharted territory. Until now, only a few studies have explored this connection. They focused mainly on the relationship between fat intake and characteristics of the menstrual cycle, such as cycle length and the duration of different phases of the cycle. In general, these studies suggest that more fat in the diet, and in some cases more saturated fat, improves the menstrual cycle. Most of these studies were very small and didn't account for total calories, physical activity or other factors that also influence reproduction. None of them examined the effect of dietary fat on fertility.

The dearth of research in this area has been a gaping hole in nutrition research. If there is a link between fats in the diet and reproduction, then simple changes in food choices could offer delicious, easy and inexpensive ways to improve fertility. The Nurses' Health Study research team looked for connections between dietary fats and fertility from a number of different angles. Among the 18,555 women in the study, the total amount of fat in the diet wasn't connected with ovulatory infertility once weight, exercise, smoking and other factors that can influence reproduction had been accounted for. The same was true for cholesterol, saturated fat and monounsaturated fat—none were linked with fertility or infertility. A high intake of polyunsaturated fat appeared to provide some protection against ovulatory infertility in women who also had high intakes of iron, but the effect wasn't strong enough to be sure exactly what role this healthy fat plays in fertility and infertility.

Trans fats were a different story. Across the board, the more trans fat in the diet, the greater the likelihood of developing ovulatory infertility. We saw an effect even at daily trans fat intakes of about four grams a day. That's less than the amount the average American gets each day.

Eating more trans fat usually means eating less of another type of fat or carbohydrates. Computer models of the nurses' diet patterns indicated that eating a modest amount of trans fat (2 percent of calories) in place of other, more healthful nutrients like polyunsaturated fat, monounsaturated fat or carbohydrate would dramatically increase the risk of infertility. To put this into perspective, for someone who eats 2,000 calories a day, 2 percent of calories translates into about four grams of trans fat. That's the amount in two tablespoons of stick margarine, one medium order of fast-food french fries or one doughnut.

Fats aren't merely inert carriers of calories or building blocks for hormones or cellular machinery. They sometimes have powerful biological effects, such as turning genes on or off, revving up or calming inflammation and influencing cell function. Unsaturated fats do things to improve fertility—increase insulin sensitivity and cool inflammation—that are the opposite of what trans fats do. That is probably why the largest decline in fertility among the nurses was seen when trans fats were eaten instead of monounsaturated fats.

The Protein Factor

At the center of most dinner plates sits, to put it bluntly, a hunk of protein. Beef, chicken and pork are Americans' favorites, trailed by fish. Beans lag far, far behind. That's too bad. Beans are an excellent source of protein and other needed nutrients, like fiber

and many minerals. And by promoting the lowly bean from side dish to center stage and becoming more inventive with protein-rich nuts, you might find yourself eating for two. Findings from the Nurses' Health Study indicate that getting more protein from plants and less from animals is another big step toward walking away from ovulatory infertility.

Scattered hints in the medical literature that protein in the diet may influence blood sugar, sensitivity to insulin and the production of insulin-like growth factor-1—all of which play important roles in ovulation—prompted us to look at protein's impact on ovulatory infertility in the Nurses' Health Study.

We grouped the participants by their average daily protein intake. The lowest-protein group took in an average of 77 grams a day; the highest, an average of 115 grams. After factoring in smoking, fat intake, weight and other things that can affect fertility, we found that women in the highest-protein group were 41 percent more likely to have reported problems with ovulatory infertility than women in the lowest-protein group.

When we looked at animal protein intake separately from plant protein, an interesting distinction appeared. Ovulatory infertility was 39 percent more likely in women with the highest intake of animal protein than in those with the lowest. The reverse was true for women with the highest intake of plant protein, who were substantially less likely to have had ovulatory infertility than women with the lowest plant protein intake.

That's the big picture. Computer models helped refine these relationships and put them in perspective. When total calories were kept constant, adding one serving a day of red meat, chicken or turkey predicted nearly a one-third increase in the risk of ovulatory infertility. And while adding one serving a day of fish or eggs didn't influence ovulatory infertility, adding one serving a day of beans, peas, tofu or soybeans, peanuts or other nuts predicted modest protection against ovulatory infertility.

Eating more of one thing means eating less of another, if you want to keep your weight stable. We modeled the effect that juggling the proportions of protein and carbohydrate would have on fertility. Adding animal protein instead of carbohydrate was related to a greater risk of ovulatory infertility. Swapping 25 grams of animal protein for 25 grams of carbohydrates upped the risk by nearly 20 percent. Adding plant protein instead of carbohydrates was related to a lower risk of ovulatory infertility. Swapping 25 grams of plant protein for 25 grams of carbohydrates shrank the risk by 43 percent. Adding plant protein instead of animal protein was even more effective. Replacing 25 grams of animal protein with 25 grams of plant protein was related to a 50 percent lower risk of ovulatory infertility.

These results point the way to another strategy for overcoming ovulatory infertility—eating more protein from plants and less from animals. They also add to the small but growing body of evidence that plant protein is somehow different from animal protein.

Milk and Ice Cream

Consider the classic sundae: a scoop of creamy vanilla ice cream crisscrossed by rivulets of chocolate sauce, sprinkled with walnuts and topped with a spritz of whipped cream. If you are having trouble getting pregnant, and ovulatory infertility is suspected, think of it as temporary health food. OK, maybe that's going a bit too far. But a fascinating finding from the Nurses' Health Study is that a daily serving or two of whole milk and foods made from whole milk—full-fat yogurt, cottage cheese, and, yes, even ice cream—seem to offer some protection against ovulatory infertility, while skim and low-fat milk do the opposite.

The results fly in the face of current standard nutrition advice. But they make sense when you consider what skim and low-fat milk do, and don't, contain. Removing fat from milk radically changes its balance of sex hormones in a way that could tip the scales against ovulation and conception. Proteins added to make skim and low-fat milk look and taste "creamier" push it even farther away.

It would be an overstatement to say that there is a handful of research into possible links between consumption of dairy products and fertility. The vanishingly small body of work in this area is interesting, to say the least, given our fondness for milk, ice cream and other dairy foods. The average American woman has about two servings of dairy products a day, short of the three servings a day the government's dietary guidelines would like her to have.

The depth and detail of the Nurses' Health Study database allowed us to see which foods had the biggest effects. The most potent fertility food from the dairy case was, by far, whole milk, followed by ice cream. Sherbet and frozen yogurt, followed by low-fat yogurt, topped the list as the biggest contributors to ovulatory infertility. The more low-fat dairy products in a woman's diet, the more likely she was to have had trouble getting pregnant. The more full-fat dairy products in a woman's diet, the less likely she was to have had problems getting pregnant.

Our advice on milk and dairy products might be criticized as breaking the rules. The "rules," though, aren't based on solid science and may even conflict with the evidence. And for solving the problem of ovulatory infertility, the rules may need tweaking. Think about switching to full-fat milk or dairy products as a temporary nutrition therapy designed to improve your chances of becoming pregnant. If your efforts pay off, or if you stop trying to have a baby, then you may want to rethink dairy—especially whole milk and other full-fat dairy foods—altogether. Over the long haul, eating a lot of these isn't great for your heart, your blood vessels or the rest of your body.

Before you sit down to a nightly carton of Häagen-Dazs ("*The Fertility Diet* said I needed ice cream, honey"), keep in mind that it doesn't take much in the way of full-fat dairy foods to measurably affect fertility. Among the women in the Nurses' Health Study, having just one serving a day of a full-fat dairy food, particularly milk, decreased the chances of having ovulatory infertility. The impact of ice cream was seen at two half-cup servings a week. If you eat ice cream at that rate, a pint should last about two weeks.

Equally important, you'll need to do some dietary readjusting to keep your calorie count and your waistline from expanding. Whole milk has nearly double the calories of skim milk. If you have been following the U.S. government's poorly-thought-out recommendation and are drinking three glasses of milk a day, trading skim milk for whole means an extra 189 calories a day. That could translate into a weight gain of 15 to 20 pounds over a year if you don't cut back somewhere else. Those extra pounds can edge aside any fertility benefits you might get from dairy foods. There's also the saturated fat to consider, an extra 13 grams in three glasses of whole milk compared with skim, which would put you close to the healthy daily limit.

Aim for one to two servings of dairy products a day, both of them full fat. This can be as easy as having your breakfast cereal with whole milk and a slice of cheese at lunch or a cup of whole-milk yogurt for lunch and a half-cup of ice cream for dessert. Easy targets for cutting back on calories and saturated fat are red and processed meats, along with foods made with fully or partially hydrogenated vegetable oils.

Once you become pregnant, or if you decide to stop trying, going back to low-fat dairy products makes sense as a way to keep a lid on your intake of saturated fat and calories. You could also try some of the nondairy strategies for getting calcium and protecting your bones. If you don't like milk or other dairy products, or they don't agree with your digestive system, don't force yourself to have them. There are many other things you can do to fight ovulatory infertility. This one is like dessert—enjoyable but optional.

The Role of Body Weight

Weighing too much or too little can interrupt normal menstrual cycles, throw off ovulation or stop it altogether. Excess weight lowers the odds that in vitro fertilization or other assisted reproductive technologies will succeed. It increases the chances of miscarriage, puts a mother at risk during pregnancy of developing high blood pressure (pre-eclampsia) or diabetes, and elevates her chances of needing a Cesarean section. The dangers of being overweight or underweight extend to a woman's baby as well.

Weight is one bit of information that the participants of the Nurses' Health Study report every other year. By linking this information with their accounts of pregnancy, birth, miscarriage and difficulty getting pregnant, we were able to see a strong connection between weight and fertility. Women with the lowest and highest Body Mass Indexes (BMI) were more likely to have had trouble with ovulatory infertility than women in the middle. Infertility was least common among women with BMIs of 20 to 24, with an ideal around 21.

Keep in mind that this is a statistical model of probabilities that links weight and fertility. It doesn't mean you'll get pregnant only if you have a BMI between 20 and 24. Women with higher and lower BMIs than this get pregnant all the time without delay or any medical help. But it supports the idea that weighing too much or too little for your frame can get in the way of having a baby.

We call the range of BMIs from 20 to 24 the fertility zone. It isn't magic—nothing is for fertility—but having a weight in that range seems to be best for getting pregnant. If you aren't in or near the zone, don't despair. Working to move your BMI in that direction by gaining or losing some weight is almost as good. Relatively small changes are often enough to have the desired effects of healthy ovulation and improved fertility. If you are too lean, gaining five or 10 pounds can sometimes be enough to restart ovulation and menstrual periods. If you are overweight, losing 5 percent to 10 percent of your current weight is often enough to improve ovulation.

Being at a healthy weight or aiming toward one is great for ovulatory function and your chances of getting pregnant. The "side effects" aren't so bad, either. Working to achieve a healthy weight can improve your sensitivity to insulin, your cholesterol, your blood pressure and your kidney function. It can give you more energy and make you look and feel better.

While dietary and lifestyle contributions to fertility and infertility in men have received short shrift, weight is one area in which there has been some research. A few small studies indicate that overweight men aren't as fertile as their healthy-weight counterparts. Excess weight can lower testosterone levels, throw off the ratio of testosterone to estrogen (men make some estrogen, just as women make some testosterone) and hinder the production of sperm cells that are good swimmers. A study published in 2006 of more than 2,000 American farmers and their wives showed that as BMI went up, fertility declined. In men, the connection between increasing weight and decreasing fertility can't yet be classified as rock solid. But it is good enough to warrant action, mainly because from a health perspective there aren't any downsides to losing weight if you are overweight. We can't define a fertility zone for weight in men, nor can anyone else. In lieu of that, we can say to men who are carrying too many pounds that shedding some could be good for fertility and will be good for overall health.

The Importance of Exercise

Baby, we were born to run. That isn't just the tagline of Bruce Springsteen's anthem to young love and leavin' town. It's also a perfect motto for getting pregnant and for living a long, healthy life. Inactivity deprives muscles of the constant push and pull they need to stay healthy. It also saps their ability to respond to insulin and to efficiently absorb blood sugar. When that leads to too much blood sugar and insulin in the bloodstream, it endangers ovulation, conception and pregnancy. Physical activity and exercise are recommended and even prescribed for almost everyone—except women who are having trouble getting pregnant. Forty-year-old findings that too much exercise can turn off menstruation and ovulation make some women shy away from exercise and nudge some doctors to recommend avoiding exercise altogether, at least temporarily. That's clearly the right approach for women who exercise hard for many hours a week and who are extremely lean. But taking it easy isn't likely to help women who aren't active or those whose weights are normal or above where they should be. In other words, the vast majority of women.

Some exciting results from the Nurses' Health Study and a handful of small studies show that exercise can be a boon for fertility. These important findings are establishing a vital link between activity and getting pregnant. Much as we would like to offer a single prescription for conception-boosting exercise, however, we can't. Some women need more exercise than others, for their weight or moods, and others are active just because they enjoy it. Some who need to be active aren't, while a small number of others may be too active.

Instead of focusing on an absolute number, try aiming for the fertility zone. This is a range of exercise that offers the biggest window of opportunity for fertility. Being in the fertility zone means you aren't overdoing or underdoing exercise. For most women, this means getting at least 30 minutes of exercise every day. But if you are carrying more pounds than is considered healthy for your frame (i.e., a BMI above 25), you may need to exercise for an hour or more. If you are quite lean (i.e., your BMI is 19 or below), aim for the middle of the exercise window for a few months. Keep in mind that the fertility zone is an ideal, not an absolute. Hospital delivery rooms are full of women who rarely, or never, exercise. Not everyone is so lucky. If you are having trouble getting pregnant, then maybe the zone is the right place for you.

Whether you classify yourself as a couch potato or an exercise aficionado, your fertility zone should include four types of activity: aerobic exercise, strength training, stretching and the activities of daily living. This quartet works together to control weight, guard against high blood sugar and insulin, and keep your muscles limber and strong. They are also natural stress relievers, something almost everyone coping with or worrying about infertility can use.

Exercise has gotten a bad rap when it comes to fertility. While the pioneering studies of Dr. Rose Frisch and her colleagues convincingly show that too much exercise coupled with too little stored energy can throw off or turn off ovulation in elite athletes, their work says nothing about the impact of usual exercise in normal-weight or overweight women. Common sense says that it can't be a big deterrent to conception. If it were, many of us wouldn't be here. Our ancestors worked hard to hunt, forage, clear fields and travel from place to place. Early *Homo sapiens* burned twice as many calories each day as the average American does today and were fertile despite it—or because of it.

Results from the Nurses' Health Study support this evolutionary perspective and show that exercise, particularly vigorous exercise, actually improves fertility. Exercising for at least 30 minutes on most days of the week is a great place to start. It doesn't really matter how you exercise, as long as you find something other than your true love that moves you and gets your heart beating faster.

JORGE E. CHAVARRO and **WALTER C. WILLETT** are in the Department of Nutrition at the Harvard School of Public Health. **PATRICK J. SKERRETT** is editor of the Harvard Heart Letter. For more information, go to health.harvard.edu/newsweek or thefertilitydiet.com.

Acknowledgements—Adapted from THE FERTILITY DIET by Forge E. Chavarro, M.D., Sc. D., Walter C. Willett, M.D., Dr. P.H., and Patrick F. Skerrett. Adapted by permission from The McGraw Hill Companies, Inc. Copyright © 2008 by the President and Fellows of Harvard College.

Originally from chapter 4 of *The Fertility Diet* (McGraw-Hill 2007) by Jorge E. Chavarro, Walter C. Willett, and Patrick J. Skerrett, pp. 54–62 excerpt. Copyright © 2007 by Jorge E. Chavarro, Walter C. Willett, and Patrick J. Skerrett. Reprinted by permission of the McGraw-Hill Companies.

Starting the Good Life in the Womb

Pregnant women who eat right, watch their weight and stay active can actually improve their unborn babies' chances of growing into healthy adults.

W. ALLAN WALKER, MD AND COURTNEY HUMPHRIES

Most pregnant women know they can hurt their babies by smoking, drinking alcohol and taking drugs that can cause birth defects. But they also may be able to "program" the baby in the womb to be a healthier adult. New research suggests that mothers-to-be can reduce the risk of their babies developing obesity, high blood pressure, heart disease and diabetes by monitoring their own diet, exercise and weight.

The science behind this is relatively new and still somewhat controversial. In the late 1980s, a British physician and epidemiologist named David Barker noticed that a group of Englishmen who were born small had a higher incidence of heart disease. Studies showed that rates of obesity, high blood pressure and diabetes—illnesses that often are associated with heart disease—are higher in men born small. Barker proposed that poor nutrition in the womb may have "programmed" the men to develop illness 50 years or more later.

The "Barker Hypothesis" is still hotly debated, but it is gaining acceptance as the evidence builds. Because organs develop at different times, it appears that the effects of too little food during pregnancy vary by trimester. One example comes from study of the Dutch Hunger Winter, a brief but severe famine that occurred during World War II. Pregnant women who didn't get enough to eat in their first trimester had babies who were more likely to develop heart disease. If they were in their second trimester, their babies were at risk for kidney disease. A poor diet in the last three months led to babies who had problems with insulin regulation, a precursor of diabetes.

More-recent research has focused on the negative effects of too much food during pregnancy. Women who gain excessive weight during pregnancy are more likely to have babies who are born large for their age and who become overweight in childhood. A recent study from the National Birth Defect Prevention Study found that obesity in pregnancy also increases a baby's risk for birth defects, including those of the spinal cord, heart and limbs.

A mother's nutrition and exercise patterns during pregnancy influence the long-term health of the baby by shaping her baby's metabolism. "Metabolism" includes everything that allows your body to turn food into energy—from the organ systems that process food and waste to the energy-producing chemical reactions that take place inside every cell. It is the collective engine that keeps you alive.

A mother's body may influence her baby's metabolism on many levels: the way organs develop, how appetite signals get released in the brain, how genes are activated, even the metabolic chemistry inside the baby's cells. Research now shows that the environment of the womb helps determine how a baby's metabolism is put together, or "programs" it for later health. The science of fetal programming is still new; it will be a long time before we have all the answers, since these health effects emerge over a lifetime. But several principles already are clear for a pregnant woman.

The first is to get healthy before pregnancy. Weighing too little or too much not only hampers fertility but can set the stage for metabolic problems in pregnancy. Doctors used to think of body fat as nothing more than inert insulation, but they know now that fat is an active tissue that releases hormones and plays a key role in keeping the metabolism running. Women should also eat a balanced diet and take prenatal vitamins before pregnancy to ensure that their bodies provide a good environment from the beginning.

The amount of weight gain is also critical. Women who gain too little weight during pregnancy are more likely to give birth to small babies, while women who gain too much weight are likely to have large babies. Paradoxically, both situations can predispose a child to metabolic disease. The weight gain should come slowly at first—about two to eight pounds in the first trimester, and one pound per week after that for normal-weight women. Obese women (with a body-mass index, or BMI, higher than 29) should gain no more than 15 pounds.

Pregnancy Pounds

Putting on too much or too little weight during pregnancy can predispose the baby to metabolic disorders. The right amount to gain:

Body-mass index (BMI) before pregnancy	Recommended weight gain
Less than 19.8 (underweight)	28–40 lb.
19.8–25 (normal weight)	25–35
26–29 (overweight)	15–25
Greater than 29 (obese)	No more than 15

Source: "Programming Your Baby for a Healthy Life" by W. Allan Walker, M.D., and Courtney Humphries

During pregnancy, women are already more susceptible to metabolic problems such as gestational diabetes and preeclampsia (high blood pressure), so choosing foods that help your metabolism run smoothly is important. Eating whole grains and foods rich in protein and fiber while avoiding foods high in sugar can help even out rises and falls in blood sugar. Pregnant women should eat about 300 extra calories per day while they're pregnant. But, as always, the quality of the calories matters even more. It's important to eat a diet rich in nutrients, since a lack of specific nutrients in the womb can hamper a baby's long-term health. A clear example is folic acid, without which the brain and spinal cord do not develop properly. But new research is uncovering other nutrients that may have subtler but long-lasting effects on health.

Studies suggest that women could benefit from taking omega-3 fatty-acid supplements, particularly those containing docosahexaenoic acid (DHA, for short), a type of fat that has been shown to help prevent prematurity and contribute to healthy brain development. A recent study found that women with more vitamin D in their bodies have children with stronger bones; adequate vitamin D is also needed for organ development.

Women may have different nutrient needs because of genetic differences, but to be safe every woman should take a daily prenatal vitamin before and during pregnancy. But supplements, whether in the form of a pill, a fortified shake or energy bar, don't replace the nutrients found in fruits, vegetables, low-fat meats, whole grains and other foods.

The energy you expend is as important as what you take in. Regular activity helps keep a woman's metabolism running smoothly and offsets problems of pregnancy like varicose veins, leg cramps and lower back pain. Pregnant women should avoid high-impact activities, especially late in their pregnancies.

All this may sound daunting, but most of the changes are simple ones that will improve a mother's long-term health as well as her children's.

W. ALLAN WALKER, MD, the Conrad Taff Professor of Pediatrics at Harvard Medical School, and **COURTNEY HUMPHRIES**, a science writer, have written "The Harvard Medical School Guide to Healthy Eating During Pregnancy." For more information, go to health.harvard.edu/newsweek.

Not Always 'the Happiest Time'

**Pregnancy and depression: a new understanding
of a difficult—and often hidden—problem.**

LISA MILLER AND ANNE UNDERWOOD

Let's just say that you are among the millions of women for whom pregnancy was not bliss. You may have felt cranky or anxious, exhausted or fat, moody, stressed, nauseated, overwhelmed, isolated or lonely. You may even have felt bad about feeling bad. Now let's say that you, like Marlo Johnson, are a veteran of depression, someone who has battled the illness on and off for years. Then pregnancy can feel like the worst thing that ever happened to you. Johnson, 35 years old and from Brentwood, Calif., felt her mood plummet almost as soon as she conceived. But she put a brave face on it at work, with her family—even with her own therapist. The only time she cried was when she visited her obstetrician. Every time. Johnson's doctor encouraged her to look on the bright side. "'Just think, at the end you're going to have this beautiful baby, the most beautiful gift'," Johnson recalls her saying, "and I said, 'I don't care. I don't want it. It doesn't matter to me'."

Contrary to conventional wisdom and medical lore, pregnancy does not necessarily equal happiness, and its hormones are not protective against depression. Doctors estimate that up to 20 percent of women experience symptoms of depression at some point during their pregnancy—about the same as women who are not pregnant. Even as postpartum depression has become morning-television fodder, the problem of depression during pregnancy has remained hidden—largely because most people still assume that pregnancy is or should be the realization of every woman's dream. When she was training as a psychiatric resident in the 1980s, Katherine Wisner, now a professor of psychiatry and Ob-Gyn at the University of Pittsburgh, remembers being told not to worry about pregnant patients who were, in her view, "very ill." Pregnant women, her teachers said, are "psychologically fulfilled."

Finally, pregnancy-linked depression is coming into the open. A series of studies, published this year in medical journals, is looking at all aspects of the problem—with special focus on the effects of anti-depressants on the health of pregnant women and newborn babies. These studies have launched, for the first time, a serious debate among doctors on the risks and benefits of treating pregnant women with medication. "There are still

unanswered questions" about SSRIs and pregnancy, says Lee Cohen, a psychiatrist at Mass General Hospital in Boston and author of one of the recent studies. "But the doctors—the psychiatrists, the OBs—can't be cavalier, and can't presume that [without treatment] things are going to be fine."

Pregnancy probably doesn't cause depression, per se, but just like a divorce or a death in the family, it can trigger it in women who may already be genetically predisposed. And the hormones don't help. The relationship between estrogen, progesterone and mood is not well understood, but scientists believe it is the *changes* in hormonal levels, rather than the levels themselves, that affect people's moods. In a series of experiments published in *The New England Journal of Medicine* in 1998, psychiatrists Peter Schmidt and David Rubinow found that women who were prone to mild depression associated with premenstrual syndrome felt better only when their hormonal cycles were artificially shut down. They guess that the same is probably true with pregnancy: massive hormonal changes affect mood, but only in susceptible women. "In some women it may be the dramatic drop in hormones at childbirth that is the trigger," says Rubinow. "In others, it may be the elevated levels at the end of pregnancy."

It's difficult to detect depression in a pregnant woman, doctors say, because so few of them admit they're depressed—and because so many of the symptoms, such as sluggishness and sleeplessness, look alike. But Linda Worley, a psychiatrist at the University of Arkansas, who has a $250,000 federal grant to raise awareness about pregnancy and depression, says too many doctors don't ask pregnant patients about their mood or administer routine screening tests; some are too busy, some assume it isn't a problem and a few—not knowing where to refer such a patient—are afraid to hear the answer. According to preliminary results of a survey Worley received from 145 obstetrical providers, more than 80 percent rely on patients to self-report depression.

Treating a pregnant woman for depression is a delicate balancing act, a constant weighing of risks and benefits to the mother and to the fetus. But intervention is critical: a recent study by Columbia's Myrna Weissman shows that a mother's mental health directly affects the mental health of her children. Without aggressive treatment, "the whole family will suffer," Weissman says. Cohen's study, in *The Journal of the American Medical Association,* showed without a doubt that depressed mothers-to-be do better on SSRIs. Women who continued taking medication while pregnant were five times less likely to have a relapse of their illness than women who didn't. This is important—and not only because it improves the mother's health. Depressed women are far likelier to smoke, drink and miss doctors' appointments; depressed mothers give birth more often to under-weight babies. Faced with these facts, Claudia Crain of Newburyport, Mass., decided to continue taking her antidepressants: "The more research I did, the better I felt about what, in the end, was my personal decision." Her twins are due this month.

Most people assume that pregnancy is the realization of every woman's dream.

At the same time, no one would argue that antidepressants are good for growing fetuses. Two new studies help people assess the risks for themselves. In one, published in *The New England Journal of Medicine,* researchers found that newborns whose mothers took Prozac, Paxil or Zoloft in the third trimester had six times the risk of persistent pulmonary hypertension, a rare blood-pressure condition that is potentially fatal.

In another, smaller study, 30 percent of infants whose mothers took SSRIs showed symptoms of neonatal abstinence syndrome, a kind of supercrankiness linked to withdrawal. Most got better within days.

Therapy is a good alternative, especially for women with mild or moderate symptoms. In today's world, where families live far apart and everyone works all the time, many pregnant women say they feel isolated. This can be alleviated by talking. Margaret Spinelli, a psychiatrist at Columbia University, was surprised to find in a 2003 study that depressed pregnant women had a 60 percent recovery rate with interpersonal psychotherapy, a short-term, focused treatment—about the same rate as with antidepressants. "We just don't have the networks of close-by girlfriends and sisters and neighbors and moms that provide support," adds Pittsburgh's Wisner.

One of the reasons Marlo Johnson kept her depression hidden was that she didn't want to take antidepressants during her second pregnancy, as she had during her first. "I don't like being on medication; I kept telling myself I could handle it," she says. But finally Johnson's doctor took action. She ordered her to take a leave from work and to come clean with her therapist; Johnson's husband, who was working hundreds of miles away, came home. On March 20, Carter Patrick Johnson was born, weighing more than eight pounds. Mom says she loves the baby, "but I'm still depressed," and is back on medication. Sometimes even happy stories have bittersweet endings.

With Joan Raymond

Adopting a New American Family

Adoption plays a key role in our nation's diversity, experts say, and merits more attention from psychology.

JAMIE CHAMBERLIN

Adoption is redefining the American family: International and transracial adoptions are speeding up the nation's diversity by creating more multicultural families and communities. And as more same-sex couples and single parents adopt, and more grandparents adopt their grandchildren following parental abuse or neglect, the 21st century American family has many looks and meanings, notes journalist Adam Pertman in his best seller *Adoption Nation: How The Adoption Revolution is Transforming America* (Basic Books, 2001).

In addition, adoption itself has changed over the last 20 years, experts say. Due to policy changes in many states, adoptions tend to be much more open than in years past, when adoption records were sealed and adopted children couldn't access their personal histories. Many adopted children have contact with their biological parents—or "birth-parents." In the case of many kinship or foster-care adoptions, they may also see members of their own extended family.

The increasingly diverse adoption population, and these changes in adoption policy and practice, are spurring the need for more research, say psychologists who study adoption. For starters, says longtime adoption researcher Harold Grotevant, PhD, of the department of family social science at the University of Minnesota (UM), researchers should be studying how to help children navigate their membership in multiple families and cultures. Research is also lacking on such issues as how adults adopted as children cope with issues of identity and loss, or with emotions that emerge when they start a family.

What's more, few practitioners specialize or receive graduate training in helping clients navigate these and related issues, such as the emotions that can accompany the decision to search out a biological mother. Those who do specialize in adoption or in disorders that may accompany international adoptions, such as attachment disorders, are likely to live in metropolitan areas and may be inaccessible to families in rural areas.

"More and more, people in small towns are adopting," says Cheryl Rampage, PhD, of the Family Institute at Northwestern University. "The factors that lead to adoption happen across the spectrum and geography of the country."

Research Strides

Among those striving to fill the adoption research gaps is UM associate professor of psychology Richard Lee, PhD, who participates in the university's multidisciplinary International Adoption Project, a large-scale survey of Minnesota parents who adopted internationally between 1990 and 1998. In the project, led by developmental psychologist Megan Gunnar, PhD, UM researchers surveyed more than 2,500 parents about their children's health, development and adjustment. They also asked participants whether their employers offered leave for the adoption, how their kids have fared academically and how they managed adoption costs, among other topics.

Lee, a second-generation Korean American, says his personal friendships with many in the Korean-American adoption community spurred his interest in this overlooked segment of the Asian American population. He's using the data to explore cultural socialization practices in families who have adopted internationally. Some adoptive parents expose their children to their birth culture by sending them to language classes and culture camps or setting up playdates with other internationally adopted children. They may also make a conscious effort to talk with their child about racism and discrimination. But what's not known, Lee maintains, is how these efforts affect their children's well-being or cultural or ethnic identity, or provide a buffer against racism or discrimination as they grow older.

"We presume that if parents socialize kids in a certain way, those outcomes will be protective factors," says Lee. "But there is actually very little research on that."

Grotevant, also of UM, heads a separate longitudinal study, the Minnesota Texas Adoption Research Project, on how openness in adoption affects the adopted child and members of the "adoptive kinship network," which includes the child, the extended adoptive family and the extended birth family. Among the salient findings of the first two waves of his study—conducted when the children were between 4 and 12 years old and 12 and 20 years old—is that, within the group of families having some birth-parent contact, higher degrees of collaboration and communication between the child's adoptive parents and birth-mothers were linked to better adjustment in the children during middle childhood. Grotevant is now gathering a third wave of data as the children—now in their 20s—become adults. He's looking at how they transition from school to work, how they have fared academically, their identity and interpersonal relationships, and if they are searching for or have contact with their birth-mother.

"We know from the research literature that many adopted children are in their 20s and 30s when they begin to seek information about their birth-relatives," says Grotevant. He's also asking the young adults what advice they have for people considering adoption, which he hopes—along with the rest of his findings—can be used to inform adoption practice and policy.

Like Grotevant, Rutgers University psychologist David Brodzinsky, PhD, is hoping his findings from a national survey of adoption agency opportunities for gay and lesbian adoptive parents can guide future policy on adoption. The study, conducted in 2003 through the Evan B. Donaldson Adoption Institute, showed that 60 percent of the agencies he surveyed were willing to accept applications from gay men and lesbians, but less then 39 percent had made such placements. Only 18 to 19 percent actively recruited adoptive parents in the gay and lesbian community, he notes.

"The trend has been for supporting gay and lesbian adoption—most states do, but a few ban it or have barriers that make it difficult," says Brodzinsky, a senior fellow at the institute.

Serving Families

The majority of adoptive parents turn to adoption agencies—or social work or adoption support groups—for postadoption counseling or services, but a handful of psychologists are also serving the adoption community. Take, for example, Martha Henry, PhD, of the Center for Adoption Research at the University of Massachusetts Medical School. As director of education and training there, Henry teaches an eight-week adoption course to medical students each semester that covers such topics as how to work with adoptive and foster-care families and to discuss adoption with couples facing infertility.

When she's not teaching medical students, Henry educates elementary school teachers on ways to keep their classrooms comfortable for children who were adopted or are in the foster-care system.

"Lots of classroom assignments are based on that perfect family model with two parents, a child, a dog and a picket fence," she says, such as asking children to bring in baby pictures to teach about change. That kind of activity is inappropriate if a class includes an adopted child, adds Henry.

"There are other ways to do the same lesson with something that doesn't put a child in a situation of having to say, 'I don't have a picture from when I was a baby,'" says Henry.

Likewise, psychologist Amanda Baden, PhD, a Chinese-American who was adopted from Hong Kong, teaches a course on adoption issues—which she believes is unique in any psychology training program—as part of a master's-level counseling program at Montclair State University in New Jersey. In it, she covers many of the issues she sees in her part-time practice working with families and individuals who are part of transracial adoptions. Many of her clients struggle with such issues as whether to search for their birth-mothers and how to manage conflicts between their birth culture and race and their adopted culture and race.

Cheryl Rampage sees many of these same issues in the Northwestern University Family Institute's Adoptive Families Program, which offers counseling and psychotherapy to adoptive families and school outreach programs that train teachers on adoption sensitivity. The program also hosts the Adoption Club, a biweekly support group for local adopted 7 to 11 year olds. The club is geared to preteens because in these years, "for the first time, loss becomes a real issue," she says. Preschool-age adopted children tend to talk about their being adopted matter-of-factly, but at 7 or 8 these same children start to feel scared and sad when they think of this other family they lost, says Rampage.

Through the club, children draw family pictures, play games and write stories or perform plays about adoption.

According to Baden, the adoption community could benefit if more psychologists specialized in adoption issues like Henry and Rampage do.

"Psychologists often think adoption is social work's domain," she says. "Psychologists have a tremendous amount to offer. . . . Adoption and the issues associated with it have moved beyond the domains of case management and adoption placements. It's time for psychologists to use their skills to develop treatment protocols and counseling process research."

UNIT 3
Family Relationships

Unit Selections

Key Points to Consider

- Is marriage necessary for a happy, fulfilling life? Why is or is not that so? When you think of a marriage, what do you picture? What are your expectations of your (future) spouse? What are your expectations of yourself?

- What are the attributes of good parents? Of bad parents? What are your thoughts on spanking?

- What do you think is the appropriate adult–adult relationship between parents and children? At what point should parents back away to let their children "fly"?

- Who do you include in your family? Is everyone legally tied to you?

Student Website
www.mhcls.com

Internet References

Child Welfare League of America
   http://www.cwla.org
Coalition for Marriage, Family, and Couples Education
   http://www.smartmarriages.com
The National Academy for Child Development
   http://www.nacd.org
National Council on Family Relations
   http://www.ncfr.com
Positive Parenting
   http://www.positiveparenting.com
SocioSite
   http://www.pscw.uva.nl/sociosite/TOPICS/Women.html

*A*nd they lived happily ever after. . . . The romantic image conjured up by this well-known final line from fairy tales is not reflective of the reality of family life and relationship maintenance. The belief that somehow love alone should carry us through is pervasive. In reality, maintaining a relationship takes dedication, hard work, and commitment.

We come into relationships, regardless of their nature, with fantasies about how things ought to be. Partners, spouses, parents, children, siblings, and others—all family members have at least some unrealistic expectations about each other. It is through the negotiation of their lives together that they come to work through these expectations and replace them with other, it is hoped, more realistic ones. By recognizing and acting on their own contribution to the family, members can set and attain realistic family goals. Tolerance and acceptance of differences can facilitate this process as can competent communication skills. Along the way, family members need to learn new skills and develop new habits of relating to each other. This will not be easy, and, try as they may, not everything will be controllable. Factors both inside and outside the family may impede their progress.

Even before one enters a marriage or other committed relationship, attitudes, standards, and beliefs influence our choices. Increasingly, choices include whether we should commit to such a relationship. From the start of a committed relationship, the expectations both partners have of their relationship have an impact, and the need to negotiate differences is a constant factor. Adding a child to the family affects the lives of parents in ways that they could previously only imagine. Feeling under siege, many parents struggle to know the right way to rear their children. These factors can all combine to make child rearing more difficult than it might otherwise have been. Other family relationships also evolve, and in our nuclear-family-focused culture, it is possible to forget that family relationships extend beyond those between spouses and parents and children.

The initial subsection presents a number of aspects regarding marital and other committed relationships, decisions about whether one wants to enter such a relationship, and ways of balancing multiple and often competing roles played by today's couples, who hope to fulfill individual as well as relationship needs. It is a difficult balancing act to cope with the expectations and pressures of work, home, children, and relational intimacy. The first article, "Free as a Bird and Loving It" addresses the issue of remaining single in a culture that expects adults to pair up. Next, David Wagner discusses the introduction of

© Keith Thomas Peoductions/Brand X Pictures/PictureQuest RF

same-sex marriage in New Jersey. What seemed like an easy task quickly became complex. "Two Mommies and a Daddy" discusses family forms that are common in some parts of the world, but illegal in the United States. The article presents positives and drawbacks of polygamous and polyamorous families, particularly with regard to the rearing of children.

The next subsection examines the parent/child relationship. In the first article, "Good Parents, Bad Results," looks at eight errors that well-meaning parents make and ways to avoid them. The next article, "Do We Need a Law to Prohibit Spanking?" addresses the fact that, although research strongly supports the drawbacks of corporal punishment, legislation may be necessary to end a practice that is commonly seen as relatively benign. "Children of Lesbian and Gay Parents" comes to the conclusion that sexual orientation of parents has no effect on the development and well-being of their children The next reading, "Prickly Père," addresses concerns regarding one's responsibilities toward an abusive parent.

The third and final subsection looks at other family relationships. "The Forgotten Sibling" draws attention to the fact that, in research on family, siblings often are forgotten. Yet, sibling relationships can be among the most important and long-lasting in one's life. They can also be one of the most challenging, especially if one's siblings have special needs. "Being a Sibling" addresses this relationship from the perspective of children. Families may be formed in nontraditional ways, with nontraditional connections. Friendships can grow in significance to become affiliative family connections that rival traditional family relationships in their meaning and significance. This expanded view of who we include as family members is presented by John Tyler Connoley in "Aunties and Uncles." The final article in this section address issues of concern among aged family members. "Roles of American Indian Grandparents in Times of Cultural Crises" depicts a significant enculturative role for grandparents, in which they teach about and reinforce their grandchildren's ties to their cultural past.

Free as a Bird and Loving It

More Americans are happy to marry later—or not at all.

Sharon Jayson

Being single means bucking the pressure to join the married half of U.S. society.

Despite lavish celebrity weddings, a multitude of dating websites and stacks of self-help books about finding your soul mate, singles are a growing segment of the population—and increasingly say they are perfectly happy with their singlehood, thank you very much.

The Census Bureau reports about 97 million unmarried Americans age 18 and over in 2006, the most recent numbers available. That represents 44% of Americans 18 and over; a quarter have never been married; 10% are divorced, 6% widowed, and 2% separated.

"It's probably the best moment for singles in our history . . . because of the attitudes of popular support and the numbers," says Pat Palmieri, a social historian at Teachers College at Columbia University, who is writing a history of singles in America since 1870. She is 60 and has never been married.

Young adults are delaying marriage and have a longer life expectancy, experts say, so more Americans will spend more of their adult lives single. As their ranks multiply, singles aren't waiting for a partner to buy a home or even have a child. They've decided to embrace singlehood for however long it lasts.

"I don't have to be dating someone to be happy," says Jennifer MacDougall, 26, an office assistant in Wilmington, N.C. She says her friends share her outlook.

"When I was younger, I thought that was how it worked. You went to college and got married. When I got to college, I realized that was not how it worked and not how I even wanted it to work. I wouldn't mind being married someday, but I want to feel comfortable with myself and what I'm doing."

That attitude may arise from the frenetic quality dating takes on after college, says Barbara Dafoe Whitehead, co-director of the National Marriage Project, a research initiative at Rutgers University.

"It is not a bad trend that we are removing the stigma from being single and talking about alternative ways to lead a single life," she says.

Households in which no one is married now make up 47.3% of the USA's 114 million households, according to recently released Census data for 2006. (Numbers from 2005 released last year showed unmarried households at a 50.3% majority, but the percentage fluctuates year to year.)

"I don't have to be dating someone to be happy."

—Jennifer MacDougall, 26 of Wilmington, N.C.

"Unmarried here means not married right now," says Andrew Cherlin, a professor of sociology and public policy at Johns Hopkins University in Baltimore. The data reflect larger numbers of elderly singles, probably widowed or divorced, and twenty- and thirty somethings who haven't tied the knot, such as unmarried people who share living quarters or romantic partners who live together.

"Most people who are single seem to want to eventually be married," says Michael Rosenfeld, author of *The Age of Independence,* about young adults living on their own. "But they're putting it off. In the past, there just weren't that many single, young adults supporting themselves. It's a new phenomenon, post-1960, and getting stronger every day."

Singles do continue to face obstacles, from work policies and tax codes that favor married couples to extra fees lone travelers must pay. But society is beginning to recognize singles' needs: Individual servings of packaged grocery items are just one example.

Also, a Pew Research Center study released last year found that most singles aren't actively looking for a committed relationship: 55% of 3,200 adults 18 and older surveyed in 2005 reported no interest in a relationship. For ages 18–29, 38% said they weren't looking for a partner.

"When I graduated from college, I spent more time not in relationships than in relationships," says Len Sparks, 37, an engineer from Boston who says he's now in a relationship.

"Most of my 20s, I just didn't date. I had one relationship. Outside of that, I just worked. I worked really hard and was getting promotions and changing jobs and moving from city to city."

Bella DePaulo, 53, a social psychologist and author of *Singled Out: How Singles Are Stereotyped, Stigmatized, and Ignored and Still Live Happily Ever After,* says most books for singles try to teach "how to become un-single. What I love about my single life are the nearly limitless opportunities it offers," she says.

Other new books touting the solo-is-fine theme:

- *Better Single Than Sorry: A No-Regrets Guide to Loving Yourself and Never Settling* by Jen Schefft, who appeared on TV in *The Bachelor* and *The Bachelorette* and rebuffed two marriage proposals.
- *I'd Rather Be Single Than Settle: Satisfied Solitude and How to Achieve It* by Emily Dubberley, a relationship and sex writer from Brighton, England.
- *Naked on the Page: The Misadventures of My Unmarried Midlife* by Jane Ganahl, who previously wrote a newspaper column called "Single Minded."

- *On My Own: The Art of Being a Woman Alone* by Florence Falk, a "60-plus" psychotherapist in New York City.
- *Singular Existence: Because It's Better to Be Alone Than Wish You Were!* by Leslie Talbot of Boston, founder of the website SingularExistence.com.

"We do have an unfortunate tendency to favor couples and perhaps disparage single people," Cherlin says. "These books are aimed at boosting the self-image of single people."

DePaulo agrees not everything is rosy. "I don't love everything about being single," she says. "I don't like the stigma or the stereotyping or the discrimination."

Talbot says she wrote her book to counter the belief that being single is "a deficiency or liability—a temporary condition that hopefully, if you're lucky, you'll get over."

She says there's a fine line between being alone and lonely. "There's nothing lonelier than being with somebody you don't want to be with."

Gay Marriage Lite

New Jersey's high court doesn't quite go all the way.

David M. Wagner

If not New Jersey, then (besides Massachusetts) where? A liberal state with no explicit prohibition on same-sex marriage in state law, and no law barring state officials from performing such marriages for out-of-staters—New Jersey would seem the perfect state in which to persuade the highest court to duplicate the Massachusetts holding. There the supreme judicial court declared that no rational basis exists for restricting marriage to opposite-sex couples, and that same-sex marriage must, then, be enacted posthaste.

Yet it didn't quite happen that way in Trenton. Instead, in *Lewis* v. *Harris,* handed down October 25, the Supreme Court of New Jersey went for what, in the present state of the marriage debate, passes for a Solomonic compromise: Hold that same-sex couples must be given all the legal benefits of marriage, but leave to the legislature the issue of whether the resulting legal relationship is to be called "marriage." This is similar to the path followed by the court in Vermont in creating those states' "civil unions." For the New Jersey court, no "substantial" basis exists for withholding from same-sex couples the benefits of marriage. Yet one may exist for reserving the name "marriage"—and the social symbolism that goes with it—to opposite-sex couples.

Remarkably, for an opinion that insists on equalizing the rights of same- and opposite-sex couples, *Lewis* v. *Harris* nonetheless recognizes that the U.S. Supreme Court's landmark 1967 decision *Loving* v. *Virginia,* striking down racial restrictions on marriage, does *not* create a "right to marry" independent of all traditional and societal understandings of what marriage is. "The heart of the [1967] case," the New Jersey court notes, "was invidious discrimination based on race, the very evil that motivated the passage of the Fourteenth Amendment."

"Despite the rich diversity of this State," the court continues (passing the hanky), "the tolerance and goodness of its people, and the many recent advances made by gays and lesbians toward achieving social acceptance and equality under the law, we cannot find that a right to same-sex marriage is so deeply rooted in the traditions, history, and conscience of the people of this State that it ranks as a fundamental right." New Jerseyans are good, it seems, but not *that* good.

After so holding, the court turns to the passage of the New Jersey Constitution that most closely tracks the U.S. Constitution's equal protection clause. For any suspect government classification (such as the one reserving marriage to male-female couples), New Jersey weighs "three factors: the nature of the right at stake, the extent to which the challenged statutory scheme restricts that right, and the public need for the statutory restriction."

The court then sums up the extensive rights that New Jersey has bestowed upon same-sex couples, and notes the "remaining" rights that are not included in the state's Domestic Partnership Act. Is there a reason, the court asks, for not sliding all the way down this slope?

"The State does not argue that limiting marriage to the union of a man and a woman is needed to encourage procreation or to create the optimal living environment for children." California did not press an affirmative case for traditional marriage either; that state's intermediate appeals court nonetheless deferred to legislative judgment. But New Jersey's legislature has *not* said that marriage is one man and one woman, and it *has* said that distinctions based on sexual orientation are to be removed. Given this legislative background, it takes perhaps only a smidgen of judicial activism to conclude: "It is difficult to understand how withholding the remaining 'rights and benefits' from committed same-sex couples is compatible with a 'reasonable conception of basic human dignity and autonomy.'" The court then ordered the legislature to correct its oversight in the next 180 days.

Despite the admittedly "extraordinary remedy," the four-judge majority nonetheless scolds its three dissenting colleagues, who wanted to order up same-sex marriage right now, Massachusetts-style. "We cannot escape," it says, "the political reality that the shared societal meaning of marriage—passed down through the common law into our statutory law—has always been the union of a man and a woman. To alter that meaning would render a profound change in the public consciousness of a social institution of ancient origin."

Speculation will swirl as to what drove this strange mixture of activism and restraint. It could be a set-up: If the legislature responds by enacting Vermont-style civil unions that are not called "marriage," the court can, in inevitable litigation to follow, hold that the legislature had not shown a "substantial" reason for a difference of nomenclature. The result would be a Massachusetts-style same-sex marriage mandate, only without an election-year backlash. Or it could be they blinked: Public resistance to same-sex marriage is being felt in the courts, and the New Jersey Supreme Court is, by its own admission—nay, proclamation—sensitive to changes in "times and attitudes."

David M. Wagner teaches constitutional law at Regent University, and blogs at ninomania.blogspot.com.

From *The Weekly Standard,* November 6, 2006, pp. 12–13. Copyright © 2006 by David M. Wagner. Reprinted by permission of the author.

Two Mommies and a Daddy

ELIZABETH MARQUARDT

This spring HBO debuted a television series, *Big Love,* that features a likable polygamous family in Utah. An article in a March issue of *Newsweek,* headlined "Polygamists Unite!" quotes a polygamy activist saying, "Polygamy is the next civil rights battle." He argues, "If Heather can have two mommies, she should also be able to have two mommies and a daddy." That weekend on the *Today Show,* hosts Lester Holt and Campbell Brown gave a sympathetic interview to a polygamous family.

Western family law has so far not permitted children to have more than two legal (biological or adoptive) parents. This limitation could soon be a thing of the past. Trends in science, law and culture are threatening the two-person understanding of marriage and of parenthood. Though most advocates of same-sex marriage say they do not support group marriage, the partial success of the gay-marriage movement has emboldened others to borrow the language of civil rights to break open further our understanding of marriage.

If two parents are good for children, are three even better?

During the same month that *Big Love* debuted, the *New York Times* devoted much attention to the subject of polygamy. One article featured several polygamous women watching *Big Love's* first episode and sharing their view that polygamy "can be a viable alternative lifestyle among consenting adults." In an article in the paper's business section, an economist snickered that polygamy is illegal mainly because it threatens male lawmakers who fear they wouldn't get wives in such a system. In a separate piece, columnist John Tierney argued that "polygamy isn't necessarily worse than the current American alternative: serial monogamy." He concluded: "If the specter of legalized polygamy is the best argument against gay marriage, let the wedding bells ring."

It is not just *Big Love* that is putting polygamy in play in North America. In a development that shocked many Canadians this winter, two government studies released by the Justice Department in Ottawa recommended that polygamy be decriminalized. One report argued that the move is justified by the need to attract skilled Muslim immigrants.

Besides this movement for polygamy ("many marriages"), there is a movement on behalf of polyamory ("many loves"). Polyamory involves relationships of three or more people, any two of whom might or might not be married to one another. Whereas polygamists are generally heterosexual, polyamorous people variously consider themselves straight, gay, bisexual or just plain "poly." Polyamorists distinguish themselves from the "swingers" of the 1970s, saying that their relationships emphasize healthy communication and what they call "ethical nonmonogamy."

Polyamorous unions have been around for a while, but now they and their supporters are seeking increased visibility and acceptance. A recent *Chicago Sun-Times* article mentioned the "Heartland Polyamory Conference" to be held this summer in Indiana. (A similar Midwestern polyamory conference was held two years ago in Wisconsin.) A *Chicago Tribune* article in February featured Fred, Peggy, Bill, John and Sue, the latter two a married couple, who share their beds in various ways. The reporter termed them an "energetic bunch" of polyamorists. And articles about polyamory routinely appear in alternative periodicals such as the *Village Voice* and *Southern Voice* and, increasingly, in campus newspapers.

Support for polyamory and polygamy is found not only on the fringes. The topic is also emerging at the cutting edge of family law. Dan Cere of McGill University cites some examples, including: a substantial legal defense of polyamory published by University of Chicago law professor Elizabeth Emens in the *New York University Law Review;* a major report, "Beyond Conjugality," issued by the influential Law Commission of Canada, which queried whether legally recognized relationships should be "limited to two people"; and *An Introduction to Family Law* (Oxford University Press), in which a British law professor observes that "the abhorrence of bigamy appears to stem . . . from the traditional view of marriage as the exclusive locus for a sexual relationship and from a reluctance to contemplate such a relationship involving multiple partners."

Columnist Stanley Kurtz recently noted that a number of legal scholars are calling for the decriminalization of polygamy, including Jonathon Turley of George Washington University, who wrote a widely noticed opinion piece in *USA Today* in October 2004. According to Kurtz, a significant number of legal scholars argue that "the abuses of polygamy flourish amidst the isolation, stigma, and secrecy spawned by criminalization." In other words, the problem is not polygamy but the stigmatizing of it.

Meanwhile, the Alternatives to Marriage Project, whose leaders are often featured by mainstream news organizations in stories on cohabitation and same-sex marriage, includes polyamory among its "hot topics" for advocacy. Among religious organizations the Unitarian Universalists for Polyamorous Awareness hope to make theirs the first to recognize and bless polyamorous relationships (see www.uupa.org).

Advocates for polyamory often explicitly mimic the language used by gays, lesbians and bisexuals and their supporters. They say they must keep their many loves in the closet; that they cannot risk revealing their personal lives for fear of losing their jobs or custody of their children; that being poly is just who they are.

Website for practitioners of polyamory devote considerable space to the challenges of being a poly parent. On a blog at LiveJournal.com, one mom says, "Polyamory is what my kids know. They know some people have two parents, some one, some three and some more. They happen to have four. Honestly? Kids and polyamory? Very little of it affects them unless you're so caught up in your new loves you're letting it interfere with your parenting."

An older mom advises a young poly mother-to-be who isn't sure how to manage a new baby and her poly lifestyle: "Having a child . . . and being poly isn't exactly a cakewalk, but . . . it is possible. Sometimes it means that you take the baby with you to go see your OSO [other significant other], or your OSO spends more time at the house with you, your husband, and the baby. . . . There is a lot of patience that is needed from all parties involved, but it can be done. The first six months are extremely hard."

A pro-poly website despairs: "One challenge that faces poly families is the lack of examples of poly relationships in literature and media." A sister site offers the "PolyKids Zine." This publication for kids "supports the principles and mission of the Polyamory Society." It contains "fun, games, uplifting Poly-Family stories and lessons about PolyFamily ethical living." Its book series includes *The Magical Power of Mark's Many Parents* and *Heather Has Two Moms and Three Dads.*

A different set of challenges to the two-person understanding of marriage and parenthood is emerging from medical labs.

Scientists are experimenting with creating artificial sperm and eggs and fusing them in unexpected ways to create human embryos for implantation in the womb. Last year, British scientists at Newcastle University were granted permission to create a human embryo with three genetic parents. A team in Edinburgh announced that it had tricked an egg into dividing and created the first human embryo without a genetic father. But evidence from experiments with animals suggests that the physical—not to mention psychological—risks for such embryos and children are enormous. In Japan in 2004, scientists created a mouse with two genetic mothers and no genetic father. To achieve this result, they created over 450 embryos, of which 370 were implanted. Only ten were born alive, and only one survived to adulthood.

In the current explosion of reproductive technology the law is gasping to stay in last place. For example, only now are some nations beginning to recognize the moral and health risks of sperm donation, a relatively low-tech reproductive technology that has been in use for at least 40 years. Responding to donor-conceived adults who say they desperately wish to know and have a relationship with their sperm-donor fathers, expert commissions last year in New Zealand and Australia recommended allowing sperm and egg donors to opt in as third legal parents for children.

Such a move promises to create as many problems as it solves. Just one likely result: as soon as children are assigned three or more legal parents, the argument for legalizing group marriage will almost certainly go something like this, "Why should children with three legal parents be denied the same legal and social protections as children with only two parents have?"

Pity the children. We frequently see the havoc wreaked on children's lives when two parents break up and fight over their best interests. Imagine when three or more adults break up and disagree over the children to whom each has an equal claim. How many homes will we require children to grow up traveling between to satisfy the parenting needs of all these adults?

If two parents are good for children, are three even better? Should scientists try to make babies from three people, or babies with no genetic father (or mother)? Is the two-parent, mother-father model important for children, or does it just reflect a passing fixation of our culture? The debate is upon us.

ELIZABETH MARQUARDT is director of the Center for Marriage and Families at the Institute for American Values. This article is based on a report to be released in August by the Commission on Parenthood's Future.

Good Parents, Bad Results

Science is providing proof of where Mom and Dad go wrong.

NANCY SHUTE

Does your 3-year-old throw a five-alarm tantrum every time you drop him off at day care? Does "you're so smart!" fail to inspire your 8-year-old to turn off *Grand Theft Auto IV* and tackle his math homework? Do the clothes remain glued to your teenager's bedroom floor, along with your antisocial teenager, no matter how much you nag or cajole? Being a parent has never been easy—just ask your own. But in this day of two-earner couples and single parents, when 9-year-olds have cellphones, 12-year-olds are binge drinking and having oral sex, and there is evidence that teens are more fearful and depressed than ever, the challenges of rearing competent and loving human beings are enough to make a parent seek help from Supernanny. Actually, there is something better: science.

Researchers have spent decades studying what motivates children to behave and can now say exactly what discipline methods work and what don't: Call it "evidence-based parenting." Alas, many of parents' favorite strategies are scientifically proven to fail. "It's intuitive to scream at your child to change their behavior, even though the research is unequivocal that it won't work," says Alan Kazdin, a psychologist who directs the Yale Parenting Center and Child Conduct Clinic. Other examples:

- Yelling and reasoning are equally ineffective; kids tune out both.
- Praise doesn't spoil a child; it's one of the most powerful tools that parents can use to influence a child's actions. But most parents squander praise by using it generically—"you're so smart" or "good job!"—or skimping.
- Spanking and other harsh punishments ("You're grounded for a month!") do stop bad behavior but only temporarily. Punishment works only if it's mild, and it is far outweighed by positive reinforcement of good behavior.

As yet, few of the bestselling books and videos that promise to turn surly brats into little buttercups make use of this knowledge. That may be because the research goes on in academia—at Yale, at Vermont's Behavior Therapy and Psychotherapy Center, and at the University of Washington's Parenting Clinic, for example. Surprisingly, many family therapists and parenting educators aren't up to speed on the research, either, so that parents who seek professional help won't necessarily get the most proven advice. Case in point: Just 16 programs designed for treating kids with disruptive behavior have been proven "well established" in randomized clinical trials, according to a review led by Sheila Eyberg at the University of Florida and published in the January *Journal of Clinical Child and Adolescent Psychology*. Kazdin, who for years has pushed clinical psychologists to adopt evidence-based methods, published a book for parents earlier this year: *The Kazdin Method for Parenting the Defiant Child*. Other lab-tested tomes include *Parenting the Strong-Willed Child* by Rex Forehand and Nicholas Long and *The Incredible Years* by Carolyn Webster-Stratton.

These discipline programs are grounded in classical behavioral psychology—the positive reinforcement taught in Psych 101. Researchers have run randomized controlled trials on all the nuances of typical parent-child interactions and thus can say just how long a timeout should last to be effective or how to praise a 13-year-old so that he beams when he takes out the trash. Who knew that effectively praising a child in order to motivate her has three essential steps? They are: 1) Praise effusively, with the enthusiasm of a Powerball winner. 2) Say exactly what the child did right. 3) Finish with a touch or hug.

What else can parents learn from the science? Researchers say these are the biggest common boo-boos:

1. Parents Fail at Setting Limits

It would be hard to find a parent who doesn't agree that setting and enforcing rules are an essential part of the job description. Yet faced with whining, pouting, and tantrums, many parents cave. "The limited time you have with your kids, you want to make it ideal for them," says Forehand, a professor of psychology at the University of Vermont whose evidence-based program is outlined in his book. "As a result, we end up overindulging our kids."

Faced with whining and pouting, many parents cave, Result: domestic inferno.

A Good Parent's Dilemma: Is It Bad to Spank?

Plenty of people argue for an occasional swat

Last year, the California Legislature considered criminalizing the spanking of toddlers. But at least half of parents, and according to some surveys as many as 94 percent, consider a swat on the bottom to be an appropriate form of discipline. "spanking has worked very well for us," says Tim Holt, a 45-year-old insurance agent and the father of four children, ages 4 to 13, in Simpsonville, S.C., who notes that he and his wife spank very rarely. He recalls spanking his 7-year-old son, Scott, after Scott hit his brother in the head with a shoe and then lied to his father about it. "I pulled Scott aside. We discussed what he had done: Why is it wrong? What does God's law say? That we don't take our anger out on others." Then Holt put Scott over his knee and smacked him on his pants with a plastic glue stick. "It's something that gets his attention and provides a little bit of pain to his bottom."

Proponents include James Dobson, a psychologist and founder of Focus on the Family, who likens squeezing a child's shoulder or spanking his behind to discomfort that "works to shape behavior in the physical world." He writes in *The New Dare to Discipline:* "The minor pain that is associated with this deliberate misbehavior tends to inhibit it. . . . A boy or girl who knows love abounds at home will not resent a well-deserved spanking." But the subject generates more heat than just about any other child-rearing issue. Sweden banned spanking in 1979. The United Nations Committee on the Rights of the Child has been seeking a ban on corporal punishment worldwide since 1996.

The evidence. The debate roils academia, too. Murray Straus, a professor of sociology at the University of New Hampshire, says 110 studies have linked spanking to increased misbehavior in childhood as well as adult problems such as increased spousal abuse and depression. In February, Straus published research linking being spanked in childhood with an adult preference for sadomasochistic sex. Straus acknowledges that most of today's parents were themselves spanked as children but says that since spanking is no more effective than other discipline methods and can cause harm it's not worth the misery. Other researchers, including Diana Baumrind, a psychologist at the University of California-Berkeley, have found that children who were spanked occasionally had no more behavior problems than children who were never spanked. But Baumrind says regular reliance on physical punishment, as well as "impulsive and reactive spanking," causes harm to a child. The bottom line: Proponents of either position can come up with enough evidence to support their belief-but not enough to convince the other side.

Demonizing spanking may leave some parents feeling they must avoid *any* discipline that makes a child feel bad, says Lawrence Diller, a developmental pediatrician in Walnut Creek, Calif., who works with children with attention deficit hyperactivity disorder. He speculates that a more coherent disciplinary approach that includes an occasional well-timed swat can make the overall system more effective and could "make the difference in whether your child will be on Ritalin or not. You don't have to spank. But if you're using spanking as one of array of tools to get control of your kid, you're not hurting them in the long term."

—N.S.

But, paradoxically, not having limits has been proven to make children *more* defiant and rebellious, because they feel unsafe and push to see if parents will respond. Research since the 1960s on parenting styles has found that a child whose mom and dad are permissive is more likely to have problems in school and abuse drugs and alcohol as teenagers. "Parents ask their 1-year-olds what they want for dinner now," says Jean Twenge, an associate professor of psychology at San Diego State University and author of *Generation Me.* "No one ever said that a generation or two ago." Using surveys dating back to the 1930s, Twenge has found significant increases in reported symptoms of depression and anxiety among today's children and teenagers, compared with earlier generations. Suniya Luthar, a psychologist at Columbia University Teachers College, reported in 2003 that children who are showered with advantages are more likely to be depressed and anxious and to abuse drugs and alcohol than the norm. Luthar says that's probably because those children are under a lot of pressure to achieve at school and think that their parents value their achievements more than themselves. They also feel isolated from their parents.

Rule-setting works best when parents give simple, clear commands and discuss the family rules with kids well in advance of a conflict, according to Robert Hendren, a professor of psychiatry at the Medical Investigation of Neurodevelopmental Disorders Institute at the University of California-Davis and president of the American Academy of Child and Adolescent Psychiatry. A common recommendation for parents who fear coming off as a meanie: Let the child choose between two options when either choice is acceptable to the parent. A half-hour of Nintendo right after school, then homework? All homework before game time?

Consistency is also key. "I have to be very strict with myself and go over and tell him the rules and walk away," says Lauren Jordan, a stay-at-home mom in Essex Junction, Vt., whose 4-year-old son, Peter, would scream and hit Jordan and her husband, Sean, then kick the wall during timeout. "It felt out of control." Jordan signed up with Vermont's Behavior Therapy and Psychotherapy Center to learn Forehand's five-week process.

The first week was spent just "attending" to Peter, watching him play and commenting without telling the preschooler what to do. "He *loved* it," says Jordan, whose older son has autism and has required an outsize share of her energy. "I realized at that point that he needs this one-on-one attention." Jordan

53

then had to learn to ignore Peter's minor bad behavior (such as screaming for attention while Mom is on the phone) and to not rush in to scold him during a timeout. "Consistency is the key. It's not easy," Jordan says. "But it's made our home a much happier place."

2. They're Overprotective

Teachers, coaches, and psychotherapists alike have noticed that parents today can't stand to see their children struggle or suffer a setback. So they're stepping in to micromanage everything from playground quarrels to baseball team positions to grades. Even bosses aren't immune. One owner of a New York public relations firm says he has gotten E-mails from parents telling him that's he's making their child work too much. The child in question is in his 20s.

"Many well-meaning parents jump in too quickly," says Robert Brooks, a clinical psychologist in Needham, Mass., and coauthor of *Raising Resilient Children.* "Resilient children realize that sometimes they will fail, make mistakes, have setbacks. They will attempt to learn from them." When parents intercede, Brooks says, "it communicates to the kid that 'I don't think you're capable of dealing with it.' We have to let kids experience the consequences of their behavior."

Otherwise, they may grow afraid to try. "I see a lot of kids who seem really unmotivated," says Kristen Gloff, 36, a clinical and school social worker in the Chicago area. "It's not that they're lazy. They don't want to fail."

3. They Nag. Lecture. Repeat. Then Yell.

If one verbal nudge won't get a kid to come to dinner, 20 surely will. Right? In fact, there's abundant evidence that humans tune out repeated commands. "So many parents think they have to get very emotionally upset, yell, threaten, use sarcasm," says Lynn Clark, a professor emeritus of psychology at Western Kentucky University and author of *SOS Help for Parents.* "The child imitates that behavior, and you get sassy talk."

Nagging also gives children "negative reinforcement," or an incentive—parental attention—to keep misbehaving. "I was kind of ignoring the good behavior, and every time he did something wrong, I would step in and give him attention," says Nancy Ailes, a 46-year-old stay-at-home mom in East Haven, Conn. She was frustrated with her 9-year-old son, Nick, who would melt down and throw things if the day's schedule changed, drag his feet about cleaning his room or doing homework, and call her "bad Mommy" if she complained.

Parent management training this spring at the Yale Child Conduct Center taught Ailes and her husband how to use positive reinforcement instead—to praise Nick immediately and enthusiastically. Now, when Nick is picking up his toys in the family room, she sits down, watches, and says: "Wow, that looks really nice!"

Ailes and her husband, David, also learned how to set up a reward system with points that Nick can cash in for Yu-Gi-Oh

cards and Game Boy time and to back up the system with timeouts for bad behavior. Within three weeks, Ailes says, Nick had made a complete turnaround. "Instead of doing things that make people unhappy," she says, "you do things that make them happy!"

4. They Praise Too Much— and Badly

It seems like a truism that praising children would make them feel good about themselves and motivate them to do better. But parents don't give children attaboys as often as they think, Kazdin says. And when they do, it's all too often either generic ("good job!") or centered on the person, not the task ("you're so smart!"). This kind of praise actually makes children less motivated and self-confident. In one experiment by Carol Dweck, a psychologist now at Stanford University, fifth graders who were praised for being intelligent, rather than making a good effort, actually made less of an effort on tests and had a harder time dealing with failure.

"It's so common now for parents to tell children that they're special," says Twenge. That fosters narcissism, she says, not self-esteem. Twenge thinks parents tell a child "You're special" when they really mean "You're special to me." Much better in every way, she says, to just say: "I love you."

5. They Punish Too Harshly

Although spanking has been deplored by child-development experts since the days of Dr. Spock in the 1940s, as many as 90 percent of parents think it's OK to spank young children, according to research by Murray Straus, a professor of sociology at the University of New Hampshire (more on the spanking controversy in the box). Kazdin and other behavioral researchers say parents commonly punish far more harshly than they need to.

After all, it's not supposed to be about payback, though that's often what's going on, says Jamila Reid, codirector of the Parenting Clinic at the University of Washington. The clinic's "The Incredible Years" program has been found in seven studies to improve children's behavior. "Often parents come looking for bigger sticks. We tell parents the word discipline means 'teach.' It's something to teach a child that there's a better way to respond."

Consider the fine art of the timeout. Parents often sabotage timeouts by lecturing or by giving hugs, according to Sheila Eyberg, a professor of psychology at the University of Florida. Her Parent-Child Interaction Therapy is used in many mental health clinics. Forehand and other researchers have spent many hours observing the use of timeout as a disciplinary strategy to determine exactly what makes it effective. The key finding: Discipline works best when it's immediate, mild, and brief, because it's then associated with the transgression and doesn't breed more anger and resentment. A timeout should last for just a few minutes, usually one minute for each year of age of the child.

Teenagers who have outgrown timeouts shouldn't lose a privilege for more than a day. Beyond that, the child's attitude shifts from regretting bad behavior to resenting the parent. "The punishment business isn't just ineffective," Kazdin says. "It leads to avoidance and escape. It puts a little wedge in the relationship between parent and child." Long groundings also make it more likely that the parents will relent after a few days. Better, Kazdin says, to ask the child to practice good behavior, such as fixing something he damaged, in order to win privileges back.

6. They Tell Their Child How to Feel

Most parenting books focus on eradicating bad behavior. But in study after study, empathy for other people leads the list of qualities that people need to successfully handle relationships at school, at work, and in the family. Children need to think about how their own feelings will be affected by what they do, as well as the feelings of others, says Myrna Shure, a developmental psychologist at Drexel University and author of *Raising a Thinking Child*. "That is what will inhibit a child from hurting others, either physically or emotionally."

And parents, by telling children "you're fine" or "don't cry," deny children the chance to learn those lessons. "The child learns empathy through being empathized with," says Stanley Greenspan, a child psychiatrist in Chevy Chase, Md., whose most recent book, *Great Kids*, tells parents how to help their child develop 10 essential qualities for a happy life. Empathy, creativity, and logical thinking top the list. A simple "We're so sorry, we know how it feels" is enough.

"Modeling empathic behavior is really very important," says James Windell, a counselor with the juvenile court system in Oakland County, Mich., and author of *8 Weeks to a Well-Behaved Child*. "How you respond to your children's needs sets the stage. It's really easy to be a supportive parent when they bring home a straight-A report card. When they get a bad grade, that's when they really need our support."

7. They Put Grades and Sats Ahead of Creativity

An overemphasis on good grades can also distort the message about how and what children should learn. "We like kids to learn rules, and we want them to learn facts," says Greenspan. "We're impressed when they can read early or identify their shapes. It's much harder for us to inspire them to come up with a creative idea." Children who can think creatively are more likely to be able to bounce back if their first idea doesn't work. They also know it can take time and patience to come up with a good solution. The goal, says Greenspan, is not to have a child who knows how to answer questions but one who will grow up to ask the important questions.

Parents can help their children become independent thinkers by asking open-ended questions like: Can you think of another way to solve the problem with your teammate? Or ask a whining preschooler: Can you think of a different way to tell me what you want?

8. They Forget to Have Fun

"When I talk to families that aren't functioning so well, and I ask, how often do you laugh together, they say: We haven't laughed together for a long time," says Hendren. Those little signs of love and connection—a laugh, a song shared in the car—are, he says, signs of health.

Do We Need a Law to Prohibit Spanking?

MURRAY STRAUS, PhD

The proposal by a member of the California legislature to prohibit spanking and other corporal punishment of children age three and younger has attracted nationwide interest—and outrage. Newspapers around the country published editorials about it. I read many of them, and all opposed the proposal. The two main objections are that spanking children is sometimes necessary and that it is an unprecedented and horrible example of government interference in the lives of families. The editorials usually also say or imply that "moderate" spanking does not harm children. These objections accurately represent the beliefs of most Americans, but they are not accurate representations of the scientific evidence on the effectiveness and side effects of spanking. They are also historically inaccurate about government interference in the family.

The research on the effectiveness of spanking shows that it does work to correct misbehavior. But the research also shows that spanking does not work better than other modes of correction and control, such as time out, explaining, and depriving a child of privileges. Moreover, the research clearly shows that the gains from spanking come at a big cost. These include weakening the tie between children and parents, and increasing the probability that the child will hit other children, hit their parents, and as adults hit a dating or marital partner. Spanking also slows down mental development and lowers the probability of a child doing well in school and in college. There have been more than a hundred studies of these side effects of spanking, and there is over 90% agreement between them. There is probably no other aspect of parenting and child behavior where the results are so consistent.

Despite this overwhelming evidence, few believe that "moderate" spanking harms children, including few psychologists. It seems to contradict their own experience and that of their children. They say "I was spanked and I was not a violent kid and I did well in school." That is correct, but the implication that spanking is harmless is not correct. Like smoking, spanking is a "risk factor"—not a one-to-one cause of problems. About a third of heavy smokers die of a smoking related disease. That is gruesome, but it also means that two thirds can say "I smoked all my life and I am OK." Does that mean smoking is OK? No, it just means that they are one of the lucky two thirds. Similarly, when someone says "I was spanked and I am OK," that is

correct. However, the implication that spanking is harmless is not correct. The correct implication is that they are one of the lucky majority, rather than one of those harmed by spanking.

> **The large and consistent body of evidence on the harmful side effects of spanking is also not believed because because so few get to know about it.**

Another reason the evidence is not believed is because the harm from spanking occurs down the road. Parents can see that the spanked child stopped what they were doing wrong. They cannot see the harmful effects that occur months or years later.

The large and consistent body of evidence on the harmful side effects of spanking is also not believed because so few get to know about it. I analyzed the content of ten child psychology textbooks published in the 1980's, ten in the 1990's, and ten published since 2000. These giant textbooks averaged only half a page on spanking, despite the fact that almost all American toddlers are spanked. None reported the fact that over 90% of the studies found harmful side-effects. Or putting it the other way around, none let their readers know that children who are not spanked, rather than being out of control brats, are more likely than spanked children to be well behaved and to have fewer psychological problems. This may be the best kept secret of American child psychology.

What about no-spanking legislation being an unprecedented interference in the family? Until the 1870's husbands had the right to use corporal punishment to correct an "errant wife." When the courts started to rule that this aspect of the common law was no longer valid, it was regarded by many as an outrageous interference in what should be a private family matter. Government now prohibits "physically chastisting an errant wife" and prohibits many other things to protect family members and to enhance the stability of the family, starting with prohibiting marriage at an early age.

The proposed California law, however, has two major problems. First, it applies only to children age three and younger. Therefore it has the ironic implication of endorsing the hitting of older children. A second irony is that this law would be doing the very thing it wants parents not to do—use harsh punishment to correct misbehavior. A better model is the 1979 Swedish no-spanking law. It has no criminal penalty. The purpose of that type of law is to set a standard for how children should be treated, and to make money available to educate the public about these standards and to provide services to help parents who are having enough difficulty with their children that they spank. The Swedish law has proven to be very effective. Spanking children has declined tremendously. Opponents of the law feared that Swedish children would be "running wild." The opposite has happened. Youth crime rates, drug use, and suicide have all decreased.

Fifteen nations now prohibit spanking by parents. There is an emerging consensus that this is a fundamental human right for children. The United Nations committee charged with implementing the Charter of Children's Rights is asking all nations to prohibit spanking. Never spanking will not only reduce the risk of delinquency and mental health problems, it will also bring to children the right to be free of physical attacks in the name of discipline, just as wives gained that human right a century and a quarter ago.

MURRAY A. STRAUS, PhD has studied spanking by large and representative samples of American parents for thirty years. He is the author of *Beating the Devil out of Them: Corporal Punishment in American Families and Its Effects on Children* (Transaction Press, 2001). He has been president of three scientific societies including the National Council On Family Relations, and an advisor to the National Institutes of Health and the National Science Foundation. He can be reached at 603 862-2594 or by email at murray.straus@unh.edu. Much of his research on spanking can be downloaded from http://pubpages.unh.edu/~mas2.

NCFR Report, *Family Focus Section,* Volume FF34, June 2007. Used by permission. Copyright 2007.

Children of Lesbian and Gay Parents

Does parental sexual orientation affect child development, and if so, how? Studies using convenience samples, studies using samples drawn from known populations, and studies based on samples that are representative of larger populations all converge on similar conclusions. More than two decades of research has failed to reveal important differences in the adjustment or development of children or adolescents reared by same-sex couples compared to those reared by other-sex couples. Results of the research suggest that qualities of family relationships are more tightly linked with child outcomes than is parental sexual orientation.

CHARLOTTE J. PATTERSON

Does parental sexual orientation affect child development, and if so, how? This question has often been raised in the context of legal and policy proceedings relevant to children, such as those involving adoption, child custody, or visitation. Divergent views have been offered by professionals from the fields of psychology, sociology, medicine, and law (Patterson, Fulcher, & Wainright, 2002). While this question has most often been raised in legal and policy contexts, it is also relevant to theoretical issues. For example, does healthy human development require that a child grow up with parents of each gender? And if not, what would that mean for our theoretical understanding of parent–child relations? (Patterson & Hastings, in press) In this article, I describe some research designed to address these questions.

Early Research

Research on children with lesbian and gay parents began with studies focused on cases in which children had been born in the context of a heterosexual marriage. After parental separation and divorce, many children in these families lived with divorced lesbian mothers. A number of researchers compared development among children of divorced lesbian mothers with that among children of divorced heterosexual mothers and found few significant differences (Patterson, 1997; Stacey & Biblarz, 2001).

These studies were valuable in addressing concerns of judges who were required to decide divorce and child custody cases, but they left many questions unanswered. In particular, because the children who participated in this research had been born into homes with married mothers and fathers, it was not obvious how to understand the reasons for their healthy development. The possibility that children's early exposure to apparently heterosexual male and female role models had contributed to healthy development could not be ruled out.

When lesbian or gay parents rear infants and children from birth, do their offspring grow up in typical ways and show healthy development? To address this question, it was important to study children who had never lived with heterosexual parents. In the 1990s, a number of investigators began research of this kind.

An early example was the Bay Area Families Study, in which I studied a group of 4- to 9-year-old children who had been born to or adopted early in life by lesbian mothers (Patterson, 1996, 1997). Data were collected during home visits. Results from in-home interviews and also from questionnaires showed that children had regular contact with a wide range of adults of both genders, both within and outside of their families. The children's self-concepts and preferences for same-gender playmates and activities were much like those of other children their ages. Moreover, standardized measures of social competence and of behavior problems, such as those from the Child Behavior Checklist (CBCL), showed that they scored within the range of normal variation for a representative sample of same-aged American children. It was clear from this study and others like it that it was quite possible for lesbian mothers to rear healthy children.

Studies Based on Samples Drawn from Known Populations

Interpretation of the results from the Bay Area Families Study was, however, affected by its sampling procedures. The study had been based on a convenience sample that had been assembled by word of mouth. It was therefore impossible to rule out the possibility that families who participated in the research were especially well adjusted. Would a more representative sample yield different results?

To find out, Ray Chan, Barbara Raboy, and I conducted research in collaboration with the Sperm Bank of California

(Chan, Raboy, & Patterson, 1998; Fulcher, Sutfin, Chan, Scheib, & Patterson, 2005). Over the more than 15 years of its existence, the Sperm Bank of California's clientele had included many lesbian as well as heterosexual women. For research purposes, this clientele was a finite population from which our sample could be drawn. The Sperm Bank of California also allowed a sample in which, both for lesbian and for heterosexual groups, one parent was biologically related to the child and one was not.

We invited all clients who had conceived children using the resources of the Sperm Bank of California and who had children 5 years old or older to participate in our research. The resulting sample was composed of 80 families, 55 headed by lesbian and 25 headed by heterosexual parents. Materials were mailed to participating families, with instructions to complete them privately and return them in self-addressed stamped envelopes we provided.

Results replicated and expanded upon those from earlier research. Children of lesbian and heterosexual parents showed similar, relatively high levels of social competence, as well as similar, relatively low levels of behavior problems on the parent form of the CBCL. We also asked the children's teachers to provide evaluations of children's adjustment on the Teacher Report Form of the CBCL, and their reports agreed with those of parents. Parental sexual orientation was not related to children's adaptation. Quite apart from parental sexual orientation, however, and consistent with findings from years of research on children of heterosexual parents, when parent–child relationships were marked by warmth and affection, children were more likely to be developing well. Thus, in this sample drawn from a known population, measures of children's adjustment were unrelated to parental sexual orientation (Chan et al., 1998; Fulcher et al., 2005).

Even as they provided information about children born to lesbian mothers, however, these new results also raised additional questions. Women who conceive children at sperm banks are generally both well educated and financially comfortable. It was possible that these relatively privileged women were able to protect children from many forms of discrimination. What if a more diverse group of families were to be studied? In addition, the children in this sample averaged 7 years of age, and some concerns focus on older children and adolescents. What if an older group of youngsters were to be studied? Would problems masked by youth and privilege in earlier studies emerge in an older, more diverse sample?

Studies Based on Representative Samples

An opportunity to address these questions was presented by the availability of data from the National Longitudinal Study of Adolescent Health (Add Health). The Add Health study involved a large, ethnically diverse, and essentially representative sample of American adolescents and their parents. Data for our research were drawn from surveys and interviews completed by more than 12,000 adolescents and their parents at home and from surveys completed by adolescents at school.

Parents were not queried directly about their sexual orientation but were asked if they were involved in a "marriage, or marriage-like relationship." If parents acknowledged such a relationship, they were also asked the gender of their partner. Thus, we identified a group of 44 12- to 18-year-olds who lived with parents involved in marriage or marriage-like relationships with same-sex partners. We compared them with a matched group of adolescents living with other-sex couples. Data from the archives of the Add Health study allowed us to address many questions about adolescent development.

Consistent with earlier findings, results of this work revealed few differences in adjustment between adolescents living with same-sex parents and those living with opposite-sex parents (Wainright, Russell, & Patterson, 2004; Wainright & Patterson, 2006). There were no significant differences between teenagers living with same-sex parents and those living with other-sex parents on self-reported assessments of psychological well-being, such as self-esteem and anxiety; measures of school outcomes, such as grade point averages and trouble in school; or measures of family relationships, such as parental warmth and care from adults and peers. Adolescents in the two groups were equally likely to say that they had been involved in a romantic relationship in the last 18 months, and they were equally likely to report having engaged in sexual intercourse. The only statistically reliable difference between the two groups—that those with same-sex parents felt a greater sense of connection to people at school—favored the youngsters living with same-sex couples. There were no significant differences in self-reported substance use, delinquency, or peer victimization between those reared by same- or other-sex couples (Wainright & Patterson, 2006).

Although the gender of parents' partners was not an important predictor of adolescent well-being, other aspects of family relationships were significantly associated with teenagers' adjustment. Consistent with other findings about adolescent development, the qualities of family relationships rather than the gender of parents' partners were consistently related to adolescent outcomes. Parents who reported having close relationships with their offspring had adolescents who reported more favorable adjustment. Not only is it possible for children and adolescents who are parented by same-sex couples to develop in healthy directions, but—even when studied in an extremely diverse, representative sample of American adolescents—they generally do.

These findings have been supported by results from many other studies, both in the United States and abroad. Susan Golombok and her colleagues have reported similar results with a near-representative sample of children in the United Kingdom (Golombok et al., 2003). Others, both in Europe and in the United States, have described similar findings (e.g., Brewaeys, Ponjaert, Van Hall, & Golombok, 1997).

The fact that children of lesbian mothers generally develop in healthy ways should not be taken to suggest that they encounter no challenges. Many investigators have remarked upon the fact that children of lesbian and gay parents may encounter anti-gay sentiments in their daily lives. For example, in a study of 10-year-old children born to lesbian mothers, Gartrell, Deck, Rodas, Peyser, and Banks (2005) reported that a substantial minority had encountered anti-gay sentiments among their peers. Those who had had such encounters were likely to report having felt angry, upset, or sad about these experiences. Children of lesbian and gay parents may be exposed to prejudice against their parents in some settings, and this may be painful for them, but evidence for the idea that such encounters affect children's overall adjustment is lacking.

Conclusions

Does parental sexual orientation have an important impact on child or adolescent development? Results of recent research provide no evidence that it does. In fact, the findings suggest that parental sexual orientation is less important than the qualities of family relationships. More important to youth than the gender of their parent's partner is the quality of daily interaction and the strength of relationships with the parents they have.

One possible approach to findings like the ones described above might be to shrug them off by reiterating the familiar adage that "one cannot prove the null hypothesis." To respond in this way, however, is to miss the central point of these studies. Whether or not any measurable impact of parental sexual orientation on children's development is ever demonstrated, the main conclusions from research to date remain clear: Whatever correlations between child outcomes and parental sexual orientation may exist, they are less important than those between child outcomes and the qualities of family relationships.

Although research to date has made important contributions, many issues relevant to children of lesbian and gay parents remain in need of study. Relatively few studies have examined the development of children adopted by lesbian or gay parents or of children born to gay fathers; further research in both areas would be welcome (Patterson, 2004). Some notable longitudinal studies have been reported, and they have found children of same-sex couples to be in good mental health. Greater understanding of family relationships and transitions over time would, however, be helpful, and longitudinal studies would be valuable. Future research could also benefit from the use of a variety of methodologies.

Meanwhile, the clarity of findings in this area has been acknowledged by a number of major professional organizations. For instance, the governing body of the American Psychological Association (APA) voted unanimously in favor of a statement that said, "Research has shown that the adjustment, development, and psychological well-being of children is unrelated to parental sexual orientation and that children of lesbian and gay parents are as likely as those of heterosexual parents to flourish" (APA, 2004). The American Bar Association, the American Medical Association, the American Academy of Pediatrics, the American Psychiatric Association, and other mainstream professional groups have issued similar statements.

The findings from research on children of lesbian and gay parents have been used to inform legal and public policy debates across the country (Patterson et al., 2002). The research literature on this subject has been cited in amicus briefs filed by the APA in cases dealing with adoption, child custody, and also in cases related to the legality of marriages between same-sex partners. Psychologists serving as expert witnesses have presented findings on these issues in many different courts (Patterson et al., 2002). Through these and other avenues, results of research on lesbian and gay parents and their children are finding their way into public discourse.

The findings are also beginning to address theoretical questions about critical issues in parenting. The importance of gender in parenting is one such issue. When children fare well in two-parent lesbian-mother or gay-father families, this suggests that the gender of one's parents cannot be a critical factor in child development. Results of research on children of lesbian and gay parents cast doubt upon the traditional assumption that gender is important in parenting. Our data suggest that it is the quality of parenting rather than the gender of parents that is significant for youngsters' development.

Research on children of lesbian and gay parents is thus located at the intersection of a number of classic and contemporary concerns. Studies of lesbian- and gay-parented families allow researchers to address theoretical questions that had previously remained difficult or impossible to answer. They also address oft-debated legal questions of fact about development of children with lesbian and gay parents. Thus, research on children of lesbian and gay parents contributes to public debate and legal decision making, as well as to theoretical understanding of human development.

References

American Psychological Association (2004). Resolution on sexual orientation, parents, and children. Retrieved September 25, 2006, from http://www.apa.org/pi/lgbc/policy/parentschildren.pdf

Brewaeys, A., Ponjaert, I., Van Hall, E.V., & Golombok, S. (1997). Donor insemination: Child development and family functioning in lesbian mother families. *Human Reproduction, 12,* 1349–1359.

Chan, R.W., Raboy, B., & Patterson, C.J. (1998). Psychosocial adjustment among children conceived via donor insemination by lesbian and heterosexual mothers. *Child Development, 69,* 443–457.

Fulcher, M., Sutfin, E.L., Chan, R.W., Scheib, J.E., & Patterson, C.J. (2005). Lesbian mothers and their children: Findings from the Contemporary Families Study. In A. Omoto & H. Kurtzman (Eds.), *Recent research on sexual orientation, mental health, and substance abuse* (pp. 281–299). Washington, DC: American Psychological Association.

Gartrell, N., Deck., A., Rodas, C., Peyser, H., & Banks, A. (2005). The National Lesbian Family Study: 4. Interviews with the 10-year-old children. *American Journal of Orthopsychiatry, 75,* 518–524.

Golombok, S., Perry, B., Burston, A., Murray, C., Mooney-Somers, J., Stevens, M., & Golding, J. (2003). Children with lesbian parents: A community study. *Developmental Psychology, 39,* 20–33.

Patterson, C.J. (1996). Lesbian mothers and their children: Findings from the Bay Area Families Study. In J. Laird & R.J. Green (Eds.), *Lesbians and gays in couples and families: A handbook for therapists* (pp. 420–437). San Francisco: Jossey-Bass.

Patterson, C.J. (1997). Children of lesbian and gay parents. In T. Ollendick & R. Prinz (Eds.), *Advances in clinical child psychology* (Vol. 19, pp. 235–282). New York: Plenum Press.

Patterson, C.J. (2004). Gay fathers. In M.E. Lamb (Ed.), *The role of the father in child development* (4th ed., pp. 397–416). New York: Wiley.

Patterson, C.J., Fulcher, M., & Wainright, J. (2002). Children of lesbian and gay parents: Research, law, and policy. In B.L. Bottoms, M.B. Kovera, & B.D. McAuliff (Eds.), *Children, social science and the law* (pp. 176–199). New York: Cambridge University Press.

Patterson, C.J., & Hastings, P. (in press). Socialization in context of family diversity. In J. Grusec & P. Hastings (Eds.), *Handbook of socialization.* New York: Guilford Press.

Stacey, J., & Biblarz, T.J. (2001). (How) Does sexual orientation of parents matter? *American Sociological Review, 65,* 159–183.

Wainright, J.L., Russell, S.T., & Patterson, C.J. (2004). Psychosocial adjustment and school outcomes of adolescents with same-sex parents. *Child Development, 75,* 1886–1898.

Wainright, J.L., & Patterson, C.J. (2006). Delinquency, victimization, and substance use among adolescents with female same-sex parents. *Journal of Family Psychology, 20,* 526–530.

Address correspondence to **CHARLOTTE J. PATTERSON,** Department of Psychology, P.O. Box 400400, University of Virginia, Charlottesville, VA 22904; e-mail: cjp@virginia.edu.

Prickly Père

What are your obligations to a parent who's smothering or abusive?

Elizabeth Svoboda

As a child, Michael Levine yearned to please his mother, but her drinking gave rise to mood swings so extreme that living at home felt like performing a high-wire act. "You didn't know what was going to happen from one day to the next," says Levine, now a Los Angeles public relations executive. "Monday you might be told you were God Almighty, and Tuesday you might have things thrown at you."

We each owe our existence to our parents, and in many cases, we'll never fully appreciate their sacrifices on our behalf. But prospective parents don't have to pass mental-health tests to procreate, and parents with difficult personalities come in as many flavors as emotionally challenged suitors. Some are "helicopter parents," always hovering, anxious and overprotective; some neglect their children's needs out of selfishness or mild depression; others seethe with anger, unhappiness, or jealousy, lashing out at their offspring—physically or verbally—on a regular basis. But such parents can nevertheless come across to outsiders as involved and loving, so children receive little independent confirmation that something is wrong with the way they're being treated.

Many people born into difficult families spend their childhoods looking forward to leaving their parents' orbit. But when they do, the parameters that define the relationship must be redrawn: How can adult children strike a balance between maintaining a healthy measure of personal freedom and keeping difficult parents satisfied? Are they obligated to keep communication lines open as a gesture of filial loyalty? Can anything positive be salvaged from the relationship? Regardless of parents' past wrongs, the duty to "honor thy father and mother" exerts a strong pull.

Parents with toxic personalities can feel threatened by their grown children's independence, making this balancing act treacherous. Other parents make drastic impositions on their adult children's lives in an effort to reassert closeness.

We want so badly to believe that our parents are perfect, and we resist the idea that they need to change. We tend to hope that with enough love from us, they'll smooth out the rough edges of their personalities. But ironically, their confidence in our unconditional support can make them feel like changing is unnecessary. "Most parents continue the behavior that has always 'worked' for them, since it gets them what they want," says syndicated advice columnist Amy Alkon. The best way to sustain a relationship with a troubled parent is to set clear boundaries for your interactions with them. Allowing parents unlimited access to your time and resources might seem like the most selfless option, but it can backfire: You'll rack up so much resentment that you lose sight of your parents' positive qualities, and what's left of the relationship shrivels.

If problem parents are confident of their kids' unconditional support, they will feel little pressure to improve.

The best way to negotiate these boundaries varies depending on the type and severity of a parent's problems, says Barbara Kane, a psychologist who specializes in family issues. One basic rule of thumb, though, is to take a calm but uncompromising stand against unreasonable demands, vicious put-downs, and other bad behaviors. If your mother insists that you drive an hour and a half just to fix her thermostat and fires off a volley like "You're a horrible daughter for not wanting to help me," or even "I'll kill myself if you don't come," stand your ground while still acknowledging your parent's feelings—which communicates a message of caring. "Try saying something like 'I understand you're disappointed I can't do this right now,'" says Kane.

"You can't change a parent," emphasizes Karen Shore, a Santa Monica, California, clinical psychologist. "What you can do is change how you react to them. Anger will push you back into the old, unbalanced parent-child dynamic."

To cultivate empathy for your parents, it helps to view them objectively, says psychologist Cheryl Dellasega, author of *Forced to Be Family*. If Dad is verbally abusive, or Mom seems forever in need of affirmation, think about what might have made them that way. As children, were they neglected? Mistreated? Bullied? Did they grow up in households where

Taming the Toxic Parent

Problem parents can dominate your life. Here's how to manage them without sacrificing happiness or autonomy.

- **Set firm boundaries** for approaching a difficult parent. If your parent is smothering or narcissistic, opt for shorter or less frequent visits.
- **If your parent is verbally abusive,** walk away when insults start to fly.
- **Stop trying to "fix" your troubled parent.** Recognize that you're not to blame for his or her shortcomings.
- **Don't let past infractions poison your relations now.** Forgiving doesn't mean forgetting, but be open to healthy new developments in the relationship.
- **Avoid situations that trigger underlying conflict.** If your parents act toxic at large family gatherings, try suggesting a park outing or a play.
- **Think about what the relationship means to you** and whether it's worth saving *even if he or she never changes.* Your parents aren't total monsters: They influence your life in positive ways as well as negative ones—so think hard before deciding to cut them off.

screaming fits were the primary mode of communication? Life experiences don't excuse rotten behavior, but understanding what's shaped someone can help you come up with more compassionate and appropriate responses to inappropriate behavior. When your investment-banker dad ridicules your job as a day-care instructor, try "I realize your priorities in life are different from mine." When your mother begs you to stay overnight with her at the assisted-living center, try "You know I'm never going to abandon you, Mom."

Interacting with an unpleasant parent on a day-to-day basis is only half the battle; adult children must also tackle the broader question of what exactly they "owe" the person who gave them life—but now makes them miserable. Some children opt to love and stand by their difficult parents no matter what, treasuring the sense of self-worth that comes from honoring the relationship.

Other offspring embrace the possibility—however disconcerting—that filial closeness is best found outside the family they were born into. "Some parents think, Ha, ha, you're stuck with me, I can do anything I want," says Alkon. "But to me, family are people who really treat you like family. People shouldn't focus so much on DNA." Shore agrees: "We should not judge children who decide to distance themselves from their parents. To the outside world, it looks callous, but if a parent has really destroyed a child's life, it can be the healthiest thing."

For children who resolve to stick it out with problem parents, the struggle is not without reward. Levine worked hard at maintaining regular contact with his mother in the years before she died. The decision to stay in touch wasn't easy—each time he visited her, the pain and bad memories came flooding back—but he doesn't regret it. "You need to be able to put the past in some kind of bracketed perspective," he says. "Opportunities to truly resolve all your issues with a parent are few and far between, but I feel a little bit more peaceful knowing that I made the effort."

ELIZABETH SVOBODA is a freelance writer based in San Jose, California.

The Forgotten Siblings

In this article I wish to argue that the qualities and dynamics of sibling relationships may have been overlooked in family therapy. In overlooking them, we have also overlooked a significant feature in the emotional life of children. I would like to suggest that sibling relationships are where children practise identity. In these relationships we can learn how to be one in a group. Family Therapy treatment may not make enough use of the dynamic of the sibling relationship.

SALLY YOUNG

Family therapists have prided themselves on their peripheral vision. Part of the claim of systemic therapy is to see the 'big picture.' In terms of families, this often means seeing the whole family. At the very least, it means that the therapist must take into account the existence and importance of family viewpoints other than those represented in the therapy room. However, it could he contended that our primary focus has been on the parent-child relationship and that the sibling relationship is on the periphery. At worst these relationships may have been taken for granted rather than analysed.

In the course of writing this article I opened many relationship and psychology books and looked up 'sibling' in the index. What was interesting was how few references there were, and that usually the word 'sibling' was coupled with 'rivalry.' That in itself was disquieting, in that it suggests that the rivalry in sibling relationships has been emphasised above other emotional dynamics.

Siblings engage in multiple, complex interactions over many years, and in the process they learn much, and could be said to 'practise' many positions they will later take in adult life and relationships. From a lifespan perspective, sibling relationships are often the longest-lasting relationships we have—outlasting relationships with parents, partners, and our own offspring. Here are some key 'sibling learnings':

- That love and hate can quickly follow each other; this is the precursor to ambivalence, where a mixture of feelings can be tolerated together.
- That we can *feel* 'murderous,' but also come to know that we would not *act* on this: an important experience in differentiating thought and action.
- That there is a thin line between a tight hug and a strangle, that we can come to know about our

desire to hurt, that in this way we become aware of our own potential for cruelty and our own potential to manage this.

- That we get to be alone together (Winnicott, 1958).
- That we can hate a sibling at home but defend him/her outside the home. That loyalty and honour involve the ability to manage our own ambivalence.
- That being a parent's favourite can ultimately be as burdensome as not being the favourite.
- That we can never overtake our older siblings—a challenge to our magical thinking.
- That we can imitate, anticipate, or dread, the developmental stages that we see our older siblings go through.
- That our sibling relationships offer an invisible continuity throughout our lives, although the grievances, the jealousy, and the competitiveness may be lifelong as well.

In the past couple of years, I have noticed a resurgence of interest in sibling relationships in the systemic and psychodynamic literature. *The Journal of Family Psychology* devoted a special edition to sibling relation-ships in 2005. This special edition emphasises the need for further research in this complex area, but looks at the state of the evidence for sibling relationships in the development of psychopathology. Juliet Mitchell's book. *Siblings* (2003) and *The Importance of Sibling Relationships in Psychoanalysis* (2003) by Prophecy Coles are another two examples. All in different ways suggest that our culture emphasises 'vertical relationships' and marginalises horizontal relationships such as those with our siblings. Sibling relationships are the prototype of peer and later collegial relationships. This idea attracted me as I have long felt that families, classrooms and workplaces survive on the capacity of individuals to find peers, as well protectors, in the face of the inevitable predators. Judy Dunn writes:

> There are powerful arguments for viewing siblings as potentially developmentally important: Their daily contact and familiarity, their emotionally uninhibited relationship, and the impact of sharing parents all suggest that the relationship may have a developmental influence (2005: 654).

Some scenarios come to mind.

Scenario 1

Sharon is a 17-year-old girl, who has a turbulent history. Her brother Mark is a source of great suffering for her. She feels tormented and intimidated by him. The intensity of their arguments has the quality of lovers' tiffs but without the love. One night, Sharon falls back on the familiar solution of cutting herself, as if in search of the lifeblood of her pain. Mark uncharacteristically tries to stop her. Sharon uncharacteristically does stop. Later in a session she says 'I stopped, as it was such a shock that he cared whether I lived'.

Scenario 2

Kathleen is in her forties. Suddenly and unexpectedly her eldest brother dies of a coronary. She awakes in the night anxious about her own mortality. The thought that she is one step closer to death strikes her: a rung has been removed in the ladder of mortality. Somewhere it reflects how deep the sense of sibling order is in her mind. As if some unconscious law dictates we must all die in timely order? Instead, reality declares an untimely disorder

I would now like to look at theoretical constructions of sibling relationships.

As suggested earlier, 'sibling rivalry' is often the only aspect of sibling relationships to receive attention, and has become somewhat clichéd. Perhaps it is worth revisiting. Rivalry is often seen as negative and destructive, yet it can be a positive spur to development. Circular questioning in family therapy often illustrates that there is more than rivalry in sibling relationships, and that siblings can understand each other well, particularly when it comes to issues of the familiar war between parents and children.

Nonetheless it is important not to deny the power and at times the secession between siblings. I think aggressive feelings between siblings are much less repressed than those between parents and children. Juliet Mitchell writes:

> I believe we have minimized or overlooked entirely the threat to our existence as small children that is posed by the new baby who stands in our place or the older child who was there before us (2003: xv).

She suggests there is little difference between the tantrumming two-year-old who feels left out by the attention given to the baby, and the hysteria of adult life. In both, she argues the demand is 'Look at me, I am unique, there is only room for me!'

Perhaps all of us in family work have come across individuals who cannot bear the sharing of emotional space that is needed in families, and in family therapy. Juliet argues that beneath this is something that may have its roots in traumatic sibling rivalry; that is, the threat of annihilation by the other, even if that annihilation is figurative rather than actual—a child feels obliterated just by the fact of its sibling's existence. Mitchell goes on to speak about the triumph which psychopaths feel in obliterating the other.

Both Mitchell and Coles argue that theoretically we have overemphasised the Oedipal complex, and as a result have looked vertically (at child—parent relationships) rather than horizontally (at the child—child level). The equivalent of this could be most graphically seen in the structural school of family therapy (Minuchin, 1974). Also the strategic school (Haley, 1976) places enormous emphasis on parental—child relationship. In family therapy perhaps this goes with the understandable stress on parents being parents, taking on their parental authority and functioning in an aware manner. All this I agree with completely, yet is it the complete story?

The danger of the parentified child is something we are all alert to. Yet many of us see single-parent families under stress, where it is necessary for the family's survival that a child carries some parental functions. I wonder if one aspect that may test the difference between functional and dysfunctional parentification is how the parent manages the differences in roles between the siblings. For instance, is it still clear that the child is a child carrying some parental functions, as opposed to being mother's partner, which can only promote aggression and rivalry between the siblings?

Psychodynamic authors suggest that siblings who are very rivalrous may reflect unresolved sibling conflict in the parent's family of origin. In my work in CYMHS, I am struck with how often a parent will, on exploration, reflect a concern that a child will be like a troublesome uncle or aunt. The parent's childhood experiences of their sibling are echoed in the child's behaviour. The child is seen like a sibling, and the parent often attempts to be like or very unlike their own parents, in the management of the sibling ghost. Byng-Hall calls this the replicative or corrective script (Byng-Hall, 1995).

The Development of Group Psychology

I think one of the most powerful areas that have been overlooked in sibling relationships is the power of identification. In childhood, it is an important experience to feel part of a group and be able to step inside the shoes of another. Mary Target (2002) refers to research that suggests that younger siblings are slightly better at reading the intentions of older siblings than their older siblings are, given that they are born into a sibling order with big sister or big brother predecessors. Peter Fonagy and Mary Target's work's (2003) highlights the concept of 'mentalisation' in emotional development. This is really the capacity to think about thinking and feeling, in ourselves and others. They suggest this capacity is vital for us in digesting the realities of our internal and external lives. The people we have the most practice in interpreting/thinking about in childhood are our siblings. After all, we often spend the most time with them, in the timeless world of childhood.

It is worth reflecting on how powerfully siblings 'wind each other up,' so equally, they bear witness to each other's emotional worlds. Sibling can bring each other alive. In theory, circular questioning may access these understandings. However, this depends on a level of verbalisation that may be beyond many children, and perhaps we need to find a 'play equivalent' of this technique to access these understandings between siblings. These sibling insights may be accessed through projective games such as the Bear Cards (St Lukes Innovative Resources) and family drawings.

Michael Rutter's studies of children from Romanian orphanages who had been adopted in England indicated that these traumatised children, from horrific institutional situations, like to be with babies—as though the baby gives them back their lost baby selves (Mitchell: 227). Similarly, one can see in many families the way in which a new baby can regenerate a capacity for feelings in siblings and in parents.

Juliet Mitchell writes of having the experience of being part of a group and not feeling annihilated by it (Mitchell, 2003: 52). Sibling relationships give us an early but important experience of being the same but different, which is an experience we have whenever we are in a group. Clearly, our parents are central in managing this experience. The capacity to be in a group is something that we have psychologically undervalued.

Stuart Twemlow (2001), in his research on bullying in schools, stresses the significance of the group, comparing schools with high and low rates of bullying. What he discovered to be the significant factor is what is called the bystander affect. If, when a victim was being bullied, the rest of the group acted as passive bystanders, this was oxygen for the bullying—it inflamed it; if the others were not prepared to be passive, but expressed a point of view, the bullying diminished. Our preparedness to participate in group life is vital, in personal life and in a democracy. In families, whether a troubled sibling is left isolated, or feels some connectedness with a sibling, is often predictive of how likely the family is to respond positively to treatment. Perhaps all family work on some level is looking for the capacity to imaginatively identify with the other.

Prophecy Coles writes:

> Emde, surveying research on infant development to date . . . suggests we need a new concept of the 'we' ego. That is children by the age of three had developed an executive sense of 'we', of the other being with them which gave them increased sense of power and control (Coles, 2003: 76).

Emde says:

> It is perhaps ironic that in our age, so preoccupied with narcissism and self, we are beginning to see a different aspect of psychology, a 'we' psychology in addition to a self psychology . . . This represents a pro-found change in our world view (Coles, 2003: 76).

The Significance of Birth Order

From Adler to the more recent work by Sulloway in his book *Born to Rebel,* theorists have asserted the determinative effects of birth order, though others have argued that these effects are exaggerated, or non-existent. Sulloway hypothesises that the eldest is more authoritarian, having lost something by his displacement by his younger siblings, and the youngest is more likely to rebel, having the security of being the baby of the family. This strikes me as over-deterministic.

However, each individual will experience and interpret family dynamics differently. Siblings growing up in the same family may report very different experiences. Research has indicated that inter-family experiences may be almost as diverse as between-family experiences (Richardson & Richardson, 1990). The differences in family experiences might partly be due to parental expectations, which vary depending on birth order. In their seminal book *Separate Lives: Why Sibling Are So Different,* Robert Plomin and Judy Dunn argue that despite siblings being brought up in the same environment, the environment only *seems* the same. Each sibling perceives their family environment differently, which explains why they turn out so different. I also wonder if a factor in identity formation is the experience of feeling individual through differentiation from one's sibling.

Michael Duffy's joint biography of politicians Mark Latham and Tony Abbott points out that

> . . . each is the eldest child of four children, the others being three girls, each had parents who were enormously ambitious for their only son, and each was as highly competitive and aggressive in sport as they were to be in Federal parliament (Fitzgerald, 2004: 11).

Whether it is completely accurate or not, this description gives a sense of the complex mixture of personality, sibling order, parental expectations and gender mix in families.

In fact, I wonder if one of the many insufficiently understood dynamics in sibling relationships is gender. Being a child with siblings of the other gender is a primary experience of a gendered relationship. Perhaps a test of this is the difference in associations in the public mind between brotherly love, sisterly love and love between a brother and a sister. I recall seeing a mother who had three sons, but who described having only sisters in her family of origin. Despite having a good relationship with her husband, she says 'I just don't understand boys.' I thought that she felt that without brothers, she had missed out on an imaginative understanding of boys, an understanding 'from the inside out,' in the way a sibling might.

Birth order can have determinative effects; take, for example, the case of the eldest child, accorded a special place with a grandparent, as the first grandchild. Yet many other factors can mitigate these effects. For instance, school gives children another chance with their peers. A youngest child who is the 'baby' at home may find herself being able to take a leadership role at school, in this way finding a possibility of being taken seriously by others and by herself.

It is important not to leave out the single child, frequently called the only child. For myself this has associations of 'only an only' child, as if the very description raises an idea of a disappointment that there aren't more children. Miriam Cosic, in her book *Only Child,* argues that culturally the drawbacks of being an only child have been overstated. Perhaps we may potentially envy the only child for not having to share! Single children frequently imagine what happened to the possibility of other children. Family therapists will be increasingly challenged to adapt when the single child family becomes more common. I think one particular difficulty is that the child then has no potential child witnesses or allies in the therapy room. Perhaps

when the family has only one child, the onus on the therapist is increased, to join with the child and allow him/her to remain a child, not a pseudo-adult in the sessions.

Single children frequently imagine what happened to the possibility of other children.

It is not unusual for children to carry the fantasy of a twin as a comforting solution to isolation. For example, Mary is complaining with great intensity about her troublesome little brother. He is indeed troublesome but something in her complaints makes me feel there is more. 'Do you wish you had a sister?' I ask. What then emerges is a very full imagining of a twin sister with whom she could play soccer. Later in the session it was possible for her to have some more hopeful imaginings of when her *brother* could manage to play soccer with her.

The Ghosts in the Nursery

We are generally alert to the influence of the parent's childhood lying like a shadow over their parenting. However, many children, too, carry ghosts—the ghosts of their sibling experiences, which can sometimes include a sibling's mental disturbance. The most poetic description I have found has been in the Oliver Sacks' autobiography, in which he describes the psychotic breakdown of his brother Michael, when Oliver was 12.

> Michael could no longer sleep or rest, but agitatedly strode to and fro in the house, stamping his feet, glaring, hallucinating, shouting. I became terrified of him, for him, of the nightmare which was becoming reality for him, the more so as I could recognize similar thoughts and feelings in myself, even though they were hidden locked up in my own depths. What would happen to Michael, and would something similar happen to me, too? It was at this time that I set up my own lab in the house, and closed the doors, closed my ears against Michael's madness. It was at this time that I sought for (and sometimes achieved) an intense concentration, a complete absorption in the worlds of mineralogy and chemistry and physics, in science—focusing on them, holding myself together in the chaos. It was not that I was indifferent to Michael; I felt a passionate sympathy for him, I half-knew what he was going through, but I had to keep a distance also, create my own world from the neutrality and beauty of nature, so that I would not be swept into the chaos, the madness, the seduction, of his (Sacks, 2001: 186).

It is not easy to deal with a child's trauma about a disturbed sibling. I have sometimes seen siblings who have such a fear of madness or emotionality, that it can be difficult to find a therapeutic engagement to support them. However, a timely family session can provide a forum for siblings to speak of their distress, and this can help rescue the parents from focusing only on the disturbed sibling.

> Rose is 13 years old. Her elder sister. Sara, has early symptoms of anorexia nervosa. Both parents are understandably preoccupied with Sara's mental and physical health. When asked in a family session how this affects her, Rose says, 'I just come home from school and go to my room. The talk is always about Sara'. Her parents are initially shocked, and mother says she feels the same as Rose, unheard above the worry about Sara. A few minutes later we are again talking about Sara, but Mother and Rose have noticeably faded into the background. It seems important to draw attention that what happens in the family's daily life is happening in the session.

I am very fond of the idea, borrowed from physics, that in a family system, every action has an opposite and equal reaction. I have been struck many times over the years by how siblings tend towards either identifying with each other or individuating by being opposite. Often a conduct-disordered teenager who takes inadequate responsibility, somewhere has a sibling who takes too much responsibility. I think it often happens that the reactions to each other can be seen on the internalising–externalising spectrum. By this I mean that one child may 'internalise' his/her emotional life, perhaps by being withdrawn and depressive, and the other sibling may 'externalise' by being actively disobedient, showing aggression, doing drugs, and the like. Perhaps this 'equal and opposite' phenomenon could be a worthy area of further research, as if proven it would give further support to the systemic model of intervention.

> Harry is part of a large single-parent family. They are a poor family, struggling to keep their heads above water. Harry has an explosive temper that is frightening to everyone in the family. Harry is seen as following in the footsteps of his father's violence. When Harry explodes it reminds everyone in the family of the terrors of the past. Jean, the eldest girl in the family, stands up to Harry, trying to support her mother. Harry hates this, saying to Jean 'You are not my mother'. One day Jean unexpectedly runs away, perhaps in search of a childhood. Later she returns, wanting to live with the family. The family work is about helping Harry free himself from his identification with his father, but also to allow Jean

to be a big sister, not to replay a mother fighting with a father.

The siblings of children with special needs themselves have particular needs. Kate Strohm's book. *Siblings: Brothers and Sisters of Children with Special Needs,* vividly describes her own experience of growing up with a sister who had cerebral palsy. This work assisted in the development of a website www.siblingsaustralia.org.au, which provides information and Internet support to siblings. On this site, children whose siblings have special needs can talk about the dangers of lack of information about the disability, and their feelings of isolation, resentment and grief. The Internet chat room functions as a cyberspace sibling group for these young people. Anecdotal evidence suggests that siblings of special needs children sometimes become health professionals, so this may be pertinent to the professional reader.

Family Sessions as 'Commissions for Truth, Justice and Reconciliation'

I have long been struck by how significant the concept of fairness is in psychological life. An article by the British analyst Eric Rayner (Rayner, 2000: 153) drew my attention the preoccupation with fairness, in both therapy and everyday life. For instance, in writing this article, my wish to create case examples that would suit my argument might conflict with my wish to do justice to those involved, even if only in my imagination. It strikes me that the original arena for this fight for justice is the sibling group, and subsequently the playground. The oft-heard retort of childhood, 'S'not fair', echoes this preoccupation.

I think family therapy has a forgotten but useful sibling, anthropology. The anthropological attitude is very valuable in its enquiry into meaning, rituals and events. Sometimes we will be dealing with hostile 'warring tribes.' And in certain situations the anthropological attitude allows us not to feel compelled to be the agents of change, and can allow a more respectful attitude towards the family, so that they can create solutions within their own culture.

This idea of justice for multiple voices is exemplified by Helen Garner:

> I went to visit my four sisters, carrying a tape recorder and my imagined map of my family. It was unsettling to learn that each sister has her own quite individual map of that territory: the mountains and rivers are in different places, the borders are differently constituted and guarded, the history and politics and justice system of the country are different according to who's talking (Garner, 1997: vi).

In a very poetic way, Garner is alerting us to the trauma of growing up and dealing with competing claims within the same psychological territory. Since I decided to write this article I have been much more consciously asking children about their relationship about their siblings. This list is my attempt at the top 10 complaints:

1. *She gets into my things and sometimes breaks them.* This seems to be the precursor to:
2. *She gets under my skin.*
3. *It's not fair, he gets away with murder.*
4. *She is such a goody-goody.*
5. *Mum and Dad don't know what she gets up to.*
6. *He's the favourite.*
7. *I wish they were dead* [and they are not].
8. *They get all the attention.*
9. *He stinks.*
10. *She spends all her time in front of the mirror.*

I have found that surprisingly often, *the acknowledgement of some feeling of unfairness* seems to take the heat out of the anger, as if the child has felt that no one sees his or her point of view, that a sense of internal justice has been lost. This fight for justice happens in families and between couples as well. I think we do not do it psychological justice if we only call it a 'power struggle.' The apparent tussle for 'power' conceals a deeper concern with fairness.

Couples

Perhaps as a part of my recent focus on siblings, it is has been striking me that over time a sibling-type dynamic can develop in couple relationships. This has positive features, such as companionship and knowing each other very well. But it can also embody negative aspects, such as knowing each other too well, and being able to get under each other's skin. From this point of view, I wonder if the wish for space within a couple is sometimes the wish *to feel less like siblings* and hence to recapture some desire. I think sometimes the ghost of sibling relationships is enacted within these couples.

Mr X was the eldest child in his family. He has been married to Mrs X for 30 years, and she was the youngest child in her family. In the early stages of their relationship, some of his protective capacities were attractive to Mrs X. Gradually, however, she has come to feel restricted in the relationship as though she can never grow up, as though she always remains the little sister. Of course this description of their relationship would not do justice to its other dynamics. Yet to ignore this aspect would mean one

might never uncover what their sibling roles had meant in their identity formation, leaving them feeling stuck forever in an unfair childhood.

Conclusion

Throughout this paper, I have tried to argue that our sibling relationships have a power and dynamism of their own, not to be tidied away as a shadow of the parent–child relationship. Family therapy may not have paid enough attention to this dynamic, both theoretically and technically. Perhaps the question of 'Where are the siblings?' is an extension of Catherine Sanders' comment that has there been 'a recurrent failure to embrace children as clients' (2003: 177). A recent family therapy book by Robert Sanders (2004), *Sibling Relationships: Theory and Issues for Practice* may be testimony to a growing interest within family therapy. Sanders raises many dilemmas for practice such as the question of siblings in care being kept together and of course the danger of assuming we know what is best without assessing the uniqueness of any sibling relationship.

One area ripe for investigation is the actual history of this neglect of conceptualisation of sibling relationships, across all therapies. I wonder if unspoken assumptions that siblings are rivalrous and destructive has meant we potentially neglect the value of these early 'we' relationships. Ironically as systemic therapists, have we neglected the group experience of siblings as a subsystem? Has there been a therapeutic reenactment of the saying, 'Two's company, three is a crowd'?

References

Byng-Hall, J., 1995. *Rewriting Family Scripts,* NY, Guilford.

Coles, P., 2003. *The Importance of Sibling Relationships in Psychoanalysis,* London, Karnac.

Cosic, M., 1999. *Only Child; A Provocative Analysis of the Impact of being an Only Child,* Sydney, Lansdowne.

Dunn, J., 2005. Commentary: Siblings in their Families, *Journal of Family Psychology,* 19, 4: 654–657.

Dunn. J. & Plomin, R., 1990. *Separate Lives: Why Siblings Are So Different.* NY, Basic.

Fitzgerald, R., 2004. Review of Michael Duffy, *Abbott and Latham: The Lives and Rivalry of Two of the Finest Politicians of their Generation,* Sydney, Random House, 2004, *Sydney Morning Herald,* Spectrum Section: 11, August 14–15, 2004.

Fonagy, P. & Target, M., 2003. *Psychoanalytic Theories, Perspectives from Developmental Psychopathology,* London, Whurr.

Garner, H., 1997. A Scrapbook, An Album. In J. Sauers (Ed.), *Brothers and Sisters: Intimate Portraits of Sibling Relationships,* Melbourne, Random House.

Minuchin, S., 1974. *Families and Family Therapy,* London, Tavistock.

Mitchell, Juliet, 2003. *Siblings,* Cambridge, Polity Press.

Rayner, E., 2000. In M. Whelan (Ed.), *Mistress of Her Own Thoughts: Ella Freeman Sharpe and the Practice of Psychoanalysis,* London, Rebus Press.

Richardson, R. W. & Richardson, L. A., 1990. *Birth Order and You,* North Vancouver, British Columbia, Self-Counsel Press.

Sacks, O., 2001. *Uncle Tungsten,* NY, Picador.

Sanders, C., 2003. Living up to our Theory: Inviting Children to Family Sessions, *ANZJFT,* 24, 4: 177–182.

Sanders, R., 2004. *Sibling Relationships: Theory and Issues for Practice,* NY, Macmillan.

Sauers, J., 1997. *Brothers and Sisters: Intimate Portraits of Sibling Relationships,* Melbourne, Random House.

Sulloway, F., 1996. *Born to Rebel: Birth Order, Family Dynamics and Creative Lives,* NY, Random House.

Target, M., 2002. Adolescent Breakdown, A Developmental Perspective [Videotape of Lecture], Sydney. NSW Institute of Psychoanalytic Psychotherapy.

Twemlow. S., 2001. An Innovative Psychodynamically Influenced Approach to Reduce School Violence, *Journal of American Academy of Child and Adolescent Psychiatry,* 40, 3 (March): 741–785.

Winnicott, D., 1958. The Capacity to be Alone, *International Journal of Psychoanalysis,* 39, 5: Sept–Oct: 416–420.

SALLY YOUNG is a Senior Social Worker at Greenslopes Child and Youth Mental Health Clinic, 34 Curd St. Brisbane 4120: yngs@bigpond.com. An earlier version of this paper was presented at the Australian Family Therapy Conference in Brisbane in 2004.

From *Australian & New Zealand Journal of Family Therapy,* Vol. 28, No. 1, March 2007, pp. 21–27. Copyright © 2007 by Australian & New Zealand Journal of Family Therapy. Reprinted by permission.

Being a Sibling

The purpose of this descriptive exploratory study was to explore the meaning of being a sibling using Parse's human becoming perspective. Twelve children between 5 and 15 years of age with a younger sibling with a cleft lip and palate or Down Syndrome participated. Through semi-structured interviews and the use of art children talked about their experiences. Major themes portrayed the complex and paradoxical nature of being a sibling. The themes also revealed that having a sibling with special circumstances includes some unique opportunities and challenges. The finding of this study is the descriptive statement, being a sibling is an arduous charge to champion close others amid restricting-enhancing commitments while new endeavors give rise to new possibilities. Implications for nursing are discussed in the context of understanding being a sibling.

STEVEN L. BAUMANN, RN, PhD
Associate Professor, Hunter College, The City University of New York, New York

TINA TAYLOR DYCHES, EdD
Associate Professor, Brigham Young University, Provo, Utah

MARYBETH BRADDICK, MS
Ingram Visiting Nurses, Lansing, Michigan

The sibling relationship can be one of the longest and most important relationships in a person's life. Having a sibling can be very formative for children and instrumental in life. In an age when many people choose not to marry, marry later in life, and many marriages end in divorce, a sibling tie can provide stability and consistency. A sibling can provide fulfilling child-rearing experiences for people who do not have their own children. Yet for many, having a sibling fails to fulfill this potential. Despite years of research on the sibling relationship it is still not well understood (Dunn, 2000). Like being a parent, being a sibling includes much that is not in our control (Baumann & Braddick, 1999). This is particularly evident when a family has a child with special circumstances, or what most of the current literature describes as a child with *special needs*. The phrase *special needs* is avoided here because it imposes meaning, and labels, on the person. In the words of one participant from this study, siblings with special circumstances are *just different*. The authors of this study do assume that siblings of children with a cleft lip and palate (CL&P) or Down Syndrome (DS) in particular, can teach us not only about their personal experiences of being a sibling, but also about being a sibling in general.

Some researchers have said that having a sibling with special circumstances is stressful and problematic for the other children in the family (Murray, 1998, 1999, 2000; Senel & Akkok, 1995; Terzo, 1999). Others have reported that there is not much difference between having a sibling with special circumstances and having a sibling in general (Benson, Gross, & Kellum, 1999; Stawski, Auerbach, Barasch, Lerner, & Zimin, 1997). Still others have identified some benefits for siblings of children with special circumstances (Derouin & Jessee, 1996). It remains unclear what it means to children to have a sibling, with or without special circumstances. Therefore, the purpose of this descriptive exploratory study was to explore what it means to be a sibling. The primary aim of this inquiry was to add to the current understanding about being a brother or sister from the perspective of Parse's (1998) theory of human becoming. Parse holds that children, like adults, live situated freedom as full participants in the cocreation of their lives.

Relevant Literature

The word *sib* is thought to be derived from an Old English word *sib,* meaning relative, and from the Germanic word *sibja,* which means both blood relation and "one's own" (American Heritage Talking Dictionary, 1994). In everyday use, the word *sibling* refers to having one or both parents in common, or having a common ancestry. The terms *sister* and *brother* have numerous meanings, mostly related to close association or shared background (American Heritage Talking Dictionary, 1994).

Family psychoanalytic theory, on the other hand, focuses primarily on parent-child family processes and attributes both the closeness and tensions among family members to conscious and unconscious dynamics (Nichols & Schwartz, 1998). Families and social groups tend to impose expectations on siblings.

Sociologists, such as Mendelson, de Villa, Fitch, and Goodman (1997), have said that adult role expectations for siblings differ with age and gender of the sibling.

A family systems theory (Nichols & Schwartz, 1998) which views the family as an interactive system where what happens to one member affects all members, posits that the siblings represent a subsystem. Some family systems theorists hold that sibling position is very important to both the family and the child development. From this perspective, sibling experiences are shaped by birth order and gender (Silver & Frohlinger-Graham, 2000), and sibling relationships cannot be understood apart from other family relationships and events.

Most social scientists now view being a sibling as both a relationship and a family role (Dunn, 2000). It is likely that this dual nature of being a sibling contributes to the conflict that is common among many siblings. Pollack (2002) suggested that expecting older children to be the primary caregivers of their younger siblings contributes to intersibling tension and can lead to long-term resentment. Family size and the age differences of siblings may also influence sibling relationships, but this effect varies with the age of the siblings, proximity of one to another in the sibling constellation, and gender (Newman, 1996). Larger families may demonstrate both more affection and conflict, whereas wider age spacing between siblings has been observed to be related to less closeness and conflict (Newman, 1996).

Parents and researchers are generally impressed with how different siblings are from one another (Dunn, 2000). These differences are particularly evident in families with a child with special circumstances. As mentioned above, some authors have reported that siblings of children with special circumstances have more stressful lives, exhibit fewer competencies, have more psychopathologies, and may have more unrealistic housework and caregiving demands than siblings in general (Fisman et al., 1996; Fisman, Wolf, Ellison, & Freeman, 2000; Murray, 1999; Williams, 1997). These children are also described as having more limited playtime and opportunities to be with their friends (Seligman & Darling, 1997). Age is considered to be an important factor in understanding how children experience the circumstances of their siblings; older siblings of children with special circumstances have been reported to have more behavioral problems than younger siblings of children in the same situation (Morrison, 1997; Skidmore, 1996; Stawski et al., 1997).

Siblings of children with special circumstances have also been described as harboring intense emotions, such as anger and guilt (Meyer, Vadasy, & Vance, 1996). In addition, unequal parental attention, insufficient information, and ineffective communication between parents and children have been associated with misunderstandings, resentment, and conflict (Brody & Stoneman, 1996; Kowal & Kramer, 1997). Dunn (2000) reported that this pattern is also common in families stressed by separation or illness.

Siblings of children with special circumstances may also face comments by others who equate differences with moral inferiority (Goffman, 1963). These siblings must then make sense of incorrect assumptions, over generalizations, and insults, and

have to respond in awkward social situations. Some siblings have been observed altering their thinking or frame of reference in relation to these family members to mitigate their emotional involvement and negative feelings (Andersson, 1997). This shift in frame of reference could be seen as a defense, which minimizes the differences among the siblings, or it could be that they appreciate underlying likeness and the gifts that their siblings possess. Some health professionals judge the quality of life of persons with special circumstances as more negative than the individuals report themselves (Albrecht & Devlieger, 1999). This *disability paradox* can be explained by the pathological orientation of many biomedical-oriented health professionals, and their failure to appreciate factors which account for health and well being, such as how all individuals cocreate meaning with their values and choices (Parse, 1998).

Cuskelly, Chant, and Hayes (1998) found no significant differences between siblings of children with DS and a comparison group of siblings from the general population in relation to parent-reported behavioral problems. In addition, siblings of children with special circumstances have been found to demonstrate greater sensitivity and nurturing behaviors (Seligman & Darling, 1997), closer family relationships, more independence, and greater satisfaction in seeing improvement in their ill sibling than children without siblings with special circumstances (Derouin & Jessee, 1996).

The contributions of children with special circumstances to the family and community have also been described. Teachers have reported that siblings of children with special circumstances were more cooperative and had greater self-control than other children (Mandleco, Olsen, Robinson, Marshall, & McNeilly-Choque, 1998). Dunn (2000) suggested that sibling relationships offer children opportunities to learn about and better understand people and themselves. Vanier (1997) referred to the family as places where *lessons of the heart* can be learned, and children with special circumstances as particularly attentive to this dimension of human and family life. For Vanier, the heart is the affective core of the human being and its most fundamental reality (Downey, 1986). Being a sibling of a child with special circumstances can contribute to the sibling's identity and career direction (Seligman & Darling, 1997).

In summary, being a sibling is a significant experience for children and the literature is mixed regarding the experience of being a sibling of a child with special circumstances. Clearly unrealistic parenting roles assigned to siblings can contribute to sibling conflict and resentment. Further information is needed to explore the meaning of being a sibling, especially from the child's perspective. Therefore, through this study the authors sought to better understand the experience of being a brother or sister from the child's own perspective.

Conceptual Framework

The human becoming theory (Parse, 1998) views individuals and families as in mutual process with the universe. It represents a synthesis of selected existential phenomenological tenets and Rogers' science of unitary human beings (Parse, 1981). Three

Table 1 Demographics of Participants

Participant	Age	Gender	Number of Siblings	Birth Order	Special Circumstance
Mary	5	Girl	2	Oldest	Cleft Lip and Palate
Joe	6	Boy	1	Oldest	Cleft Lip and Palate
Marvin	8	Boy	7	3rd youngest	Cleft Lip and Palate
Marie	9	Girl	2	Middle	Cleft Lip and Palate
Jane	10	Girl	7	4th youngest	Cleft Lip and Palate
Peter	12	Boy	2	Oldest	Cleft Lip and Palate
Bob	13	Boy	2	Middle	Cleft Lip and Palate
Rebecca	14	Girl	7	Oldest	Cleft Lip and Palate
Mark	15	Boy	2	Oldest	Cleft Lip and Palate
Maura	9	Girl	1	Oldest	Down Syndrome
Sue	10	Girl	1	Oldest	Down Syndrome
Barbara	11	Girl	1	Oldest	Down Syndrome

major themes emerging from Parse's assumptions are meaning, rhythmicity, and cotranscendence. In Parse's (1998) terms, meaning is cocreating reality through the languaging of valuing and imaging. In other words, individuals, including young children, choose personal meaning in situations based upon their values. Rhythmicity is explained by Parse (1998) as patterns of relating which are paradoxical in nature, such that in the process of revealing something, one is also concealing, and likewise with enabling-limiting and connecting-separating. This view shows appreciation for the many levels and complexities that unfold in relationships of all kinds. It acknowledges that possibilities and limitations arise from choice-making. Cotranscending with the possibilities describes how one continually transforms one's view of the world based on life experiences (Parse, 1981). The theory holds that children, like adults, define what health and well-being is for them. Parse's theory guided the researchers in focusing on how siblings construct language to make sense of their experiences, how siblings live their patterns of relating, and how they participate in constructing their view of the future. The research question is, *What does it mean to be a sibling?*

Method

This descriptive exploratory study used the philosophical assumptions and the framework of the human becoming theory (Parse, 1998) to guide the researchers in viewing the participants, being with the participants, and designing objectives and questions to ask the participants. The objectives were: (a) to describe the meaning of being a sibling, (b) to describe changing relationship of living with a sibling, and (c) to describe views of the future in light of having a sibling.

Participants

Twelve biological siblings (ages 5–15), from eight families with a child with cleft lip and palate or DS participated in this descriptive exploratory study. Eight were the oldest children in their family, four were middle children, and all were older than

their sibling with special circumstances (see Table 1). Most participants were recruited after their parents responded to notices in newsletters of support groups in the northeast or midwestern United States; three were referred by others. All of the participants were Caucasian, but they represented several different cultures and religions. The human subjects institutional review board of a university approved the study; steps to safeguard minor-age participants' rights for self-determination and confidentiality were taken. The use of informed consent/assent and all other guidelines for protection of human subjects were followed, including the right to withdraw at any time. Each participant was given a pseudonym.

Procedure

Children were asked to describe (a) what it means to be a brother or sister, (b) how their relationships with others were different because they had a brother or sister, and (c) how their view of the future or what they wanted to be when they grew-up, had been altered by being a brother or sister. The special circumstances of their siblings were not mentioned in the questions used by the researchers, but it was in the consent. Specific questions included, What is it like for you to be a brother or sister? What is most important for you about being a brother or sister? How has being a brother or sister changed the way you relate to the people who are most important to you? How has it changed your relationships with others? Do you feel you relate differently to people because of your experiences as a brother or sister? What do you want to be when you are older, and has that changed because you are a brother or sister? Have your dreams changed? How has your view of life been changed by your experience of being a brother or sister? Tape-recorded interviews, guided by the open-ended questions, were conducted in a private area of the participants' homes. After being interviewed, participants were invited to draw or use a laptop with art software (Adobe Illustrator 7.0 or Microsoft Paint) and talk about their artwork. Children's art has been used with human becoming theory by the primary researcher in two previous studies (Baumann,

Table 2 The Findings Reflecting the Human Becoming Theory

Objectives of the Study	Theoretical Concepts	Participants' Language	Researchers' Language
To describe the meaning of being a sibling.	Structuring meaning multi-dimensionally	Being a brother or sister was a big responsibility, especially when they have something like Down's, "because you have to watch out for them," "you have to be there for them, defend them, protect them, or stand up for them."	An arduous charge to champion close others
To describe the changing relationship of living with a sibling.	Cocreating rhythmical patterns of relating	Having a sister or brother had "not changed their relationships with others much," they had less time to play with their friends, "learned how to treat others, to share, take care of people, and be nice to people who are different."	Restricting-enhancing commitments
To describe the views of the future in light of having a sibling.	Cotranscending with the possibilities	"Plans for the future had not changed," "interested in what their siblings like to do," "wanted to do things differently than their siblings had done," "careers where they would protect or care for others."	New endeavors give rise to new possibilities

1999a, 1999b). From this perspective, the interpretation of the art is left to the participant. The children were asked to talk about their drawings. The interviews and art sessions with each participant lasted 30–60 minutes.

Data Analysis

In a process Parse (2001) referred to as analyzing-synthesizing, major themes were identified according to the objectives of study. In this study, all interviews were transcribed and major themes of what being a brother or sister was like for the participants were determined by reading and contemplating participants' comments and artwork (Parse, 2001, 1987). These data contained answers to the specific questions asked by the researchers. Themes arose directly from the language of the participants, and were then synthesized to construct a descriptive statement in the language of the researcher, reflecting Parse's theory (Parse, 1998, 2001). All of the analysis-synthesis in this study was conducted by the primary researcher (SB). An earlier work by two of the authors on fathering used a similar methodology (Baumann & Braddick, 1999).

Findings

The finding of this study is the descriptive statement: *being a sibling is an arduous charge to champion close others amid restricting-enhancing commitments while new endeavors give rise to new possibilities.* The process of going from objectives to findings is outlined in Table 2. In Table 2, column 1 contains the objectives of the study and column 2 contains the themes of the human becoming theory. Column 3 presents participants' comments and column 4 presents the researchers' synthesis of being a sibling in the researcher's language.

Discussion
The Meaning of Being a Brother or Sister

Although the participants' comments clearly identified who is older, or *bigger* using their words, and the gender of each sibling, they were less likely to refer to the special circumstances of their brother or sister. One participant's comment regarding a sibling's special circumstances demonstrates this relative lack of attention to the special circumstance: In Barbara's (age 11) words, "I kind of forget that he has DS and I just see him as a boy." Some authors see this inattention to details as related to siblings' lack of information and awareness about the medical and other special circumstances of their sibling (McHale & Pawletko, 1992).

The participants' comments could also be seen as part of their way of "constructing reality through assigning significance to events" (Parse, 1998, p. 35). For example, when asked about being a sister, Mary (age 5) talked about her cousin, who was older than her, and about her brother who died without coming home from the hospital (at age 7 days), and not much about her two sisters with whom she lived. She also named one of her favorite stuffed animals after her brother who had died, which can also be seen as her defining of the membership of her family and how she is keeping her deceased brother present in her life.

For most of the participants in this study, being a sister or brother is a "big responsibility," which at times is fun. Participants said they have to "be there for their sibling, to stand up for them and protect them." Jane (age 10) said, "It's tough, you have to watch out for the others." Peter (age 12) said,

If someone is pushing my brother I have to be there, or if my sister gets into trouble I have to be there, I have to defend them. That's what being a brother or sister is all about. If I'm a big brother I have to defend littler kids than me, like the kid next door, I'll do that. One time I saw these kids go over to this kid and say, "Do you want to play Power Ranger?" The kid was little, he picked him up and threw him on the ground, so I went over there and stared at him and told him not to, he just stared right back at me. You kind of pester these kids or they don't listen.

Rebecca (age 14) said, "Well, it's hard sometimes because there are things to be taken care of, and you have to help them, but it's still fun, because they help you and they can be fun. So it's fun, but it's hard." Rebecca's comments reveal that being a sibling is both a duty and a source of enjoyment or amusement.

The participants in this study described the role of older sibling as being *fill-ins*. One participant said that when her mother was not around she had to tell her siblings what to do and what not to do. Mark (age 15) said, "for me as the oldest, I always felt that I had to look out for Dan, like when my mother has to go out." Bob (age 13), the middle brother in that same family, said, "I have to fill in for Mark, when he is not around, in looking out for Dan." Pollack (2002) referred to the caregiving role of older siblings as *auxiliary parents*. She said that in the United States since the 1970s older children spend less time in this role, than in earlier generations. She stated that this has reduced the resentment and conflict that can arise when older children's own needs and education were to some degree shortchanged because of their caregiving responsibilities.

Several participants discussed the moods and behaviors of their siblings, which they described as *difficult*. Sue (age 10) said, "Well, it gets kind of annoying sometimes, but if you don't have a really restless sister, it can be kind of fun. My sister, as she is younger than me, she's kind of restless and sometimes it bothers me, she bugs me so much. Sometimes I wish she was not even there." Maura (age 9) said, "Well, I think it is sort of a responsibility, because you have to look after your brother. I think it is a little harder with a kid having DS, but it's not that much harder. It's a big responsibility." She described him as "rough" and having a "tough build," and that used to bother her until she realized that this is "the way he is." Peter (age 12) created a computer image of an oval face and described it as his brother when he gets mad—he gave him concentric red circles in his eyes. He also drew himself offering his brother who fell while skating on the sidewalk a band aid from a first aid kit.

When asked what was the most important thing about being a brother or sister, several participants again mentioned having to be responsible. Others mentioned caring, listening, and "cheering each other up." Maura (age 9) said, "I think it's really important for me to listen to him and understand what he's saying, not to ignore him, to understand that he has feelings too." While none of the participants focused on the learning differences of their siblings, this comment by a very articulate sibling of a child with DS, hints at the effort she has to make to understand what her brother is saying and her choice to see it as important. Rebecca (age 14) said, "to be able to help them and care about them." Sue (age 10) said what was most important for her was when her sister was there for her, "Like when my

grandpa died . . . she pats you on your back. It's like when you cry, she cries." Peter (age 12) said,

> Being there for them when they are sad or depressed, or mad about something, I go there and talk to them, I sought out the problems that they are having, like when Jim got mad at something, I got mad at him, I gave him a piece of gum, and he was happy again, he came downstairs and we went outside. I help Marie (age 9) sometimes, when Mom yells at her, I comfort her.

The synthesis of the participants' comments related to the first objective, which was to describe the meaning of being a brother or sister, in the language of the researcher is: *an arduous charge to champion close others*. Being a sister or brother is a mix of feelings, including feeling dutiful, antagonism, and enjoyment, from which a mutually nurturing presence can arise. This synthesis also exemplifies the complexity of being a sibling. Longitudinal studies of sibling relationships have suggested that close relationships between siblings can become closer as siblings provide assistance and support for each other (Dunn, 2000). The participants' comments also suggest that courage and commitment is required when being a brother or sister, particularly when *being there* for a younger sibling with special circumstances. This finding is related in this study to the first principle of human becoming theory (Parse, 1998), structuring meaning multidimensionally is cocreating reality through the languaging of valuing and imaging (p. 35). Being a sibling is a paradoxical rhythm of confirming-not confirming that one is neither alone nor without obligations.

The Way Relationships Unfold

Several participants said they did not think having a brother or sister changed their relationships with others very much. However, others said their mothers spent more time with younger siblings than they did with them. Mary (age 5) said her youngest sister (who has a cleft lip and palate) slept in her mother's bed, "because she could suffocate." She also said, "My daddy used to be home more. He used to buy me rainbow cookies, but when my sister was born he had to work all the time." Some participants said being a brother or sister decreased the time they had to be with and play with their friends.

Several participants described how being a brother or sister had altered their relationships with other people. As mentioned above, some participants reported that there had been times when having to take care of their sibling reduced the time they could spend with their friends. A few reported incidents when their sibling's *difficult* behaviors were directed at their friends, or were embarrassing. What they said also suggested that having a sibling, especially one with special circumstances, can deepen relationships with others. Peter (age 12) said,

> Sometimes my friends tease my brother, so I say, "Don't do that;" but I am not too harsh on them. My friends have been there for Marie and my brother too, they like them and care for them too. When I baby sit my brother, and Linda comes over and she helps me, or Tracy, they come

over and help me with my brother and Marie. They help out, almost like they are part of the family.

In this way several participants came to value and appreciate their friends who had shown understanding and helpfulness to their siblings. Several said that they had looked out for the well-being of other young children as well, recalling how their own brother or sister had been treated by other people. Having a sibling at times interfered with their plans. Having a sibling also served to encourage children to try things, they might not have done alone, such as a pair of brothers in this study who chose to be in their school plays.

The way relationships unfold when being a sibling was stated in the language of the researcher as the paradox: *restricting-enhancing commitments*. At times participants had to forego their own plans because they had a sibling, but most times this was not without satisfaction and learning. While the conflict and tensions evident in some of the participants' comments could be related to their perception of having less time to be with their parents or friends, it can also reflect their annoyance that siblings wanted what they had. Marie's (age 9) drawing of being a sibling was very similar to her brother's (Peter, age 12) which she had seen, but she was happy to point out the differences. The annoyance of having younger siblings imitate them was evident in Sue's (age 10) comment that her sister "loves every single thing that I have." Girard (1996) saw rivalry for the same object as a basis of most social conflict, and he said such conflicts arise because a person wants to be like their model. He called this phenomenon *mimetic desire* and he saw this in most cultures and religions. Girard (1996) did not see this as a bad thing, because imitating ultimately involved "opening oneself out" (p. 64).

One participant (Sue, age 10) mentioned how unfair some children are to children with DS. She described children with DS as "just different." Her use of the word *just* suggested that to her they were essentially like other children, despite their obvious differences. She was also referring to the importance of including all children, and this reveals her growing awareness of the importance of being sensitive to the feelings of others. Some participants also found ways to cheer up their siblings when they were feeling down, and learned how to accept their anger without needing to retaliate. The second principle of human becoming theory (Parse, 1998) is: Cocreating rhythmical patterns of relating is living the paradoxical unity of revealing-concealing and enabling-limiting while connecting-separating (p. 42). For example, Peter's computer graphic of one of his brother's anger, could be seen as his revealing, while concealing, his own differences and difficult feelings. The second part of the finding of this study, restricting-enhancing, can be described as reflecting the enabling-limiting of connecting-separating of being a sibling. Being a sibling involves decisions which alter one's view of the past, and living out of one's present and future possibilities.

How One's View of Life Has Changed When Being a Sibling?

Several participants said being a brother or sister had not changed their view of their future or the world, but some children said they had learned from their sibling's mistakes. Others

identified their own interests by trying and liking things their siblings liked. For example Bob (age 13) got involved in school plays like this older brother Mark (age 15), and both wanted to continue to be in plays in high school and maybe go into acting.

Several participants were able to connect their thoughts about their future with their current family situation. Peter (age 12) said he wanted to be a police officer so that he could "be responsible to take care of other people." Another said she wanted to be a pediatrician to take care of children. One participant planned to go into business with her siblings. Dunn (1999) observed that in sibling interactions, play, and conversations, there is evidence that children read each other's feelings and intentions and explore their abilities and differences. Most participants' comments suggested that they accepted their situation as siblings of children with special circumstances, and accept these children for who they were. This appeared to be a transformative process for them.

The concept of psychosocial adjustment as applied to the situation of siblings of children with special circumstances (Murray, 2000), fails to appreciate the transformative possibilities in the experience. In the present study, the researchers, led by the assumptions of human becoming theory, synthesized these comments as the theme: *new endeavors give rise to new possibilities*. Children participate in cocreating their world by their choices in given circumstances. Often children are particularly imaginative in their envisioning of new possibilities.

The possibilities that arise for young children reflect their exposure to various experiences and to close others, including parents, siblings, and teachers. The personal meanings and imaginations of children also reflect this cocreating process. For example, they and their siblings are from time to time transformed into various characters from their favorite stories. The special circumstances of siblings in this study did not hamper these participants' abilities to make choices, to play, or to use their imagination; however, it did give them some different options to consider. The third principle of the human becoming theory is cotranscending with the possibles is powering unique ways of originating in the process of transforming (Parse, 1998, p. 46). The tasks and challenges of being a sibling faced by the participants of this study were different from most of their friends and it gave rise to personal uniqueness, if not distinction.

Conclusions and Implications

Like all qualitative research, the findings of this study are not meant to be generalized to other groups or suggest causal relationships. This study is also limited because it did not include children of color. It also did not include enough varied participants to explore the differences between the experiences of siblings of children with CL&P and DS and those without siblings with special circumstances. The reader is also encouraged to keep in mind that most of the participants were the oldest child in these families.

For the most part, the participants of this descriptive exploratory study talked about being a brother or sister in general, but some of their comments related to having siblings with special circumstances. The participants' comments suggest that the *special circumstances* of their siblings were generally accepted and relatively unimportant to them. Only one participant said there were times she wished her sibling "wasn't even there." All participants found both challenges and opportunities in having a sibling, for example, they generally understood that younger children need more attention from their mothers, and they realized that some children require special arrangements. The participants generally took their responsibilities very seriously, and for the most part, felt it gave them a sense of purpose and direction. Many admitted their experiences contributed to how they were with other people. There were three sets of participants from the same family in this study. These sibling pairs seemed to share much in common and be cohesive, perhaps in part because of their relationship and duties with their sibling with special circumstances.

The findings related to Parse's (1998) theory suggest being a sister or brother is *an arduous charge to champion close others amid restricting-enhancing commitments while new endeavors gives rise to new possibilities.* Being a sibling is a complex, paradoxical and ever-changing experience. It includes making choices and being responsible. This investigation also uncovered a definition of being a sibling that reflects shifting rhythms and changing perspectives of what is possible.

Parents and nurses should provide opportunities for children to talk about their feelings and thoughts regarding being a sibling in general and in particular about being a sibling of a child with special circumstances. The use of art can be a particularly helpful means of communicating with such children. It may also be helpful if nurses can get to know children's favorite stories and toys, to explore new meaning in difficult situations, such as discovering that a child's favorite stuffed animal was named after a family member who had died. The tendency of many children, especially older children of siblings with special circumstances, to feel overly responsible can interfere with their ability to enjoy the pleasure of being a child (Pollack, 2002). Childhood is the secret place where imagination, uniqueness, and hope are most alive. This place is a vital resource not only for them but also for their families and close others. Some families with unexpected birth events and children with special circumstances have a difficult time finding new meaning. For them there is incongruence between what they had previously hoped and dreamed for and their present lives. This is a particularly good opportunity for nurses who practice nursing in a way which is "illuminating meaning, synchronizing rhythms and mobilizing transcendence" (Parse, 1998, pp. 69–70).

This study also suggests that nurses can help families find ways to understand the difficult behaviors of children, especially those with special circumstances. These behaviors can be difficult for siblings to understand and live with. While providing siblings with more information may be needed at times, each child's view of his or her family and sibling's circumstances should be respected. Longitudinal studies of being a sibling, and a sibling of children with special circumstances would provide valuable understanding of this important and common life experience.

References

Albrecht, G. L., & Devlieger, P. J. (1999). The disability paradox: High quality of life against all odds. *Social Science & Medicine, 48,* 977–988.

The American heritage talking dictionary of the English language (3rd ed.). (1994). New York: Houghton Mifflin.

Andersson, E. (1997). Relations in families with a mentally retarded child from the perspective of the siblings. *Scandinavian Journal of Caring Sciences, 11,* 131–138.

Baumann, S. (l999a). Art as a path of inquiry. *Nursing Science Quarterly, 12,* 106–110.

Baumann, S. (1999b). The lived experience of hope: Children in families struggling to make a home. In R. R. Parse, *Hope: An international human becoming perspective* (pp. 191–210). Boston: Jones & Bartlett.

Baumann, S., & Braddick, M. (1999). Out of their element: Fathers of children who are not the same. *Journal of Pediatric Nursing, 14,* 369–377.

Benson, B. A., Gross, A. M., & Kellum, G. (1999). The siblings of children with craniofacial anomalies. *Children's Health Care, 28,* 51–68.

Brody, G. H., & Stoneman, Z. (1996). A risk-amelioration model for sibling relationships: Conceptual underpinning and preliminary findings. In G. H. Brody (Ed.), *Sibling relationships: Their cause and consequences* (pp. 231–247). Norwood, NJ: Ablex.

Cuskelly, M., Chant, D., & Hayes, A. (1998). Behaviour problems in the siblings of children with Down Syndrome: Associations with family responsibilities and parental stress. *International Journal of Disability, Development & Education, 45,* 295–311.

Derouin, D., & Jessee, P. O. (1996). Impact of a chronic illness in childhood: Siblings' perceptions. *Issues in Comprehensive Pediatric Nursing, 19,* 135–147.

Downey, M. (1986). *A blessed weakness: The spirit of Jean Vanier and l'Arche.* New York: Harper & Row.

Dunn, J. (1999). Making sense of the social world: Mindreading, emotion and relationships. In P. D. Zelazo, J. W. Astington, & D. R. Olson (Eds.), *Developing theories of intention: Social understanding and self control* (pp. 229–242). Mahwah, NJ: Lawrence Erlbaum.

Dunn, J. (2000). State of the art: Siblings. *The Psychologist, 13,* 244–248.

Fisman, S., Wolf, L., Ellison, D., & Freeman, T. (2000). A longitudinal study of siblings of children with chronic disabilities. *Canadian Journal of Psychiatry, 45,* 369–375.

Fisman, S., Wolf, L., Ellison, D., Gillis, B., Freeman, T., & Szatmari, P. (1996). Risk and protective factors affecting the adjustment of siblings of children with chronic disabilities. *Journal of the American Academy of Child & Adolescent Psychiatry, 35,* 1532–1541.

Girard, R. (1996). *The Girard reader* (J. G. Williams, Ed.). New York: Crossroad.

Goffman, E. (1963). *Stigma: Notes on the management of spoiled identity.* Englewood Cliffs, NJ: Prentice-Hall.

Kowal, A., & Kramer, L. (1997). Children's understanding of parental differential treatment. *Child Development, 68,* 113–126.

Mandleco, B., Olsen, S., Robinson, C., Marshall, E., & McNeilly-Choque, M. (1998). Social skills and peer relationships of siblings of children with disabilities: Parental and family linkages. In P. Slee & K. Rigby (Eds.), *Children's peer relations: Current issues and future directions* (pp. 106–120). London: Routledge.

McHale, S. M., & Pawletko, T. (1992). Different treatment of siblings in two family contexts: Implications for children's adjustment and relationship evaluations. *Child Development, 63,* 68–81.

Mendelson, M. J., de Villa, E. P., Fitch, T. A., & Goodman, F. G. (1997). Adult expectations for children's sibling roles. *International Journal of Behavioral Development, 20,* 549–572.

Meyer, D. J., Vadasy, P., & Vance, R. S. (1996). *Living with a brother or sister with special needs: A book for sibs* (Rev. ed.). Seattle, WA: University of Washington Press.

Morrison, L. (1997). Stress and siblings. *Pediatric Nursing, 9,* 26–27.

Murray, J. S. (1998). The lived experience of childhood cancer: One sibling's perspective. *Issues in Comprehensive Pediatric Nursing, 21,* 217–227.

Murray, J. S. (1999). Siblings of children with cancer: A review of the literature. *Journal of Pediatric Oncology Nursing, 16.* 225–234.

Murray, J. S. (2000). Attachment theory and adjustment difficulties in siblings of children with cancer. *Issues in Mental Health Nursing, 2,* 149–169.

Newman, J. (1996). The more the merrier? Effects of family size and sibling spacing on sibling relationships. *Child Care, Health and Development, 22,* 285–302.

Nichols, M. P., & Schwartz, R. C. (1998). *Family therapy: Concepts and methods* (4th ed.). Boston: Allyn & Bacon.

Parse, R. R. (1981). *Man-living-health: A theory of nursing.* New York: Wiley.

Parse, R. R. (1987) Parse's man-living health theory of nursing. In R. R. Parse, *Nursing science: Major paradigms, theories, and critiques* (pp. 181–204). Philadelphia: Saunders.

Parse, R. R. (1998). *The human becoming school of thought: A perspective for nurses and other health professionals.* Thousand Oaks, CA: Sage.

Parse, R. R. (2001). *Qualitative inquiry: The path of sciencing.* Sudbury, MA: Jones and Bartlett.

Pollack, E. G. (2002). The children we have lost: When siblings were caregivers, 1900–1970. *Journal of Social History, 36,* 31–61.

Seligman, M., & Darling, R. B. (1997). *Ordinary families, special children: A systems approach to childhood disability* (2nd ed.). New York: Guilford Press.

Senel, H. G., & Akkok, F. (1995). Stress levels and attitudes of normal siblings of children with disabilities. *International Journal for the Advancement of Counseling, 18,* 61–68.

Silver, E. J., & Frohlinger-Graham, M. J. (2000). Brief report: Psychological symptoms in healthy female siblings of adolescents with and without chronic conditions. *Journal of Pediatric Psychology, 25,* 279–284.

Skidmore, K. L. (1996). Childhood cancer, families and siblings. (Doctoral dissertation, Loyola University, 1996), *Dissertation Abstracts International, 56*(12B), 7056.

Stawski, M., Auerbach, J. G., Barasch, M., Lerner, Y., & Zimin, R. (1997). Behavioral problems of children with chronic physical illness and their siblings. *European Child and Adolescent Psychiatry, 6,* 20–25.

Terzo, H. (1999). Evidence-based practice: The effects of childhood cancer on siblings. *Pediatric Nursing, 25,* 309–311.

Vanier, J. (1997). *Our journey home: Rediscovering a common humanity beyond our differences* (M. Parham, Trans.). Maryknoll, NY: Novalis.

Williams, P. D. (1997). Siblings and pediatric chronic illness: A review of the literature. *International Journal of Nursing Studies, 34,* 312–323.

Aunties and Uncles

John Tyler Connoley

When Mom was a kid, her nuclear family consisted of her mom and dad, one sister, two brothers, one cousin and his wife, and Grandpa and Grandma. They all lived together in an Indiana farmhouse, where 40 relatives (the extended family) would arrive each Sunday afternoon for chicken and dumplings. Family holidays, like Thanksgiving and Christmas, included even more people, many of whom were not strictly relatives but were "church family." Like a quilt, Mom's childhood family was constructed from many pieces sewn together with love.

When Mom grew up and left home, she became a missionary and moved to Africa with her husband and two kids, but she took her family values with her. Family in our house meant all the people we cared about. Of course, we had relatives in the United States, but we also had our missionary family.

My sister and I called all the missionaries Auntie and Uncle, which I suppose made their children our "cousins." When I think of my earliest memories, I think of eating Auntie Eleanor's cheesecake, being scared by Auntie Rosemary's funny faces, and visiting Uncle Ora and Auntie Linda in South Africa.

The first time we came back to the United States, the terms grandma and grandpa confused my sister and me: We kept calling them Auntie Grandma and Uncle Grandpa because that's how one referred to relatives.

These aunties and uncles who made up my familial world are the people I learned to depend on. They're the ones who taught me what it meant to be a grown-up. Their children were the kids I wrestled with and fought with and played Star Wars with. Later they would become the people I'd pick up the phone and call for help if I needed it. It never occurred to me that family should be related by blood or marriage, or that familial responsibility might extend only to the people to whom you are legally bound.

I've grown up and moved away, but I've taken my mom's inclusive definition of family with me. Like my grandparents in their Hoosier farmhouse and my parents on their mission station, my partner, Rob, and I have a door that's always open. We intentionally moved to a small town here in New Mexico so we could afford to buy a big house with lots of space for guests and where we would have a close community of people we cared about. We don't have kids yet, but we know when we do they'll be raised in an extended family that includes lots of relatives and lots of friends.

We believe children should be raised by a community—of aunties and uncles, of friends and relatives, of all the people we love. And we trust that if our child's immediate household doesn't include a mother and a father, well, that's OK, because the quilt is bigger than our little corner. And there will always be adult role models around.

Rob and I have embraced a traditional meaning of family that is expansive enough to include the whole world. And this family tradition of inclusiveness has made us wary of "traditional family" rhetoric. Why would anyone want to limit the definition of family to a mother, father, and two kids? It's like substituting a quilted place mat for a warm bedspread.

The way we understand it, family is just another word for the people we love, and the nuclear family is everyone we can fit under our roof. If one of our friends loses his job and needs a place to stay, he might become part of the nucleus. If Rob's mom decides to move to New Mexico, she might join the nucleus too. It doesn't matter how or if we're legally related; what matters is that family takes care of each other.

Instead of limiting the legal definition of family, we would like to expand it. Let the patchwork connections we make with one another be reflected in the way the government treats us. Let people choose their families, and then write the laws to support those choices. To do anything else seems contrary to my family's values.

John Tyler Connoley cowrote *The Children Are Free: Reexamining the Biblical Evidence on Same-Sex Relationships.* He lives in Silver City, N.M.

Roles of American Indian Grandparents in Times of Cultural Crisis

This study examined the roles of contemporary American Indian grandparents in the lives of their grandchildren. Structured interviews were conducted with 20 American Indian grandparents. Analysis of interviews followed a sequence of strategies traditionally identified with the process of data reduction and analysis using qualitative methodologies. Participants reported enculturative responsibilities for their grandchildren in regard to traditional tribal values and knowledges such as tribal spirituality and protocol, cooperative interaction, tribal language and appreciation of nature. Methods of enculturation took the form of stories, modeling, direct teaching and playful interaction.

ROCKEY ROBBINS, PHD, ET AL.

Given the dearth of articles about American Indian grandparents in psychological journals, it is necessary to briefly review relevant articles in order to provide an enriched context for this study. In many cultures, grandparents are seen as "fun relatives," offering treats and activities that parents were unable or unwilling to provide, such as social games, companionship, community events and domestic help (Kennedy, 1992). Grandparents are also seen as the designated repository of family histories, culture and memories (Williams, 1995). In some cultures, grandparents are viewed as community leaders, mediators and to some extent, lawgivers (Bahr, 1994). Grandparents are also seen as transmitters of family values, such as morality, altruism, social identity, a sense of accomplishment, competency and affiliation (Timberlake & Chipungu, 1992).

Grandparents are frequently mentioned as providers of emotional and tangible support for their grandchildren (Scherman, Goodrich, Kelly Russell, & Javidi, 1988; Scherman, Beesley, & Turner, 2003). However, this varies, due in part to the grandparents' health, geographical proximity and financial ability. Grandparents often provide support for their children who have young children of their own. The support can be monetary, advice giving, baby sitting or emotional support. This role changes depending on the perceived needs of the family, and the grandparents situation. The grandparents may become the ones needing care and support due to health problems (Creasey & Kahiler, 1994, Sander & Trygstad, 1993). The frequency and quality of contact between grandparents and grandchildren also affect the roles adopted by the grandparents, as well as the level of perceived support (Creasey & Kahiler, 1994).

Few articles have been written specifically about American Indian grand parenting. Those have focused primarily on grandmothers, changing status, and social culture (Barr, 1994;

Nahemow, 1987; Schweitzer, 1987; Williams, 1995) and their place in the American Indian extended family (Coleman, Unau, & Manyfingers, 2001). They have also been described as storytellers (Barnett, 1955) and mentors (Elmendorf & Kroeber, 1960). Weibel-Orlando (1990) conducted interviews with 28 American Indian grandparents to determine grand-parenting styles. She found five basic styles: ceremonial, which entails grandparents acting as models of appropriate ceremonial behavior; fictive, which entails older persons nurturing children as an alternative to the lack or absence of biological grandchildren; custodial, which entails grandparents taking on full child care responsibilities for their grandchildren; distanced, which entails almost complete lack of contact with grandchildren; and cultural conservator, which entails grandparents and ways of life.

Williams (1995) differentiated the roles American Indian grandfathers and grandmothers played. Grandfathers are more likely than grandmothers to view grand-parenting as an opportunity to share information with grandchildren and to take pride in grandchildren's accomplishments. Noor Al-Deen (1997) lists American Indian women's traditional roles as life-givers, healers, caregivers, mothers, guardians, nurturers, family counselors, providers, and sources of wisdom and knowledge to their nations, including council decisions and participation in battle. She noted that female American Indian elders experience conflict that may result from divergent tribal and dominant culture's pressures and expectations regarding their grand-parenting roles. Noor Al-Deen proposes three factors which contribute to these conflicts: 1) cultural deprivation caused by prejudice from Euro-American mainstream populations; 2) restricted traditionalism from governmental and societal pressures coupled with the loss of tribal lands; and 3) federal bureaucratic health care from Indian Health Services.

According to Coleman, Unau, and Manyfingers (2001), the extended family plays a central role in raising Indian children. Grandparents and community elders are considered potent sources of influence for children, families, and communities as a whole. It is common for grandparents to willingly assume childcare responsibilities for their grandchildren and for parents to seek advice from community elders. This study attempts to explore and explicate the specific contents of the roles of American Indian grandparent's roles in the enculturation process of passing down values, stories and songs, as well as the cultural costumes, and their function as a nurturer and protector.

Methodology

Three American Indian and one Euro-American interviewers met with 20 American Indian grandparents. Interviews were conducted in American Indian mental health centers and in the homes of participants. A structured interview schedule was used to conduct the interviews (a copy of the structured interview is available from the first author). Information was collected on contents of grandparents roles play in lives of their grandchildren, the relationships between grandparents.[sic] Each interview was summarized and transmitted electronically to the person analyzing the data.

Eighteen of the twenty participants in this study were from Oklahoma. The tribes represented were: Cherokee, Creek, Chickasaw, Commanche, Lakota, Pawnee, Pottawatomi, Seminole, and Shawnee. Participants included seven grandfathers and thirteen grandmothers, ranging in age from 42 to 79, averaging 59. Eight participants reported that they spoke their tribal language fluently and two participants reported they could understand their tribal language, but could not speak it fluently. Two other participants reported being able to speak their tribal language as young children but could not speak it now. Ages of participants ranged from 42 to 79, averaging 59. The grandchildren participants described ranged in age from 2 to 18 years and averaged 11. Seven participants reported that the grandchild they described lived with them. Six participants reported that the grandchild they described lived over 30 minutes away from them. Six grandparents reported that they and their families participated in the Relocation Program for American Indians during the 1960's. Three grandparents had attended Indian Boarding Schools and none of the grandchildren described attended Indian Boarding Schools.

Participants were asked to describe the roles they played in the lives of one of their grandchildren. The questions were open-ended, and throughout the interview each grandparent was provided as much time and autonomy to answer the questions as she needed. The interviewer was allowed to rephrase or probe as a way to elicit clarification, additional information, detail, or elaboration (Bodgan & Biklen, 1992; Survey Research Center, 1982). When supplemental questioning occurred, non-directive probing techniques (Survey Research Center, 1982), whereby the interviewer's response is only a simple acknowledgement using a neutral follow-up question or comment (such as "could you tell me more," or "what do you mean by that"), were used

to insure that the interviewer did not influence the grandparents' responses.

Analysis of the interviews followed a sequence of strategies traditionally identified with the process of data reduction and analysis using qualitative methodologies (Bogdan & Biklin, 1992; Creswell, 1998; Huberman & Miles, 1994; Lincoln & Guba, 1985). The analysis began by independently reviewing the transcripts through multiple readings, taking a micro analytic perspective, and using grounded theory methodology to identify concepts and generate potential categories to represent participant responses (Strauss & Corbin, 1994, 1998). Categories and themes that existed across all interviews, as well as those within the context of specific questions, were identified. A series of meetings were then held where identification and discussion of potential concepts, their properties and constructions, and metaphors to realistically represent grandparents' responses were shared. Over the course of these meetings, initial themes and coding conventions were established, resulting in a process often referred to as "open coding" (Strauss & Corbin, 1998). It was also determined that in most cases the level of coding would anchor on phrases or sentences (Strauss & Corbin, 1998), and that frequency counts (Huberman & Miles, 1994) would be collected to aide in the representation of themes and concepts.

Having identified the coding conventions, two raters independently returned to the transcripts and coded the responses to each question. The process of coding and data analysis in qualitative research is one that is fluid and dynamic, and can often result in intuitive modifications regarding the labeling and meaning of themes and categories (Creswell, 1998; Strauss & Corbin, 1998). Therefore during this phase of the coding process, the raters continued to document new or alternative constructions of themes and concepts. Huberman and Miles (1994) view data analysis as an interactive process where data reduction, data display, and conclusion drawing interact with one another. These components do not occur in a single linear sequence, rather they revolve around each other, indicating that the process of data analysis can go through a number of iterations. Subsequent to independent analysis, the raters held a second set of meetings, and applied procedures consistent with the principle of multiple investigator corroboration (Lincoln & Guba, 1985) and the value of employing multiple perspectives during analytic interpretations (Strauss & Corbin, 1998). They reviewed and compared their analyses, held additional discussion, and combined their interpretations, finally reaching a consensus regarding how each participant's responses were coded for each question.

Results

In many ways contemporary American Indian grand-parenting roles are similar to grand-parenting roles in general. For instance, participants in this study frequently reported partaking in general custodial and care taking responsibilities such as babysitting, transporting, disciplining, coordinating extended family gatherings and cooking for their grandchildren (Scherman, 2003). They also emphasized their role of cultural conservator through telling traditional and family stories (Scherman, 1988). The styles with which they performed these roles were also often commensurate to the styles described in previous studies. For instance, participants spoke of "spoiling," "giving more space," and offering unconditional love to their grandchildren (Scherman et al., 2003). Nonetheless, contemporary American Indian grand-parenting roles and styles emerge from unique socio-economic and cultural conditions that dress them in unique costumes.

All of the participants expressed feelings of enculturative responsibilities, in greater and lesser degrees. Only one person was tentative, stating that he would not take an assertive role in this area, but would wait to respond to his granddaughter's own interest to discuss tribal history and beliefs. All other participants reported that they engaged in active efforts to pass on American Indian traditional knowledge. Nineteen of the twenty grandparents interviewed expressed grave fears about the possibility of tribal culture being lost. One grandfather said, "Our ways are dying out with the death of every elder."

The most commonly mentioned strategy of cultural preservation took story form. Sixteen participants mentioned that they told stories to their grandchildren. The stories that were retold during the interviews might be categorized as nature, prudence, historical and ghost stories. In one story a duck rescues a man from drowning and in another a reed offers life saving air to a girl who is hiding from a fight at home. Stories such as these seem to imply that if nature is respected it will provide human beings with survival. Several participants told stories suggesting a prudence theme, recommending that children should think before acting. For instance, one interviewee related a story about Indian boys thoughtlessly playing a game of shooting arrows straight up into the air. One day an arrow came down onto the head of one of the boys, injuring him. Another person told a story of how "White people" came onto their land wanting to set up a trading post, which many feared would disrupt their way of life, and were directed to locate on a hill away from the Indian community. Some told stories of spirits. One warned of not telling ghost stories to grandchildren until they "grew older" and another warned not to tell ghost stories after dark. The stories suggest that many Indian grandparents are intent on their grandchildren knowing that the world consists of more than its material surface and that traditional rules function as forms of protection.

American Indian grandparent participants almost unanimously provided active support in their grandchildren's' participation in both tribal and pan-Indian activities, ceremonies, and ways of interacting. The list of these activities include facilitating grandchildren's participation in pow-wows, gourd dances, sweats, Indian church, dressing out in appropriate traditional regalia, Indian games, naming ceremonies, adoption ceremonies, stomp dances, bread dances, making tribal foods, crafts, and drumming. Several grandparents expressed great concern that their grandchildren know the differences and protocol regarding tribal dress at pow-wows, understanding different perspectives regarding "stomp dancers" and "pow-wow people," and distinguishing between stomp dance beliefs and Indian church beliefs. Another grandmother claimed to be so concerned that her son learn to drum and sing his tribal songs that she had taken the lead to teach him rather than leaving it to

males in her tribe. Also, the majority of the participants mentioned that it was important to teach at least some words of their tribal language to their grandchildren. Their language teaching ranged from teaching their grandchildren to be fluent to teaching them basic introductions, words for relatives, and songs. Almost all participants spoke of tribal language being an important element or their tribal culture.

Every American Indian grandparent interviewed stressed a concern for passing down values, which she believed to be colored by their ethnicity. Thirteen participants discussed their desire to teach their children a love and respect for nature. For some an ecological mindedness for clean water and respect for plants and animals was expressed, while for some it was an appreciation for nature's beauty. Just under half the participants said that "respect" was a value they wished to pass on. When asked to define this word it was usually defined as "honoring your elders." Other values mentioned at from three to six times were: showing appreciation, courage, unselfishness, hard work, giving, quietness, kindness, pride in being Indian, balance, and regular prayer. Participants said they taught these values by role modeling and through direct verbal communication. Several participants complained that their children were not teaching the above values to their grandchildren.

Acting as a facilitator in "bringing the family together" was another role participants believed that they regularly performed to help grandchildren. This idea was expressed in the following ways: "I feel a responsibility to bring the family together for meals. My grandchild can get to know his family this way." "I bring him to Indian church and show him off." "I look forward to the day I can bring her to my tribal pow-wow. When she gets old enough, her white father won't be able to stop me. My tribal people know she is alive and they will be so happy to meet her." "It is important for me to have her mix with her cousins and aunts. She will need them for support." "It is great to get the nephews and nieces together to fish and play softball." "Our land has been in our family for 150 years. We clean it up and I get everybody together there. My grandchild fishes there with his cousins." "My grand daughter sits right there next to me and her family at the pow-wows." The preceding remarks reflect the grandparents' values of regular interaction and closeness across generations and among extended family members. While one does not detect a law like regularity that governs interactions, there appears to be an expectation of continuous exchanges. Grandparents also appear to view this role as a source of self-worth.

All participants expressed the belief that as grandparents they had unique offerings for their grandchildren. Several mentioned the love, support and interaction that they had with their grandchildren as more egalitarian and less structured, characterizing it as "less directive," "more imaginative" and "more flexible" than parent/child interactions. One grandmother described her role with her granddaughter as being a "playmate." Others spoke again of their responsibilities to transmit "old ways" and "family history" and to gather the extended family together. One person reflected comments several others made when she described herself as a "safety net" when problems arose with her grandchild's parents. One grandparent said his unique contribution to his grandson's life was starting a drum group for his grandson to participate in.

When asked about what they would prefer to do as a grandparent, comments reflected desires to be useful and attached, yet not overused and inextricably bound to their grandchildren everyday. Several wished for greater proximity in order to interact more frequently with their grandchildren. One grandfather wished his granddaughter lived with him, while three, who had custodial care of their grandchildren, expressed a desire to live separately and to have fewer obligations, including financial responsibility. Two participants suggested that their interactions contrasted with mainstream grandparents because they lacked financial resources. They were proud to offer their grand children "stories," "histories" and "good cooking" rather than "finances." Two said that they "just wanted to be there to soothe" their grandchildren emotionally when they needed it, contrasting this relationship with parents' interactions which one described as "picky or critical." Another's comment reflected many of the comments when she said, "I just want to be useful, you know, to be needed, like to be asked for something. I can give good advice because I have lived a lot."

Discussion

The status of American Indian grandparents has until recently been of an exalted nature. Today there are traces or this past reverence in speeches made about grandparents at pow-wows and other ceremonies, but as indicated in the above fragments of interviews the deferential attitude shown is often a matter of form and devoid of power. Many elders feel the wisdom they believe they possess is too often unappreciated. The grandparents in this study often expressed low levels of antagonism toward their children for not working to preserve tribal culture. Still they reported that they continue to transfer tribal values and knowledge to their grandchildren through telling stories, modeling, direct communicative teaching, and playful interaction.

Almost all of the American Indian grandparents interviewed in this project felt great responsibility for mediating American Indian religion and culture. They felt they were at a crossroads at which they could let the old ways go forever or try to pass some of the ways down to their grandchildren. For some the possibility of preserving heritage was seen as remote. In spite of the cultural bombs dropped to annihilate beliefs and tribal unity by the American government, almost all participants in this study took active roles to pass down at least a few of the old ways. Nonetheless, there appeared to be an anxious awareness among participants that their present predicament was not purely a matter of personal choice but it arose from a historical situation. They were all too aware that economic, political, cultural, psychological and military pressures have quite a strangle-hold on tribal culture.

Such responses indicate that American Indian grandparents want the cultural needs of their grandchildren met despite the fact that they themselves were taught by educators who were probably emphatic assimilationists. American Indian elders have lived through periods when tribal customs and ways were either disregarded or vehemently opposed as uncivilized and

anti-Christian (Szasz, 1984). Nonetheless, the grandparents in this study expressed the desire to teach aspects of American Indian culture to their grandchildren. But because of past and present, covert and overt discrimination and assimilation policies they are limited. It is no accident that grandparents in this study frequently mentioned language and love of the land, values often used to define American Indian peoples (Sue & Sue, 2003), as two of the most important gifts they might impart to their grandchildren.

The interviewers in this study could not help but be cognizant of the contradiction of having American Indian grandparents define their roles in terms of a language (English) of imperialist imposition. Possibly the most meaningful information offered regarding the grandparent's relationship to their grandchildren came when they used the Indian names of their grandchildren. One musically breathed, "My grandson's Indian name is Onsehoma . . . Red Eagle." From such tribal words, phrases, and names one can glean norms, attitudes and values of tribal grandparents in regard to their grandchildren. Some researchers contend that language is the primary factor of cultural identity because it connects persons to their cultures' traditions, customs, unique styles of humor, history, and understandings of ceremonies (Eastman, 1985; Dividoff, 2001). Unfortunately, while many American Indian grandparents wish to pass on their tribal language, many are limited by their own lack of fluency that comes as a consequence of having had it forbidden for generations. Some grandparents expressed despair about having lost their tribal language. Stealing language from a people is the bullet of spiritual subjugation. Many of the participants in this study are attempting to pass down tribal language with all its cultural attachments to their grandchildren.

For American Indians love of the land and nature in general (Highwater, 1982), is one of the most essential values because, unlike many values, it is concrete and bound up with history and contemporary politics. The valuing of land and the protection of natural sites is a passionate concern for many American Indians. In fact, many claim that the Great Spirit has given American Indians a special vocation to model respect and love Mother Earth for other races (Highwater, 1982). But tribal lands were taken away by conquest, unequal treaties, or by genocide. American Indian grandparent participants in this study wished to teach their children about the importance of the unique historical character of American Indians' connections to their land and nature. Tragically, for many of the participants, tribal land has been wrested from their families, which has had devastating consequences. For example, American Indians are now the most poverty stricken of all races in the United States (Sue & Sue, 2003), which undermines cohesiveness among tribal members who find themselves fighting against each other for limited resources. In Oklahoma, where all the land was taken from tribes and redistributed according to checkerboard plans (farms given to Whites to separate American Indian families) in the early twentieth century, American Indians find themselves separated from other tribal members, as well as from their historical and spiritual connections to their land (Sue & Sue, 2003). Nonetheless, though the American government robbed American Indians of their land, they were not successful in stealing their dignity. In heroic fashion, the participants in this research project expressed a profound love of the land and a passionate desire to pass this love of land on to their grandchildren.

Grandparents also asserted that telling stories to their grandchildren was important. Stories act as mechanisms through which grandparents can teach succeeding generations how to live life consistent with tribal values (Robbins, 2002). Both traditional and personal stories were told by participants to add meaning and coherence to their grandchildren's lives and to offer structures with which to frame their experiences. They were told to grandchildren to help clarify their cultural and personal self-concepts and to unravel confusing rules, ceremonial expectations and relationships. Many of the traditional stories had animals as main characters. While sometimes small and weak, they were full of wit and cunning when claiming victory over stronger enemies or saving someone from hostile nature. The stories appeared to reflect past and present real life psychological and political struggles. Dances, songs, and ceremonies taught and promoted by grandparents served similar purposes. But for participants in this study, storytelling roles no longer could be assumed in the same fashion as they were historically. For instance, many grandparents in this study were separated geographically not only from their grandchildren, but also from tribal gatherings where they might have told their grandchildren seasonally appropriate stories. The grandparents in this study told their stories in situations when the opportunity presented itself.

In addition to the values often taught indirectly through stories, there were many taught directly and others were demonstrated through modeling. Spiritual and community values appeared to be the most cherished. Grandparents taught grandchildren to pray and continue customs as well as to show appreciation, to be generous, and unselfishness) as the ultimate good their communities. Grandparents taught values that might provide the foundation for tribal renewal and cooperative communities. It is not easy for American Indians to maintain traditional values in the wake of years of gradual accumulation of Euro-American values, which easily over time become almost self-evident truths governing what is right and wrong, and good and bad. Still, the grandparents in this study expressed a commitment to preserve and renew traditional tribal values.

Lastly, the grandparents in this study repeatedly expressed the complex predicament of being somewhat marginal in their grandchildren's' lives, yet also in better positions to joke and laugh with their grandchildren. Their marginality was typically explained as being the result of living at a distance from grandchildren, lack of mobility, feelings of a decline in influence and loss of culture. Their "special" intimacy was often either directly or indirectly explained as being the result of being freed from the disciplinarian role. Those who had not been forced to become custodial described teasing, kind, close, playful and affectionate relationships with their grandchildren. Some grandparents' descriptions of their interactions contrasted with the severity of the parents' involvement with their children. While custodial grandparents complained of the tension associated with establishing rules and enforcing punishments on their

grandchildren, non-custodial grandparents could indulge their grandchildren, being in positions where they were free from the taboos of parental discipline.

Recommendations, Limitations, and Further Directions

The recommendations of this study are for democratic initiatives and human liberation. They directly address the deepest fears of many of the grandparents' of this study who feel they are at a dramatic crossroads that requires nothing less than fundamental social and political transformation. It is a call for rediscovery and for regenerative reconnections. This begins with the resumption of tribal languages. Tribal governments should employ American Indian grandparents who speak their tribal languages to teach their grandchildren their tribal languages before those languages, with their unique cultural nuances, are irrevocably erased. To lose one's tribal language is to lose, to a large extent, a tribal sensibility and to be alienated from much of one's tribal culture. Language is an enormous carrier of culture, and many American Indian grandparents have this part of culture to share. Secondly, tribes could employ grandparents to teach tribal arts and crafts, tribal religions, and tribal history to their grandchildren. All this must be done soon, taking into account that many elders are taking traditional tribal culture with them and that children must be taught early in life before the values of Euro-American society become implanted and nearly impossible to eradicate. Thirdly, there must be a systematic effort to reclaim tribal lands. Many tribes are already attempting this. Grandparents might lobby for this sort of political directive. Without a doubt the reacquisition of tribal lands would provide renewed dignity and greater cohesiveness among tribal members. Support in these endeavors from culturally sensitive, non-American Indians is welcomed.

Due to the fact that almost all of the participants in this study live in Oklahoma and do not live on reservations, the generalizability of the study is limited. There was a profound commitment Researchers expected a lower level of commitment to the transference of tribal values among this non-reservation sample. One might expect an even greater commitment among American Indians living on reservations. A replication of this study might bear this hypothesis out.

Future research might also explore the impact of American Indian grandparents' efforts in the role of cultural conservator in specific areas such as story telling, participation in tribal activities and in the transference of tribal values on their grandchildren. Such a study may entail interviewing grandchildren as well as grandparents. Efforts to develop reliable and valid acculturation instruments might facilitate further research.

References

Bahr, K. S. (1994). The strength of Apache mothers: Observations on commitment, culture and caretaking. *Journal of Comparative Family Studies, 25,* 233–248.

Barnett, H. (1955). *The Coast Salish of British Columbia.* Eugene, Oregon: University of Oregon.

Bogdan, R. C., & Biklen, S. K. (1992). *Qualitative research for education.* Boston: Allyn & Bacon.

Coleman, H., Unau, Y.A, & B. Manyfingers, (2001). Revamping Family Preservation Services for Native Families. *Journal of Ethnic & Cultural Diversity in Social Work, 10* (1), 49–65.

Cooney, T., & Smith, L. (1993). Young adults relations with grandparents following parental divorce. *Journal of Gerontology Services B: Psychological Sciences and Social Sciences, 51B,* 591–595.

Creasey, G. L., & Kaliher, G. (1994). Age differences in grandchildren's perceptions of relationship quality with grandparents. *Journal of Adolescence, 17,* 411–426.

Creswell, J. W. (1998). *Qualitative inquiry and research design: Choosing among five traditions.* Thousand Oaks, CA: Sage Publications.

Elmendorf, W. W., & Kroeber, A. (1960). *The structure of Twona with notes on Yurals culture.* Pullman, WA: Washington State University.

Gladstone, J. W. (1988). Perceived changes in grandmother-grandchild relations following a child's separation or divorce. *The Gerontologist, 28,* 66–72.

Highwater, J. (1982). *The primal mind.* Hammondsworth: Penguins Books.

Huberman, A. M., & Miles, M. B. (1994). *Data management and analysis methods.* In N. K. Denzin, & Y. S. Lincoln, Handbook of qualitative research (pp. 428–444). Thousand Oaks, CA: Sage Publications.

Jaskowski, S., & Dellasega, C. (1993). Effects of divorce on grandparent-grandchild relationship. *Issues in Comprehensive Pediatric Nursing, 16,*125–133.

Kennedy, G. E. (1992). Shared activities of grandparents and grandchildren. *Psychological Reports, 70,* 211–227.

Lincoln, Y. S., & Guba, E. G. (1985). *Naturalistic inquiry.* Newbury, CA: Sage Publications.

Nahemow, N. O. (1987). Grandparenthood among the Baganda: Role option in old age. In Sokolovski, J. (ed.). *Growing old in Societies.* Belmont, CA: Wadsworth.

Noor Al-Deen, Hana S. (Ed.) (1997). *Cross-cultural communication and aging in the United States.* Mahwah, NJ: Lawrence Erlbaum Associates.

Robbins, R. R. (2002). The role of traditional American Indian stories and symbols in counseling adolescents with behavior problems. *Beyond Behavior, 16,* 12–19.

Sander, G. F., & Trygstad, D. W. (1993) Strengths of grandparents and grandchildren relationships. *Activities, Adaptation and Aging, 17,* 43–53.

Scherman, A., Beesley, D., & Turner, B. (2003). Grandparents' involvement with grandchildren during times of crisis in the family. *Oklahoma Association of Teacher Educators, 7,* 47–61.

Scherman, A., Goodrich, C., Kelly, C., Russell, T., & Javidi, A. (1988). Grandparents as a support system for children. *Elementary School Guidance and Counseling Journal, 37,* 16–22.

Schweitzer, M. M. (1987). The elders: Cultural dimensions of aging in two American Indian communities. In Sokolovski, J. (ed.). *Growing old in Societies.* Belmont, CA: Wadsworth.

Strauss, A., & Corbin, J. (1998). *Basics of qualitative research: Techniques and procedures for developing grounded theory.* Thousand Oaks, CA: Sage Publications.

Sue, D. W., & Sue, D. (2003). *Counseling the culturally diverse.* New York: John Wiley & Sons.

Survey Research Center (1982). *General interviewing techniques.* Ann Arbor, MI: Institute for Social Research.

Szasz, M. C. (1984). *Education and the American Indian.* Albuquerque: University of New Mexico.

Timberlake, E., & Chipungu, S. S. (1992). Grand motherhood: Contemporary meaning among African American middle class grandmothers. *Social Work, 37,* 216–222.

Weibel-Orlando, J. (1990). Grand parenting styles: Native American Perspectives. In Sokolovski, J. (ed.). *The cultural context of aging* (pp 109–125). Westport, CT: Greenwood Press.

Williams, E. (1995). Father and grandfather involvement in childrearing and the school performance of Ojibwa children: An exploratory study. (Doctoral dissertation, University of Michigan, 1995). *Dissertation Abstracts International, 56* (4-A), 1530.

ROCKEY ROBBINS, PhD (Cherokee/Choctaw), is in the Counseling Psychology Department at the University of Oklahoma in Normal, OK 73019. **AAVRAHAM SCHERMAN,** EdD, is also in the Counseling Psychology Department at the University of Oklahoma. **HEIDI HOLEMAN,** MS and **JASON WILSON,** MS are doctoral students in the Counseling Psychology Department at the University of Oklahoma. Dr. Robbins may be reached at 405/325-8442 or E-mail: Rockey@ou.edu.

From *Journal of Cultural Diversity,* Summer 2005, pp. 62–68. Copyright © 2005 by Tucker Publications, Inc. Reprinted by permission.

UNIT 4

Challenges and Opportunities

Unit Selections

Key Points to Consider

- How does an abusive relationship develop? What, if anything, can be done to prevent it?
- What are the risk factors for child abduction? Why do we hold the belief that it is strangers who are more likely to abduct children? What can be done to protect children from family abduction?
- What are the particular risks for children of alcoholics? What contributes to resilience for them?
- If you felt your intimate relationship was troubled, how would you act? Would you discuss it with your partner? Would you hope that it would correct itself without your doing anything?
- What is the best way to work out the competing demands of work and family?
- How do you think you would respond if your child or partner was diagnosed with a life-threatening disease? What is the relationship among loss, grief, and care?
- How can you go about helping a family cope when a member is deployed?
- Discuss how the breakup of a relationship or a divorce affects the people involved. Is it possible to have a "good" divorce? What would that good divorce look like? What are the particular issues related to remarriage and the family dynamics associated with it?

Student Website
www.mhcls.com

Internet References

Alzheimer's Association
http://www.alz.org
Caregiver's Handbook
http://www.acsu.buffalo.edu/~drstall/hndbk0.html

National Crime Prevention Council
http://www.ncpc.org
Widow Net
http://www.widownet.org

Stress is life and life is stress. Sometimes stress in families gives new meaning to this statement. When a stressful event occurs in families, many processes occur simultaneously as families and their members cope with the stressor and its effects. One thing that can result is a reduction of the family members' ability to act as resources for each other. Indeed, a stressor can overwhelm the family system, and family members may be among the least effective people in coping with each other's behavior.

In this unit, we consider a wide variety of crises. Family violence is the focus of the first articles. "Recognizing Domestic Partner Abuse" presents warning signs and resources for those who experience or those who hope to help those experiencing domestic partner abuse. "Domestic Abuse Myths" addresses common myths about partner violence—even when the victim is a popular celebrity, teens appear to believe that she must have "done something to deserve it."

Substance abuse is next addressed in "Children of Alcoholics" and "Impact of Family Recovery and Pre-Teens and Adolescents." The first article looks at ways in which children of alcoholics (COA) are put at risk by substance abuse in their families, while it also presents surprising resilience factors that may serve to protect these children from their family dysfunction. The second looks at the nature of family recovery, the traumatic effect of family recovery on the young, and potential treatments.

Next, infidelity is addressed in "My Cheatin' Heart" and "Love but Don't Touch." The former concerns the choices people make that lead to infidelity. The latter addresses emotional infidelity, a form of unfaithfulness that many see as less serious than sexual infidelity, but others view as just a damaging to a couple's relationship. In this article, Mark Teich addresses a variety of ways of spotting emotional cheating as well as ways of strengthening a relationship after or in anticipation of its happening. A new phenomenon, "Is This Man Cheating on His Wife?," is explored in the final article in this subsection.

The subsection that follows, Economic Concerns, looks at the work/family connection with interesting results. The "Opt-Out Myth" questions a common belief that women are leaving the workforce to focus on their home life. The view that family and work life must arrive at some form of appropriate balance is the focus of "Making Time for Family Time."

The nature of stress resulting from a life-threatening illness as well as loss and grief are the subject of the next subsection. Life-threatening illnesses can place tremendous strain on couples' relationships. "Partners Face Cancer Together" documents the ways in which couples survive breast cancer together with a stronger relationship in the bargain. The same is true when the person affected is a child, as discussed in "Dealing Day-to-Day with Diabetes." The next two articles address issues of caregiving. In the first, "Caring for the Caregiver," addresses an often invisible health risk—the stress experienced by caregivers. This stress puts them at risk and this article provides suggestions on how caregivers can care for themselves. The next article, "Bereavement after Caregiving," shows that the stress of caregiving does not end with death. The struggle faced by bereaved

© Image Source/PunchStock RF

parents, addressed in "Love, Loss–and Love," is how and when to open one's heart to the thought of having another child after losing a child.

In the next section, the many crises of war is portrayed. "Stressors Affecting Families during Military Deployment" catalogues stressors faced by military families when a member is deployed to a war zone. "Children and the Wars" looks specifically at the issues of the children of those deployed.

Divorce and remarriage are the subjects of the final subsection. The first articles in this subsection, "A Divided House" and "Civil Wars," both address ways in which the divorcing (and then divorced) couple may use their children as pawns in their battles with each other. The needs of the children must be paramount when a couple divorces—this is too often not the case. Finally, "Stepfamily Success Depends on Ingredients" details characteristics of successful stepfamilies, paying particular attention to ways of building resilience into the family system.

Recognizing Domestic Partner Abuse

With its daunting complexities, the path to change takes courage and support.

Domestic abuse. Battering. Intimate partner violence. These are terms that make us wince. And they should: The phenomenon is widespread in the United States, and its effects can be long-lasting and life-threatening. Breaking the pattern of domestic violence can be extremely difficult and may take a long time. It requires courage, planning, and a support network.

The U.S. Department of Health and Human Services defines domestic violence as "a pattern of assaultive and/or coercive behaviors . . . that adults use against their intimate partners to gain power and control in that relationship." It includes not only physical and sexual abuse but also emotional abuse. All can have serious health consequences.

Domestic violence affects people of all ethnic backgrounds; it occurs among the poor and the rich and among the well educated and the poorly educated. Men are usually (though not always) the abusers, and women are usually on the receiving end. In the United States, a woman's lifetime risk of being a victim of such violence is 25%. Women who were abused as children are at an increased risk for being in an abusive relationship as an adult.

First Signs

Women don't consciously choose to have an abusive partner. In fact, the abuser may be charming and well liked by most of the people who know him, but at home he shows a different side. Friends, family, and colleagues are often shocked when his abusive behavior becomes known. In the beginning, it may also be a shock to the abused woman. She may have regarded her relationship with this man as the most

wonderful, romantic, fairy tale–like experience imaginable, says Susan Neis, executive director of Cornerstone, a shelter that serves five suburbs of Minneapolis.

Changes in the relationship can be difficult to see at first. The abuser's need for control often begins to show itself in little things he says and does. He may criticize the way his partner acts or looks. He may say deeply hurtful things, such as accusing her of being a bad mother. "When somebody says this to you, somebody you're in love with, it's devastating," says Neis, who is herself a survivor of domestic abuse.

Over time, the abuser's words can chip away at a woman's sense of herself. She starts to doubt her perceptions and may even come to believe the horrible things he says about her. She feels isolated, ashamed, and helpless, but at the same time may feel an obligation to keep herself convinced of the fairy tale because "there's nothing else to hold onto," says one 35-year-old woman who received help from Cornerstone.

Control and Power

At the center of domestic violence is the issue of control. The abuser is intent on gaining and maintaining power over his partner through fear and intimidation. Abuse doesn't necessarily involve physical harm. Threats can also be highly effective and should not be minimized, suggests Dr. Judith Herman, clinical professor of psychiatry at Harvard Medical School and training director of the Victims of Violence Program at Cambridge Health Alliance in Cambridge, Mass. A man who says "If you leave me, I'll track you down and kill you and anyone who helps you" can instill as much (or more) fear as one who strikes his partner.

The abusive partner uses various tactics to achieve control. He may intimidate and demean his partner by constantly criticizing her, monopolizing household finances, or telling her what she can wear, where she can go, and whom she can see. He may play "mind games," such as suggesting that she's hypersensitive, hysterical, or mentally unbalanced. Often he isolates the woman from family, friends, and colleagues, either by removing her from them physically or by limiting her employment options and social contacts. Abuse may also take the form of pathological jealousy, such as false accusations of adultery. Soon, the woman may find that she's cut off from all outside connections, no longer in touch with the people and services that could help her.

Isolation may also disconnect her from a sense of what's normal. She may not even think of herself as a victim of domestic violence, says Dr. Megan Gerber, an internist at Cambridge Health Alliance who specializes in women's health and an instructor of medicine at Harvard Medical School. After an incident, the abuser often apologizes and tries to placate his victim. There may be periods of relative calm. It may take a victim a long time to recognize that her partner's behaviors aren't random but form a pattern of abuse.

Selected Resources

National Domestic Violence Hotline
800-799-7233 (toll free)
800-787-3224 (for the hearing impaired; toll free)

National Sexual Assault Hotline
800-656-4673 (toll free)

National Women's Health Information Center, "Violence against Women"
womenshealth.gov/violence/domestic/
800-994-9662 (toll free)

United Way First Call for Help
800-231-4377 (toll free)

Intimate Partner Abuse Is a Health Issue

Intimate partner abuse can have profound effects on a woman's health, both physical and mental. Physical harm, including fractures, lacerations, and soft tissue trauma, is one obvious effect. Intimate partner abuse is also linked to chronic health problems and even death—from either suicide because of depression or murder (or manslaughter) by the partner.

The intense, ongoing stress may result in chronic pain or gastrointestinal symptoms. Victims of domestic abuse are more likely to have arthritis, neck pain, pelvic pain, and migraine headaches. They also have an increased risk of menstrual problems and difficulties during pregnancy, including bleeding, low birth weight, and anemia.

Domestic abuse is closely linked with mental illness and substance abuse. A recent study found that 47.6% of battered women were depressed and 63.8% had post-traumatic stress disorder; 18.5% used alcohol excessively; 8.9% used drugs; and 7.9% committed suicide.

Because women in abusive relationships often need emergency room and primary care services, physicians, nurses, and other clinicians are often the first outsiders to learn about the emotional or physical abuse. Women are often reluctant to mention the subject on a patient history form, but if asked by a clinician, they may be relieved to acknowledge it.

Getting Out

Walking away from an abusive relationship is a process more than a single action. Women usually make several attempts—five, on average—before they leave the partner for good. Isolation and fear may prevent a woman from leaving, even when she knows it is probably for the best. She may still love her partner or worry about what will happen to her children if she leaves. She may be unsure how to escape or how to survive financially and care for her children.

Community support can be crucial (see "Selected Resources"), although a woman in an abusive relationship often has difficulty taking advantage of that support. The abuser may track her computer use, looking for visits to websites and evidence of keyword searches. If that's a concern, says Rita Smith, executive director of the National Coalition Against Domestic Violence in Boulder, Colo., she should use a computer outside the home—for example at a library or a friend's home or work place. As a safeguard, the coalition's own site (www.ncadv.org) features a red "Escape" button that immediately switches the user to an Internet search engine.

Care for the Children

Each year, up to 10 million children witness the abuse of a parent or caregiver. Many women stay in an abusive relationship because they think it's best not to disrupt the children's lives so long as they're not being abused themselves. But children who live with domestic violence are at serious risk for behavioral and cognitive problems. In later life, they may suffer depression and trauma symptoms, and they may tolerate or use violence in their own relationships.

Experts say that women leaving an abusive relationship should take their children with them. Otherwise, it can be difficult to get the children later, because police may not want to remove them from the home if the abusive partner is their biological father. Also, the abuser may later try to get custody by arguing that the woman abandoned her children.

What Can I Do to Help?

You suspect that your friend is in an abusive relationship. For example, she seems anxious and fearful when she recounts arguments with her husband. Or she may mention having to ask him each time she needs money. (While by itself not a sign of abuse, controlling finances can be part of a pattern of abuse.)

Part of you wants to rescue her and take her to a safe place where her husband can't find her. Yet you worry that any action you take could make things worse, increasing the danger she's already in. You know the decision is hers to make, not yours. But you can do a lot to help. Here are some things to consider:

- Think about your relationship with your friend. When and where might you talk with her safely, and what could you say? Does she trust you? Does she feel that she can confide in you without fearing that you'd judge her harshly or dismiss her concerns?
- Ask questions that let her know of your suspicions and concern. One question might be: Are you afraid of your husband? Understand that she might be hesitant to talk about this directly—or might deny or minimize what's happening. Assure her that you'll keep what she says strictly confidential.
- When she talks about the situation, believe what she says and validate her concerns. Let her know you don't think she's crazy or it's all in her head. And let her know that she's not to blame, despite what her partner may have told her.
- Help your friend make use of local resources—public health services, a hospital or clinic, a women's shelter, or a legal assistance program. If she thinks the abuser is monitoring her phone calls, offer her the use of your home phone or cell phone to make these contacts.
- Work with your friend to develop a personal safety plan. One resource for this step is the National Coalition Against Domestic Violence, www.ncadv.org/protectyourself/MyPersonalSafetyPlan_131.html.
- Help her prepare to leave if the danger and abuse escalate. Your friend should have coins with her at all times for phone calls, or a phone card. She should prepare a small bag with clothes, cash, and copies of important documents (birth certificate and passport, for example) and keep it in a safe place. Would you be willing to keep the bag for her in case of need?
- Knowing that someone believes her and is ready to help can be crucial to your friend's safety and eventual escape from the abusive relationship. Be patient, listen, and offer her hope. Recognize that it may take a long time, and often several attempts at leaving, for the relationship to end.

Domestic Abuse Myths

Five mistakes we make when we talk about Rihanna and Chris Brown's relationship.

RAINA KELLEY

Last week, R&B singer Chris Brown was formally charged with two felonies, assault and making criminal threats, in connection with the alleged beating of his pop-star girlfriend Rihanna on Feb. 8. Though we will never know exactly what happened that night, many of us have seen Rihanna's bruised and bloodied face on the front pages and read horrific details of the alleged attack from the affidavit of a LAPD detective in which he describes contusions on the singer's body. At same time, rumors are that the 21-year-old singer is back in a relationship with Brown, whom she has accused, according to the affidavit, of biting, choking and punching her until her mouth filled with blood.

While we can argue about how much of all that is true, it really doesn't matter. This sad story doesn't have to be verifiable for it to potentially warp how Rihanna's hundreds of thousands of tween fans think about intimate relationships. We've all heard that this should be a "teachable moment"—a chance to talk about domestic violence with our kids. But children and teens aren't just listening to your lectures, they're listening to the way you speculate about the case with other adults; they're absorbing how the media describes it; they're reading gossip websites. When you tune into to all the talk about Rihanna and Chris Brown, it's scary how the same persistent domestic-violence myths continue to be perpetuated. Celebrity scandals may have a short shelf life, but what we teach kids about domestic violence will last forever. So rather than "raise awareness," here are five myths that anyone with a child should take time to debunk:

Myth No. 1: It Was a Domestic Argument, and She Provoked Him

We need to remember that any discussion of domestic violence should not revolve around what the couple may have been arguing about, or as one CNN anchor put it: "the incident that sparked

the fight." Nor should we be using the word "provoked" when describing this case, as in the Associated Press account that said the "argument" was "provoked" by Rihanna's "discovery of a text message from another woman." Domestic violence has to do with, well, physical violence, not arguments. There isn't a verbal argument that should "spark" or "provoke" an attack of the kind that leaves one person with wounds that require medical attention.

Cable news has to stop referring to this incident as a "violent fight." A "fight" involves two people hitting each other, not—as is alleged in this case—a woman cowering in a car while a man punches and bites her. If Rihanna had called the police beaten and bloodied and alleging an attack of this nature by a stranger, no one would be calling it a "fight." They'd say that a man was being accused of severely beating and choking a young woman half his size.

Myth No. 2: Evolution Makes Us Do It

Steven Stosny, a counselor and founder of an organization that treats anger-management issues believes that the tragic tendency of women to return to the men who hurt them (battered-woman syndrome) is a product of evolution. Stosny was quoted on CNN.com as saying "To leave an attachment relationship—a relationship where there's an emotional bond—meant certain death by starvation or saber-tooth tiger."

Apologies to Mr. Stosny, but that is the most ridiculous thing I have ever heard. This is the kind of argument that really boils my blood because it seems to naturalize the torture of women. Very little is known about the emotional attachments of early humans. And trust me, after 50,000 years, our fear of saber-tooth tigers has abated. In most domestic-abuse cases, we're talking about a situation where one person is wielding power over an individual through pain, fear, and domination. It's not about being scared to leave because of the dangers that await you in the world, it's about being too scared of what's at home to leave.

Myth No. 3: People Make Mistakes. Give the Guy a Break

When singer Kanye West talked about the Rihanna-Brown case with his VH1 audience recently, he asked: "Can't we give Chris a break? . . . I know I make mistakes in life." Kanye's not the only one saying this kind of thing, so let's get something straight: People leave the oven on or fry turkeys in the garage and burn their house down. One may even accidentally step on the gas instead of the brake and run over the family cat. Mistakes resulting in tragic consequences happen all the time. But one cannot mistakenly beat someone up. You do not accidentally give someone black eyes, a broken nose, and a split lip.

Myth No. 4: Brown Said He Was Sorry and They're Working It Out

Experts will tell you that domestic violence is an escalating series of attacks (not fights) designed to increase a victim's dependence on her abuser. According to the police documents released last week, Rihanna told police that Brown had hit her before and it was getting worse. Sorry means you don't do it again. In discussions about abuse, we need to make it clear that sorry is not enough.

Myth No. 5: She's Young, Rich and Beautiful. If It Was Really as Bad as the Media Says, She'd Leave

The secret to the abuser's power is not only making his victim dependent on him, but convincing her that she is to blame for the attack. No amount of money or fame can protect someone from the terrible cycle of emotional dependence, shame and fear that keeps them with abusive partners. Women who are abused look for ways they may have "provoked" an attack, finding fault with their own behavior to explain the unexplainable—why would someone they love hurt them? And it doesn't help when people outside the relationship blame the victim. In this case, Phylicia Thompson, a cousin of Brown's, told "Extra TV" that, *"Chris was not brought up to beat on a woman. So it had to be something to provoke him for Chris to do it."* As the rumors swirl about whether Rihanna is back with Brown, understand that those who are abused do not stay with their abusers because they want to be beaten again, or because they are really at fault; it's usually because they feel trapped and guilty.

You may have noticed that the words *power, control,* and *domination* running through my rant. That was purposeful. What we need to remember, and what we need to teach our children, is that yes, you should never hit anybody and you should never let anybody hit you. But, we also need to tell them that love does not guarantee respect and that any relationship they find themselves involved in should be based on both equally.

Children of Alcoholics
Risk and Resilience

Cara E. Rice, MPH, et al.

In 2002, over 17 million people in the United States were estimated to suffer from alcohol abuse or alcohol dependence (NIAAA, 2006). These alcohol disorders have devastating effects on the individuals, their families, and society. It has been reported that one in four children in the United States has been exposed to alcohol abuse or dependence in the family (Grant, 2000). A 1992 survey revealed that over 28 million children in the United States lived in households with one or more adults who had an alcohol disorder at some time in their lives, while nearly 10 million children lived with adults who reported alcohol disorders in the past year (Grant, 2000). Children of alcoholics (COAs) are at increased risk for a variety of negative outcomes, including fetal alcohol syndrome, substance use disorders, conduct problems, restlessness and inattention, poor academic performance, anxiety, and depression (West & Prinz, 1987). Furthermore, children of alcoholics are more likely to be exposed to family stressors such as divorce, family conflict, parental psychopathology, and poverty, which, in turn, may contribute to their negative outcomes.

In particular, COAs show increased risk of alcoholism and other substance use disorders. Genetic factors have been identified as increasing the risk of developing substance use problems among COAs (Schuckit, 2000). However, the risk faced by COAs is best understood as resulting from the interplay of both genetic and environmental factors (McGue, Elkins, & Iacano, 2000). We will discuss the factors that influence the development of substance abuse and other negative outcomes in COAs. We will also review three models in the development of substance disorders for COAs. These models are not mutually exclusive, and all three may influence a child. We will also discuss protective factors that may decrease COAs' risk for the development of future negative outcomes.

Prenatal Risk

One pathway for increased risk among COAs is through prenatal exposure to alcohol. Fetal alcohol syndrome (FAS), which can occur if a woman drinks alcohol during pregnancy, is a condition characterized by abnormal facial features, growth retardation, and central nervous system problems. Children with FAS may have physical disabilities and problems with learning, memory, attention, problem solving, and social/behavioral problems (Bertrand et al., 2004).

Pathways of Risk for the Development of Substance Disorders

Multiple pathways have been studied in the development of substance use disorders. Three important ones are the deviance proneness model, the stress/negative affect model, and the substance use effects model (Sher, 1991). Although these models were originally proposed to explain the development of alcohol disorders among COAs, they can also be extended to a consideration of other negative outcomes.

Deviance Proneness Pathway

The deviance proneness pathway theorizes that parental substance abuse produces poor parenting, family conflict, difficult child temperament and cognitive dysfunction. Poor parenting along with conflicted family environment are thought to interact with a child's difficult temperament and cognitive dysfunctions, which raises the child's risk for school failure and for associating with peers who themselves have high levels of conduct problems. Affiliation with these antisocial peers then increases the likelihood of antisocial behavior by COAs, including substance use (Dishion, Capaldi, Spracklen, & Li, 1995). Conduct problems in childhood and later adolescence predict the development of substance use disorders in young adulthood (Chassin et al., 1999; Molina, Bukstein, & Lynch, 2002).

One component of the deviance proneness model is difficult temperament or personality. The temperament and personality traits that are associated with adolescent substance use include sensation seeking, aggression, impulsivity, and an inability to delay gratification (Gerra et al., 2004; Wills,

Windle, & Cleary, 1998). For example, 3-year-old boys observed to be distractible, restless, and impulsive were more likely to be diagnosed with alcohol dependence at the age of 21 (Caspi, Moffitt, Newman, & Silva, 1996). Importantly, these characteristics, which are associated with adolescent substance use, have also been shown to be more common among COAs and children of drug users. (e.g., Carbonneau et al., 1998). This suggests that COAs may be at risk for substance use, in part, because of their personality traits.

One in four children in the United States has been exposed to alcohol abuse or dependence in the family.

Another component of the deviance proneness model is a deficit in cognitive function. Children of alcoholics may also be at risk for substance abuse because of deficits in cognitive functioning that have been called "executive" functions. Executive functioning refers to the ability to adjust behavior to fit the demands of individual situations and executive functioning includes planning, working memory and the ability to inhibit responses (Nigg et al., 2004). COAs have demonstrated poor response inhibition (Nigg et al., 2004), and impairments in executive functioning have found to predict drinking among young adult COAs (Atyaclar, Tarter, Kirisci, & Lu, 1999).

The deviance proneness pathway also suggests that COAs may be at risk because of the poor parenting that they receive. Decreased parental monitoring of the child's behavior, inconsistent discipline, and low levels of social support from parents are associated with increased levels of adolescent substance use and conduct problems (Brody, Ge, Conger, Gibbons, Murry, Gerrard, & Simons, 2001; Wills, McNamara, Vaccaro, & Hirky, 1996). These negative parenting behaviors have been found in substance-abusing families (Chassin, Curran, Hussong, & Colder, 1996; Curran & Chassin, 1996), suggesting that alcoholic parents may engage in poor parenting practices, which may in turn place their children at risk for substance use and/or conduct problems.

Most researchers have assumed that poor parenting leads to behavior problems in children, making it the basis for many prevention and intervention programs. However, developmental researchers have suggested that child behavior also affects parenting (Bell & Chapman, 1986). For example, Stice and Barrera (1995) found that low levels of parental control and support predicted adolescent substance use. However, adolescent substance use, in turn, predicted decreases in parental control and support. Therefore, the link between parenting and adolescent conduct problems and substance use may best be thought of as a system in which parents affect children, and children affect parents.

Stress and Negative Affect Pathway

The stress and negative affect pathway suggests that parental substance abuse increases children's exposure to stressful life events such as parental job instability, familial financial difficulty, parental legal problems, etc. (Chassin et al., 1993; Sher, 1991). These potentially chronic stressors may lead to emotional distress in COAs such as depression and/or anxiety. Substance use may then be used to control this distress.

Research has shown a link between negative affect and substance use in adolescence (see Zucker, 2006, for a review). For example, depression has been found to co-occur with adolescent substance abuse (Deykin, Buka, & Zeena, 1992) and heavy alcohol use (Rohde, Lewinson, & Seely, 1996). Moreover, negative life events have been associated with adolescent substance use (Wills, Vaccaro, & McNamara, 1992). However, not all findings support a negative affect pathway to adolescent substance use problems.

One explanation for the conflicting findings is that not all adolescents with negative affect will be at risk for substance use. Rather, adolescents who suffer from negative affect may only use alcohol and drugs if they also lack good strategies to cope with their negative moods and/or if they believe that alcohol or drugs will help them cope. Therefore, helping COAs to develop coping strategies can potentially serve as an intervention. There may also be gender differences in the extent to which COAs use substance use to cope with stress and negative mood (Chassin et al., 1999).

Substance Use Effects Model

The substance use effects model focuses on individual differences in the pharmacological effects of substances. It is hypothesized that some individuals are more sensitive to the pleasurable effects of alcohol and substance use and/or less sensitive to the adverse effects. For example, Schuckit and Smith (1996) found that male COAs with extremely low levels of negative responses to alcohol were more likely be to diagnosed with alcohol abuse/dependence almost a decade later. It is possible that individuals who do not experience negative effects from drinking may lack the "natural brakes" that limit drinking behavior. Some researchers have also suggested that COAs receive greater stress reduction effects from drinking alcohol (Finn, Zeitouni, & Pihl, 1990). Thus, COAs would be expected to engage in more stress-induced drinking than non-COAs because they derive greater physiological benefit from it. It is important to note, however, that not all studies have supported this finding and more research is needed to draw concrete conclusions concerning COAs' physiological response to alcohol (see Sher, 1991, for a review).

Resilience/Protective Factors

Despite the risks presented by genetic, social, and psychological variables, not all COAs experience negative outcomes. These individuals who, despite high-risk status, manage to defeat the odds, are labeled resilient (Garmezy & Neuchterlein, 1972). Resilience has been extensively studied in a variety of populations, but resilience among COAs remains an area that needs further research (Carle & Chassin, 2004). Sher (1991) hypothesized that factors that can help protect COAs from developing alcoholism include social class, preservation of family rituals, amount of attention received from primary caregivers, family harmony during infancy, parental support, personality, self-awareness, cognitive-intellectual functioning, and coping skills.

COAs show increased risk of alcoholism and other substance use disorders.

Carle and Chassin (2004) examined competence and resilience of COAs and found a significant difference between COAs and non-COAs in competence with regards to rule-abiding and academic behaviors, but no differences in social competence. A small subset of resilient COAs demonstrated at or above average levels of academic and rule-abiding competence. These resilient COAs also had fewer internalizing symptoms and reported increased levels of positive affect than did the general COA population (Carle & Chassin, 2004). This suggests that COAs with average or above average academic and rule-abiding competence as well as low levels of internalizing symptoms and high positive affect may be resilient to the risk associated with having an alcoholic parent.

Another potential source of resilience for COAs may be the recovery of the alcoholic parent. Hussong and colleagues (2005) found support for this idea in a study of social competence in COAs. Results from this study indicated that children of recovered alcoholics demonstrated comparable levels of social competence when compared to children of nonalcoholic parents, suggesting again that not all COAs are at equivalent levels of risk.

Along with recovery of parental alcohol symptoms, previous research has also demonstrated the importance of a number of familial factors in buffering the risk associated with parental alcoholism. For example, parental social support, consistency of parental discipline, family harmony, and stability of family rituals have all been shown to protect COAs from the development of alcohol and drug use and abuse (King & Chassin, 2004; Marshal & Chassin, 2000; Stice, Barrera, & Chassin, 1993).

Although there is evidence to suggest that family factors play a protective role in children's risk for substance use and substance use disorders, there is evidence to suggest that this protection may not be equal for all children (Luthar, Cicchetti, & Becker, 2000). In other words, the protective family factor may reduce the negative effect of parental alcoholism for some children, but may lose its effectiveness at the highest

levels of risk. For example, King and Chassin (2004) found that parental support reduced the negative effect of family alcoholism for children with low and average levels of impulsivity and sensation seeking, but not for children with high levels of impulsivity and sensation seeking. In other words, parental support was protective for most children, but not for those with the highest levels of risk. Similarly, Zhou, King, and Chassin (2006) found that the protective effect of family harmony was lost for those children with high levels of family alcoholism. Together these studies provide evidence that consistent and supportive parenting and family harmony are protective for many children of alcoholics, but those children at especially high risk may not benefit from these familial protective factors.

Family relationships, though clearly an important aspect of resilience in COAs, are not the only relationships that appear to contribute to positive outcomes in children of alcoholics. There is also evidence to suggest that, for older children, peer relationships may be as influential as family relationships on adolescents' decision to use substances (Mayes & Suchman, 2006). Therefore, peer relationships may also provide protection against the risk associated with having an alcoholic parent. For example, Ohannessian and Hesselbrock (1993) found that COAs with high levels of social support from friends drank at levels similar to non-COAs, indicating that friendships may also work to reduce the negative effects of parent alcoholism.

Conclusion

Although much work remains to be done in understanding both risk and resilience among COAs, the work that has been done provides important implications for preventive interventions. For example, family factors appear to protect many COAs from negative outcomes. This knowledge supports the need for family-based preventive interventions, which seek to improve both parenting practices and family relationships among families of alcoholics. As research in this area continues to uncover the complex interplay of both the genetic and environmental factors that contribute to COA risk and resilience, prevention researchers will be afforded the opportunity to design and implement interventions to assist this prevalent and heterogeneous population of children.

References

Atyaclar, S., Tarter, R.E., Kirisci, L., & Lu, S. (1999). Association between hyperactivity and executive cognitive functioning in childhood and substance use in childhood and substance use in early adolescence. *Journal of the American Academy of Child and Adolescent Psychiatry, 38,* 172–178.

Bell, R.Q., & Chapman, M. (1986). Child effects in studies using experimental or brief longitudinal approaches to socialization. *Developmental Psychology, 22,* 595–603.

Bertrand, J., Floyd, R.L., Weber, M.K., O'Connor, M., Riley, E.P., Johnson, K.A., Cohen, D.E., National Task Force on FAS/FAE.

(2004). *Fetal Alcohol Syndrome: Guidelines for Referral and Diagnosis.* Atlanta, GA: Centers for Disease Control and Prevention. Available online at http://www.cdc.gov/ncbddd/fas/documents/FAS_guidelines_accessible.pdf

Brody, G.H., Ge, X., Conger, R., Gibbons, F.X., Murry, V.M., Gerrard, M., & Simons, R.L. (2001). The influence of neighborhood disadvantage, collective socialization, and parenting on African American children's affiliation with deviant peers. *Child Development, 72*(4), 1,231–1,246.

Carbonneau, R., Tremblay, R.E., Vitaro, F., Dobkin, P.L., Saucier, J.F., & Pihl, R.O. (1998). Paternal alcoholism, paternal absence, and the development of problem behaviors in boys from age 6 to 12 years. *Journal of Studies on Alcohol, 59,* 387–398.

Carle, A.C., & Chassin, L. (2004) Resilience in a community sample of children of alcoholics: Its prevalence and relation to internalizing symptomatology and positive affect. *Applied Developmental Psychology, 25,* 577–595.

Caspi, A., Moffitt, T., Newman, D., & Silva, P. (1996). Behavioral observations at age 3 years predict adult psychiatric disorders. *Archives of General Psychiatry, 53,* 1,033–1,039.

Chassin, L., Curran, P., Hussong, A., & Colder, C. (1996). The relation of parent alcoholism to adolescent substance use: A longitudinal follow-up study. *Journal of Abnormal Psychology, 105,* 70–80.

Chassin, L., Pillow, D., Curran, P., Molina, B., & Barrera, M. (1993). The relation between parent alcoholism and adolescent substance use: A test of three mediating mechanisms. *Journal of Abnormal Psychology, 102,* 1–17.

Chassin, L., Pitts, S.C., DeLucia, C., & Todd, M. (1999). A longitudinal study of children of alcoholics: Predicting young adult substance use disorders, anxiety, and depression. *Journal of Abnormal Psychology, 108,* 106–118.

Curran, P.J., & Chassin, L. (1996). Longitudinal study of parenting as a protective factor for children of alcoholics. *Journal of Studies on Alcohol, 57,* 305–313.

Deykin, E.Y., Buka, S.L., & Zeena, T.H. (1992). Depressive illness among chemically dependent adolescents. *American Journal of Psychiatry, 149,* 1,341–1,347.

Dishion, T.J., Capaldi, D., Spracklen, K.M., & Li, F. (1995). Peer ecology of male adolescent drug use. *Development and Psychopathology. Special Issue: Developmental Processes in Peer Relations and Psychopathology, 7*(4), 803–824.

Finn, P., Zeitouni, N., & Pihl, R.O. (1990). Effects of alcohol on psychophysiological hyperreactivity to nonaversive and aversive stimuli in men at high risk for alcoholism. *Journal of Abnormal Psychology, 99,* 79–85.

Garmezy, N., & Neuchterlein, K. (1972). Invulnerable children: The fact and fiction of competence and disadvantage. *American Journal of Orthopsychiatry, 42,* 328–329.

Gerra, G., Angioni, L., Zaimovic, A., Moi, G., Bussandri, M., Bertacca, S., Santoro, G., Gardini, S., Caccavari, R., & Nicoli, M.A. (2004). Substance use among high-school students: Relationships with temperament, personality traits, and personal care perception. *Substance Use & Misuse, 39,* 345–367.

Grant, B.F. (2000). Estimates of U.S. children exposed to alcohol use and dependence in the family. *American Journal of Public Health, 90,* 112–115.

Hussong, A.M., Zucker, R.A., Wong, M.M., Fitzgerald, H.E., & Puttler, L.I. (2005). Social competence in children on alcoholic parents over time. *Developmental Psychology, 41,* 747–759.

King, K.M., & Chassin, L. (2004). Mediating and moderated effects of adolescent behavioral under control and parenting in the prediction of drug use disorders in emerging adulthood. *Psychology of Addictive Behaviors, 18,* 239–249.

Luthar, S.S., Cicchetti D., & Becker, B. (2000). The construct of resilience: A critical evaluation and guidelines for future work. *Child Development, 71*(3), 543–562.

Marshal, M.P., & Chassin, L. (2000). Peer influence on adolescent alcohol use: The moderating role of parental support and discipline. *Applied Developmental Science, 4,* 80–88.

Mayes, L.C., & Suchman, N.E. (2006). Developmental pathways to substance use. In D. Cicchetti & D.J. Cohen (Eds.), *Developmental Psychopathology: Vol. 3. Risk, Disorder, and Adaptation* (2nd ed., pp. 599–619). New Jersey: John Wiley & Sons.

McGue, M., Elkins, I., Iacono, W.G. (2000). Genetic and environmental influences on adolescent substance use and abuse. *American Journal of Medical Genetics, 96,* 671–677.

Molina, B.S.G., Bukstein, O.G., & Lynch, K.G. (2002). Attention-deficit/hyperactivity disorder and conduct disorder symptomatology in adolescents with alcohol use disorder. *Psychology of Addictive Behaviors, 16,* 161–164.

National Institute on Alcohol Abuse and Alcoholism. (2006). NIAAA 2001–2002 NESARC [Data File]. Accessed August 1, 2006. from http://niaaa.census. gov/index.html.

Nigg, J.T., Glass, J.M., Wong, M.M., Poon, E., Jester, J.M., Fitzgerald, H.E., Puttler, L.I., Adams, K.A., & Zucker, R.A., (2004). Neuropsychological executive functioning in children at elevated risk for alcoholism: Findings in early adolescence. *Journal of Abnormal Psychology, 113,* 302–314.

Ohannessian, C.M., & Hesselbrock, V.M. (1993). The influence of perceived social support on the relationship between family history of alcoholism and drinking behaviors. *Addiction, 88,* 1,651–1,658.

Rohde, P., Lewinson, P.M., & Seeley, J.R. (1996). Psychiatric comorbidity with problematic alcohol use in high school students. *Journal of the American Academy of Child and Adolescent Psychiatry, 35,* 101–109.

Schuckit, M.A. (2000). Genetics of the risk for alcoholism. *The American Journal on Addictions 9,* 103–112.

Schuckit, M.A., & Smith, T.L. (1996). An 8-year follow-up of 450 sons of alcoholic and control subjects. *Archives of General Psychiatry, 53*(3), 202–210.

Sher, K.J. (1991). *Children of Alcoholics: A Critical Appraisal of Theory and Research.* Chicago: University of Chicago Press.

Stice, E., & Barrera, M. (1995). A longitudinal examination of the reciprocal relations between perceived parenting and adolescents' substance use and externalizing behaviors. *Developmental Psychology, 31*(2), 322–334.

Stice, E., Barrera, M., & Chassin, L. (1993). Relation of parental support and control to adolescents' externalizing symptomatology and substance use: A longitudinal examination of curvilinear effects. *Journal of Abnormal Child Psychology, 21,* 609–629.

West, M.O., & Prinz, R.J. (1987). Parental alcoholism and childhood psychopathology. *Psychological Bulletin, 102*(2), 204–218.

Wills, T.A., McNamara, G., Vaccaro, D., & Hirky, A.E. (1996). Escalated substance use: A longitudinal grouping analysis from early to middle adolescence. *Journal of Abnormal Psychology, 105,* 166–180.

Wills, T.A., Vaccaro, D., & McNamara, G. (1992). The role of life events, family support, and competence in adolescent substance use: A test of vulnerability and protective factors. *American Journal of Community Psychology, 20,* 349–374.

Wills, T.A., Windle, M., & Cleary, S.D. (1998). Temperament and novelty seeking in adolescent substance use: Convergence of dimensions of temperament with constructs from Cloninger's theory. *Journal of Personality and Social Psychology, 74*(2), 387–406.

Zhou, Q., King, K.M., & Chassin, L. (2006). The roles of familial alcoholism and adolescent family harmony in young adults' substance dependence disorders: mediated and moderated relations. *Journal of Abnormal Psychology, 115,* 320–331.

Zucker, R.A. (2006). Alcohol use and the alcohol use disorders: A developmental-biopsychosocial systems formulation covering the life course. In D. Cicchetti & D.J. Cohen (Eds.), *Developmental Psychopathology: Vol 3. Risk, Disorder, and Adaptation* (2nd ed., pp. 620–656). New Jersey: John Wiley & Sons.

CARA E. RICE, MPH, is Project Director of the Adult and Family Development Project at Arizona State University. **DANIELLE DANDREAUX,** MS, is a doctoral student in applied developmental psychology at the University of New Orleans and is currently employed by the Department of Psychology at Arizona State University. **ELIZABETH D. HANDLEY,** MA, is a doctoral student in clinical psychology at Arizona State University. Her research and clinical training are focused on at-risk children and families. **LAURIE CHASSIN,** PhD, is Professor of Psychology at Arizona State University. Her research focuses on longitudinal, multigenerational studies of risk for substance use disorders and intergenerational transmission of that risk.

Preparation of this article was supported by grant AA16213 from the National Institute of Alcohol Abuse and Alcoholism to Laurie Chassin.

Impact of Family Recovery on Pre-Teens and Adolescents

VIRGINIA LEWIS, PhD AND LOIS ALLEN-BYRD, PhD

When discussing parental alcoholism, it is often assumed that the parent's entry into recovery will resolve all problems. However, our research, which examined the impact of family recovery from alcoholism, shows that rather than being a unifying force for all family members, this process is traumatic, with pre-teens and adolescents frequently becoming the "forgotten" members of the family. The effects upon these forgotten members can be explained and understood in the context of recovery stages and family types. The purpose of this article is threefold: (1) to present a very complex process called family recovery, (2) to describe its traumatic impact on pre-teens and adolescents, and (3) to provide treatment suggestions for supporting young people.

The Family Recovery Project

In 1989, Drs. Stephanie Brown and Virginia Lewis were the first researchers to study the processes of family recovery from alcoholism. This research marked a dramatic shift from understanding how alcoholism affects all family members, to identifying the dynamics of family recovery and its influence on all aspects of family and individual functioning.

There were three questions of interest to this project: 1) What happens to the family when one or both parents stop drinking? 2) Is there a normal developmental process of recovery? and 3) What allows some alcoholic families to maintain recovery while others relapse (often repeatedly)?

Methodology

The research methodology was a cross-sectional design, studying 54 volunteer families who ranged in sobriety from a few months to 18 years. The study was multi-perspective (participants' data and researchers' observations) and multi-level (tests that measured individual, dyad, and family dynamics) in order to obtain a comprehensive picture of family recovery dynamics. In addition, two types of data analysis were used—qualitative (research team analyzing video tapes to determine individual and family functioning) and quantitative (a battery of paper/pencil measures administered to each family member). (Specific information on research methodology and results can be found in Brown & Lewis, 1995, 1999; Brown, Lewis, & Liotta, 2000;

Petroni, Allen-Byrd, & Lewis, 2003; Rouhbakhsh, Lewis, & Allen-Byrd, 2004.)

Due to the focus of this research, the drinking stage and its impact upon family members were studied retrospectively. Families were asked to describe the drinking years which, when combined with the data collected, provided a before and after sobriety perspective. Although painful for many, this journey into the past was necessary as family recovery cannot be fully understood without knowing what life was like, individually and systemically, during the drinking years.

Important Findings

Information from this research revealed that: a) there are normal developmental stages of recovery, b) there are different types of recovering families, and c) the early years of recovery are very traumatic. These latter two findings were surprising and clinically significant. For example, we found that the type of recovering family impacts stage development and requires different treatment approaches for both type of family and stage of recovery. The concept that the early years of recovery were traumatic came from the families' descriptions that this time was very disruptive, frightening, and dynamic. However, rather than being a negative, this "trauma" was normal, allowing for the disequilibrium and collapse of the addictive processes at the individual and system levels. In its place was a void without a map of how to navigate this necessary state. In time, the void was replaced with new knowledge, coping skills, and real-time functioning, providing the parents stayed in recovery through participation in 12-step programs, remained abstinent, and used various treatment modalities (individual, marital, familial) at different times during the recovery journey.

The early years of recovery are very traumatic.

These findings led to the emergence of two theoretical models: The Family Recovery Model and The Family Recovery Typology Model. Both models are briefly discussed below.

The Family Recovery Model

The Family Recovery Model captures the complex nature of family recovery. This complexity is critical for clinicians to understand because *rather than being the end point, abstinence is the beginning of a long and arduous journey that affects all functioning within a family.*

The Family Recovery Model has two dimensions: time and domain. Time is noted by four developmental stages: (1) drinking, (2) transition, (3) early recovery period, and (4) ongoing recovery period. Each domain is examined at three levels: the environment (family atmosphere); the system (family functioning—roles, rules, routines, communication patterns); and the individual (all family members, their emotions, cognitions, behaviors). The three domains are described in detail in *The Alcoholic Family in Recovery* (Brown & Lewis, 1999).

Developmental Recovery Stages

The following is a brief discussion of the three developmental recovery stages. See Box 1 for a summary of this information.

Transition Stage. This stage, which is characterized by the individual moving from drinking to abstinence, can last for several years during which there may be frequent shifts by the alcoholic between drinking and sobriety. The alcoholic feels completely out of control and the family system is in total chaos. The abstinence sub-stage is referred to as the "trauma of recovery"— there is the relief of sobriety and the utter terror of relapse. For example, although the adults in the family are feeling confused, frightened, and out of control, they are attempting to attend meetings and learning that recovery is possible. Their children, however, typically have no one available to them for support, information, or guidance, leaving them also feeling frightened and confused.

Early Recovery Stage. In this stage, the learning curve is steep for the parents as they are learning self-responsibility and self-care, and are slowly acquiring non-addictive lifestyles. It is a time of tremendous acquisition and application of knowledge. The alcoholic and co-alcoholic (spouse) are breaking addictive interactive patterns and learning to "separate" in order to develop their own individuality. Children and adolescents may cope by withdrawing, acting-out, "adopting" a friend's family, or attending 12-step meetings.

Ongoing Recovery Stage. In this stage, the process of recovery is becoming internalized. Recovery has become a central organizing principle (main force of focus) for the alcoholic and co-alcoholic. Life feels manageable and healthy. Problems, when they do occur, are addressed and resolved whenever possible. Parents can tolerate hearing about their children's pain and anger during the drinking and early recovery years. There is a process of healing between the parents and their now late adolescent or adult children.

Family Recovery Typology Model

The second theoretical model with significant implications for understanding recovery emerged from the finding that there were three types of families who differed dramatically from one another in terms of their recovery process. There were families who, regardless of time in recovery, seemed successful in their recovery processes while others appeared trapped in their dysfunctional patterns despite abstinence by the alcoholic.

The "successful" family style was the Type I family— both spouses were in recovery attending 12-step programs, accepting responsibility for change, and participating in therapy at different points in time. They practiced their sobriety, and recovery was a central organizing principle. The more rigid, stuck, and dysfunctional styles were found in the Type II and Type III families. In the Type II family, only one spouse was in recovery (typically the alcoholic who attended AA meetings), and the family environment and system retained the alcoholic dynamics, influences, and tensions. The alcoholic straddled two worlds: individual recovery and marital/family non-recovery. In the Type III family (of which there were only a few and the alcoholics were all males with short-term recovery), the alcoholics just quit drinking without participation in any 12-step program. Although they "looked" the best on the tests

---

Box 1
Family Recovery Model: Three Developmental Recovery Stages

	Drinking Transition	Early Recovery	Ongoing Recovery
Alcoholic/Spouse:	Alcoholic moves from drinking to abstinence; may involve frequent shifts between drinking and sobriety, lasting several years.	Alcoholic and spouse are breaking addictive interactive patterns.	The family recovery process is becoming internalized.
Children:	Alcoholics' children typically have no supports, information, or guidance available at this time. They are left feeling frightened and confused.	Alcoholics' children may be left to cope by withdrawing, "acting out," "adopting" a friend's family, or attending 12-step meetings.	By this point, most children are now adult age. A possible healing process between the parents and children may begin.

(probably due to denial of any problems), they were the most rigid and stilted in the interviews.

Effects of Recovery on Pre-Teens and Adolescents

Recovery is a life-long process for families that is very complex, traumatic, and utterly confusing in the early years. One major and disheartening discovery in our research was that pre-teens and adolescents were generally ignored in recovery (similar to their experiences during the drinking years). When one or both spouses became sober and began participating in 12-step programs, they became immersed in working at staying sober. For example, they attended meetings, spoke a new language (recovery terms), and developed new relationships. They were told that their number one focus was to stay abstinent. The result was that their children lacked much-needed effective and active parenting.

For pre-teens and adolescents, the early years of recovery were often worse than the drinking years. For example, they had learned how to "function" in the alcoholic system while the alcoholic was drinking; but with recovery, everything changed with no understanding of what was happening to their family. According to several adult children in the study, they "preferred" the drinking period to early recovery for a variety of reasons. For example, they had learned how to read some of the "signs" associated with drinking, (such as the alcoholic going on a binge, the first drink of the day), and, consequently, knew how to affect damage control. Initial recovery, on the other hand, was fraught with unpredictable, traumatic and out-of-control dynamics resulting in uncertainty on the part of the adolescent on how to deal with these new issues.

The following vignettes demonstrate the impact of alcoholism and recovery on adolescents.

Vignette 1

In one family, the oldest adolescent overdosed on over-the-counter medication (an attempt to break the denial that there was a problem). As she was going to the hospital, she handed her mother a note saying, "Please go to AA, you are an alcoholic." Initially her mother refused, but in time she became sober, both parents went into recovery, and they became a Type I family. For the first few months in the Transition Stage, the teens would come home, find no food on the table, and become angry. "Our parents got their own place (e.g., AA and AlAnon) and new 'parents' (sponsors), and we lost the parents we knew." Six months later, the youngest child left home as he found the changes and abandonment too painful. When this family was interviewed, they were in the Ongoing Recovery Stage and the parents had developed close relationships to their now adult children. This closeness and healing was hard-earned, requiring individual, couple, and family therapy at different times in the recovery years.

Vignette 2

A late adolescent child in the study became very anxious during the research interview. His parents had been in recovery for years and were a Type I family in the Ongoing Recovery Stage. While they were describing the drinking years, he became aware of how much he had denied that there was a problem in the family while growing up. His mother (who kept her alcohol stash in a closet in his room) would frequently drive him to school functions while drunk—behavior he would say was normal or not his problem. He began to frequently stay over at his friend's house thus "adopting" another set of parents in his early teens. Since no one commented, he thought it was normal. As the interview progressed, he said, "This is making me question my reality checks, my perceptions of life." What had been his constructed reality of himself and his family was being shattered. This is threatening for young people launching into adulthood as it questions their identity and their ability to understand reality and their place in the family system. His father said that there was one regret in recovery—that they had abandoned their son to meetings and new people (sponsors, AA members, etc.), and did not help him understand what was happening or how important he was to his parents. This was a common regret expressed by parents who had years of recovery and the ability to reflect on the past (Brown & Lewis, 1999).

Vignette 3

This last vignette is adapted from Lewis and Allen-Byrd (in press) as a brief portrayal of what an adolescent may experience in the transition/early periods of recovery.

Kayla, the oldest child, was the identified caregiver in the family and was gratefully supported by the non-alcoholic parent. She assisted in household decisions and duties, provided parental guidance to the younger children, and had special privileges because of her elevated role and status in the family system. When the parents/family went into recovery, Kayla was, in essence, demoted because as the recovering parent became more actively involved in the family, Kayla's role and functions were no longer needed. Her sense of worth and power, her identity and understanding of her family's reality were taken away when her parents went into recovery leaving Kayla feeling resentful, angry, and bewildered. Without appropriate intervention, adolescents in situations similar to Kayla's will typically act out and/or withdraw from the family.

Treatment Suggestions to Support Young People

With the awareness that family recovery is difficult for pre-teens and adolescents, positive and therapeutic action can be taken. Practitioners can play a vital role in helping children make the transition from drinking into early family sobriety. They can educate the parents, normalize the process of recovery, and provide a safe place for young people to express their fears and feelings. Box 2 provides a number of examples.

The family type will dictate how practitioners can approach parents and provide parenting guidelines. The Type I family will be open and receptive to new ideas and knowledge as both parents are in recovery and accept responsibility for change,

Box 2
Strategies for Facilitating Adolescents' Healthy Transition from Family Drinking to Early Family Sobriety

- Work with parents on basic parenting skills, inform them of the importance of these skills for abating turmoil within the pre-teen and/or adolescent.
- Explain alcoholism and recovery to the pre-teen and adolescent in age-appropriate terms.
- Educate parents on the needs of adolescents who are developmentally leaving the family and may not be interested in becoming involved in the new recovery family structure and dynamics.
- Provide safe parental substitutes for their children.
- Provide opportunities for children and adolescents to become involved in Alateen, Alakid, Alatot.
- Let children know they are not responsible for their parents' alcoholism, recovery, or relapse.
- Encourage parents to ask for help before parent-child problems become a crisis.
- Refer pre-teens and adolescents for individual therapy with a therapist who understands the recovery process and can help the young person navigate through the bewildering and newly emerging family system. The therapy focus should be on helping teens define their own individuality; work through new roles, rules, boundaries; and find their own voice.

(Adapted from Lewis & Allen-Byrd, in press)

growth, and the hope of a healthy family. In the early years, they will require a great deal of external support in the form of sponsors, 12-step members, and therapists.

The Type II and III families present additional issues. In the Type II family, one member is in recovery while the family system remains alcoholic. There is chronic marital and environmental tension that, while unnamed, is typically experienced by the children. For example, the recovering alcoholic becomes the scapegoat as a way to explain problems and tension in the family, or splitting may occur when the adolescent aligns with one parent against the other. Initially the therapist can effect change by working at the marital level and educating the adults on family recovery (e.g., the three domains of recovery, how every member in the family is impacted by alcoholism, and the danger for relapse when only one parent is in recovery).

Hopefully, with intervention, the Type II family will transition into a Type I family. If the "non-alcoholic" parent refuses marital treatment in order to change the alcoholic system into a recovery system, he/she could join a group that educates families about family recovery.

Pre-teens and adolescents may join another group to become educated about family recovery, to find alternative ways to cope with the tensions and changes, and to acquire healthy ways to begin the separation and individuation process. Frequently, without appropriate intervention, the adolescents in Type II and Type III families become involved in the rebellious, acting-out phase of life.

The Type III families (who were typically in therapy for parent-child issues because their children were identified as the "cause" of the family problems) presented unique challenges. Although the alcoholic stopped drinking, nothing else changed. The alcoholic may have cognitive rigidity (black and white thinking), emotional intolerance, and be on a collision course with the adolescent who is acting out and/or attempting to break away from a stifling, straight jacket, family dynamic. During our research Type III families remained the least clear because of their defensive stance in the interviews and paper-pencil measures. For them, the first step is to break individual and systemic denial. The least threatening approach is an educational format where the adults can attend a parent group to learn about the impact of alcoholism on family members, even though no one is currently drinking, and learn healthier parenting skills (e.g., learn what the developmental needs of the pre-teen and adolescent are). There could be a parallel education group for pre-teens and adolescents wherein they could learn the effect alcoholism had on their lives and the toll it took on their personality development, as well as help them become empowered to alter internalized alcoholic processes and develop healthy choices for their future.

Limitations

There were several limitations to the study, noted by the following: (1) the participants were all volunteers; (2) they were educated (high school graduates to all levels of college degrees); (3) they were predominantly Caucasians (multiple attempts were made to recruit a greater ethnic diversity) and, (4) small sample size. Further contribution to family recovery could be made by studying single-parent families, court-ordered families, and families from other cultures.

Summary

Family recovery from alcoholism is still an unfamiliar concept in the field of addictions and treatment (Lewis & Allen-Byrd, in press; Brown & Lewis, 1995, 1999). The more knowledgeable practitioners are in the dynamics of recovery, the more effective they will be in helping families and their children move through the normal developmental processes of recovery and launching young people into healthy adulthood.

Practitioners are on the front lines providing vital and appropriate treatment plans and referrals for recovering families with children. Their understanding of the normal processes in the stages of recovery and the knowledge of the different types of families can assist them in creating more successful interventions while minimizing family relapses and preventing adolescents from acting out or withdrawing. Pre-teens and adolescents need a voice and therapists can provide a safe and knowledgeable format for them to be heard and to help guide them through the bewildering times of adolescence in general, and in family systems of recovery, in particular.

References

Brown, S. (1985). *Treating the Alcoholic: A Developmental Model of Recovery.* New York: Wiley.

Brown, S., & Lewis, V. (1995). The alcoholic family: A developmental model of recovery. In S. Brown (Ed.), *Treating Alcoholism* (pp. 279–315). San Francisco: Jossey-Bass.

Brown, S., & Lewis, V. (1999). *The Alcoholic Family in Recovery: A Developmental Model.* New York: Guilford Press.

Brown, S., Lewis, V., & Liotta, A. (2000). *The Family Recovery Guide.* Oakland, CA: New Harbinger Publications.

Lewis, V., & Allen-Byrd, L. (2001). Family recovery typology: A new theoretical model. *Alcoholism Treatment Quarterly, 19*(3), 1–17.

Lewis, V., & Allen-Byrd, L. (in press). Coping strategies for the stages of family recovery. *Alcoholism Treatment Quarterly,* special edition.

Lewis, V., Allen-Byrd, L., & Rouhbakhsh, P. (2004). Understanding successful family recovery: Two models. *Journal of Systemic Therapies, 23*(4), 39–51.

Petroni, D., Allen-Byrd, L., & Lewis, V. M. (2003). Indicators of the alcohol recovery process: Critical items from Koss-Butcher and Lachan-Wrobel analysis of the MMPI-2. *Alcoholism Treatment Quarterly, 21*(2), 41–56.

Rouhbakhsh, P., Lewis, V., & Allen-Byrd, L. (2004). Recovering alcoholic families: When normal is not normal and when is not normal healthy. *Alcoholism Treatment Quarterly, 22*(2), 35–53.

VIRGINIA LEWIS, PhD, is co-founder and co-director of the Family Recovery Project and a Senior Research Fellow at the Mental Research Institute (MRI) in Palo Alto, California. LOIS ALLEN-BYRD, PhD, is a Research Associate at MRI. Dr. Lewis has co-authored two books on family recovery and both she and Dr. Allen-Byrd have published numerous articles on the subject.

From *The Prevention Researcher,* November 2006, pp. 14–17. Copyright © 2006 by Integrated Research Services, Inc. Reprinted by permission. www.tpronline.com

My Cheatin' Heart

When love comes knocking, do you answer the door?

Daphne Gottlieb

Let's just get this out in the open.

I was 14 and madly in love for the first time. He was 21. He made me suddenly, unaccustomedly beautiful with his kisses and mix tapes. During the year of elation and longing, he never mentioned that he had a girlfriend who lived across the street. A serious girl. A girl his age. A girl he loved. Unlike inappropriate, high school, secret me.

The next time, I was 15 and visiting a friend at college. It was a friend's friend's boyfriend who looked like Jim Morrison and wore leather pants and burned candles and incense. She was at work and I wanted him to touch me. She found out. I don't know what happened after that.

I was 19 and he was my boyfriend's archrival. I was 20 and it was my lover's girlfriend and we had to lie because otherwise he always wanted to watch. I was 24 and her girlfriend knew about it but then changed her mind about the open relationship. We saw each other anyway. I was 30 when we met—we wanted each other but were committed to other people; the way we look at each other still scorches the walls. I turned thirtysomething and pointedly wasn't invited to a funeral/a wedding/a baby shower because of a rumor.

I am a few years older now and I know this: That there are tastes of mouths I could not have lived without; that there are times I've pretended it was just about the sex because I couldn't stand the way my heart was about to burst with happiness and awe and I couldn't be that vulnerable, not again, not with this one. Waiting to have someone's stolen seconds can burn you alive, and there is nothing more frightening than being willing to take this free fall. It is not as simple as we were always promised. Love—at least the pair-bonded, prescribed love—does not conquer all. It does not conquer desire.

Arrow, meet heart. Apple, meet Eve.

Call me Saint Sebastian.

Out there in self-help books, on daytime television shows, I see people told that they're wrong to lust outside their relationships. That they must heal what's wrong at home and then they won't feel desire "inappropriately." I've got news. There's nothing wrong. Desire is not an illness. We who are its witnesses are not infected. We're not at fault. Not all of us are running away from our relationships at home, or just looking for some side action. The plain fact about desire is that sometimes it's love.

If it were anything else, maybe it would be easier. But things are not as simple as we were always promised: Let's say you're a normal, upstanding, ethical man (or woman) who has decided to share your life with someone beloved to you. This goes well for a number of years. You have a lot of sex and love each other very much and have a seriously deep, strong bond. Behind door number two, the tiger: a true love. Another one. (Let's assume for the moment that the culture and Hollywood are wrong—we have more than one true love after all.)

The shittiest thing you can do is lie to someone you love, yet there are certain times you can choose either to do so or to lie to yourself. Not honoring this fascination, this car crash of desire, is also a lie. So what do you do? Pursue it? Deny it? It doesn't matter: The consequences began when you opened the door and saw the tiger, called it by its—name: love. Pursue it or don't, you're already stuck between two truths, two opportunities to lie.

The question is not, as we've always been asked, the lady—beautiful, virtuous, and almost everything we want—or the tiger—passionate, wild, and almost everything we want. The question is, what do we do with our feelings for the lady *and* the tiger? The lady is fair, is home, is delight. The tiger is not bloodthirsty, as we always believed, but, say, romantic. Impetuous. Sharing almost nothing in common with the lady. They even have a different number of feet. But the lady would not see it this way. You already know that.

You can tell the second love that you can't do this—banish the tiger from your life. You can go home to the first, confess your desire, sob on her shoulder, tell her how awful you feel, and she (or he) will soothe you. Until later, when she wonders if you look at all the other zoo animals that way, and every day for a while, if not longer, she will sniff at you to see if you've been near the large cat cages. Things will not be the same for a long time. And you've lost the tiger. Every time the housecat sits on your lap, you tear up thinking of what might have been, the love that has been lost. Your first love asks you what's wrong and you say "nothing." You say nothing a lot, because there's nothing left, nothing inside.

So instead, let's say you go home and tell your first love, *This new love is a love I can't live without. What can we do?* She will say, *All right, I want to meet her right away. I get all holidays and weekends with you, and there will be no sleepovers with the new love, and I expect the same for myself, and you are never to call her any of the nicknames you have ever used for me,* and the whole thing starts to remind you of a high school necking session—under the sweater; over the bra, but not under it.

You feel like an inmate all the time, and, moreover, where is your first love tonight? She's out with someone you've never met while you're out with your second love, who once had been amenable to an affair. She looks at you sadly and says, "So you think I'm only a half-time tiger?" Her fangs are yellowed and sharp and she finds herself unable to stop staring at the clock, which shows when you will have to leave her to return to the lady.

Maybe there is no "happily ever after" here, but I think there's an "after." I have been the first love; I have been the second; and I have tried to decide between my own firsts and seconds. I have walked through each ring of fire, and I've found no easy answers. It could be that hearts are dumb creatures, especially mine. It could be that there are no good answers. Whether we're admitting desire, lying about it, denying it, or fulfilling it, the consequences are staggering, sometimes ruinous.

So, heart firmly sewn onto sleeve, assured that there is an "after," what can we do but stride forth? It seems clear that no system—polyamory, monogamy, or stand-on-your-head-for-me—will sanitize the astonishing highs and the bereft lows of desire and betrayal. And even if they did, who wants a sanitized heart? So it's up to us: to work together, to love what's so human about us, to understand that the risk of love is loss, and to try to grant desire without eviscerating ourselves. I'm not sure how to do this, but I'm still trying. Because above all, I know this: It's grace to try, and fail, and try again.

A version of this essay appeared as the introduction to *Homewrecker: An Adultery Reader* (Soft Skull Press, 2005), edited by Daphne Gottlieb.

Love but Don't Touch

Emotional infidelity is intense but invisible, erotic but unconsummated. Such delicious paradoxes make it every bit as dangerous as adultery.

Mark Teich

She was the first girl Brendan ever kissed, the first he made love with, the first he truly loved. They'd lost their virginity together on a magical trip to Amsterdam. He felt they were soul mates and believed that their bond would never be severed. But she had suddenly broken up with him after eight months, and they lost touch until 2000, when he paid her a visit. Their exchange was unremarkable, but they traded e-mail addresses. At first, they merely sent an occasional message, chatting superficially. But the correspondence became more frequent and personal. It was easy— she was sunnier and more passionate than Brendan's wife, Lauren, who was bleary-eyed from caring for their sick son while working full-time to pay the bills. Without the burden of these responsibilities, his old love divided her days between visits to the gym and e-mails to him. Yes, she had a husband: but while Brendan was "witty and creative," she said in her lustful notes, her husband was a drone. What a high it was for Brendan to see himself through this complimentary lens after Lauren's withering view of him: hypercritical, angry, money-obsessed.

At the same time, Lauren found herself drawn to a love interest with roots in *her* past: a man she met through a website devoted to the neighborhood she grew up in. In short order, Lauren was deeply involved in an Internet relationship that kept her mood aloft throughout the day. In every way, her new companion was superior: While Brendan had set out to be a novelist, he now worked for a little health newsletter. It was Lauren's online friend, a research biologist, who spent his free hours writing a novel, and what a gifted writer he was! While Brendan talked about bills past due and criticized everything from her clothes to her weight, her online partner was fascinated by her thoughts and the minutiae of her day. He abounded in the type of wit and imagination Brendan had lacked for years. Sure, her online partner was married, too; he described his wife as remote and inaccessible—a scientist like himself, but so involved with her work that she left the child-rearing to him and almost never came home.

The New Anatomy of Infidelity

Brendan and Lauren never slept with or even touched their affair partners. Yet their emotional involvements were so all-consuming, so blinding, that they almost blew off their marriage for the disembodied fantasies of online love. Infidelity, of course, is older than the Bible. And garden-variety cheating has been on the rise for 25 years, ever since women swelled the workforce. But now, infidelity has taken a dangerous—and often profoundly stirring—new turn that psychologists call the biggest threat marriage has ever faced. Characterized by deep emotional closeness, the secret, sexually charged (but unconsummated) friendships at issue build almost imperceptibly until they surpass in importance the relationship with a spouse. Emotional involvement outside of marriage has always been intoxicating, as fictional heroines such as Anna Karenina and Emma Bovary attest. But in the age of the Internet and the egalitarian office, these relationships have become far more accessible than ever before.

The late psychologist Shirley Glass identified the trend in her 2003 book, *Not Just Friends.* "The new infidelity is between people who unwittingly form deep, passionate connections before realizing they've crossed the line from platonic friendship into romantic love," Glass wrote. Eighty-two percent of the unfaithful partners she'd counseled, she said, had had an affair with someone who was at first "just a friend." What's more, she found 55 to 65 percent of men and women alike had participated in relationships she considered *emotionally* unfaithful—secret, sexually energized and more emotionally open than the relationship with the spouse.

Glass cited the workplace as the new minefield for marriage; 50 percent of unfaithful women and 62 percent of unfaithful men she treated were involved with someone from work. And the office has only grown more tantalizing, with women now having affairs at virtually the same rate as men. Factor in the explosive power of the Internet, and it's clear that infidelity has become an omnipresent threat. No research exists on how many affairs are happening online, but experts say they're rampant— more common than work affairs and multiplying fast.

> You go on the Internet and ask, 'Whatever happened to so and so?' Then you find him. As soon as you do, all of those raw emotions flood back.

The Slippery Slope

An emotional affair can threaten any marriage—not just those already struggling or in disrepair.

"No one's immune," says Peggy Vaughan, author of *The Monogamy Myth* and creator of the website, DearPeggy.com, where surveys and discussion reflect the zeitgeist. Although those with troubled marriages are especially susceptible, a surprising number of people with solid relationships respond to the novelty and are swept away as well.

Because it is so insidious, its boundaries so fuzzy, the emotional affair's challenge to marriage is initially hard to detect. It might seem natural to discuss personal concerns with an Internet buddy or respond to an office mate having trouble with a spouse. But slowly, imperceptibly, there's an "emotional switch." The friends have built a bubble of secrecy around their relationship and shifted allegiance from their marriage partners to the affair.

Web of Deceit

The perfect petri dish for secret, sexually charged relationships is, of course, the Internet. The new American affair can take place right in the family room; within feet of children and an unsuspecting spouse, the unfaithful can swap sex talk and let emotions run amok.

Often, it's the anonymity of online encounters that invites emotional disclosure, says Israeli philosopher Aaron Ben-Ze'ev, president of the University of Haifa and author of *Love Online*. "Like strangers on a train who confess everything to an anonymous seatmate, people meeting online reveal what they might never tell a real-world partner. When people reveal so much, there is great intimacy." But the revelations are selective: Without chores to do or children to tend, the friends relate with less interference from practical constraints, allowing fantasy to take hold. Over the Internet, adds Ben-Ze'ev, the power of imagination is especially profound.

In fact, says MIT psychologist Sherry Turkle, author of *Life on the Screen: Identity in the Age of the Internet,* it's particularly what's *withheld*—the "low bandwidth" of the information online partners share—that makes these relationships so fantasy-rich and intense. She compares the phenomenon to that of transference in psychotherapy—where patients, knowing little about their therapists, invest them with the qualities they want and need. Similarly, the illicit partner is always partly a fantasy, inevitably seen as wittier, warmer and sexier than the spouse.

So is online love real? "It has all the elements of real love," says Ben-Ze'ev: obsessive thoughts of the lover, an urgent need to be together and the feeling that the new partner is the most

---

Are You an Emotional Cheat? 7 Telltale Signs

Ever since Scarlett O'Hara flirted in front of Rhett Butler, the jury has been out on extramarital friendships that are sensual, even intimate, yet don't cross the line to actual sex. With emotional affairs so prevalent, psychologists studying the issue have finally drawn some lines in the sand. You may be emotionally unfaithful, they say, if you:

- Have a special confidante at the office, someone receptive to feelings and fears you can't discuss with your partner or spouse.
- Share personal information and negative feelings about your primary relationship with a "special friend."
- Meet a friend of the opposite sex for dinner and go back to his or her place to discuss your primary relationship over a drink, never calling your partner and finally arriving home at 3 A.M.
- Humiliate your partner in front of others, suggesting he or she is a loser or inadequate sexually.
- Have the energy to tell your stories only once, and decide to save the juiciest for an office or Internet friend of the opposite sex.
- Hook up with an old boyfriend or girlfriend at a high school reunion and, feeling the old spark, decide to keep in contact by e-mail.
- Keep secret, password-protected Internet accounts, "just in case," or become incensed if your partner inadvertently glances at your "private things."

---

wonderful person on earth. You experience the same chemical rush that people get when they fall in love.

"But the chemicals don't last, and then we learn how difficult it is to remain attached to a partner in a meaningful way," points out Connecticut psychologist Janis Abrahams Spring, author of *After the Affair.*

Blasts from the Past

People may be exceptionally vulnerable to affairs when they reconnect with someone from their past, for whom they may have long harbored feelings. "It's very common online," says Vaughan. "You go on the Internet, and the first thing you say to yourself is, 'What happened to so and so?' Then you go find them."

Lorraine and Sam had been high school friends during the Sixties, and even camped out together at Woodstock in 1969. In love with Sam but "awed by his brilliance," Lorraine remained too shy to confess. Then he went off to the University of Chicago while she stayed in New Jersey. She married and had a family, but the idea of Sam still smoldered: If only she had admitted her love!

One day she Googled him and located him in Chicago—and they began to correspond by e-mail. He was a partner in a law firm, had a physician wife and coached his daughter's

Inoculating Your Relationship

The biggest mistake couples make is taking monogamy for granted. Instead, they should take affairs for granted and protect themselves by heading infidelity off at the pass.

As part of a proactive approach, psychologist Barry McCarthy suggests couples discuss the importance of fidelity from the outset, identifying the type of situation that would put each at greatest risk. Is drinking on a business trip your downfall, or the novelty of an exotic individual from a far-off locale? Whatever your weakness, work together to make sure you help each other walk past it.

As for Internet relationships, Peggy Vaughan says the safest way to protect the primary relationship is to "make sure that no online interactions are secret. This means having your partner agree that neither of you will say anything to someone online that you aren't willing for the other one to read. If they resist and invoke privacy rights," she adds, "it is probably because they already have something to hide."

Miami Beach psychologist M. Gary Neuman recommends that in addition to setting limits, you actively build the bond with your partner every day. Among the protective strategies he suggests are exchanging "five daily touch points," or emotional strokes, ranging from bringing your partner a cup of tea to a kiss and hug. He also suggests that partners talk for 40 minutes, uninterrupted, four times a week and go on a weekly date. "It's so easy," Neuman says, "to forget why we fell in love."

—MT

Little League team. "Originally I e-mailed just to say, 'hi,'" she explains. But after a few friendly notes, Sam sent a confession. He'd always been in love with her. But her beauty had daunted him, so he'd settled for a plain, practical woman—his wife—instead. E-mails and then phone calls between Lorraine and Sam soon became constant, whipping both of them into a frenzy of heat and remorse. "I can't stop thinking about you. I'm obsessed," one of Sam's e-mails said. But Sam could never get away, never meet face-to-face. "I feel so guilty," he confessed.

That's when Lorraine stopped sending e-mails or taking his calls. "He was a coward," she says, adding that he disappointed her even more by "begging to continue the affair over the phone."

What kind of person chooses to remain immersed in fantasy? It could be someone who "compartmentalizes the two relationships," psychologist Janis Abrahms Spring suggests. "The person may not want to replace the marriage partner, but may want that extra high."

A woman may languish for years in the throes of her "special friendship," while her male counterpart considers it a nice addition to his life.

Women in Love

Frank Pittman, author of *Private Lies,* says that Lorraine lucked out. If she's like most of those involved in Internet affairs, "the face-to-face meeting would have killed it." And if she'd run off with Sam, it probably would have been far worse. "In the history of these crazy romantic affairs, when people throw everything away for a fantasy, the success rate of the new relationship is very low," he explains.

But Lorraine was just acting true to her gender. It is the woman who typically pushes the relationship from friendship to love, from virtual to actual, says Pittman. It's the woman who gets so emotionally involved she sees the affair as a possible replacement for her marriage—even if her marriage is good—and wants to test that out.

American University professor of psychology and affair expert Barry McCarthy explains that for men, "most affairs are high opportunity and low involvement. For women, an affair is more emotional. President Clinton and Monica Lewinsky are the prototypes," he says.

How does this translate to emotional infidelity, where opportunity may be thwarted but emotion reigns supreme? Some men have begun following female patterns, placing more emphasis on emotion than in the past, while women are increasingly open to sex, especially as they achieve more financial independence and have less to fear from divorce.

Even so, says Peggy Vaughan, women are usually far more involved in these relationships than men. A woman may languish for years in the throes of her "special friendship," while her male counterpart considers it a nice addition to the life he already has. As a result, men and women involved in emotional dalliances often see the same affair in different ways. The woman will see her soul mate, and the man will be having fun. Sometimes, says Ben-Ze'ev, a woman will feel totally invested in an affair, but her partner will be conducting two or even four such affairs at once. (The pattern holds for consummated affairs, too.)

For women, the dangers are great. When an emotional affair results in sex, the man's interest usually cools instantly, says Pittman. Meanwhile, husbands are less forgiving than wives, making it more likely for a woman caught up in such an entanglement to be slammed with divorce.

Total Transparency?

With easy access to emotional relationships so powerful they pass for love, how can we keep our primary relationships intact? Psychotherapist M. Gary Neuman of Miami Beach, author of *Emotional Infidelity,* draws a hard line, advocating a rigorous affair-avoidance strategy that includes such strictures as refusing to dance or even eat lunch with a member of the opposite sex. Vaughan suggests we put transparency in our Web dealings—no secret e-mail accounts or correspondence a partner wouldn't be welcome to see.

Others say such prescriptives may be extreme. "Some Internet relationships are playful," Turkle comments. "People may take on different identities or express different aspects

After Infidelity: The Road Back

An emotional affair can deliver a body blow to a marriage, but it rarely results in divorce. Instead, couples can navigate recovery to make their union stronger than before.

The first step in recovery, says psychologist Barry McCarthy, is honesty. "It is secrecy that enables affairs to thrive. The cover-up, for most people, is worse than the actual infidelity," he says. "So it's only by putting everything on the table that you'll be able to move on."

"The involved partner must be honest about all aspects of the affair," says author Peggy Vaughan. Moving on too fast usually backfires, leaving the injured party reeling and the problem unresolved. "Many people believe that too much discussion just reopens the wound; but, in fact, the wound needs to be exposed to the light of day so that it can heal." The involved partner must answer questions and soothe the injured partner for as long as that person needs.

Psychologist Janis Abrahms Spring says the ultimate goal is restoring trust and suggests couples make a list of the trust-enhancing behaviors that will help them heal. Both partners may need compassion for their feelings, she says, but "the hurt partner shoulders a disproportionate share of the burden of recovery and may require some sacrificial gifts to redress the injury caused." These may range from a request that the unfaithful partner change jobs to avoid contact with the "special friend" to access to that partner's e-mail account.

McCarthy, meanwhile, emphasizes that sexual intimacy should resume as soon as possible, as part of the effort to restore closeness and trust.

"In the course of an emotional affair, you open the window to your affair partner and wall off your spouse," McCarthy says. "To repair the marriage, you must open your windows to your partner and wall off the affair."

—MT

"Someone may want just a chess partner, and the technology allows for that."

But if you're going to permit some leeway in the context of your marriage, where do you draw the line? "It's a slippery slope," says Ben-Ze'ev. "You may set limits with your spouse—no phone contact, don't take it off the screen. But people can break the deal. It is a profound human characteristic that sometimes we cross the line."

At best, notes Turkle, a serious emotional affair can alert you to problems in the primary relationship. The injured partner can view it as "a wake-up call" that needs are not being met.

It was perhaps no more than the glimmer of that alarm that enabled Brendan and Lauren to navigate back home. For both, that happened when fantasy clashed with reality—especially when they needed to pull together and care for their sick son. Brendan told Lauren he wanted to take some time to "visit his dad," when his intent was to see his old girlfriend. "I'm so exhausted. Please don't go," Lauren had said, finally asking for help. Using the excuse of a book deadline, she soon began answering e-mails from her online partner only sporadically, then hardly at all.

The illicit partner is always partly a fantasy, she or he is inevitably seen as wittier, warmer and sexier than the spouse.

What had caused them to pull back? On one level it was the need to care for their child, but on another, it was the realization that their online affairs had been a diversion from intimacy, not intimacy itself.

"The idea of actually meeting made me feel ill. I was relieved when Lauren asked me to help at home," Brendan confesses.

"There was so much about my life I never discussed in those e-mails," says Lauren. "In the end, all that witty, arch banter was just a persona, and another job."

of self; an introvert can play at extroversion, a man at being a woman." The experience may be transformative or casual.

MARK TEICH is publications manager of the Skin Cancer Foundation.

Is This Man Cheating on His Wife?

ALEXANDRA ALTER

On a scorching July afternoon, as the temperature creeps toward 118 degrees in a quiet suburb east of Phoenix, Ric Hoogestraat sits at his computer with the blinds drawn, smoking a cigarette. While his wife, Sue, watches television in the living room, Ric chats online with what appears on the screen to be a tall, slim redhead.

He's never met the woman outside of the computer world of *Second Life,* a well-chronicled digital fantasyland with more than 8 million registered "residents" who get jobs, attend concerts, and date other users. He's never so much as spoken to her on the telephone. But their relationship has taken on curiously real dimensions. They own two dogs, pay a mortgage together, and spend hours shopping at the mall and taking long motorcycle rides. This May, when Ric, 53, needed real-life surgery, the redhead cheered him up with a private island that cost her $120,000 in the virtual world's currency, or about $480 in real-world dollars. Their bond is so strong that three months ago, Ric asked Janet Spielman, the 38-year-old Canadian woman who controls the redhead, to become his virtual wife.

The woman to whom he's legally wed is not amused. "It's really devastating," says Sue Hoogestraat, a 58-year-old export agent who married Ric just seven months ago. "You try to talk to someone or bring them a drink, and they'll be having sex with a cartoon."

While many busy people can't fathom the idea of taking on another set of commitments, especially imaginary ones, *Second Life* and other multiplayer games are complicating many lives besides the Hoogestraats.' With some 30 million people now involved worldwide, there is mounting concern that some are squandering, even damaging their real lives by obsessing over their "second" ones. According to a recent survey of 30,000 gamers, nearly 40 percent of men and 53 percent of women who play online games said their virtual friends were equal to or better than their real-life friends. More than a quarter of gamers said the emotional highlight of the past week occurred in a computer world.

A burly man with a long gray ponytail and a handlebar mustache, Ric Hoogestraat looks like the cross between a techie and the Grateful Dead fan that he is. He drives a motorcycle and wears faded black Harley-Davidson T-shirts around the house. A former college computer graphics teacher, Ric was never much of a game enthusiast before he discovered *Second Life.* But since February, he's been spending six hours a night as Dutch Hoorenbeek, his 6-foot-9, muscular, motorcycle-riding cyberself.

In the virtual world, he's a successful entrepreneur with a net worth of about $1.5 million in the site's currency, the linden, which can be purchased through the site at a rate of about 250 lindens per U.S. dollar. He owns a mall, a private beach club, a dance club, and a strip club. He has 25 employees, online persons known as avatars who are operated by other players, including a security guard, a mall concierge, and the "exotic" dancers at his club. He designs bikinis and lingerie, and sells them through his chain store, Red Headed Lovers. "Here, you're in total control," he says, moving his avatar through the mall using the arrow keys on his keyboard.

Virtual worlds like *Second Life* have fast become a testing ground for the limits of relationships, both online and off. The site's audience of more than 8 million is up from 100,000 in January 2006, though the number of active users is closer to 450,000, according to the site's parent company, Linden Lab. A typical "gamer" spends 20 to 40 hours a week in a virtual world.

Though academics have only recently begun to intensively study the social dynamics of virtual worlds, some are saying that they are astonished by how closely virtual relationships mirror real life. On a neurological level, says Byron Reeves, a Stanford University professor, players may not be distinguishing between virtual and real-life relationships. "Our brains are not specialized for 21st-century media," he says. "There's no switch that says, 'Process this differently because it's on a screen.'"

On a Saturday afternoon in July, Ric Hoogestraat decides to go to the beach. So he lights a cigarette and enters *Second Life,* becoming one of 42,752 people logged on at the time. Immediately, he gets an instant message from Tenaj Jackalope, his *Second Life* wife, saying she'll be right there.

They meet at their home, a modern-looking building that overlooks the ocean, then head to his beach club. A full-blown dance party is under way. A dozen avatars, digital representations of other live players, gyrate on the sand, twisting their hips and waving their arms. Several dance topless and some are fully nude. Dutch gets pelted with instant messages.

"What took you so long, Dutch?" a dancer asks.

"Howdy, Boss Man," an avatar named Whiskey Girl says.

Before discovering *Second Life,* Hoogestraat had bounced between places and jobs, working as an elementary school-teacher and a ski instructor, teaching computer graphics, and spending two years on the road selling herbs and essential oils at Renaissance fairs. Along the way, he picked up a bachelor's degree and took graduate courses at both the University of Wyoming and the University of Arizona. He currently works as a call-center operator for Vangent Inc., a corporation that outsources calls for the government and private companies. He makes $14 an hour.

Hoogestraat learned about *Second Life* in February, while watching a morning news segment. His mother had just been hospitalized with pancreatic cancer—she died two weeks later—and he wanted a distraction. He was fascinated by the virtual world's freewheeling atmosphere. With his computer graphics background, he quickly learned how to build furniture and design clothing. He upgraded his avatar, buying stomach muscles and special hair that sways when he walks. Before long, Hoogestraat was spending most nights and weekends acting out his avatar's life.

When Hoogestraat was diagnosed with diabetes and a failing gallbladder a few months ago, he was homebound for five weeks. Some days, he played from a quarter to 6 in the morning until 2 in the morning, eating in front of the computer and pausing only for bathroom breaks.

During one marathon session, Hoogestraat met Tenaj (Janet spelled backward) while shopping. They became fast friends, then partners. A week later, he asked her to move into his apartment. In May, they married in a small ceremony in a garden over-looking a pond. Thirty of their avatar friends attended. "There's a huge trust between us," says Spielman, who is a divorced mother of two living in Calgary, Alberta. "We'll tell each other everything."

That intimacy hasn't spilled into real life. They never speak and have no plans to meet.

Still, Hoogestraat's real-life wife is losing patience with her husband's second life. "Everybody has their hobbies," says Sue Hoogestraat, who is dark-haired and heavy-set. "But when it's from 6 in the morning until 2 in the morning, that's not a hobby, that's your life."

The real Mrs. Hoogestraat is no stranger to online communities—she met her husband in a computer chat room three years ago. Both were divorced and had adult children from previous marriages, and Sue says she was relieved to find someone educated and adventurous after years of failed relationships. Now, as she cooks, does laundry, takes care of

three dogs, and empties ash-trays around the house while her husband spends hours designing outfits for virtual strippers and creating labels for virtual coffee cups, she wonders what happened to the person she married.

One Saturday night in early June, she discovered his cyber wife. He called her over to the computer to show her an outfit he had designed. There, above the image of the redheaded model, it said "Mrs. Hoorenbeek." When she confronted him, he huffily replied that it was just a game.

Two weeks later, Sue joined an online support group for spouses of obsessive online gamers called EverQuest Widows, named after another popular online fantasy game that players call Evercrack.

"It's avalanched beyond repair," says Sharra Goddard, 30, Sue Hoogestraat's daughter. Goddard says she and her two brothers have offered to help their mother move out of the house.

Sue says she's not ready to separate though. "I'm not a monster; I can see how it fulfills parts of his life that he can no longer do because of physical limitations, because of his age. His avatar, it's him at 25," she says. "He's a good person. He's just fallen down this rabbit hole."

Ric, for his part, doesn't feel he's being unfaithful. "I tried to get her involved so we could play together," he says. "But she wasn't interested."

Early in the morning on the day after Dutch and Tanej's virtual beach party, Ric Hoogestraat is back at his computer, wearing the same Harley-Davidson T-shirt he had on the day before. Four hours after logging on, he manipulates his avatar, who is wearing cut-off denim shorts and renovating the lower level of his mall. "Sunday is my heavy-duty work day," he explains.

From the kitchen, Sue asks if he wants breakfast. Ric doesn't answer. She sets a plate of breakfast pockets on the computer console and goes into the living room to watch a dog competition on television. For two hours, he focuses intently on building a coffee shop for the mall. Two other avatars gather to watch as he builds a counter, using his cursor to resize wooden planks.

At 12:05, he's ready for a break. He changes his avatar into jeans and motorcycle chaps, and "teleports" to a place with a curvy mountain road. It's one of his favorite places for riding his Harley look-alike. The road is empty. He weaves his motorcycle across the lanes. Sunlight glints off the ocean in the distance.

Sue pauses on her way to the kitchen and glances at the screen.

"You didn't eat your breakfast," she says.

"I'm sorry, I didn't see it there," Ric responds.

Over the next five hours, he is barely aware of his physical surroundings. He adds potted palms to his cafe, goes swimming through a sunken castle off his water-front property, chats with friends at a biker clubhouse, meets a new store owner at the mall, counsels an avatar friend who had recently split up with her avatar boyfriend, and shows his wife, Tenaj, the coffee shop he's built.

By 4 P.M., he's been in *Second Life* for 10 hours, pausing only to go to the bathroom. His wrists and fingers ache from manipulating the mouse. His back hurts. Yet he feels it's worth the effort. "If I work a little harder and make it a little nicer, it's more rewarding," he says.

Sitting alone in the living room in front of the television, Sue says she worries it will be years before her husband realizes that he's traded his real life for a pixilated fantasy existence, one in which she's been replaced.

"This other life is so wonderful; it's better than real life," she says. "Nobody gets fat, nobody gets gray. The person that's left can't compete with that."

The Opt-Out Myth

E. J. GRAFF

On October 26, 2003, *The New York Times Magazine* jump-started a century-long debate about women who work. On the cover it featured "The Opt Out Revolution," Lisa Belkin's semipersonal essay, with this banner: Why don't more women get to the top? They choose not to. Inside, by telling stories about herself and eight other Princeton grads who no longer work full-time, Belkin concluded that women were just too smart to believe that ladder-climbing counted as real success.

But Belkin's "revolution"—the idea that well-educated women are fleeing their careers and choosing instead to stay home with their babies—has been touted many times before. As Joan C. Williams notes in her meticulously researched report, "Opt Out or Pushed Out? How the Press Covers Work/Family Conflict," released in October 2006 by the University of California Hastings Center for WorkLife Law, where she is the director, *The New York Times* alone has highlighted this "trend" repeatedly over the last fifty years: in 1953 (Case History of an Ex-Working Mother), 1961 (Career Women Discover Satisfactions in the Home), 1980 (Many Young Women Now Say They'd Pick Family over Career), 1998 (The Stay-at-Home Mother), and 2005 (Many Women at Elite Colleges Set Career Path to Motherhood).

And yet during the same years, the U.S. has seen steady upticks in the numbers and percentages of women, including mothers, who work for wages. Economists agree that the increase in what they dryly call "women's participation in the waged workforce" has been critical to American prosperity, demonstrably pushing up our GDP. The vast majority of contemporary families cannot get by without women's income—especially now, when upwards of 70 percent of American families with children have all adults in the work force, when 51 percent of American women live without a husband, and when many women can expect to live into their eighties and beyond.

The moms-go-home story keeps coming back, in part, because it's based on some kernels of truth. Women *do* feel forced to choose between work and family. Women *do* face a sharp conflict between cultural expectations and economic realities. The workplace is still demonstrably more hostile to mothers than to fathers. Faced with the "choice" of feeling that they've failed to be *either* good mothers or good workers, many women wish they could—or worry that they should—abandon the struggle and stay home with the kids.

The problem is that the moms-go-home storyline presents all those issues as personal rather than public—and does so in misleading ways. The stories' statistics are selective, their anecdotes about upper-echelon white women are misleading, and their "counterintuitive" narrative line parrots conventional ideas about gender roles. Thus they erase most American families' real experiences and the resulting social policy needs from view.

Here's why that matters: if journalism repeatedly frames the wrong problem, then the folks who make public policy may very well deliver the wrong solution. If women are happily choosing to stay home with their babies, that's a private decision. But it's a public policy issue if most women (and men) need to work to support their families, and if the economy needs women's skills to remain competitive. It's a public policy issue if schools, jobs, and other American institutions are structured in ways that make it frustratingly difficult, and sometimes impossible, for parents to manage both their jobs and family responsibilities.

So how can this story be killed off, once and for all? Joan Williams attempts to chloroform the moms-go-home storyline with facts. "Opt Out or Pushed Out?" should be on every news, business, and feature editor's desk. It analyzes 119 representative newspaper articles, published between 1980 and 2006, that use the opt-out storyline to discuss women leaving the workplace. While business sections regularly offer more informed coverage of workplace issues, the "opt out" trend stories get more prominent placement, becoming "the chain reaction story that flashes from the *Times* to the columnists to the evening news to the cable shows," says Caryl Rivers, a Boston University journalism professor and the author of *Selling Anxiety: How the News Media Scare Women* (April 2007).

There are a number of problems with the moms-go-home storyline. First, such articles focus excessively on a tiny proportion of American women—white, highly educated, in well-paying professional/managerial jobs. Just 8 percent of American working women fit this demographic, writes Williams. The percentage is smaller still if you're dealing only with white women who graduated from the Ivies and are married to high-earning men, as Belkin's article does. Furthermore, only 4 percent of women in their mid-to late thirties with children have advanced degrees and are in a privileged income bracket like that of Belkin's fellow Princeton grads, according to Heather Boushey, a senior economist with the Center for Economic and Policy Research. That group is far more likely than average women to be married when they give birth (91 percent, as opposed to 73 percent of all women), and thus to have a second income on which to survive. But because journalists and editors increasingly come from and socialize in this class, their anecdotes loom large in our personal rearview mirrors—and in our most influential publications. Such women are chastised for working by Caitlin Flanagan (a woman rich enough to stay home and have a nanny!) in *The Atlantic,* and for lacking ambition by Linda Hirshman in *The American Prospect.* But such "my-friends-and-me" coverage is an irresponsible approach to major issues being wrestled with by every American family and employer.

The stories are misleading in a second important way. Williams's report points out that "opt-out stories invariably focus on women in one particular situation: after they have 'opted out' but before any of them divorce." The women in those articles often say their skills can be taken right back onto the job. It's a sweetly optimistic notion, but studies show that, on average, professional women who come back after time away—or even after working part-time, since U.S. women working part-time earn 21 percent less per hour worked than those who work full-time—take a hefty and sustained pay cut, and a severe cut in responsibility level. Meanwhile, nearly 50 percent of American marriages end in divorce, according to the latest census figures. While numbers are lower for marriages in the professional class, divorce remains a real possibility. Williams points to Terry Martin Hekker, one of the opt-out mothers, who in 1977 published an op-ed in *The New York Times* entitled, "The Satisfactions of Housewifery and Motherhood in 'An Age of Do-Your-Own-Thing.'" In 2006, Hekker wrote—again in the *Times,* but demoted to the Sunday Style section—about having been divorced and financially abandoned: "He got to take his girlfriend to Cancun, while I got to sell my engagement ring to pay the roofer."

In other words, interview these opt-out women fifteen years later—or forty years later, when they're trying to live on skimpy retirement incomes—and you might hear a more jaundiced view of their "choices."

The opt-out stories have a more subtle, but equally serious, flaw: their premise is entirely ahistorical. Their opening lines often suggest that a generation of women is flouting feminist expectations and heading back home. At the simplest factual level, that's false. Census numbers show no increase in mothers exiting the work force, and according to Heather Boushey, the maternity leaves women do take have gotten shorter. Furthermore, college-educated women are having their children later, in their thirties—after they've established themselves on the job, rather than before. Those maternity leaves thus come in mid-career, rather than pre-career. Calling that "opting out" is misleading. As Alice Kessler-Harris, a labor historian at Columbia University, put it, "I define that as redistributing household labor to adequately take care of one's family." She adds that even while at home, most married women keep bringing in family income, as women traditionally have. Today, women with children are selling real estate, answering phone banks,

or doing office work at night when the kids are in bed. Early in the twentieth century, they might have done piecework, taken in laundry, or fed the boarders. Centuries earlier, they would have been the business partners who took goods to market, kept the shop's accounts, and oversaw the adolescent labor (once called housemaids and dairymaids, now called nannies and daycare workers).

Which brings us to an even deeper historical flaw: editors and reporters forget that Belkin's generation isn't post-feminism; it's mid-feminism. Women's entrance into the waged work force has been moving in fits and starts over the past century. Earlier generations of college-educated women picked either work *or* family, work *after* family, or family *after* work; those who graduated in the 1980s and 1990s—Belkin's cohort—are the first to expect to do both at the same time. And so these women are shocked to discover that, although 1970s feminists knocked down the barrier to entering the professions in large numbers, the workplace still isn't fixed. They are standing on today's feminist frontier: the bias against mothers that remains embedded on the job, in the culture, and at home.

Given that reality, here's the biggest problem with the moms-go-home storyline: it begins and ends with women saying they are *choosing* to go home, and ignores the contradictory data sandwiched in between.

Williams establishes that "choice" is emphasized in eighty-eight of the 119 articles she surveyed. But keep reading. Soon you find that staying home wasn't these women's first choice, or even their second. Rather, every other door slammed. For instance, Belkin's prime example of someone who "chose" to stay home, Katherine Brokaw, was a high-flying lawyer until she had a child. Soon after her maternity leave, she exhausted herself working around the clock to prepare for a trial—a trial that, at the last minute, was canceled so the judge could go fishing. After her firm refused even to consider giving her "part-time" hours—forty hours now being considered part-time for high-end lawyers—she "chose" to quit.

More than a third of the articles in Williams's report cite "workplace inflexibility" as a reason mothers leave their jobs. Nearly half mention how lonely and depressed those women get when they've been downgraded to full-time nannies. Never do such articles cite decades of social science research showing that women are happier when occupying several roles; that homemakers' well-being suffers compared to that of working women; or that young adults who grew up in dual-earner families would choose the same family model for their own kids. Rarely do such articles ask how husband and wife negotiated which one of them would sacrifice a career. Only by ignoring both the women's own stories and the larger context can the moms-go-home articles keep chirping on about choice and about how such women now have "the best job in the world."

Underlying all this is a genuinely new trend that the moms-go-home stories never mention: the all-or-nothing workplace. At every income level, Americans work longer hours today than fifty years ago. Mandatory overtime for blue- and pink-collar workers, and eighty-hour expectations for full-time professional workers, deprive everyone of a reasonable family life. Blue-collar and low-wage families increasingly work "tag-team" schedules so that someone's always home with the kids. In surveys done by the Boston College Sloan Work and Families Research Network and by the New York-based Families and Work Institute, among others, women and men increasingly say that they'd like to have more time with their families, and would give up money and advancement to do it—if doing so didn't mean sacrificing their careers entirely. Men, however, must face fierce cultural headwinds to choose such a path, while women are pushed in that direction at every turn.

Finally, the opt-out articles never acknowledge the widespread hostility toward working mothers. Researching the book I wrote for Evelyn Murphy in 2005, *Getting Even: Why Women Don't Get Paid Like Men—and What to Do About It*, I was startled by how many lawsuits were won because managers openly and publicly told women that they couldn't be hired because they were pregnant; or that having a child would hurt them; or that it was simply impossible for women to both work and raise kids. Many other women we talked with had the same experience, but chose not to ruin their lives by suing. One lawyer who'd been on the partner track told us that once she had her second child, her colleagues refused to give her work in her highly remunerative specialty, saying that she now had other priorities—even though she kept meeting her deadlines, albeit after the kids were asleep. She was denied partnership. A high-tech project manager told me that when she was pregnant in 2002, she was asked: Do you feel stupider? Her colleague wasn't being mean; he genuinely wanted to know if pregnancy's hormones had dumbed her down. Or consider the experience of Dr. Diane Fingold, an internist at Massachusetts General Hospital in Boston and an assistant professor at Harvard Medical School, where she won the 2002 Faculty Prize for Excellence in Teaching, the school's highest teaching award. Her credentials are outstanding, yet when she asked to work three-and-a-half fewer hours a week so that she could manage her family demands—"just a little flexibility for a short period in my life!"—her practice refused. She was enraged. "I thought hard about leaving medicine altogether," she said. Her husband is a successful venture capitalist whose "annual Christmas bonus is what I make in a year!"

Had Fingold left, in other words, she would have fit neatly with Belkin's hyperachievers. But she loves practicing and teaching medicine, and realized she couldn't reenter at the same level if she walked away entirely. So she moved to another practice that was willing to accommodate her part-time schedule until, in a few years, she can return to full-time. Had she chosen the Belkin course, would she have opted out—or been pushed out?

Experiences like Fingold's bear out what social scientists are finding: strong bias against mothers, especially white mothers, who work. (Recent research shows bias against African American mothers of any class who don't work, a subject that deserves an article of its own.) Consider the work being done by Shelley Correll, a Cornell sociology professor, described in an article in the March 2007 *American Journal of Sociology*. In one experiment, Correll and her colleagues asked participants to rate a management consultant. Everyone got a profile of an equally qualified consultant—except that the consultant was variously described as a woman with children, a woman without children, a man with children, and a man without children. When the consultant was a "mother," she was rated as less competent, less committed, less suitable for hiring, promotion, or training, and was offered a lower starting salary than the other three.

Here's what feminism hasn't yet changed: the American idea of mothering is left over from the 1950s, that odd moment in history when America's unrivaled economic power enabled a single breadwinner to support an entire family. Fifty years later we still have the idea that a mother, and not a father, should be available to her child at every moment. But if being a mom is a 24-hour-a-day job, and being a worker requires a similar commitment, then the two roles are mutually exclusive. A lawyer might be able to juggle the demands of many complex cases in various stages of research and negotiation, or a grocery manager might be able to juggle dozens of delivery deadlines and worker schedules—but should she have even a fleeting thought about a pediatrics appointment, she's treated as if her on-the-job reliability will evaporate. No one can escape that cultural idea, reinforced as it is by old sitcoms, movies, jokes—and by the moms-go-home storyline.

Still, if they were pushed out, why would smart, professional women insist that they chose to stay home? Because that's the most emotionally healthy course: wanting what you've got. "That's really one of the agreed-upon principles of human nature. People want their attitudes and behavior to be in sync," said Amy Cuddy, an assistant professor in the management and organizations department at Northwestern Kellogg School of Management. "People who've left promising careers to stay home with their kids aren't going to say, 'I was forced out. I really want to be there.' It gives people a sense of control that they may not actually have."

So yes, maybe some women "chose" to go home. But they didn't choose the restrictions and constrictions that made their work lives impossible. They didn't choose the cultural expectation that mothers, not fathers, are responsible for their children's doctor visits, birthday parties, piano lessons, and summer schedules. And they didn't choose the bias or earnings loss that they face if they work part-time or when they go back full time.

By offering a steady diet of common myths and ignoring the relevant facts, newspapers have helped maintain the cultural temperature for what Williams calls "the most family-hostile public policy in the Western world." On a variety of basic policies—including parental leave, family sick leave, early childhood education, national childcare standards, after school programs, and health care that's not tied to a single all-consuming job—the U.S. lags behind almost every developed nation. How far behind? Out of 168 countries surveyed by Jody Heymann, who teaches at both the Harvard School of Public Health and McGill University, the U.S. is one of only five without mandatory paid maternity leave—along with Lesotho, Liberia, Papua New Guinea, and Swaziland. And any parent could tell you that it makes no sense to keep running schools on nineteenth century agricultural schedules, taking kids in at 7 A.M. and letting them out at 3 P.M. to milk the cows, when their parents now work until 5 or 6 P.M. Why can't twenty-first century school schedules match the twenty-first century workday?

The moms-go-home story's personal focus makes as much sense, according to Caryl Rivers, as saying, "Okay, let's build a superhighway; everybody bring one paving stone. That's how we approach family policy. We don't look at systems, just at individuals. And that's ridiculous."

E. J. GRAFF is senior researcher at Brandeis University's Schuster Institute for Investigative Journalism. From "The opt-out myth: most moms have to work to make ends meet. So why does the press write only about the elite few who don't?" *Columbia Journalism Review* 45.6 (March-April 2007): 51(4).

Making Time for Family Time

Advice from early-career psychologists on how they juggle family and career.

Tori DeAngelis

Starting your psychology career is one of the most exciting—and stressful—times of your life. It's also a period when many early-career psychologists take on new personal responsibilities, such as marrying, starting families and caring for aging parents.

Pulling this off is a lot like spinning plates, and the field's expectations don't make it any easier, says Carol Williams-Nickelson, PsyD, associate executive director of the American Psychological Association of Graduate Students (APAGS), herself working at APA and raising a family.

"There's still a pretty strong undercurrent, especially for women, that career needs to come first if you want to advance," she says.

Other factors make this scenario even more complex, other early-career experts say. For some women, it's the ticking biological clock; for many men, it's changing roles in relation to family and work.

Capt. Jason Prinster, PhD, whose internship led into his current job heading the mental health clinic at the Nellis Air Force Base in North Las Vegas, reflects this attitude.

"Three years from now, my wife could be the one making more money, and I could be the one taking the kids to work and working part time," Prinster says. "I don't think my dad ever had that thought 30 years ago."

Yet to some extent, work places still stigmatize men who openly say they value family as much as work, which puts such men in a bind, Williams-Nickelson adds.

Given these complexities, it helps to get advice from people on the front lines. Early-career experts recommend that you:

- **Communicate.** It's Psych 101, but it's true: Good communication greases the wheels of family sanity, other early-career experts say. A case in point is Jay Robertson-Howell, PsyD, a psychologist at Seattle University's counseling and psychological services center who is raising two young children with his partner, veterinarian Travis Robertson-Howell, DVM. He and Travis make sure to talk not only about each other's needs, but also the needs of the family and their professional concerns, Robertson-Howell says. As time

pressures mount, it's easier to avoid hard topics: "We constantly have to remind ourselves to keep at it," he says.

- **Negotiate.** A central tenet of good communication is agreeing on the particulars of duties and schedules, other early-career psychologists say. While couples arrange these basics in different ways, it's important for both people to discuss and agree on the arrangements and be willing to tweak them as necessary, Prinster says.

Balancing work and family is a lot like spinning plates, and psychology's expectations don't make it any easier.

For instance, Prinster and his wife, Colleen, had many discussions before deciding to split their duties along fairly traditional gender lines, with Colleen staying home with their two children and Prinster bringing home the paycheck. "We talked a lot about our respective roles and made peace with that, at least while the kids are young," Prinster says. "That's really helped. I don't feel guilty working all day, because I know we've already talked about what she expects and what I expect."

- **Schedule time for your family and yourself.** Make sure to ink in family time as an explicit part of your schedules, adds Kristi Sands Van Sickle, PsyD, who is starting her career as an assistant professor at the Florida Institute of Technology and is raising a young daughter with her husband, retired business executive Paul Van Sickle.

"We carve out family time so that even if I'm really busy, we have one day on the weekend when we're all together," says Van Sickle. The two also plan regular visits with Paul's two children from a previous marriage, who live about an hour away. "It's important to put in extra effort to make sure they feel included," she says.

Schedule time for yourself, too, for exercise, hobbies or just to regroup, advises Robertson-Howell. "Sometimes we get going so fast in this society that we forget about that."

- **Trim the excess.** Just as important as good communication is a strategy many of our parents advised us to use: Boil things down to the basics, Prinster says. He and Colleen went from being a couple that pursued many individual interests before they had children, to a team that pursued their family's interests, he says.

"I work to make money to support my family, and I spend time with my wife and kids," Prinster says. "Beyond that, only the things that are really, really important get the resources." That applies to money, too: Colleen works at their children's cooperative preschool in exchange for reduced tuition, and they cut out cable TV—a sensible move, because "we don't have time for TV!" Prinster says.

- **Pick a job that makes sense.** Some early-career psychologists consciously choose jobs that may lack outward razzle-dazzle but offer reasonable hours, decent pay and good boundaries. To spend more time with his partner, David, and their young twins, Seth Williams, PsyD, left a job that expected him to be on "24/7, 365" to one with more reasonable hours and expectations.

"If the kids are sick, I can leave any time if there's nothing life-or-death hanging on it," says Williams, associate director of clinical training at the online graduate school Capella University. He got lucky with his supervisor, too: She has a family and "walks the talk" of work-family balance, he notes.

- **Get more creative.** While there's nothing wrong with traditional job trajectories, other early-career experts

say it's worth thinking outside the typical career box to accommodate family needs.

Although her graduate program emphasized academic careers, Eileen Kennedy-Moore, PhD, chose to write books and have a small clinical practice instead. The combination allowed her to work and meet the needs of her four children.

"It gave me flexibility," Kennedy-Moore explains. "If a kid was sick one day, I could handle that and just work harder the next day." It also proved a smart career move: Her books have been published by major publishing houses, and she's garnered many therapy clients and speaking engagements as a result.

- **Find support.** Relying on trusted others is vital, whether it's fellow moms or dads to vent with, or relatives or babysitters who can give you breaks, Van Sickle says.

But your most important support may be your spouse, so nurture that relationship, she recommends. "Paul is my anxiety barometer," she says. "He's better at reading when I'm feeling anxious and overwhelmed than I am."

- **Put family first.** You only have one chance to raise your children, says Williams-Nickelson, who has two young daughters with her husband, psychologist and attorney David Nickelson, PsyD, JD. An avid careerist before she had children, she was overwhelmed by the strength of her feelings toward her girls and now knows they will be her top priority for a long time.

"I feel like I've given a lot to my career and to the profession, and now it's time to give to my kids," she says.

Williams-Nickelson adds that she now understands what mentors advised her in the years before she had children.

"You can have it all," they told her. "Just not all at once."

Partners Face Cancer Together

Couples identify with struggle of Elizabeth and John Edwards.

ELIZABETH SZABO

When Al Shockney's wife was diagnosed with breast cancer, he was gripped by fear. For about half an hour.

But her diagnosis, which could have paralyzed him, instead gave Shockney a mission.

"It did cross my mind, 'What would I do if she wasn't around?'" says Shockney, 66, of Reisterstown, Md.

"But then I thought, 'What can I do now? I know I can't stop this from happening, but I've got to make her realize that whatever she is going to go through, I'm going to be there with her.'"

With a woman as special as his wife, Lillie, "you do what you have to do," he says, "because you want that girl with you for the rest of your life."

> "There is not always an answer to 'Why me?' At some point, you have to mobilize around what you're going to do instead of why it happened."
>
> —Laurel Northouse

The Shockneys are among a growing number of couples living with breast cancer. Nearly 2.3 million women in the USA have had breast tumors, making them the largest group of cancer survivors, according to a report in 2005 from the Institute of Medicine, which advises Congress on health.

Couples such as the Shockneys say they've been inspired by presidential candidate John Edwards and his wife, Elizabeth, who announced last month that her breast cancer has spread to her bones, an incurable condition.

Experts praise John Edwards for supporting his wife and commend Elizabeth Edwards for speaking openly about a disease that women once commonly hid. Yet experts say Elizabeth Edwards' fighting spirit, along with her desire for normalcy and her reluctance to let cancer define her, is not uncommon, even among women who have advanced cancer.

Laurel Northouse, a professor at the University of Michigan School of Nursing who studies the needs of families with cancer, says a diagnosis of advanced cancer forces couples to find ways to live fully—often for several years—under the shadow of a fatal disease.

"While the 'temporarily well' look at someone who is ill as beyond the pale and in the land of the dying, the patient just wants whatever time they have to be as rich as possible," says Diane Meier, director of the Center to Advance Palliative Care.

"They are thinking about how to live and how to live better."

Although all diseases are difficult, breast cancer poses special challenges for couples, Northouse says. According to the American Cancer Society, the average age at diagnosis for breast cancer is 61—six years younger than for cancer in general. One-quarter of patients are under 50. Like Elizabeth Edwards, 57, many patients are still raising children.

The partners of cancer patients face tremendous stress, Northouse says.

"Having to watch someone die in slow motion is about the hardest thing you can do," says John Noss, 55, of Round Hill, Va., whose wife, Karin, has advanced cancer. "There is not a day that goes by that I don't think about the fact that I'm going to be on my own.

"I try to steel myself against it. I don't know if it helps."

A Sense of Isolation

Male caregivers grapple with unique burdens, says Marc Silver, who wrote *Breast Cancer Husband* after his wife developed the disease. Many fear saying something that might make their wives more upset, he says.

Husbands often feel isolated when their wives fall ill, he says. Unlike women, who may find emotional sustenance from a wide network of friends, men often confide only in their wives. And friends who shower attention on patients may forget their husbands also feel terrified and overwhelmed.

Spouses of cancer survivors are as likely to be depressed as patients, yet are less likely to receive help, according to a study of nearly 500 people published online Tuesday in the *Journal of Clinical Oncology*. Spouses were lonelier than patients, with worse spiritual well-being and marital satisfaction.

Spouses also were less likely to report personal growth because of the experience. In the study, 27% of husbands reported marital distress, compared with 11% of wives.

John Noss says spouses often experience a mixture of grief and guilt. Many careen between such thoughts as "Why is this happening to me?" and "Oops, it's not happening to me. Get over it."

"Men assume that if they're not the ones with cancer, then they're not suffering as much," Northouse says. "But the depth of their suffering is pretty extensive, whether they recognize it or not."

Though spouses don't need to "beat themselves up" for feeling vulnerable or tired, Northouse says, couples eventually need to move past their initial shock.

"There is not always an answer to 'Why me?'" Northouse says. "At some point, you have to mobilize around what you're going to do instead of why it happened."

'The Breast Cancer Husband's Motto Should Be: Shut Up and Listen'

Experts and cancer veterans say husbands can help their wives cope with breast cancer in many ways:

- Couples often feel hopeless and helpless when facing cancer, says Laurel Northouse of the University of Michigan School of Nursing. They can regain some sense of control by focusing on short-term achievable goals, such as finishing chemotherapy or staying healthy enough to attend a wedding.

  Tom Foley of Somerset, Mass., says he has learned to savor "small victories," such as finding his wife a drink she likes while she's in the hospital.

- Couples should try to stay positive, Northouse says. Though a good attitude has no effect on the cancer itself, it can improve a patient's quality of life. She also suggests avoiding people who are critical or negative.

  "As long as you can find one thing to be happy about each day, you're OK," says John Noss, 55, of Round Hill, Va., whose wife has advanced breast cancer.

- Marc Silver, author of *Breast Cancer Husband,* says many men want to "fix" a woman's cancer. Others act as cheerleaders, trying to convince their wives that things aren't so bad.

  "Not only does that not help, but it makes your wife feel like she doesn't have a right to her feelings," Silver says. "The breast cancer husband's motto should be: Shut up and listen. Sometimes you just need to listen and learn to say, 'Yup, that sucks.'"

- Husbands should take positive action, such as attending as many medical visits as possible, Silver says. Even better, men should take notes or record the conversation. That can reduce stress later, because couples won't worry about whether they misunderstood critical details.

- Although certain treatments can wreak havoc on a couple's love life, such as wiping out a woman's libido and making intercourse painful, Silver says couples can continue to show affection. Men shouldn't withdraw just because the couple has put their sex life on hold.

  "Sometimes a back rub or foot rub can mean a lot, just to help you stay physically connected."

Even the most devoted husbands can become exhausted, Northouse says. Men are often a family's sole financial provider, working full time while ferrying their wives to medical appointments, providing complex nursing care and assuming additional household duties, such as child care, cleaning and errands.

"I used to feel like I was walking around with a big plate on my hand, and people kept piling on it and worrying, 'When am I going to drop it?'" Silver says.

Yet husbands can give their wives great strength.

Shockney says he tried to be prepared to see his wife's mastectomy scar for the first time. He remembers how she scrutinized his reaction. "She could have stared a hole through me. I knew I couldn't let her see that I was shocked or disappointed. I said that everything looks fine and tried to look as normal as I could. I guess I pulled it off."

Making a Woman Feel Beautiful

Experts say women may need extra nurturing during therapy, which can strip them of their hair, sexual organs and libido. Some medications can make intercourse difficult or even painful, says Lillie Shockney, 53.

She says her husband helped her make peace with her scars. Al Shockney, a former truck driver, says she wasn't losing her breast, she was gaining a chance at life.

"I never looked down in the shower and said 'My breast is gone,'" recalls Lillie, whose cancer has not spread to other organs. "I said, 'My cancer is gone.'"

Al also found ways to make his wife feel beautiful after she underwent a second mastectomy, two years later. During a drive in the country, he surprised her by announcing that they were actually heading to a honeymoon suite in the Pocono Mountains. When she protested that she hadn't packed a bag, he informed her that they wouldn't need a change of clothes.

"He said, 'I don't plan on us leaving the hotel room. I heard when you lose one of your senses, the others become more intense. So maybe when you lose your breast, your other erotic zones become more significant, too. I plan to test out this hypothesis over the next 48 hours.'"

Planning a Legacy

And though cancer can be grueling, Northouse says, it also can prompt couples to change their lives for the better. When faced with a life-threatening illness, many look to leave a legacy.

Many cancer patients say they long to spare others from the pain or loneliness they endured. Silver says he wrote his book to provide other husbands with the kind of guidance he wished he had had.

Karin Noss, 49, says anger made her want to change the system. A doctor in 1994 initially dismissed her breast lump, which allowed the tumor to grow for more than a year before it was correctly diagnosed. In 2000, cancer returned in her spine and hip. Now, as a member of the board of the National Breast Cancer Coalition, she campaigns to improve quality and access to care.

Breast cancer also gave Lillie Shockney a new direction. She says it forced her to ask, "How do I want to leave my mark on this world?"

Today, she organizes college "breastivals" to teach young women about cancer, using humor to make the topic more approachable. Participants can even earn "booby" prizes.

Lillie, an oncology nurse, began volunteering at the Johns Hopkins Avon Foundation Breast Center in Baltimore shortly after her cancer returned. Although she initially planned to volunteer six hours a week, she soon was working 20.

She is now the breast center's administrative director. "My husband said this is what I was destined to do," she says. "And I feel energized by every woman that I have the privilege of healing."

Dealing *Day-to-Day with* Diabetes
A Whole Family Experience

Karen Giles-Smith, MS, RD

When a child is diagnosed with diabetes, it's a time of upheaval for the entire family. Gayle Hood, a dietitian and mother of two young boys, was devastated when one of her sons was diagnosed with type 1 diabetes. Hood experienced myriad emotions: denial, fear, sadness, guilt, and anger. "I knew life would never be the same from that moment on," she says. "I was right. We have a new 'normal' now."

Unless they've experienced it themselves, most people don't realize how diabetes affects families. A basic understanding of what families of children with diabetes go through and a willingness to offer encouragement and support can help these families adjust to their "new life."

A Devastating Diagnosis

Life was relatively carefree for the Hood family—Gayle, her husband Mike, and their two sons, Matt and Jacob—until nearly one year ago when Matt, then aged 8, was diagnosed with diabetes. The diagnosis was unexpected; neither side of the family has a history of diabetes. When Matt began drinking large amounts of water and getting up several times during the night to use the bathroom, Gayle subconsciously recognized the symptoms. She took Matt to the doctor but didn't allow herself to seriously consider the possibility of diabetes until the pediatrician said, "Matt has glucose in his urine. I'm on the phone right now with the hospital. They're expecting him in the pediatrics unit." As Gayle gathered their belongings, she replied, "That's what I was afraid of," and began to cry.

Gayle called Mike at work. He heard the distress in her voice but didn't fully understand the implications of the diagnosis. When Mike arrived at the hospital and saw the physicians and nurses crowded around Matt's bed, he also realized life would never be the same. He likens it to the sobering feeling many men experience the moment their baby is born.

"This is something families live with 24 hours a day," says Gayle. "When I counseled diabetics, I saw them once, and as a clinical dietitian, that was the most important time to me. But health professionals have to see the bigger picture." The bigger picture is the family dynamics—the milieu of emotions and worries and the ways families deal with the initially overwhelming aspects of learning about and living with diabetes.

The Parents' Experience

Parents of children newly diagnosed with diabetes are given all the facts about managing diabetes from a clinical standpoint. However, according to Alicia McAuliffe-Fogarty (formerly Alicia McAuliffe), PhD, who has type 1 diabetes and is the founder and director of the Circle of Life Camp, Inc., a nonprofit camp for children and young adults with diabetes, the social and emotional aspects of diabetes are probably underemphasized.[1]

Denial, guilt, and fear are often the first feelings parents face. McAuliffe-Fogarty's mother explains her reaction when her daughter was diagnosed with diabetes at the age of 11: "Not my little girl! I had nursed her forever, three years to be exact. She ate all the right homemade food, had sun and fresh air. What could we have done differently? We wracked our brains as to how we could have done this to her. We feared the same for her sister. We feared for her future as well as ours. How could fate be so cruel?"[1]

Gayle had had a similar reaction. "All I could think about was why this was happening to our family," she says, "and I was worried about giving Matt the insulin shots." In fact, during the first few days at home, Gayle was terrified that she might harm Matt by giving him the wrong amount of insulin.

Mike worried about the future. He wondered how he and his family would cope. In the hospital, he watched a video of parents of children with diabetes explaining that life can be normal again. During the video, Mike wondered how they would ever reach that point.

According to McAuliffe-Fogarty, who wrote the book *Growing Up With Diabetes: What Children Want Their Parents to Know,* parents have more difficulty accepting and adjusting to diabetes than children. "It is more difficult to fit diabetes into an adult lifestyle and to relearn a new routine while unlearning old habits," she says. McAuliffe-Fogarty recalls one parent saying, "At first, you feel like your entire life has been taken away and you are a slave to diabetes."[1]

McAuliffe-Fogarty counsels parents to move past feelings of guilt and anger as soon as possible and focus on their children and managing their diabetes. An optimistic attitude about diabetes and making sure diabetes doesn't limit the child helps him or her live a normal life. McAuliffe-Fogarty tells parents,

Gayle's Recommended Readings

A First Book for Understanding Diabetes by H. Peter Chase, MD

Growing Up with Diabetes: What Children Want Their Parents to Know by Alicia McAuliffe

Helping the Student with Diabetes Succeed: A Guide for School Personnel, The National Diabetes Education Program (Available at: http://www.ndep.nih.gov/resources/school.htm)

Safe at School (information packet), American Diabetes Association, 1-800-DIABETES

Taking Diabetes to School by Kim Gosselin and Moss Freedman

A Typical School Day

- 6:30 AM: Matt gets up and tests his blood sugar level.
- 7 AM: Gayle gets up and the family eats breakfast. Gayle counts the carbs that Matt eats and inputs the data into his pump.
- 7:30 AM: Gayle packs school lunches and a snack for Matt. She writes the amount of carbs in the snack on the snack bag and the amount of carbs in Matt's lunch on a piece of paper for him to carry in his pocket.
- 8 AM: The boys go to school.
- 10 AM: In class, Matt tests his blood sugar, eats his snack, and enters the data into his pump.
- 12 PM: Matt tests his blood sugar, eats lunch, and walks to the school office. The secretary checks the note in Matt's pocket and makes sure Matt enters the correct data into the insulin pump. She may need to refigure the carbs if Matt didn't eat all of his lunch.
- 3 PM: Matt tests his blood sugar before he gets on the bus. If his blood sugar is low, he takes fast-acting glucose and the teacher calls Gayle to pick him up. If Matt feels "low" during the bus ride, the driver gives Matt a snack from the stash Gayle has supplied.
- 4 PM: Matt has a snack at home and enters the data into his pump.
- 6 PM: Matt tests his blood sugar, eats dinner, and inputs the data into his pump.
- 8 PM: Matt tests his blood sugar, eats a snack, and inputs the data into his pump.
- 9 PM: The boys go to bed.
- 3 AM: Gayle tests Matt's blood sugar while he sleeps if changes have been made to the pump settings during the day or if a high or low blood sugar is suspected.
- Every 72 hours: Change infusion set.
Additional glucose checks may be needed if Matt is feeling "high" or "low."
- Once per week: Data from the meter/pump is uploaded to the pump company's website where the pediatric endocrinologist's office can access the data and suggest any necessary changes to the care plan.

"Your child is able to do anything as long as she fits her diabetes regimen into her schedule."[1]

The Child's Experience

When some children are diagnosed with diabetes, they become angry and feel sorry for themselves or deny they have diabetes—and they should be allowed to feel this way. Deanne Kelleher, RD, a pediatric endocrinology dietitian with Sparrow Health System in Lansing, Mich., says children's feelings of self-pity come and go, but it's important not to give in to pity parties, especially with teens. "I allow the tears initially, then encourage them to move on," says Kelleher. "They'll say it's not fair that they have to manage their diabetes, and I say, 'No, it's not fair, but it's lifesaving therapy,'" Kelleher also stresses the importance of listening to the family and letting them lead the education. "It helps me get the family's perspective—how they're doing and how they're handling things," she says. "I just ask them to tell me about it. I've learned a lot from my patients."

Parents, too, must listen to their child's concerns, questions, and feelings. McAuliffe-Fogarty says, "Children lean on their parents for support and encouragement, and for a child living with diabetes, this is even more important." She tells parents, "You taught your child how to crawl, walk, and talk. Now you must teach her to live, to survive, and to thrive."[1]

The Hood Family: Surviving and Thriving

After becoming comfortable with the basics, such as insulin injections, calculating carbohydrates and exchanges, and interpreting food labels, Gayle says the most helpful part in managing Matt's diabetes was working with the endocrinology team to set up a flexible routine. "It's important to consider the family as a whole," says Gayle, "instead of only treating the clinical symptoms."

Together, the endocrinology team and the Hood family made accommodations in Matt's care plan for his activities and sports, family traditions, and the family's lifestyle, such as who would manage what (eg, grocery shopping, meal preparation, counting carbs). "At Christmastime, we put less candy and more fun stuff in their stockings," Gayle says. "And instead of giving the boys giant Easter baskets, we have a scavenger hunt." She explains that, especially with children, it's important to be lenient with what they're allowed to eat. "They shouldn't have to feel left out, deprived, or that they have to hoard candy bars."

When working with families, Kelleher gets a comprehensive idea of what goes on at home to customize the education: How is food viewed in the family? Are any foods considered a treat or a reward? What were mealtimes like before the diagnosis? "Parents' No. 1 concern," says Kelleher, "is that they're stuffing their child with food when the child doesn't want to eat." To make it possible for children to honor their feelings of hunger and fullness, Kelleher develops a more flexible insulin plan—based on what they're actually going to eat—as early as possible. She also teaches children how to manage insulin to enjoy a birthday treat or a snack at school. "Kids with diabetes don't need special snacks," Kelleher says. "With proper guidance, planning, and family support, we can help them feel not so different from other kids."

The ABCs of Diabetes

Even though Gayle has a background in nutrition and counseled type 2 diabetics as a clinical dietitian, she was floored by how much she had to learn about diabetes management after Matt was diagnosed. For many months, Gayle's full-time "job" was to educate herself and others to ensure Matt received proper care at home and school. "The most important thing you can do for your child is to educate the adults surrounding [him or] her, so your child is not excluded or treated differently," McAuliffe-Fogarty says. "Also, educate your child about diabetes and the misconceptions surrounding the condition so [he or] she is prepared . . . When schools, peers, and the general public are educated and understand diabetes, their misconceptions are dispelled, they are less afraid of it, and they will feel more comfortable around people with diabetes."[1]

Kelleher agrees: "Part of my responsibility is to make sure we educate as many people in the patients' lives as possible: the nanny or the day care provider, siblings, Grandpa and Grandma, and the schoolteacher."

To educate the school employees, Gayle did her homework and a lot of legwork. Armed with information about how to help the school staff and students feel comfortable caring for and being around Matt, Gayle visited the school several times to talk to school staff and Matt's classmates.

Gayle met with several staff members individually: the principal, secretary, Matt's third grade teacher, art teacher, music teacher, gym teacher, and bus driver. She had to start at square one since there hadn't been a student with newly diagnosed diabetes in need of insulin injections for as long as the principal could remember. To make matters more complicated, there wasn't a school nurse at the elementary school. Gayle explained Matt's needs and provided the staff with detailed verbal and written instructions for school days and field trips. She also added information about diabetes to the school's 504 (laws prohibiting discrimination against someone with a disability) and medical management plan. (Visit www.diabetes.org for more information.)

When Matt started third grade in the fall, Gayle visited the school every day at lunch to give Matt an injection until the special education teacher, the only staff member willing to wield a needle, took over. "I let the teacher practice on me," says Gayle.

How Parents Can Help Educate Schools

- Ask for the school district policy on medication administration, blood glucose testing, and injections.
- Meet with the teacher and principal one week or more before the school informs them that your child has diabetes. Explain daily management and effects of high and low blood glucose.
- Obtain the daily class schedule: recess, gym class, lunch time, snack time, etc.
- Establish a box of emergency snacks in locations such as the main office, homeroom, gym teacher's desk, and on the bus.
- Teach how to give injections to someone at the school, particularly if there is no school nurse. Even if your child has a pump, someone still needs to know how to administer glucagon in an emergency.
- Meet with any staff member at the school that your child has regular contact with: music teacher, art teacher, librarian, playground supervisors.
- Talk to the bus driver. Make sure he or she knows that your child must be able to eat on the bus, if necessary.
- Find out where blood glucose testing will occur (may be in the office or classroom).
- Get the menu from the school cafeteria to determine carbohydrates.
- Educate your child's classmates about diabetes.
- Prepare a 504 plan and a medical management plan.

"Practicing on an orange isn't the same, and I wanted to be sure she was comfortable." The special education teacher called Gayle every day to ask how many units Matt needed, which depended on his blood glucose before lunch and how many carbs he ate. In October, Matt switched from insulin shots to the pump, and Gayle visited the school twice every day—at 10 am and 12:30 pm—to help Matt enter data into the computerized pump until he felt confident doing it while supervised by the school secretary. Gayle says the school staff has been supportive and followed through responsibly several times, such as calling her when Matt's low blood sugar didn't improve after a snack. The school staff also makes sure substitute teachers receive information about Matt's condition, including the symptoms to watch for and what to do.

To make sure Matt's classmates didn't think something was "wrong" with him, Gayle read them the book *Taking Diabetes to School*. The book is written from the perspective of a child with diabetes in a way that's easy for children to understand: "Doctors and nurses don't know how or why I have diabetes. I didn't do anything wrong (like eat too many sweets), and it's nobody's fault! Doctors and nurses do know you can't catch diabetes from me. It's okay to play with me and be my friend."[2]

Education can prevent value judgments that may hurt a child's feelings and self-esteem. Word choices, for instance, make a big difference. Instead of calling a child "a diabetic," the child is "a person with diabetes." Instead of calling diabetes a "disease" (although technically, it is), it can be referred to as "a condition." And glucose readings should be called "low," "normal," or "high" instead of "good" or "bad." Without this type of age-appropriate education, children may believe Matt did something wrong to have diabetes, that he's sick and may die, or that he should be treated differently or avoided.

"I feel like I'm broadcasting [Matt's diabetes] to the world," says Gayle. "I communicate with everyone: all of Matt's coaches and the staff at all the summer day camps. But if I don't let everyone know, they might think he's just acting goofy when his blood sugar is low. It's a delicate balance. I want Matt to be treated normally, but the adults taking care of him need to know about his diabetes."

The New Normal

"I've been able to deal with everything pretty well," says Gayle, "because I have a type A personality. But to avoid getting overwhelmed, I have to think ahead and be very organized." Mike says he feels things are "pretty normal" now, but it's tough to be spontaneous. "You always have to remember to bring the meter, glucose tabs, and a cooler with you and eat on a fairly regular schedule," says Mike. "I'm not very organized, so I'm grateful that Gayle is."

Events that are fun and exciting for Matt are usually stressful for Gayle. "I still worry when there's a substitute teacher or when Matt goes on a field trip, to a birthday party, or stays at a friend's house overnight," she says. "But I let him go and have fun and be a kid." Something as simple as a trip to a nearby beach requires a lot of time planning and packing. Gayle developed a checklist of 18 items to pack. The list helps her remember everything, which gives her peace of mind.

Matt has learned to do some age-appropriate self-care, such as blood glucose monitoring, ketone testing, and entering his blood glucose levels into the computerized insulin pump. It took him more than three months to muster the courage to do his own finger sticks, but now it's as routine as brushing his teeth. Matt has a mind-over-matter approach to his diabetes management, recently telling his mom, "If you believe something won't hurt, it won't."

Gayle treats Matt the same as always and encourages others to do the same. "I don't allow diabetes to be used as an excuse or a crutch. I want him to be a normal kid," she says, "and to do all the things other kids can do. He's a kid with diabetes, but he's still a kid."

References

1. McAuliffe A. *Growing Up with Diabetes: What Children Want Their Parents to Know.* New York: John Wiley & Sons, Inc.; 1998.
2. Gosselin K, Freedman M. *Taking Diabetes to School.* Plainview, N.Y.: Jayjo Books; 1998.

KAREN GILES-SMITH, MS, RD, is the manager of nutrition communications for the Dairy Council of Michigan and a freelance writer.

Navigating Practical Dilemmas in Terminal Care

HELEN SORENSON, MA, RRT, FAARC

Introduction

It has been stated that one-fourth of a person's life is spent growing up and three-fourths growing old. The aging process is universal, progressive, irreversible and eventually decremental.[1] Cellular death is one marker of aging. When cells are not replaced or replicated at a rate constant enough to maintain tissue or organ function, the eventual result is death of the organism.

Although not an unexpected endpoint for any human being, death unfortunately is often fraught with turmoil and dilemmas. Patients, family, friends, caregivers and health care professionals often get caught up in conflicting opinions regarding how terminal care should be approached. For the patient, the result often is suboptimal symptom management, an increased likelihood of being subjected to painful and often futile therapy and the unnecessary prolonging of death. For the family and friends of the patient, the psychosocial consequences can be devastating. Conflict at the bedside of a dying loved one can result in long-lasting and sometimes permanent rifts in family relationships.

There are some complicated issues surrounding terminal care, such as fear, lack of trust, lack of understanding, lack of communication, and stubbornness on the part of both the physicians and family members. There are moral, ethical, economic, cultural and religious issues that must be considered. Some of the dilemmas in terminal care come up more frequently than others. This paper will discuss some of the more commonly encountered ones. And possible interventions and/or alternate ways of coming to concordance regarding end-of-life care will be presented for consideration by the reader.

Fear/Death Anxiety

A degree of fear is the natural response of most individuals to the unknown. Despite many attempts at conceptualization and rationalization, preparing for death involves coming to terms with a condition unknown in past or present experience. Fear of death has been referred to in the literature as death anxiety. Research indicates that younger people have a higher level of death anxiety than older people.[2] The reasons are not difficult to understand. Younger adults in our society are often shielded from death. Many young adults may not have had close contact with individuals dying from a terminal or chronic disease. When younger people confront death, it is most likely that of a grandparent, a parent, a sibling or a friend. Death is commonly from an acute cause. Grief is intense, with many unanswered questions and psychological ramifications.

Older adults have had more experience with death, from having lost a spouse, colleagues, a friend or relatives over the years. They undoubtedly will have experienced grief and worked through loss at some time in their life. Older adults may be more apt to express the fear of dying alone.

When facing a terminal diagnosis and impending death older adults are more likely to be concerned with "mending fences" and seeking forgiveness for perceived wrongdoing. There is a need on the part of many adults to put their affairs in order and resolve any outstanding financial matters. Some interesting research on death anxiety and religiosity conducted by Thorson & Powell[3] revealed that persons higher in religiosity were lower in death anxiety.

How can the potential dilemma caused by fear be circumscribed? Possibly allowing patients to discuss the issue may ease death anxiety, but patients may be advised not to talk about funeral arrangements, since "they're not going to die." While well intended, the statement may not be helpful. Instead of preventing the patient from discussing "depressing thoughts," encouraging frank discussions about end-of-life issues may ease death anxiety. Asking the patient to verbalize his or her fears may lead to understanding the fears and alleviate the anxiety they cause.

It is important to guard against treating dying patients as though they are no longer human. For example, asking if a person would like to talk to a minister, priest or rabbi does not impinge the religious belief of the patient—it simply allows another avenue to reduce death anxiety.

Issues of Trust

Patients who have been under the care of a personal physician for an extended period of time generally exhibit a high level of trust in the diagnosis, even when the diagnosis is that of a terminal disease. Good end-of-life care requires a measure of continuity among caregivers. The patient who has had the same physician from the onset of a serious illness to the terminal stages of the disease has a substantial advantage.[4]

Planning, family support and social services, coordinated to meet the patient's needs, can be more easily arranged if there is an atmosphere of trust and confidence.

Health care today however, has become increasingly fragmented. A physician unknown to the family and/or patient may be assigned to a case. It is difficult for very sick patients to develop new relationships and establish trust with an on-going stream of care providers.[5] When circumstances are of an immediate and critical nature, issues of trust become paramount. Lack of trust in the physician and/or the health care system can erode into a lack of confidence in a diagnosis, which often results in a conflict between the patient, the family and the health care system.

Navigating this dilemma can be challenging. Recommending that the services of a hospitalist or a palliative care team be requested may be beneficial. Patients and families who are versed in the standard of care for the specific terminal disease may be in a better position to ask questions and make suggestions. Trust is associated with honesty. Conversely, trust can be eroded by what is perceived as the incompetence of or duplicity by health care providers.

An increased, concerted effort to communicate effectively all pertinent information to a patient and family and members of the health care team caring for the patient may not instantly instill confidence, but it may forestall any further erosion of trust. It is a good feeling to think that everyone on the team is pulling in the same direction.

Issues of Communication

Communication, or lack of adequate communication, is problematic. A recent article published in *Critical Care Medicine* stated, "In intensive care settings, suboptimal communication can erode family trust and fuel so called 'futility disputes'."[6] Lack of communication does not imply wrongdoing on the part of the caregivers, nor does it imply lack of comprehension or skills in patients and families. The message is delivered, but not always in language that is readily understandable. While the message may be received, at times it is not comprehended due to the nature of the message or the emotional state of the recipient.

A few years ago, during a conversation about end-of-life care, a nurse shared with the author a situation she had encountered. The patient, an elderly female, had undergone a biopsy of a tumor. The physician, upon receiving the biopsy report, asked the nurse to accompany him to the patient's room to deliver the results. The patient was told "the results of the biopsy indicate that the tumor was not benign, so I am going to refer you to Dr. ***, an oncologist, for further treatment." The physician asked for questions from the patient and, receiving none, left the room. The patient then got on the phone, called her family and stated: "Good news, I don't have cancer." The nurse left the room and called the physician, who expressed surprise that the patient had misunderstood the message. Reluctantly, he returned to the patient's room and in simple terms told her that she did indeed have cancer and that Dr. *** was a cancer specialist who would discuss treatment options with her and her family. Did the physician, on the first visit, tell the patient she had cancer—of course. Did the patient receive the message—unfortunately, no.

Although anecdotal, the case demonstrates a situation in which there was poor communication. Had the nurse not intervened, how long would it have been before the patient was adequately apprised of her condition?

Because quality communication with patients and families is imperative, the dilemma deserves attention. Many articles have been written, discussing optimal times, situations and environments best suited for end-of-life care discussions. Unfortunately, end-of-life does not always arrive on schedule or as planned.

Because of the severity of some illnesses, intensive care units may be the environment where the futility of further care becomes apparent. Intensive care units are busy places, sometimes crowded, and replete with a variety of alarms and mechanical noises on a continual basis. About 50 percent of patients who die in a hospital are cared for in an intensive care unit within three days of their death. Over thirty percent spend at least ten days of final hospitalization in an intensive care unit.[7] This is a particularly sobering reality for patients with chronic lung disease. Many COPD patients have had serious exacerbations, have been admitted to intensive care units, and many have been on mechanical ventilation. Fortunately, the medications, therapeutic interventions, and disease management skills of physicians and therapists often can turn the exacerbation around. Unfortunately, the airway pathology may not be reversible.

How and when and with whom should communication about the gravity of a situation be handled? Ideally, it should occur prior to any crisis; realistically, when it becomes obvious that a patient is unlikely to survive. Regardless of the answer, effective communication is vitally important.

Because few intensive care unit (ICU) patients (less than 5%) are able to communicate with the health care providers caring for them at the time that withholding/withdrawing life support decisions are made,[8] there is a real need to share information with and seek input from the family.

A recent article published as a supplement to *Critical Care Medicine* reviewed the importance of talking with families about end-of-life care. Although few studies provide hard evidence on how best to initiate end-of-life discussions in an ICU environment, Curtis, et al.[9] provides a framework that could serve as a model for clinicians and families alike. The proposed components of the conference would include: preparation prior to the conference, holding the conference, and finishing the conference.[9]

Preparing in Advance of the ICU-Family Conference

It is important for the participating clinician to be informed about the disease process of the patient, including: diagnosis, prognosis, treatment options, and probably outcomes of various treatments. It is important also for the clinician to identify areas of uncertainty or inconsistencies concerning the diagnosis, prognosis, or potential treatments. Any disagreements between sub-specialists involved in the care of the patient should be resolved before the family conference. Additionally, in preparing for the family conference, it is advantageous for the clinician to have some familiarity with the attitudes of the family and the patient toward illness, life-extending therapy, and death. When possible, the determination of who will attend the conference should be done advance of the conference. The location of the conference should also be pre-determined: a quiet private setting with adequate comfortable seating is ideal. Asking all participants to turn off cell phones and pagers is appropriate and will prevent unwanted distraction. (If the patient is able to participate in the conference but is too ill to leave the ICU, then the conference should take place in the patient's room in the ICU.)

Holding the ICU Family-Conference about End-of-Life Care

Assuring that all participants are introduced and understand the reason for the conference will facilitate the process. It is also helpful to discuss conference goals and determine what the patient and his or her family understand about the prognosis. If the patient is unable to participate in the conference, it may be opportune to pose the question: "What would the patient want?" Explaining during the conference that withholding life-sustaining treatment is not withholding care is an important distinction. Another recommended approach to achieve concord in the conference is to tolerate silence. Giving the family time to absorb any information they have just received, and allowing them to formulate questions, will result in better and more goal-oriented discussions.

When families are able to communicate the fears and emotions they may have, they are better able to cope with difficult decisions.

Finishing the Conference

After the patient and/or family have been provided with the facts and have achieved an understanding of the disease and the treatment issues, the clinician should make recommendations regarding treatment options. It is a disservice, for example, to give family members the impression that they are single-handedly making the decision to "pull the plug" on a loved on. Soliciting any follow-up questions, allowing adequate time, and making sure the family knows how to reach you, should end the conference on a positive note.

Understanding Choices

Another commonly encountered dilemma in terminal care is the number of choices involved, as well as the medical terminology that sometimes mystifies the choices. Advanced directives, living wills, health care proxies, durable powers of attorney for health care; what they are, what they mean, how much weight they carry, are they honored, and does everyone who needs them have them? Not long ago during a conversation with a chaplain at a hospital, the advice shared with me—to pass on to others—was to give family members the gift of knowledge. The final gift you give them may be the most important gift of all. Let them know your wishes.

When advanced directives became available in the late 1980s, it was presumed that the document would solve all the problems and that terminal care would adhere to the patient's wishes. The Study to Understand Prognoses and Preferences for Outcomes and Risks of Treatment (SUPPORT), initiated in 1988, however, showed severe shortcomings in end-of-life care.[10]

Advanced directives, as a legal document, have not necessarily lived up to expectations. A viable option is a Durable Power of Attorney for Health Care, in which a trusted individual is designated to make health care decisions when the patient cannot.

Another option is to have advanced planning sessions with family members. If the patient and his or her family can come to consensus about terminal care in advance, and the doctor is in agreement with any decisions, unnecessary suffering probably can be avoided. (When death becomes imminent and the patient's wishes are not followed, waste no time in seeking a meeting with the hospital ethics committee.)

Adaptive Techniques

There is no "recipe" that, if followed precisely, will allow for the successful navigation of all potential dilemmas. There is no way to prepare for each eventuality that accompanies terminal illness and death. Knowledge remains the safest shield against well-meaning advice-givers. Asking questions of caregivers is the best defense against misunderstanding and mismanagement of the patient.

The University of Iowa Research Center is working on an evidence-based protocol for advanced directives, which outlines in a step-by-step fashion assessment criteria that factor in the patient's age, primary language, and mental capacity for making health care treatment decisions. The protocol also provides a check-list format for health care providers, the documentation thereof is easily accessible and in a prominent position in the patient's chart.[11]

Another alternative health care benefit being proposed is called MediCaring, which emphasizes more home-based and supportive health care and discourages hospitalization and use of aggressive treatment.[12] While not specifically aimed at solving end-of-life care issues, there may be parts of MediCaring that mesh well with terminal care of the oldest old.

Whether in a home setting, a community hospital or an intensive care unit, terminal care can result in moral, ethical, economic, religious, cultural and/or personal/family conflict. Even when death is universally accepted as a normal part of the life cycle, there will be emotional dilemmas to navigate around. Additional education and research initiatives, however, may result in increased awareness that this currently is an unsolved problem, for the patient, the family, and the health care providers. Notwithstanding, however, the medical community should continue to persevere in trying to understand patients' and families' fears and needs, the need for quality communication with questions and answers in lay vocabulary. The clinician's task is to balance communication and understanding with medical delivery.

References

1. Thorson JA. *Aging in a Changing Society,* 2000. 2nd Ed. Taylor & Francis, Philadelphia, PA.
2. Thorson JA & Powell FC. Meaning of death and intrinsic religiosity. *Journal of Clinical Psychology.* 1990;46: 379−391.
3. Thorson JA & Powell FC. Elements of death anxiety and meanings of death. *Journal of Clinical Psychology.* 1998;44: 691−701.
4. Lynn J. Serving patients who may die soon and their families. *JAMA.* 2001;285(7): 925–932.
5. Pantilat SZ, Alpers A, Wachter RM. A new doctor in the house: ethical issues in hospitalist systems. *JAMA.* 1999;282: 171−174.
6. Fins JJ & Soloman MZ. Communication in the intensive care setting: The challenge of futility disputes. *Critical Care Medicine.* 2001;29(2) Supplement.
7. Quill TE & Brody H. Physician recommendations and patient autonomy: Finding a balance between physician power and patient choice. *Ann Internal Med.* 1996;25: 763−769.
8. Prendergast TJ & Luce JM. Increasing incidence of withholding and withdrawal of life support from the critically ill. *Am J Respir Crit Care Med.* 1997;155: 15−20.
9. Curtis JR et al. The family conference as a focus to improve communication about end-of-life care in the intensive care unit: Opportunities for improvement. *Critical Care Medicine.* 2001;29(2) Supplement. PN26−N33.
10. Pioneer Programs in Palliative Care: Nine Case Studies (2000). The Robert Wood Johnson Foundation in cooperation with the Milbank Memorial Fund, New York, NY.
11. Evidence-based protocol: Advanced Directives. Iowa City, IA: University of Iowa Gerontological Nursing Interventions Research Center. 1999. Available; [http://www.guideline.gov/index.asp].
12. Lynn. J. et al. MediCaring: development and test marketing of a supportive care benefit for older people. *Journal of the American Geriatric Society.* 1999;47(9) 1058−1064.

HELEN SORENSON, MA, RRT, FAARC Assistant Professor, Department of Respiratory Care, University of Texas Health Science Center at San Antonio in San Antonio, Texas. Ms. Sorenson is also Managing Editor of "Emphysema/COPD: The Journal of Patient Centered Care."

Bereavement after Caregiving

RICHARD SCHULZ, PHD, RANDY HEBERT, MD, MPH, AND KATHRIN BOERNER, PHD

O f the approximately 2.4 million deaths that occur in the United States each year, nearly 70% are the result of chronic conditions such as heart disease, cancer, stroke, and respiratory diseases. The large majority of decedents are older persons suffering from one or more disabling conditions which compromised their ability to function independently prior to death. As a result, a typical death is preceded by an extended period of time during which one or more family members provide unpaid care in the form of health and support services to their disabled relative.[1] A recent survey estimates the out-of-pocket cost of caring for an aging parent or spouse averages about $5500 a year.[2]

Our understanding of bereavement is undergoing fundamental changes as a result of recent prospective studies of bereavement that focus on circumstances surrounding the death of a loved one. One important finding to emerge in recent years concerns the impact of family caregiving on caregiver response to death of a loved one.[3,4] Family members involved in care provision before death show remarkable resilience in adapting to the death of their relatives. Symptoms of depression and grief decline rapidly after the death and return to near normal levels within a year of the death.[5] This may be due to multiple reasons, including having time to prepare for the impending death and life afterward, relief from the burdens of caregiving, an end to the suffering of their loved one, and the absence of guilt over having done the "work of caregiving."

Despite the generally positive prognosis for most bereaved caregivers, a sizable minority continues to experience high levels of stress and psychiatric problems after death. Approximately 10% to 15% of people experience chronic depression.[6] In our own work with caregivers of patients with dementia, we found that 30% of caregivers were at risk for clinical depression 1 year post-death, and 20% experience complicated grief.[4,5] As described below, complicated grief is distinct from both depression and normal grief reactions.

Understanding the variability in response to death and the role of caregiving factors as predictors of bereavement outcomes is critical to developing effective interventions for this group. To address this issue, we distinguish among 2 types of predictors of pathologic depression and grief outcomes among caregivers: Factors associated with the caregiving experience prior to death, and factors associated with depression and grief assessed postbereavement. The rationale for making this

Approximately 20% of bereaved caregivers will experience a variety of psychiatric symptoms including depression and/or complicated grief, a disorder characterized by persistently high levels of distress that impair functioning in important life domains. We identify prebereavement risk factors for poor adjustment after the death of a loved one along with preventive strategies that can be implemented prior to death as well as diagnostic procedures and therapeutic strategies that can be used to identify and treat individuals who develop complicated grief disorder after death.

Schulz R, Hebert R, Boerner K. Bereavement after caregiving, *Geriatrics*, 2008:63(1):20–22.

distinction is that each factor provides a different opportunity for intervention. Identifying which caregiving factors contribute to poor bereavement outcomes provides us with important leads about interventions that could be delivered during caregiving. Likewise, postbereavement factors linked to poor bereavement response may help identify intervention options that can be delivered after death.

Caregivers at Risk for Poor Bereavement Outcomes

The most common finding across multiple studies is that prebereavement levels of mental distress such as depression and anxiety are predictive of postbereavement adjustment. A related finding is that high levels of burden, feeling exhausted and overloaded, lack of support, and having competing responsibilities such as work or caring for younger children are all associated with negative postbereavement outcomes.[3,7,8] The fact that increased burden is a risk factor for poor bereavement outcomes may explain in part the higher mortality rate observed among caregivers of terminal patients who do not use hospice services when compared to those who do.[9] Demographic factors also play a role. Individuals with lower income, lower education, and those who are African Americans are also more likely to exhibit greater depression and complicated grief after the death.

Table 1 Questions to Identify Caregivers at Risk for Negative Postbereavement Outcomes

Do you feel overwhelmed by the responsibilities of providing care to your relative?

Do you feel isolated from family and friends?

Do you feel prepared for the death of your loved one?

In the past month have you felt depressed, sad, or anxious much of the time?

Table 2 Symptoms of Complicated Grief

Trouble accepting the death

Inability to trust others since the death

Excessive bitterness related to the death

Feeling uneasy about moving on

Detachment from formerly close others

Feeling life is meaningless without the deceased

Feeling that the future holds no prospect for fulfillment without the deceased

Feeling agitated since the death

A recent randomized trial of dementia in caregivers showed that psychosocial-behavioral interventions designed to decrease caregiver burden and distress had the added benefit of preventing complicated grief after the death of their loved one.[4] This suggests that adverse effects of bereavement can be addressed through preventive treatments delivered to family caregivers prior to the death of their loved one. Individuals at risk for negative postbereavement outcomes can be identified by asking a few questions to determine how stressful caregiving is, the availability of support from family and friends, how depressed and anxious they feel, and whether or not they feel prepared for the death of their loved one (see Table 1). Treatment options for caregivers thus identified include interventions to reduce caregiver burden, such as hospice care, behavioral and pharmacologic treatment of depression and anxiety, and referral to religious counselors.

Diagnosis and Treatment of Complicated Grief

One of the hallmarks of poor response to death is persistent (ie, 6 months or longer) complicated grief. This disorder is distinct from normal grief reactions or depression. It is characterized by an intense longing and yearning for the person who died and by recurrent intrusive and distressing thoughts about the absence of the deceased, making it difficult to concentrate, move beyond an acute state of mourning, form other interpersonal relationships, and engage in potentially rewarding activities. Complicated grief is a source of significant distress and impairment and is associated with a range of negative psychiatric and physical health consequences.[10]

Formal diagnostic criteria for complicated grief disorder have been proposed for inclusion in the *Diagnostic and Statistical Manual of Mental Disorders, Fifth Edition (DSM-V)*.[11] A diagnosis of complicated grief disorder requires that the bereaved person must have persistent and disruptive yearning, pining, and longing for the deceased. The individual must experience 4 of the 8 symptoms at least several times a day and/or to a severely distressing disruptive degree (see Table 2). Symptoms of distress must endure for at least 6 months and significantly impair functioning in important life domains.

Complicated grief often occurs along with other disorders such as major depression and post-traumatic stress disorder (PTSD) and is associated with suicidality and self-destructive behaviors,[12] but it is a distinct disorder requiring treatment strategies different from those used with major depression and PTSD. A recent randomized trial found higher and faster rates of improvement among persons with complicated grief using loss-focused, cognitive behavioral therapy techniques when compared to rates obtained with a standard interpersonal therapy approach used to treat depression.[13] Components of effective treatment included repeated retelling of the story of the death, having an imaginary conversation with the deceased, and working on confronting avoided situations. In general, although traditional treatments for depression after bereavement such as referral to a psychiatrist or psychologist for medications and/or psychotherapy can be effective in treating depression and to some extent, complicated grief, there is added benefit to treatments that are specifically tailored to address symptoms of complicated grief.[6]

Hundreds of studies carried out in the past 2 decades have documented the negative health effects of caregiving, showing that caregivers are at increased risk of psychiatric and physical morbidity.[14] The challenges of caregiving become even more extreme as the care-recipient nears death. When the death does occur, the caregiver enters bereavement already compromised with high levels of depression and anxiety and sometimes physical exhaustion brought about by the caregiving experience. Even with these vulnerabilities, caregivers, for the most part, adapt well to the death of their loved one. Psychiatric symptomatology typically improves and caregivers are able to effectively reengage in activities that may have lapsed while caregiving.

Opportunities for Intervention

Despite this generally positive picture of caregiver adaptation to bereavement, a minority of caregivers exhibit adverse bereavement outcomes in the form of high levels of depression and/or complicated grief. High levels of burden, physical exhaustion, lack of social support, along with traditional predictors, such as prebereavement anxiety and depression, are all associated with negative postbereavement outcomes. Although empirical support for the efficacy of bereavement interventions to enhance adaptation to bereavement is mixed at best,[13,15] researchers have generally not tested preventive approaches in which interventions are delivered prior to death. In addition, new treatment strategies described above specifically designed to treat complicated grief hold promise for helping individuals who are not able to effectively cope with the death of a loved one.

References

1. Emanuel EJ, Fairclough DL, Slutsman J, et al. Assistance from family members, friends, paid care givers, and volunteers in the care of terminally ill patients. *N Engl J Med,* 1999; 341(13):956–63.

2. Gross J. Study finds higher outlays for caregivers of older relatives. *New York Times,* November 19, 2007:A18.

3. Schulz R, Boerner K, Hebert RS, Caregiving and bereavement. In Stroebe MS, Hansson RO, et al, eds. *Handbook of Bereavement Research and Practice: 21st Century Perspectives.* Washington, DC: American Psychological Association Press; in press.

4. Schulz R, Boerner K, Shear K, et al. Predictors of complicated grief among dementia caregivers: a prospective study of bereavement. *Am J Geriatr Psychiatry,* 2006;14(8):650–658.

5. Schulz R, Mendelsohn AB, Haley WE, et al. End of life care and the effects of bereavement on family caregivers of persons with dementia. *N Engl J Med.* 2003;349(20): 1936–1942.

6. Hensley PL, Treatment of bereavement related depression and traumatic grief. *J Affect Disord.* 2006;92(1):117–124.

7. Hebert RS, Dang Q, Schulz R. Preparedness for the death of a loved one and mental health in bereaved caregivers of patients with dementia: findings from the REACH study. *J Palliat Med.* 2006;9(3):683–693.

8. Boerner K, Schulz R, Horowitz A. Positive aspects of caregiving and adaptation to bereavement, *Psychol Aging.* 2004;19(4):668–675.

9. Christakis NA, Iwashyna TJ. The health impact of health care on families: a matched cohort study of hospice use by decedents and mortality outcomes in surviving, widowed spouses, *Soc Sci Med.* 2003;57(3):465–475.

10. Prigerson HG, Bierhals AJ, Kasi SV, et al. Traumatic grief as a risk factor for mental and physical morbidity, *Amer J Psychiatry.* 1997;154(5):616–623.

11. Zhang B, El-Jawahri A, Prigerson HG, Update on bereavement research: evidence-based guidelines for the diagnosis and treatment of complicated bereavement. *J Palliat Med.* 2006;9(5):1188–1203.

12. Latham AE, Prigerson HG. Suicidality and bereavement: complicated grief as psychiatric disorder presenting greatest risk for suicidality. *Suicide Life Threat Behav.* 2004;34(4): 350–362.

13. Shear K, Frank E, Houck PR, et al. Treatment of complicated grief: a randomized controlled trial. *JAMA.* 2005;293(21):2601–2608.

14. Schulz R, Beach S. Caregiving as a risk factor for mortality: the caregiver health effects study. *JAMA.* 1999;282: 2215–2219.

15. Schut H, Stroebe MS. Interventions to enhance adaptation to bereavement. *J Palliat Med.* 2005;8(suppl 1):S140–147.

Dr Schulz is Professor of Psychiatry, Director, University Center for Social and Urban Research, University of Pittsburgh, Pittsburgh, Pa. **Dr Hebert** is Assistant Professor of Medicine, Division of General Internal Medicine, University of Pittsburgh. **Dr Boerner** is Senior Research Scientist, Jewish Home Lifecare, Research Institute on Aging, New York, NY.

Disclosures: Drs Schulz, Hebert, and Boerner disclose that they have no financial relationship with any manufacturer in this area of medicine.

Love, Loss—and Love

The death of a young child can devastate a family. How couples decide they're ready to try again.

KAREN SPRINGEN

Two years ago, 5-month-old Cody Schmurr died from multiple congenital myopathy—a rare condition that made his muscles so weak he could not exhale the carbon dioxide from his lungs. Doctors told Cody's parents, Tracy and Steve Schmurr, that there was a one in three chance that their next child might suffer from the same problem. For the Livermore, Calif., couple, it was a risk worth taking. "I didn't want to ever turn back and say, 'I wish we would have'," says Tracy. "Even the five months with Cody were the best five months of my life." In June 2006, 13 months after Cody's death, Tracy delivered a healthy baby boy named Levi.

Every year, about 25,000 kids under age 10 die, most from congenital anomalies, unintentional injury (mainly car accidents), premature birth and cancer. It is the ultimate tragedy: kids aren't supposed to pass away before their parents. But sometimes they do. And then what? "Every family, at some point, evaluates whether they should have another child," says Kristin James, bereavement counselor at Children's Memorial Hospital in Chicago. "When that loss occurs, they're suddenly incomplete. You've defined yourself as a family of five, and now you're a family of four." The fear factor (will another child die, too?) often looms large.

The loss of a child can put tremendous stress on even the best marriages and the closest families. "Losing a kid makes you lose faith in life," says child psychiatrist Alvin Rosenfeld. "To reclaim that faith in living, that it's worth doing this again, is an act of enormous courage." No one knows how many parents gather that courage—or how they fare. It's difficult to study. "You certainly can't randomly assign people to have a child or not have a child," says Douglas Hawkins, a pediatric oncologist at Seattle Children's Hospital. Yet, anecdotally, many experts say parents seem to do better when they try again. "The most profound attachment in human life is mother and child," says John Golenski, executive director of the George Mark Children's House, a residential facility in San Leandro, Calif., for kids with terminal illnesses and their families. "The best adaptation to [the loss of a child] is another attachment."

Still, another attachment is not for everyone. "Some families are willing to risk anything to hold a healthy baby. Some families can't imagine going through that pain again," says James. "It's very hard to convince them that this won't happen again. Their bubble of what they think is safe and normal is forever shattered." Even if they want to conceive again, some couples run into fertility problems. These families may—or may not—decide to adopt.

For one couple, the decision was made easier by their children, including their dying son. On Christmas Day in 1997, Joey Albrecht, 8, died of a rare pediatric cancer. "Two weeks before Joey died, he told us that when he got to heaven, he was going to tell God to send us a baby," says his mother, Cheryl Albrecht. Right after the funeral, Cheryl's daughter, Kelly, now 21, said, "Mom, the house is so quiet. Can we have another baby?" The answer: yes. In January 1999, Cheryl gave birth to Julia, now 8, followed by Nick, now 7. Cheryl remembers seeing Julia's heart beat on the ultrasound. "I thought, 'Oh, my God, my heart is starting to grow again'," she says. "I can love again. There is going to be happiness in my life."

Such feelings cause some parents to feel guilty. "What I do hear a lot is the feeling of, 'Am I betraying my child who died?'" says Barbara Sourkes, director of the pediatric palliative-care program at Lucile Packard Children's Hospital at Stanford. "'How can I throw myself wholeheartedly into a new child and leave the child who died behind?'" Cheryl Albrecht says Julia and Nick have not replaced her Joey. "But they helped us love again and helped us keep happy," she says.

All parents worry about their kids' health and safety—more so when they've lost a child. Michelle and Bill McGowan's daughter Katie died last year, just before her first birthday. (She was born with a blockage in her intestine.) Four months ago, the McGowans, of Glenview, Ill., had a healthy baby boy, John. Michelle still attends a support group at Children's Memorial in Chicago, where moms talk about their fears that other offspring will die. "As a mom anyway, you can be paranoid. Now I'm paranoid to the nth degree," says McGowan. Even her older kids, Kylie, now 4, and Bill, now 6, worry. One day Kylie, concerned about John's getting a cold, said, "We can't touch him. He's going to die." Michelle reassured her that John would be OK. And every week after church, they visit Katie's gravestone, with a small butterfly etched at the top of the cross. (Experts say this sort of ritual is normal.) Michelle tells her kids, "Sometimes butterflies fly away, and you don't see them again." But sometimes they stay—and sometimes new ones are born.

Stressors Afflicting Families during Military Deployment

Gina M. Di Nola

Operation Iraqi Freedom is a stressful time for many military families. Help is available, if one knows where to look. The U.S. Army has implemented a program to address the needs of family members–the Family Readiness Group or FRG. Before any program or group can assist spouses, it is necessary to name and understand the issues families face. In doing so, leaders can be better prepared to help family members handle the stressors associated with the current deployments in support of Operation Iraqi Freedom (OIF) and the Global War on Terrorism (GWOT).

History of the FRG

Involvement of spouses in the military started with the Revolutionary War. In May of 1780, Esther Reed (her husband was an aide to George Washington) and 39 wives started the first wives' club, which became known as "the Association". The Association performed fundraising for supplies, cooking, mending, nursing, and equipment caddying in exchange for rations to feed their families (1).

During World War II, the Association became known as the "waiting wives club", an established support system for family members back home. The club eventually evolved and was institutionalized after the Persian Gulf War (2) to today's family support group known as the Family Readiness Group (FRG). The FRG serves as the link between units and their spouses; it is the support system for family members, especially during wartime or deployment.

Role of the FRG

The FRG plays an important role in the military. The effectiveness of family support groups has been apparent since the Vietnam War (2). After the First Gulf War, the U.S. Army mandated that all units have an established family support group, or FRG (3). "Commanders have an obligation to provide assistance to establish and maintain personal and family affairs readiness . . . . Examples include Family Readiness Groups . . . ." (3). The role of the FRG is to keep families informed and updated during times of deployment, training, or military exercises. Although it doesn't practice the same formalities and structures as the military, the FRG is beneficial during the difficult times that military spouses must face.

Stressors During Deployments

There is no doubt that deployments cause much stress to the service member and the family. Operation Desert Storm/Shield was the largest military mobilization since the Vietnam War (4). Three categories of stressors were identified in a study done during Operation Desert Storm (5): emotional (missing the soldier, safety concern for the soldier), deployment-related (managing budget, Powers of Attorney, and increase in child-care costs), and general life events (non-English speakers, new to installation, etc.). The list of stressors noted at that time were loneliness, financial insecurities, children's discipline, and an overall feeling that the military was not concerned for their well-being. Some spouses did not use programs available to them for fear of being classified as unable to handle their problems. Others were not able to seek family support because they were not stationed near them. Family roles had to be changed and required adjustment by both parents and children.

Other factors affecting spouses during Operation Desert Storm were rumors. In 1992, the US Army War College reported that "family support groups helped, in some cases, to reduce rumors" (6). However, in a subsequent study conducted by the U.S. Army Research Institute (ARI) and the Walter Reed Army Institute of Research (WRAIR), "unit leaders' support for families was strongly related to rumors . . . ." The case study demonstrated that family support groups may facilitate the spread of rumors and any attempts to control rumors actually enhanced them (6).

Another stresser faced by families is spousal aggression. A study done between 1990 and 1994 revealed that there was a significant probability of aggression for soldiers who had deployed than those who did not (7). In 1996 Caliber Associates interviewed 96 couple participants in the Army's Family

Advocacy Programs. Half of the abusers had been deployed an average of 110 days and cited deployment as the triggering stressor (8). Between 2002 and 2004, Fort Bragg, NC alone reported 832 victims of domestic violence (9), which were deployment-related.

Children's reactions to deployments vary with age and developmental stage. Children's system levels are similar to the stress level experienced by their parents or caregiver. One would think the source of the stress would be the immediate family. Instead of being informed by their parents, active-duty children received most of their information from teachers. Media coverage also added to the concerns of safety of the deployed service member. There is an additional stress factor—concern for the service member's safety (10). Active duty children worried that the military parent would die during the deployment (11). Watanabe and Jensen state that children who were not prepared for the deployment fared not as well as those who were (12).

Current OIF Stressors

The National Military Family Association surveyed military spouses in 2005. Stress levels were measured for the various points of the deployment cycle. Fifteen percent experienced heightened stress levels upon notification of the deployment and 18 % upon the departure of the service. During the deployment or absence of the service member, 62 % felt the greatest stress. The respondents emphasized the need for good communication between the unit and the families. Some family members felt that "when entering a second or third deployment, they carry the unresolved anxieties and expectations from the last deployment(s)" (13).

Redeployment and reintegration were also times of much stress for families. The constant deployment left little time for adjustment for each phase of the deployment cycle. Family members expressed an interest in knowing what to expect prior to, during, and after the redeployment phase. Yet few participated in formal training or briefings offered by the installation (13).

Stressors and the FRG

Stressors may vary with each deployment, and everyone copes differently. By establishing family support groups, families were thought to be better equipped to handle the challenges of the military lifestyle, up to the point where the support group becomes a stressor. Whether it is the Army's Family Readiness Group, the Air Force's Key Spouse Program, the Navy's Ombudsman Program, or the Marine Corps's Key Volunteer Network, group dynamics within the support system can affect the coping mechanism of the family members.

The commitment of support group leaders was questioned in a survey conducted recently of 100 family members of deployed soldiers in 2007. Commitment concerns that were stated by the family members included lack of communication from leaders, slow dissemination of information from leaders, cliques within the family support groups (or the FRG), gossip, drama in the group, and limited group activities. Of those who did not like their FRG, 20 % still attended the meetings. Three percent of the participants did not know how to contact their leader in the event of an emergency. One family member suggested that a social worker be present at the meetings. Although 74 % remained on or near the installation, only 54 % attended support group meetings.

Conclusion

According to Webster (2006), readiness is defined as being "prepared mentally or physically for some experience or action." According to the Army's Training and Doctrine Command Public Affairs Office, "Family readiness is the state soldiers, spouses and family members proactively prepare for, and in which they are able to cope with mobilization, deployments and prolonged separations." (14). Independence, financial responsibility, etc. are a few of the attributes of readiness for today's family. Yet, no one knows how ready the family will be until the family separation or deployment occurs.

Deployments are inevitable while serving in the military. Families have many programs or resources available to them to help them cope with the challenges of the deployments, yet many do not use them. The intent of the FRG was to provide families these resources. Unfortunately, the dilemma can stem from the FRG. Addressing the stressors that families face is the first step to attaining readiness. With current and prolonged deployments in support of OIF or GWOT, time is of the essence.

References

1. Crossley A and Keller CA: The army wife handbook: Updated and expanded, Second edition, Sarasota, FL, ABI Press, 1993.
2. Rosen LN, Durand DB: Coping with the unique demands of military family life. In The military family: A practice guide for Human Service providers, ed. Martin JA, Rosen LN, Sparacino LR, Westport, CT: Praeger, 2000; 55–72.
3. Department of the Army: Army Regulation 600–20: Army Command Policy. 2006.
4. Black Jr WG: Military-induced family separation: A stress reduction intervention. Social Work 1993; 38; no. 3.
5. Rosen LN, Durand DB, Martin JA: Wartime stress and family adaptation. In The military family: A practice guide for Human Service providers, ed. J. A. Martin, Rosen LN, Sparacino LR, Westport, CT, Praeger, 2000: 123–138.
6. Schumm WR, Bell DB, Knott B: Predicting the extent and stressfulness of problem rumors at home among army wives of soldiers deployed overseas on a humanitarian mission. Psychol Rep 2001; 89; 1: 123–34.
7. McCarroll JE, Ursano RJ, Liu X, Thayer LE, Newby JH, Norwood AE, Fullerton CS: Deployment and the probability of spousal aggression by US Army soldiers. Mil Med 2000; 165, 1: 41–4.
8. Brannen SJ, Hamlin II ER: Understanding spouse abuse in military families. In The military family: A practice guide for

Human Service providers, ed. Martin JA, Rosen LN, Sparacino LR; 169–183. Westport, CT: Praeger, 2000.

9. Houppert K: Base crimes: The military has a domestic violence problem. Retrieved on February 6, 2008 from http://www. motherjones.com/cgibin/print_article.pl?url=http://www. motherjones.com/news/featurex/2005/07/base_crimes.html

10. Stafford EM, Grady BA: Military family support. Pediatric Annals 2003; 32:2: 110–115.

11. Ryan-Wenger NA: Impact of the threat of war on children in military families. American Journal of Orthopsychiatry 2001: 71; 2: 236–244.

12. Watanabe HK, Jensen PS: Young children's adaptation to a military lifestyle. In The military family: A practice guide for Human Service providers, ed. Martin JA, Rosen LN, Sparacino LR: 209–223. Westport, CT, Praeger, 2000.

13. National Military Family Association: Cycles of deployment: An analysis of survey responses from April through September, 2005: 20. San Diego, Defense Web Technologies, 2005.

14. US Army's Training and Doctrine Command: Family Readiness Group Leader's Command Information Pocket Guide, 2003: Fort Monroe, VA, Headquarters, U.S. Army Training and Doctrine Command, 2003.

Children of the Wars

Students whose parents are called to active duty face challenges and stresses that schools must be ready to address.

LAWRENCE HARDY

"Why does Daddy have to go back?" 7-year-old Tyler kept asking.

It had been three years since Tyler's father, a U.S. Army captain, returned from Iraq after a seven-month deployment. Now he was leaving again—for an even longer tour—and the boy was nervous and upset. "Well, there are other daddies who have been in Iraq, and they have to come home to see their kids," Tyler's mother, Alison Sakimura explained as best she could. "And other daddies have to go" and take their place.

The boy asked: "Will Daddy come back?"

Sakimura answered truthfully: "Daddy wears a helmet to protect his head, and a vest to protect his heart, and carries a weapon. We just have to pray to God to watch over him."

That was in 2006, shortly before Capt. Greg Sakimura, a company commander in the 82nd Airborne, began a 15-month tour of northern Iraq. He returned to Fort Bragg, N.C., last fall; Tyler, who had bravely dubbed himself "Little Dad" to help his mother and two younger siblings in his father's absence, went back to being just another third-grader at Ed V. Baldwin Elementary School.

But Baldwin Elementary is not just another school. More than half its students have parents in the military; and, like similar children attending other schools on or near military bases, they must confront challenges and stresses that most children would never dream of. These include long separations from a parent and fears that loved ones may not return.

"We've had teachers lose spouses," says William C. Harrison, superintendent of the Cumberland County Schools, which includes Baldwin Elementary. "We've had—thank God, not many—students lose parents."

The stresses have intensified in recent years as the military, stretched thin from the ongoing wars in Iraq and Afghanistan, has had to send combat troops back to the war zones multiple times. Downtime has been shortened and deployments extended to as long as 15 months. That can be especially tough for families with school-age children.

"Some people miss two Christmases—that's very hard," says Shannon Shurko, a former science teacher who recently assumed the new position of Military Child Support Liaison for the Cumberland County Schools.

Trauma and Resilience

There are 700,000 children in the United States with at least one parent serving in Iraq, Afghanistan, or other military bases around the world—nearly 40 percent of the 1.8 million military children. According to a July 2007 report coauthored by Stephen Cozza, an expert on the mental health of military children and their families, it is estimated that more than 2,500 children have lost a parent in the Iraq war alone, and nearly 20,000 have had parents injured.

Despite these numbers, Cozza cautions against assuming that military children are uniformly traumatized by the increased stress. Many are extremely resilient, he says, and may even be made stronger by the challenges they face. "To assume either widespread trauma or uniform resilience is harmful to our efforts as concerned professionals," wrote Cozza and coauthor Alicia F. Lieberman, of the University of California, San Francisco. "The truth lies somewhere between these two extremes."

Stress is not the same as psychological trauma, the authors note; it is something we all experience in varying degrees. However, the stress level among military families in this period of extended conflict is substantial.

Last October, Army Secretary Pete Geren alluded to this stress when he said the Army's well-regarded system of family supports could have trouble keeping up with demand.

"For 500,000 spouses and 700,000 children, six years of war is uncharted territory," Geren told a meeting of the Association of the United States Army. "Our family systems . . . did not contemplate the operational tempo our families are experiencing today."

The Front Lines

Alison Sakimura is on the front lines of those family support systems. The wife of an infantry officer who was in charge of 130 soldiers in Iraq, she feels a responsibility to the "Family

Preparing and Supporting Military Children Are Critical

Maybe they develop attention problems, and their grades slip. Or maybe they don't show any signs at all that they are among the "suddenly military" children.

These are children of reservists and National Guard troops whose parents have been sent overseas, says Larry W. Moehnke, chief of staff of the Military Child Education Coalition in Harker Heights, Texas. Moehnke says more than 480,000 children between the ages of 5 and 18 have parents in these service branches, but the coalition has no estimate of the number of these whose parents are deployed.

For schools on or near military bases, the needs of military children are well-known. That may not be the case with children of National Guard members and reservists, who are spread out in school districts across the country. Indeed, some districts may not even know they have children whose parents are deployed, and, even if they do, they may not know how to help them.

The coalition sponsors professional development institutes for school counselors and special education teachers who serve military children. A special institute also trains educators in how to support children with parents in the National Guard and reserves who have been deployed.

"Basically, it's a matter of schools trying to open the lines of communication—letting parents know the schools are supportive and will do what they can to ease anxieties during this period of time," Moehnke says.

An online booklet, *How to Prepare Our Children and Stay Involved in Their Education During Deployment*, is also available for parents and educators (See www. militarychild.org).

Readiness Group" back home. She has a time-consuming volunteer job sending e-mails to its members—parents of soldiers, other relatives, fiancées, and 60 spouses—with information and messages of support.

"We've been in the military for 12 years," she says, using the plural pronoun to describe a commitment that extends to her entire family.

The e-mails let families know about impending deployments, tell them of family-related events on the base, and offer support while they wait for their spouses and loved ones to come home.

When her husband would call from Iraq, he would tell her little more than, "It's hot. It's busy."

"I already know it's hot. I already know it's busy," she recalls telling him. "Will you tell me something else?"

But actually, she didn't want to know too much more, and he was more interested in hearing news from her, things like how the children were doing in school and who got an A on a test.

Kimberly Nieto, a social studies teacher at a Cumberland County middle school, said it helped to keep her children busy and maintain family routines while her husband was deployed in Iraq for 12 months (his second deployment). Counselors at her now-6- and 7-year-old daughters' elementary school regularly checked on them and the children of other deployed parents.

"That was definitely helpful," Nieto says.

It also helped that her husband, a technical inspector for helicopters, didn't have to travel much during most of his tour and could talk to the family most nights via Internet and Webcam.

The day he came home to Fort Bragg and strode down the "Green Ramp" that has become a symbol of joy to military families, her daughters got excited, and that made now-3-year-old Alexander excited as well—and anxious to meet the parent he'd known only from the Webcam.

"Their Only Memory Is War"

Adrianne Hakes remembers growing up during World War II and the air raid drills that enveloped her hometown of Studio City, Calif. She remembers the darkened windows and the streetlights that gave off a muted yellow glow instead of the bright white light of today. Back then, everyone knew there was a war going on, and everyone was involved. But not now.

"I can go through my daily activities and not give a thought to it," says Hakes, a school board member for the Oceanside Unified School District near the Marine Base at Camp Pendleton. "But for our military families, this is a reality every day of their lives."

Three of Oceanside's elementary schools are located on Camp Pendleton, and the school board has been studying ways to ease transitions for the typically mobile military child. "Just being a military child is stressful," Hakes says, "but having the war is more."

She said deployment is a three-part process, each with its own stressors. There is the anxiety of waiting for the family member to be deployed, the adjustment to life during the parent's absence, and another adjustment when he or she returns. A lot can happen to a family over 12 or 15 months. Children change, take on new responsibilities, and may not relate to their parents as they did when they were younger. This can be stressful and confusing for both the returning parent and the rest of the family.

School can be a place of comfort during wartime. Hakes described a first-grade class in which the teacher read the book *A Long, Long Time* about a parent in the military. Children who thought they were alone realized there were other classmates going through the same thing.

"They each thought they were by themselves," Hakes says. "It was a very poignant moment for the children."

She adds: "There are children in school who were 2 when this war started. Their only memory is war. They don't know anything but war."

"I Hope My Dad Doesn't Die in Iraq"

At Santa Margarita School on Camp Pendleton, 100 percent of the students are children of active duty military personnel, some in the Navy, but most in the Marines. Principal Pat Kurtz says the atmosphere is different than at other schools.

"Just the stress. The stress is just enormous," Kurtz says. "The children really are emotional. And, as anyone would be when there's this kind of stress, they sometimes lose it."

At the same time, Kurtz says she's "always in awe that they handle the stress as well as they do." There are no more discipline problems at Santa Margarita than at most schools, and the students are close to one another. When teachers and administrators do have to discipline students, they try to do so with reason and compassion.

There are many activities to do during lunch and recess. A Japanese club meets in one room (many children's families had been based in Okinawa). There's a Chess Club and a Spirit Club and just quiet spaces to be alone and read. In one class students gather to play LEGOs while the teacher does prep work. ("He's got the mother lode of LEGOs," Kurtz says.)

Kurtz and her staff see their work as a calling and their school as a sanctuary for military children. "As I see it," she says, "we can provide our little piece of patriotism, contribute something to make the families' lives a little better."

Chris Woodard teaches first grade at Santa Margarita. She says the stress level is higher than at the schools "in town." Children sometimes have trouble paying attention, following directions, and getting along with one another.

"'I hope my dad doesn't die in Iraq'—this is something my kids write in their journals," Woodard says.

And yet, she adds, "I'm just amazed that in my class my children operate at or above grade level, which is just, I think, a sign of their resilience."

The children are very interested in geography and want to know just where their parents are deployed. On one wall is a large chart that reads: "I'm a Military Child. My Military Parent is. . . ." The children put sticky tabs on the places, around the world, where they are stationed.

"We're Marines," Woodard says, "so we're based on ships, or headed toward Iraq, or training here." Of her 18 students, nine have a parent who is either on a ship headed toward Iraq, or in Iraq. "That's half my class. It's coming and going time here at Camp Pendleton. We're in transition."

Even on the base, the children are reminded of the conflicts, Kurtz says. They see helicopter flyovers and hear gunfire from the shooting range.

"We're very much children of the wars."

LAWRENCE HARDY (lhardy@nsba.org) is a senior editor of *American School Board Journal.*

A Divided House

In an era of bitter divorce battles, parents often use children as hammers to bash each other, manipulating not only the legal system but also their children's affections. Can a broken parent-child bond be restored?

Mark Teich

In 1978, after Cathy Mannis and her future husband moved into the same cooperative at U.C. Berkeley, they ran into each other often. She was not immediately smitten. "I detested him at first, and I should have stayed with that feeling," recalls Cathy Mannis of her now ex-husband. "He was overweight and always very critical. Then he lost weight, became cuter, and started paying attention to me. He was going to be a doctor and he seemed so trustworthy; he said he would never desert his family as his own father had done to him." They started dating, and she ultimately cared for him enough to marry him. "I thought he'd be a good father, and I was dying to be a mother. I thought we'd have a good life."

She worked full-time as a legal secretary to put him through medical school. She also bought the two of them a town house with money she'd saved before marriage. When she gave birth to a boy, Matt (not his real name), she was as happy as she'd ever been. Over time, she saw signs that her husband was cheating on her, but she always forgave him.

Their second son, Robby, was born autistic, and things went downhill fast. The boy had speech and learning problems and was frequently out of control. Her husband was appalled. "He's dumber than a fish," he said.

Still, they had one more child, Harry (the name has been changed), hoping to give Matt a sibling without Robby's problems. Harry turned out normal, but he bonded most closely with Robby; they became inseparable.

When Cathy once again became convinced her husband was cheating—he inexplicably never came home one night—she finally threw him out. He filed for divorce before she could forgive him again.

Cathy was granted primary custody of the kids, and her ex soon married the woman he'd been seeing on the side. Because of all she had to do to help Robby as well as her other two kids, Cathy could no longer hold a full-time job. Meanwhile, her ex declared two bankruptcies and, at one point, even mental disability, all of which kept alimony payments to a trickle.

Eventually Cathy was so broke that her electricity was turned off; she and the boys ate dinner by candlelight. Then she became so ill she had to be hospitalized for life-threatening surgery. She had no choice but to leave the kids with her ex. "He promised to return them when my health and finances improved," she says.

That was almost seven years ago. Her health has long since returned and she has a good job she can do from home, but the only child ever restored to her, despite nonstop court battles, was Robby. In fact, her ex got the courts to rule that the children should be permanently separated, leaving the other two children with him, since Robby was a "threat" to his younger brother's well-being.

Through all those years, Cathy says she faced a campaign of systematic alienation from Matt and Harry. "When I called to speak to them, I was usually greeted with coldness or anger, and often the boys weren't brought to the phone. Then my ex sent letters warning me not to call them at home at all. Whenever the kids came to stay with me, they'd report, 'Dad says you're evil. He says you wrecked the marriage.'" Then he moved thousands of miles away, making it vastly more difficult for her to see her children.

As time has passed, the boys have increasingly pulled away. Matt, now grown and serving in the military, never speaks to Cathy. Thirteen-year-old Harry used to say, "Mommy, why can't I stay with you? All the other kids I know live with their moms," before leaving visits with her. Now he often appears detached from her and uninterested in Robby, whom he once adored. His friends at his new home think his stepmother is his mom, because that's how she introduces herself. "She told me she would take my kids, and she did. The alienation is complete," rues Cathy. "All I ever wanted was to be a mom."

Divorcing parents have long bashed each other in hopes of winning points with kids. But today, the strategy of blame encompasses a psychological concept of parental alienation that is increasingly used—and misused—in the courts.

On the one hand, with so many contentious divorces, parents like Cathy Mannis have been tragically alienated from the children they love. On the other hand, parental alienation has been seized as a strategic tool in custody fights, its effects exploited in the courtroom, often to the detriment of loving parents protecting children from true neglect or abuse. With the impact of alienation so devastating—and false accusations so prevalent—it may take a judge with the wisdom of Solomon to differentiate between the two faces of alienation: a truly toxic parent and his or her victimized children versus manipulation of the legal system to claim damage where none exists.

> **The maligning of an ex need not be conscious—or even particularly extreme—to inflict lasting damage on a parent-child relationship.**

A Symptom of Our Time?

Disturbed by the potential for alienation, many divorce courts have today instituted aggressive steps to intervene where they once just stood by. And with good reason: Alienation is ruinous to all involved. "In pathological or irrational alienation, the parent has done nothing to deserve that level of hatred or rejection from the child," explains University of Texas psychologist Richard Warshak, author of *Divorce Poison: Protecting the Parent-Child Bond from a Vindictive Ex.* "It often seems to happen almost overnight, and neither the rejected parent nor even the rejecting child understands why."

Often, in fact, it's the emotionally healthier parent who gets rejected, Warshak adds. That parent tends to understand that it's not in the child's best interests to lose the other parent. In contrast, the alienating parent craves revenge against the ex—then uses the child to exact that punishment. "It's a form of abuse," Warshak says. "Both parent and child are victims."

The alienating parent could vilify the ex to rationalize the dissolution of the relationship, explains Atlanta family therapist Frank Pittman, M.D. "Even though they managed to stay married to that person for 10 or 15 years, they now see him or her as the devil's spawn. It's the only way they can justify the breakup of their marriage, because otherwise, it would be their own fault." Once they've convinced themselves of that, it's easy enough to see why their children should be kept away from the other parent.

The maligning of an ex need not be conscious—or even particularly extreme—to inflict lasting damage on a parent-child relationship. "The child can hear negative comments inadvertently," notes Diane McSweeney, a marriage, family, and child counselor for the San Diego Unified School District. "Mom is on the phone with a friend, or Dad is talking to his girlfriend and the child happens to hear negative things. I don't think most people mean to insult the other parent to the child, but they're caught up in their grief for their failed marriage and don't appreciate that the kid can hear everything."

Alienation is especially damaging when one parent can't contain the anger—Mom cheated, or Dad hasn't visited or paid child support—and the wounded parent starts venting to the child. "They're just so desperate to talk to someone, and there's no one else they trust left to talk to. They would never do that to

---

Divorce without Devastating the Kids

Clearly, some parents—those who are physically or emotionally abusive—should be separated from their children. But these are the rarity, and in virtually all other cases, children would do better if their divorced parents stayed amicable partners in raising them. To keep a divorce as healthy as possible for children, follow these rules:

- **Never put** the other parent down. Divorce uproots children's feelings of stability badly enough—trashing or eliminating one of the parents magnifies the instability exponentially.
- **Rather than using** kids as a sounding board, divorced parents who are struggling with each other should seek outside emotional help.
- **Hold any charged** or volatile discussions far out of earshot of the children.
- **Do everything in** your power to accept your ex's next mate, since this person will also play an important role in your child's future stability and happiness.

Parents Who Alienate May Use the Following Tactics

- **Limiting the time** a child can spend with the other parent, and even violating court-ordered visitation schedules.
- **Making false** or unfounded accusations of neglect or abuse, especially in a legal forum. The most damaging expression of this is the false accusation of sexual abuse.
- **Creating fear** of rejection and threatening to withhold affection should the child express positive feelings about the absent parent.
- **Saying negative things** about the other parent in front of or within earshot of the child.
- **Blaming the other** parent for the collapse of the marriage.
- **Moving far away,** making it difficult for the other parent to have a regular relationship with a child.

---

their child in any other situation, but now they are in no shape or form ready to parent," says McSweeney. "The child is then thrown into confusion, feeling the need to take sides. 'I love Mom, but Mom hates Dad, so how can I love them both?' Or, 'I'll make Dad mad if I keep loving Mom, so I have to choose him over her.' "

"I was an adolescent when my parents were divorced," recalls Michelle Martin. "You were either on my mother's side or against her, and if you were on her side, you had to be against my father. She was so angry at him for walking out on her, felt so much shame and betrayal, that you couldn't possibly have a relationship with him if you wanted one with her."

Decades later, Michelle recalls her father (who has since died) as a gentle, caring man. But from the moment he left, her mother systematically worked to convince her that he had been abusive. "She really could not have portrayed him more negatively. 'How can you love him?' she'd say. 'You can't count on him.' He'd call, and she'd tell him my siblings and I didn't want to talk to him, then she'd tell me he didn't want to talk with us."

Afraid to lose her mother's love on top of having had her father walk out, Michelle ended up buying the brainwashing. Eventually, her father married another woman and moved away. At first he came into town regularly to visit, but the ever-renewing hostility gradually became too much for him, and the visits became few and far between.

Her father's reluctance to criticize her mother allowed Michelle's misconceptions to continue unabated, keeping up the walls her mother had created between them. It wasn't until she was 17 that her father finally said to her, " 'You know, a lot of the things you've been told about me were untrue.' It was instantly eye-opening." By her early twenties she'd reconnected with her father, but they only had about 15 years together; he died when she was 38. "I'd lost all those years with a wonderful man, as well as with the members of his family that I loved."

Strategies of War

There's another side to the alienation phenomenon: the hard-edged legal one. Although it is a psychological issue, parental alienation can be truly addressed only in the legal system. Remedy for alienation, say experts, requires an order from a court to allow a manipulated child time to bond with the alienated parent. It is critical, therefore, that there be proof that alienation has in fact occurred. If a parent seeking custody can document the phenomenon, the system—if it is working—will adjust a custody arrangement to promote relationship repair.

The courts worked fairly for Larry Felton, an orthodontist in Detroit (identifying details changed). His wife, an architect who had put her career on hold to raise their daughter, Emily, left Larry and later divorced him. Immersed in his practice, he settled for the once a week plus every other weekend visits the court imposed. "I was devoted and determined to make it work. I wasn't going to let anything keep me from having a relationship with my daughter," he says.

But when Emily grew older and he asked for a little more time with her, things turned ugly. By unilateral decree of his ex, he stopped getting even the limited time that was his due. By the time the court got involved, Emily had grown distant and withdrawn, blaming him for all that had happened. She resisted seeing him at all.

He might have lost his bid for more time with his daughter if not for a key piece of evidence. His ex called to tell him she was canceling yet another weekend with Emily. Then, thinking

she'd disconnected the phone when she had not, she said to the daughter and Felton's answering machine, "Your father is evil, a bad man, but we need him for his money. At least he's good for that."

After hearing the tape, the judge awarded primary custody to Larry in hopes of reversing the alienation that had been ongoing for years. Seven years later, 17-year-old Emily has reaped the benefits. Though it took time to earn her trust back, her father now has a solid relationship with her, and her time with her mother is more positive. "I think it saved her," Felton says.

Things are hardly ever so clear-cut in court. Often, judges don't have access to proof like Felton's incriminating voice mail. In the end, after listening to expert witnesses from both sides, decisions are often based on impressions and even the testimony of the children, the very ones who are brainwashed and may be least reliable of all.

"Even when a judge acknowledges that alienation occurred, the court can end up siding with the alienating parent because of the child's wishes," Warshak says. "Otherwise, they fear, the child in his anger might hurt himself or someone else."

In fact, it takes a sophisticated judge to realize what psychologists might see as obvious: Deep down, the child has never really stopped loving the other parent. He or she has just been brainwashed like a prisoner of war or a cult victim, programmed to accept destructive beliefs until critical thinking can be restored.

"Even if they say they don't want to see the parent, underneath they might be longing to reconnect," says Warshak. "These kids need more time with that parent rather than less. Only then will they have a chance to see that the poisoned thoughts are wrong." In the most extreme cases, children are permitted to see the alienating parent only during therapy sessions until the alienation has been resolved.

Other times judges listen mostly to the parent who says he or she has been wronged—and that too can be misleading. According to John E. B. Myers, a professor of law at the University of the Pacific McGeorge School of Law in Sacramento, California, false accusations of parental alienation do "tremendous harm to many children and their parents, particularly mothers seeking custody in family court."

According to Myers, fathers accused of sexual or other abuse by mothers often hide under the protective mantle of "parental alienation" in court, pitting accusation against accusation. The alleged alienator may be dismissed as manipulative, an assumption not always representing truth. The charge could paint a protective parent as a liar trying to poison a child instead of keeping him from harm.

University of California at Davis law professor Carol Bruch adds that the theory of parental alienation fails to account for the anger often felt by children of divorce, especially the kind of contentious divorce that results in custody fights in the first place. "Sometimes the child's feelings are prompted by the behavior of the noncustodial parent. That parent may not be abusive, but just deficient in some way. A parent can become estranged from a child without any provocation whatsoever from the other parent."

The estranged parent could accuse the custodial parent of alienating behavior through blindness to his or her own role.

It takes a sophisticated judge to realize what psychologists might see as obvious: that deep down, the child has never stopped loving the other parent.

Loss and Repair

With knowledgeable experts and astute judges, real alienation can be discerned from false accusations. When alienation is accurately recognized, appropriate intervention on the part of the court can certainly help families heal the damage.

Without the right intervention, however, the result is a scenario of loss and unresolved grief like that of Cathy Mannis. Ironically it is Robby, Cathy's autistic son, who is most acutely in touch with his pain.

"What his father did, first trying to institutionalize him as dangerous, then separating him from his brothers, gave him a devastating signal that he was not worthy, that he deserved punishment rather than help and love," explains Stephen Stahl, MD, PhD, Robby's psychiatrist and a professor of psychiatry at the University of California at San Diego.

Now 18, Robby feels rejected by both his father and his younger brother, both of whom have very little to do with him anymore. "My father never cared about me, so I don't care about him anymore," he says. "But I loved being with Harry every day and every night. I try to call him a lot, but my stepmom is often mean to me or hangs up on me. I almost never get to see him, and he doesn't call. It all makes me so sad."

Parents' grief is also profound. "The child is alive but still lost to you, so close but yet so far, there but not seeing you, and you're uncertain if you'll ever have the relationship back again," Warshak says. "You can't grieve the final loss, because you can never accept that it's final."

As for Cathy Mannis, she recently had Harry with her in San Diego for a one-week court-ordered visit. She and Robby were both thrilled to have the chance to reconnect with him. But as wonderful as that week was, it only set Mannis up for further heartbreak. "He left on Sunday," she says, "and I won't see him again for four months."

MARK TEICH is a writer in Stamford, CT.

Civil Wars

Psychologists who work as parenting coordinators help moms and dads keep the peace.

CHRISTOPHER MUNSEY

Research suggest that it's not divorce in itself that most harms children, but the tension between divorcing parents, some of whom repeatedly appear before judges to battle over drop-off times or visitation rights.

One review of studies in *Children and Divorce,* for example (Vol. 4, No. 1, pages 165–182), found that children whose parents bitterly fight over divorces scored as significantly more disturbed on standardized measures of maladjustment.

"In a lot of these cases, the individual parents 'parent' fine. It's when they interface that all hell breaks loose," says Matt Sullivan, PhD, a Santa Clara, Calif., psychologist, who works with many divorcing clients.

But help is at hand: Through the growing practice area of parenting coordination, psychologists are helping feuding parents call a truce, communicate and work out their disagreements with the goal of better-adjusted children and less-burdened courts.

"It can be helpful for parents to have someone who can help them work out how they're going to keep conflict away from the kids, and help them focus on what the kids need, as opposed to what's going on between the two of them," says Judge Judith Bartnoff of the District of Columbia Superior Court, who has seen the benefits of parenting coordination in several custody disputes.

With their communication skills, psychologists are uniquely qualified for parenting coordination, says Robin Deutsch, PhD, of Harvard Medical School who has served in the role and provided training as well. "Psychologists can help people stuck in ineffective communication patterns learn to communicate better," she says. "It's the bread and butter of what [we] know how to do."

A Growing Field

Parenting coordination typically starts with a court-ordered parenting agreement establishing a detailed custody schedule, with exact drop-off and pickup times listed, plus arrangements for vacations and holidays. When a dispute arises—such as which sport a child should play—the parenting coordinator can step in, halt the angry back-and-forth between the parents and gather feedback from all parties involved.

Besides hearing from the adults involved, a parenting coordinator pays close attention to the child's needs. After gathering the different perspectives, the coordinator—depending on the state where the parents live—either makes the decision, or recommends a solution.

Eight states have passed laws setting up parenting coordination procedures since 1989: Minnesota, Oklahoma, Idaho, Oregon, Colorado, Texas, Louisiana and North Carolina. Meanwhile, a number of other states rely on existing laws that give judges leeway to appoint parenting coordinators (see sidebar).

Demanding Work

Sullivan and co-author Karl Kirkland, PhD, recently completed a survey of 54 parenting coordinators. They found that 44 percent of the responding parenting coordinators were licensed psychologists. Other mental health professionals such as master's level social workers and licensed professional counselors also do the work, with attorneys forming the third-largest share.

For all the different ways parenting coordination is carried out, psychologists say common issues arise for practitioners who move into the area of practice: chiefly, the need for balance, and avoiding falling into dual roles, Deutsch says. Parenting coordinators can't become therapists to their clients, and they have to make decisions fairly, Deutsch says.

"Maintaining impartiality is very important," she says.

From a practitioner's perspective, parenting coordination can be lucrative, without the hassle of third-party payers. In most cases, parents pay the parenting coordinator on a fee-for-service basis, says Sullivan, adding that many coordination agreements spell out the hourly cost of the service, how

State by State

Here's a snapshot of how parenting coordination works and is developing in several states and the District of Columbia:

- **California:** If both parents agree, a judge can appoint a parenting coordinator, using a statute already on the books. Called "special masters," these coordinators make legally binding decisions when disputes arise between parents.

- **Maryland:** Although efforts are under way to draft legislation to define parenting coordination, judges in several Maryland counties began turning to parenting coordinators several years ago, says Paul Berman, PhD, a psychologist who also serves as the professional affairs officer for the Maryland Psychological Association. If both parties sign off, the judge can name a parenting coordinator once a child custody order has been signed.

  In his work, Berman is empowered to decide what's best, presenting his decision in writing to both parents.

- **Massachusetts:** Legislation establishing a parent coordination program hasn't moved out of committee in the state legislature in the past two years, but judges do appoint parenting coordinators, says parenting coordinator Robin Deutsch, PhD, relying on their traditional discretion to take action in the best interest of children. If both parents agree, the state allows judges to appoint a parenting coordinator at the time of divorce to help resolve disputes that the parties can't resolve on their own.

- **District of Columbia:** As part of a pilot project of APA, Argosy University, the D.C. Bar and the D.C. Superior Court, family law judges can appoint a licensed clinical psychologist as a special master, who works in a team format with advanced doctoral students from Argosy University in Washington, D.C., to provide parent coordinator services to caregivers who otherwise couldn't afford it, says Giselle Hass, PsyD, an associate professor at Argosy who serves as clinical director for the program.

  Besides helping caregivers learn to communicate effectively with each other, the students can help connect them with resources for themselves and their children, Hass says. Those resources might include helping arrange the evaluation of a child for a possible developmental disability, referring a caregiver for treatment of a mental health issue or helping connect with free legal help.

- **Texas:** Under a state statute, a judge can order a parenting coordinator to get involved if parents agree or if there is evidence of high conflict. However, Texas parenting coordinators do not have authority to make decisions, says Lynelle Yingling, a marriage and family therapist in Rockwall, Texas. Instead, parenting coordinators talk with both parents and help parents develop solutions, Yingling says.

—C. Munsey

---

the parents will split the costs, and what happens if fees go unpaid. Some programs offer pro[[check]] bono parenting coordination to low-income parents, such as one based in Washington, D.C.

The work is also attractive to many psychologists because of its flexible scheduling. And the field is growing, as more judges turn to the idea of using parenting coordinators to help defuse the most problematic cases, several observers say.

It can be very demanding though, judging from the comments of several psychologists experienced in parenting coordination. Getting in the middle of disputes where the parties are often very angry at each other requires a thick skin.

"It's just tough work," says Sullivan. "These are difficult people to work with." He adds that having a "directive, take-charge" personality helps a psychologist succeed as a parenting coordinator. "It takes a particular brand of psychologist to fit this role."

APA's Pilot Parenting Coordination Program

An APA-initiated program enables family law judges in Washington, D.C., to appoint licensed clinical psychologists as special masters who work with Argosy University doctoral students to smooth out disputes between caregivers. Since the program started in January 2005, parenting coordinators have handled 19 cases.

In June, APA's Practice Directorate honored several people who consulted on and helped develop the program including APA's Shirley Ann Higuchi, JD; Dr. Robert Barrett, of the American School of Professional Psychology at Argosy University—Washington, D.C., campus; Judge Judith Bartnoff of the District of Columbia Superior Court; and Dr. Bruce Copeland, formerly of Washington, D.C.

—C. Munsey

Stepfamily Success Depends on Ingredients

One in three Americans is part of a stepfamily, each with its own flavor. How can psychologists help them thrive?

Tori DeAngelis

If Tolstoy were alive today, he might have penned his famous line like this: Happy families are all alike—and every stepfamily is complex in its own way.

Take one example. If a stepparent is frequently battling his former spouse, research shows that his children suffer. But if he is *close* with his ex-partner, his new spouse may feel anxious and insecure. On top of this, say experts, many children don't view their stepparents as "real parents" for the first few years—if ever—and parents in second marriages may treat their biological children differently from their stepchildren.

"Stepparents once were viewed as 'replacing' biological parents, thus recreating a two-parent family," notes University of Virginia (UVA) psychology professor Robert E. Emery, PhD, author of *The Truth about Children and Divorce: Dealing with the Emotions So You and Your Children Can Thrive* (Viking/Penguin, 2004). "Economically, there may be some truth to this, but psychologically, that is not the reality. Remarriage and stepparenting are new, tricky transitions for children, the stepparent and the biological parents."

Fortunately, researchers and clinicians today better understand the common pitfalls of such "blended" families and how they can overcome them. That's important because one in three of us is a member of a stepfamily, according to the Stepfamily Association of America, and that number is likely to grow as traditional family bonds grow more fragile. The demographics of stepfamilies are as complex as the psychological ones: About a quarter are headed by unmarried parents, for example, and stepfamilies make up the full spectrum of our nation's citizens, according to the association.

The Role of Children

Given the complexity of the subject matter, researchers and clinicians are looking at stepfamilies through many lenses. A major one is via the children, who often suffer the most through divorce, remarriage and stepfamily situations. They are particularly at-risk if their biological parents are in conflict

(see box, next page), the divorce situation is protracted, they receive less parenting after the divorce or they lose important relationships as a result of the divorce, according to a 2003 article in *Family Relations* (Vol. 52, No. 4, pages 352–362) by Emery of UVA and Joan B. Kelly, PhD, a psychologist and divorce expert in Corte Madeira, Calif.

> **"When the kids aren't happy, they'll say things like, 'I don't like your new husband—he's mean to me.' That creates conflict in the marriage. In a first-marriage family, if a kid says, 'I don't like my dad,' the mom says, 'So?'"**
>
> James H. Bray
> Baylor College of Medicine

Indeed, children of divorce—and later, remarriage—are twice as likely to academically, behaviorally and socially struggle as children of first-marriage families: About 20 to 25 percent struggle, compared with 10 percent, a range of research finds. They're also more likely to get divorced themselves, reports University of Utah sociologist Nicholas H. Wolfinger, PhD, in his book, *Understanding the Divorce Cycle* (Cambridge University Press, 2005). Adults whose parents divorced but didn't remarry are 45 percent more likely to divorce than adults whose parents never divorced, he notes, and 91 percent more likely to divorce if their parents divorced and remarried.

Furthermore, children often "calls the shots" on the emotional trajectory of family life, says psychologist and stepfamily expert James H. Bray, PhD, of the Baylor College of Medicine.

"When people get married for a second time, the biological parent really feels they need to attend to the kids," explains Bray, author with writer John Kelly of *Stepfamilies* (Broadway, 1998). "And when the kids aren't happy, they'll say things like,

Containing Conflict in Divorce Battles

As a parent coordinator who helps to resolve custody disputes in divorce cases, Bruce Copeland, PhD, JD, has seen his share of high-drama conflict.

"I had one case involving the father's infidelity with a close relative of the mother's," the Bethesda, Md., psychologist and attorney recalls. "You can imagine the level of intensity around that issue."

Despite the high-octane feelings between the couple, Copeland acted as a conduit so they could exchange information about their two young children. The process went well enough that six months later, "They were able to have a conversation, to make some decisions and to coordinate their children's care," he says.

Parent coordination–a growing niche for qualified psychologists (see the September 2004 *Monitor*)—addresses an important research finding: The level of conflict between parents is one of the key predictors of children's long-term adjustment following a divorce.

"Children in these cases are often caught in a tug of war," says Michelle Parker, PhD, a clinical psychologist and parent coordinator in Washington, D.C. "Much of the energy of the family is being diverted toward the conflict, which doesn't leave an appropriate level of energy and space for the children to grow and develop."

Parent coordinators are meant to help create that space. Unlike mediators and custody evaluators, they have, in many instances, quasi-judicial clout allowing them to make binding recommendations to the courts about parenting arrangements, even if the parents can't agree. Often their work centers on helping parents create specific, developmentally appropriate schedules and plans for their children and teaching them communication skills so they can eventually co-parent without intervention.

Because of the complexity of the work, parent coordinators need special backgrounds, including expertise in child psychology, dispute resolution, marital conflict and legal issues, says Copeland. They also need a solid emotional foundation, since their task is to remain neutral vis á vis the parents, while ensuring—and enforcing if necessary—that children receive the best possible arrangements.

"You need all your clinical skills and more," he says.

The role is gaining in importance, Copeland adds: Courts are calling in coordinators at increasingly early stages of the process to help contain conflict before it gets too toxic for children. Such early intervention also can serve a reporting function, he notes, where coordinators are able to give courts useful psychological information if the case ends up litigating.

—T. DeAngelis

Parenting Plans with Kids in Mind

Many courts still order a one-size-fits-all custody arrangement in which fathers see their children every other weekend, and mothers assume parenting duty the rest of the time.

However, psychological research suggests families fare better with individualized custody plans tailored to fit children's developmental stage and individual circumstances, as well as the particular relationship between children and their parents.

That research shows that children experience cookie-cutter plans as confusing and arbitrary, notes clinical psychologist and divorce expert Joan B. Kelly, PhD. Especially affected are children who have good relationships with their fathers and those so young they "have no cognitive capacity to understand why this abrupt decrease in their contact with the object of their affection occurred," she notes.

Other research she cites in a paper in press at the *Journal of the American Academy of Matrimonial Lawyers* finds that:

- About half of children want more contact with their noncustodial fathers than they have.
- Children are rarely asked about living arrangements, but when they are and their input is used, they report high levels of satisfaction with postdivorce living arrangements.
- Children whose fathers are more involved with them postdivorce generally do better socially, behaviorally and academically than those whose fathers are less involved.
- Children in joint-custody arrangements have better emotional, behavioral and general adjustment than those living only with their mother, according to a 2002 meta-analysis of 33 studies.

University of Virginia psychology professor Robert E. Emery, PhD, co-author with Kelly of a 2003 paper in *Family Relations* (Vol. 52, No. 4, pages 352–362) on children's postdivorce adjustment, puts some of these findings into concrete and user-friendly terms on his Web site at http://emeryondivorce.com/parenting_plans.php. Using a review of the developmental literature, Emery spells out specific custody schedules for children in six developmental periods from birth to 18 years old. He further separates them into categories for angry, distant and cooperative divorce situations.

Meanwhile, APA has embarked on a number of projects to aid the work of psychologists working in the child-custody area. These include collaborative ventures with a range of children-and-law organizations, including the Family Law Section of the American Bar Association (ABA), says Donna Beavers of APA's General Counsel's Office. APA and the ABA section have joined on a number of projects, including a successful joint conference on children, divorce and custody in 1997. Now, the two groups are establishing an interdisciplinary committee aiming to develop projects to ease child-custody conflict.

—T. DeAngelis

'I don't like your new husband—he's mean to me.' That creates conflict in the marriage. In a first-marriage family, if a kid says, 'I don't like my dad,' the mom says, 'So?'"

That said, UVA psychologist and professor emeritus E. Mavis Hetherington, PhD, found in a much-publicized 20-year study that the vast majority of children of divorce do well. As adults, many still feel pain and sadness when they think about their parents' divorce, but they still build productive and satisfied lives, and they don't experience clinical levels of depression, anxiety or other mental health disorders, Hetheringon concludes in her and writer John Kelly's book, *For Better or For Worse: Divorce Reconsidered* (Norton, 2002).

Fostering Resilience

Indeed, many researchers are focusing on these young people's resilience and how to build on it. Psychology professor Allen Israel, PhD, of the University at Albany of the State University of New York, for example, has been developing and evaluating a model of family stability that he believes has special relevance to children in divorce and stepfamily situations.

Family stability, he and his team are finding, isn't contingent on whether you live in a first-marriage, stepfamily or single-parent family, but more particularly on the environment that parents create for their kids, such as the presence of regular bed- and meal-time hours.

That's heartening, Israel believes, because it suggests intervention potential: "You can't always prevent the big things that are causing stress in these kids, such as parents moving or parents who have periods of low contact," he says. "But you might be able to affect the little things that are happening in the home."

In a related 2002 study in the *Journal of Marriage and Family* (Vol. 64, No. 4, pages 1,024–1,037), Kathleen Boyce Rodgers, PhD, a child and family studies researcher at Washington State University, found that outside influences like friends and neighbors can help youngsters undergoing such transitions cope better.

Analyzing data on 2,011 children and adolescents in first-marriage families, stepfamilies and single-parent divorced families, she found that teens who lived with a single, divorced parent and who said they received little support from that parent were less likely to have internalizing symptoms like depression, suicidal ideation and low self-esteem if they had a friend to count on.

In addition, Hetherington has found that consistency in school settings helps predict positive adjustment in children, especially when their home lives are chaotic.

Successful Stepfamilies

Bray examined factors that may predict stepfamilies' success in a nine-year, National Institute of Child Health and Human Development-funded study of 200 Texan stepfamilies and first-marriage families.

Classifying stepfamilies into categories of neotraditional, matriarchal and romantic, he found that neotraditional families fared the best. These parents formed a solid, committed partnership so they could not only nurture their marriage, but effectively raise their children. They didn't get stuck in unrealistic expectations of what the family should be like.

A Sea Change in Family Values?

Researchers consistently find that children of divorce do as well as their nondivorced peers on academic, social and behavioral measures.

But what about their internal lives? And how will their experiences shape their future family choices?

In a March paper in the *Journal of Sociology* (Vol. 4, No. 1, pages 69–86), Katie Hughes, PhD, a senior lecturer in the department of communication, culture and languages at Victoria University in Melbourne, Australia, explores those questions via in-depth interviews with 31 gen Xers, ages 29 to 44–all children of divorced parents who grew up in single-parent or stepfamily homes.

These young adults demonstrated:

- An emphasis on individual growth, as opposed to a family or couple focus. "They argue very strongly that personal and intimate relationships are about personal growth," Hughes notes. "They've almost completely replaced old-fashioned notions about gender roles, obligation and duty, and sticking to things, with notions of self-actualization."
- The willingness to abandon a relationship if it turns sour or is not promoting growth.
- The use of subliminal "exit strategies," such as deciding not to have children or declining to pool resources with one's partner.

When Hughes probed the interviewees on their transient views of relationships, many expressed a strong belief that all relationships would inevitably end.

"That's where the divorce patterns kick in," she notes, "because people from intact families don't have that belief."

Reasons they held this notion, interviewees told her, included their own bad memories about their parents' breakup, and their observations that if their parents did remarry, their second marriages often were happier than their first, Hughes says.

While Hughes' study lacks a control group, her subjects' demographics parallel the quantitative literature on children of divorce, she notes. In her sample, 36 percent lived alone, 18 percent cohabited only with a partner, 10 percent lived in stepfamilies and 15 percent lived in shared-house arrangements, she notes.

—T. DeAngelis

Relatively successful were matriarchal families, headed by strong, independent women who remarried not to gain a parenting partner, but a companion. While their husbands were devoted to these women, the men had fairly distant relationships with the children, Bray found.

Matriarchal families functioned well except in parenting matters, Bray found. Conflicts arose, he says, either when the men decided they wanted to play a greater role in parenting—in which case the women were loathe to relinquish their parenting power—or when the women decided they wanted their partners to get more involved. In one common scenario, the woman asked her husband for parenting help but he prevaricated. "She'd ask him to pick up the kids, for example, and he'd forget," Bray says. "That created a lot of conflict."

Romantic families were the most divorce-prone, Bray found. Couples in these families had unrealistic expectations, wanting to immediately create the perfect family atmosphere, and they took their stepchildren's ambivalent reactions to the family transition personally instead of seeing them as normal reactions to a stressful situation.

Tips for Clinicians

Bray and others also have put their heads to creating research-based clinical suggestions for those working with stepfamilies (Bray's suggestions, called "Making Stepfamilies Work," are summarized at www.apahelpcenter.org/articles/article.php?id=41).

These include encouraging second-marriage parents to:

- Discuss and decide on finances before getting married.
- Build a strong marital bond "because it will benefit everybody," says Bray.

- Develop a parenting plan, which likely will involve having the stepparent play a secondary, nondisciplinary role for the first year or two. "Otherwise, even if you're doing a good job, the children will rebuff you," he says.

Family psychologist Anne C. Bernstein, PhD, author of *Yours, Mine and Ours: How Families Change When Remarried Parents Have a Child Together* (W.W. Norton, 1990), additionally advises parents to:

- Take time to process each transition.
- Make sure that big changes are communicated adult-to-adult, not via the children.
- Work with therapists who are specially trained in step-family dynamics.

Finally, parents in these families need to "take the long view," Emery advises. "You're going to be a parent forever," he says. "For the sake of the kids, you want to at least make that a working relationship."

TORI DEANGELIS is a writer in Syracuse, N.Y.

UNIT 5

Families, Now and into the Future

Unit Selections

Key Points to Consider

- What changes do you see yourself making in your life? How would you go about gathering the information you need to make these decisions?

- What role does spirituality play in the life of your family?

- What is the state of rituals in your family? What rituals might you build in your family? Why? How might you use family gatherings and other traditions to build family integration?

Student Website

www.mhcls.com

Internet References

National Institute on Aging
http://www.nih.gov/nia/

*W*hat is the future of the family? Does the family even have a future? These questions and others like them are being asked. Many people fear for the future of the family. As previous units of this volume have shown, the family is a continually evolving institution that will continue to change throughout time. Still, certain elements of family appear to be constant. The family is and will remain a powerful influence in the lives of its members. This is because we all begin life in some type of family, and this early exposure carries a great deal of weight in forming our social selves—who we are and how we relate to others. From our families, we take our basic genetic makeup, while we also learn and are reinforced in health behaviors. In families, we are given our first exposure to values, and it is through families that we most actively influence others. Our sense of commitment and obligation begins within the family as well as our sense of what we can expect of others.

Much that has been written about families has been less than hopeful and has focused on ways of avoiding or correcting errors. The five articles in this unit take a positive view of family and how it influences its members. The emphasis is on health rather than dysfunction.

Knowledge is the basic building block of intelligent decisions regarding family relationships. Information is important in planning for our family's future. One way to gather this information is through interviews, and "Get a Closer Look" explains just how this can be done. Family rituals are examined as being a powerful force for family cohesion and change, and the nature of family rituals is described in "The Joy of Rituals" and "Sustaining Resilient Families for Children in Primary Grades." Families are changing their approach to spending, as Michael Mandel attests in "The Consumer Crunch." Finally, leisure activities and time spent in nature can strengthen families, according to "Sparking Interest in Nature—Family Style."

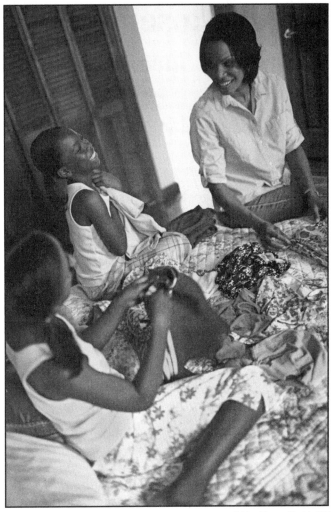

© Max Power/Corbis RF

Get a Closer Look
12 Tips for Successful Family Interviews

IRA WOLFMAN

How do you get relatives talking? A good family history interview isn't easy to conduct. You need to combine the best attributes of caring friend, hard-nosed reporter, and sensitive psychologist. But do it well and you may be rewarded with wonderful stories.

Interviews are different from normal conversations. One person has a goal: to get information from another person (let's call him or her the "talker"). You want the talker to feel comfortable, but you also need to direct the conversation to the points you are interested in.

You also have to be flexible. Sometimes an unexpected topic can turn out to be wonderful. Other times you'll need to lead your talker back to the main point—without hurting his or her feelings. This can be difficult, but you will become better at it as you go along—practice will make you skilled. Be patient with yourself and expect some mistakes. To make things easier, keep these tips in mind:

1. Before any interview, give advance warning. Explain what you want to do, why you want to do it, and why the talker is important to you and your research. You can call or write a letter or e-mail. Here's an example of the kinds of things you should say:

Dear Aunt Gus:

I'm working on a history of our family, and it would be very helpful if I could sit down and talk with you. I'm particularly interested in your memories of my great-grandparents (your mother and father) and the family's early years in Minnesota. I'd also love to look at any old photographs or documents you have.

I won't need much more than an hour of your time and would like to hold our talk at your home. Any weekend day would be fine. Can you let me know a date that is convenient for you?

Thanks so much for your help.

By writing this letter, you've given your relative a chance to start thinking about the topics you're interested in, and you may have even jogged her memory. Of course, not all your relatives will be close by, and your arrangements may be more difficult than "any weekend day." That just makes your writing—and planning—even more important.

2. Prepare before your interview. Find out whatever you can about the talker *before* the interview. Where does she fit in the family? What documents might she have? What other genealogical jewels might she have?

Gather as much information as you can ahead of time about her relationship to everyone in your family. Your parents can probably help you with this.

3. Think out all your questions beforehand. Interviewing requires structure. Write your questions on a sheet of paper, organized by subject. One easy way to organize what you want to ask is by year: Start with your relative's earliest years and then move on from there.

"So, Aunt Gus, you lived in the house in a town outside Minneapolis till you were 10—about 1922, right? Then where did you move?" Or "You say Great-grandpa worked as a tailor in St. Paul. Did you ever visit his shop? Where was it? What years did he have the business there?" As this interviewer did, it's a good idea to summarize what you already know so that your subject can verify your facts. Then move on to a request for more detail.

Sometimes the simplest questions can hit the jackpot. I asked my great-uncle Max, "How old were you when you went from Poland to America?" I didn't get an answer; I got a story:

I must have been about 15 when I went to Warsaw to get a visa to emigrate. I got the visa, but then the counselor at the examination said, "Listen, boy, you are underage. You can't go without your father." He crossed out my stamp.

I went back to our town and told my father. He said, "Don't worry, we'll take care of that."

My father was a religious man, but he also knew how to get things done. He called a policeman from our town and asked him to make me older.

Ready, Set, Research . . .
Your Family Tree

- Interview your parents about their family history. Practice interviewing with them.
- Make appointments to interview other family members.
- Prepare your questions. (For a list of good questions for family interviews, see www.workmen.com/familytree.)
- Type up your notes from interviews. Ask the relatives you interviewed to review them and correct or add to them.
- Write a thank-you note to every family member you interviewed.

I got new papers. Now I turned from 15 to 18 or 19. I went back to Warsaw, and I was able to leave. And on February 20, 1920, I took the boat Susquehanna *from Danzig to New York.*

Remember to also ask open-ended questions. "What do you remember most about the apartment on Division Street?" or "Tell me about your relationship with your brothers" may yield something unexpected and wonderful.

4. Bring a video or tape recorder if possible.
A small tape recorder usually doesn't disturb anyone, and it catches every bit of information, including the way your talkers sound and exactly how they answer questions. If you plan to videotape, be sure someone comes with you to run the camera. You need to focus on your talker.

5. In any case, bring a notebook and a pen.
Even if you have [an audio tape or video] recorder, always take handwritten notes. Recorders can break down.

During the interview, write down names and dates and double-check them with your subject. Facts are important, but the most important information your talkers offer are their stories. Try to capture the way they talk and their colorful expressions: "That ship was rolling on the ocean like a marble in your hand."

There's another good reason to bring pen and paper with you. You won't have to interrupt when you think of a question; just write a note to yourself so you'll remember to ask it at an appropriate time.

6. Start with easy, friendly questions.
Leave the more difficult or emotional material for later in the interview, after you've had time to gain your talker's trust. If things aren't going well, you may want to save those questions for another time.

It's also a good idea to begin with questions about the person you're interviewing. You may be more interested in a great-grandfather if he is the missing link in your family chart. But first get some background information about your talker—your aunt, for example. This serves two purposes. First, it lets her know she's important to you, that you care about her, and that her life is interesting, too. Second, as she talks, she may reveal some other information that you would never have known about otherwise.

7. Bring family photographs with you.
Look for photos, artwork, or documents that will help jog your subject's memory. Bring the pictures out and ask your talker to describe what's going on. "Do you remember when this was taken? Who are the people? What was the occasion? Who do you think took the picture?" You may be amazed at how much detail your relative will see in a photograph and also at the memories that come spilling forth.

8. Don't be afraid of silence.
You might feel uneasy and want to rush in with another question when your talker stops speaking. *Don't.* Silence is an important part of interviewing and can sometimes yield to interesting results. Because people often find silence uncomfortable, they often try to fill it if you don't—and in doing so, they may say something you might not have heard otherwise.

Sometimes silence is also necessary for gathering thoughts. Don't forget—you are asking your subjects to think back on things they may not have considered for years. Calling up these memories may spark other thoughts, too. Allow your subject time to ponder. You may be thrilled by what he or she remembers.

9. Ask the same question in different ways.
People don't know how much they know, and rephrasing a question can give you more information. This happens all the time. "I don't know," a relative will tell you, sometimes impatiently. They do know—they just don't know that they know. The most common version of this occurs when an interviewer asks, "What was your father's mother's name?" The relative answers, "I never knew her. I don't know." Then a few minutes later, in response to "Whom were you named after?" this answer comes; "My father's mother."

Try to find a couple of ways to ask important questions. You may feel like you're being repetitive, but you never can be sure what you will learn.

10. Be sensitive to what you discover.
Sometimes people become emotional talking about the past. They may remember long-dead relatives or once-forgotten tragedies. If your talker is upset by a memory, either remain silent or quietly ask, "Is it all right if we talk some more about this? Or would you rather not?" People frequently feel better when they talk about sad things; you should gently give your relative the *choice* of whether or not to go on.

11. Try not to interrupt.
If your talker strays from the subject, let him or her finish the story and then say, "Let's get back to Uncle Moe" or "You said something earlier about . . . " By not interrupting, you make the conversation friendlier, and the story may lead you to something you didn't expect.

Of course, there is always the exception to the rule. If a story goes on forever and seems useless, the best way to handle it may be to say, "Gee, Aunt Gus, could you hold the rest of that story for later? I'd like to get the facts out of the way and then come back to that."

12. Ask for songs, poems, unusual memories.
You may discover something wonderful when you ask your subject if she recalls the rhymes she used to recite while jumping rope as a little girl or the hymns she sang in church. Probe a little here—ask about childhood games and memories, smells and tastes and sounds.

The Joy of Rituals
Simple Strategies for Strengthening Family Ties

Reading Bible stories before bedtime, sitting down to Sabbath dinner, and saying grace before each meal brings warmth and joy to many families. Now, researchers are discovering that such activities enhance child development as well.

DAWN MARIE BARHYTE

Rituals are repeated and shared activities that carry meaning and provide an emotional reward to family members. Although routines are also repetitious family behavior and vital to family life, they lack the symbolic content and compelling nature that rituals possess. Unlike rituals, routines are purely instrumental rather than symbolic; they are activities family members *have* to do rather than *want* to do.

Meg Cox, expert on rituals and author of *The Heart of a Family—Searching America for Traditions that Fulfill Us,* believes that a ritual is anything—big or small—that families perform together deliberately. She says they must be repetitious and provide some dramatic flourish that elevates the activity above the ordinary grind.

Even simple activities can be transformed into satisfying and memorable rituals, such as always singing a certain song whenever you give your child medicine, or declaring an evening study break for hot cocoa on cold winter weeknights. Cox writes, "The more we understand [rituals], the more their power will enrich our lives."

William J. Doherty, professor of family social science at the University of Minnesota, and author of *The Intentional Family* adds, "Children are natural ritualists. They crave connection and love predictability. Family rituals give children a sense of steady love and connection, and give order to their lives."

Shared Experience

Rituals are significant not so much for the act itself but for the results they yield; the sense of togetherness that grows out of shared experience and the feeling of rightness that comes from its repetition.

According to research, these repeated positive experiences form strong connections between neurons in the brain and foster a sense of security in children. They also help kids learn what to expect from their environment and how to understand the world around them.

Other studies have shown that young people who are best equipped to face the challenges of life and stay centered are those who feel close to their families. That closeness comes from the routine reassurances and shared experiences found in everyday rituals.

At one time or another, all families experience stress. Rituals have the capacity to provide stability even during trying times. Researchers have found that rituals are integral family resources that can act as a coping mechanism during those challenging moments. Professor Doherty adds that family rituals are what children can fall back on when under stress. He says that regular meals with parents provide emotional protection from every major risk factor.

Little Celebrations

When you think of family rituals, you probably picture the grand annual events such as Thanksgiving, Christmas, Hanukah, birthdays, weddings, or baby dedications. But you may want to consider adding some everyday rituals that can serve as glue that binds families together right in the midst of our harried lives. These common, often repeated happenings can become extraordinarily vital and act as a powerful buffer against this complex world. These rituals will build a bridge that connects the past to the future and allows children to pick up the torch and pass it on to the next generation.

According to Meg Cox, "Scientists tell us that many animals have rituals, and anthropologists report they haven't found any human societies without them, which alone is compelling evidence that rituals must be a human necessity."

Psychologists insist that rituals help us keep track of where we came from and essentially who we are. While this is key for all family members, it's profoundly significant for children who are forming their own identities. Rituals become a road map for kids, offering a comforting sense of predictability and order to life. When children have a clear sense of where they come from, they have a better sense of where they are going. Knowing what to do and being able to predict what comes next helps a boy or girl feel competent, and feeling competent is key to emotional well-being.

Grounded by Constancy

Children delight in rituals, look forward to them, learn from them, and feel comforted and grounded by their constancy. Positive family rituals leave indelible imprints on children's minds and form treasured memories ready to be passed on from generation to generation. For instance, knowing that every fall the family will load themselves into the minivan and go pumpkin or apple picking makes the season something to look forward to and savor.

Knowing that, each night, dad will talk to his child about his or her day and read a story at bedtime gives often-lonely children something to which they can look forward. In fact, developing a bedtime ritual is an excellent way to unwind and quietly embrace the day's happenings.

Whether it's reading a story, saying a prayer, or giving a hug and kiss, these nightly rituals offer security and comfort that fold gently into pleasant slumber.

The challenge, of course, lies in making the decision to create this time and saying no to any intrusions. With the myriad of demands on our time, it will require some effort. But the payoff will be well worth it.

Takes Work

Once you have good family rituals in place, keeping them alive takes work. If it's centered on a specific day, like Sabbath dinner, and you're not able to do it one week, don't let it slip away. Squeeze it in later in the week if you have to do so.

With some attentiveness, your family rituals will survive the demands of life and may endure for generations to come. Know that no matter what life brings, rituals will act as a safety net for your family members. Establishing your own distinctive activities now and faithfully repeating them will offer a much-needed

shelter in unsettling times. Rituals are like keepsakes that live in your heart.

Springboard for Action

If you are inspired but feel at a loss at the thought of starting your own family ritual, here are some ideas to use as a springboard for action.

- If you're like many families today and can't manage family dinners seven nights a week, try for **breakfasts together or special fruit-juice treats in the evening.** These relaxed moments of sharing nourishment and conversation provide a much-needed platform for reconnecting.

- Recognition night. A fun way to celebrate your child's achievements in the classroom or extracurricular activity is to serve an **"Honoree Dinner"** on a special plate reserved for that occasion with all the healthy foods they crave.

- Designate one night a week as **"Family Night"** created solely for family members to connect, interact, and communicate while having wholesome fun. One week you could play board games, another rent a DVD and serve popcorn, and yet another allow various family members to plan the meal and help cook it as a team.

- Hold an **"Unbirthday"** where you surprise your child by unexpectedly celebrating the fact that they exist. Include their favorite foods, a cake, and small tokens of affection.

- Create a **"Give a Helping Hand Day"** to help children cultivate altruism and focus on others less fortunate. As a family, participate in some community service like volunteering at a nursing home or soup kitchen, or collecting food for a local food pantry.

Life is hard. Rituals can help soften the edges and bring a sense of togetherness back into the lives of every family member. Why not start one today?

Freelance writer **DAWN MARIE BARHYTE** of Warwick, New York, is a stepmother of two and grandmother of six. She's a former junior volunteer coordinator at St. Anthony Community Hospital and teacher at the First Baptist Child Care Center.

Sustaining Resilient Families for Children in Primary Grades

JANICE PATTERSON AND LYNN KIRKLAND

The adversities that today's families face are well-documented and staggering (Children's Defense Fund, 2004). Even in the midst of tough times, however, many families are able to display resilience. Family resilience refers to the coping mechanisms the family uses as a functional unit to recover from life's setbacks. The purpose of this article is to provide parents and teachers with guidelines for creating resilient families, thereby helping primary-grade children withstand the challenges in their lives. In this article, we will consider what is known about family resilience, examine the role of protective factors and recovery processes, and suggest specific strategies that families and teachers can use to support resilience.

Family Resilience

Much of the work on family resilience is anchored in studies about the resilience of children. Werner and Smith (1982, 1992; Werner, 1984), authors of arguably the most important study on childhood resilience, spent 40 years studying children on the island of Kauai who were judged to be at risk of living in hardship. The children were born into poor, unskilled families, and were judged to be at risk based on their exposure before age 2 to at least four risk factors, such as serious health problems, familial alcoholism, mental illness, violence, and divorce. By age 18, about two-thirds of the children had fared poorly, as predicted by their at-risk status. The remaining one-third had developed into competent, confident, and caring young adults living productive lives, as rated on a variety of measures. In a follow-up study, the overwhelming majority of this group, now at age 40, were still living successful lives. In fact, many of them had outperformed Kauai citizens from more advantageous backgrounds. They were more likely to be stable in their marriages and fewer were unemployed. The key factors that promoted individual resilience were:

- Caring and support were provided by at least one adult who knew the child well and cared deeply about that child's well-being
- Positive expectations were articulated clearly for the child, and the support necessary to meet those expectations was provided

- Meaningful involvement and participation provided the child the opportunity to become involved in something she cared about and to contribute to the well-being of others

Although it is not impossible for an individual child from a non-resilient family to bounce back from adversity, the child's health and well-being is best supported if the family functions as a resilient unit. When a crisis upsets the life of a primary-grade child, the impact of that crisis on the child is determined largely by the extent to which the family's normal functioning is disrupted. Even when the child is not directly affected by a situation, he or she is touched by the changes in relationships that result from the changes or crises for others in the family.

As we reflect on the image of a resilient family, note how changes in society contribute to that image. Traditionally, the model of a resilient family, those who successfully navigated the ups and downs of life, was the image of a white, affluent, nuclear family led by the breadwinning father and a mother working as full-time homemaker. Enormous social changes in recent decades highlight the fact that resilient families can be non-white, upper or lower income, represent a variety of ethnic and cultural traditions, and include single parents, non-custodial parents, grandparents, stepparents, and same-gender parents. Changes in the definition of family are dynamic. In one landmark court decision supporting the rights of gay parents, the judge recognized changing definitions of "family" by acknowledging, "It is the totality of the relationship, as evidenced by the dedication, caring and self-sacrifice of the parties, which should, in the final analysis, control the definition of family" (quoted in Stacey, 1990, p. 4).

Protective and Recovery Factors

An understanding of family resilience incorporates research on *protective factors* and *recovery factors* (Cowan, Cowan, & Schultz, 1996; Garmezy & Rutter, 1983; Hawley & DeHaan, 1996; McCubbin, Thompson, Thompson, & McCubbin, 1992). Protective factors are behaviors that help give people strength in times of stress (Patterson, Patterson, & Collins, 2003). Examples of such factors include family celebrations, planned family time, consistent routines, and family traditions. In addition, family resilience can be sustained by maintaining open communication within the family and building a solid support network beyond the family.

Recovery factors refer to the family's ability to develop and use adaptation strategies when confronted with a crisis. Families can and do bounce back and adapt by changing their habits, their patterns of functioning, or the situation that has created the problem. Some evidence exists that there may be variation in the nature of the needed recovery factors, depending upon the situation. For instance, families having to deal with chronically ill children (e.g., cystic fibrosis) made use of the following strategies:

- *Family integration.* The mother's and father's optimism and efforts to keep the family together were important to the child's health.

- *Family support and esteem building.* The parents made concerted efforts to reach out to family, friends, and the larger community, thereby helping them to develop their self-esteem and self-confidence.

- *Family recreation orientation, control, and organization.* A family emphasis on active involvement in recreational and sporting activities is positively associated with improvements in the child's health. The greater the family's emphasis on control and family organization, rules, and procedures, the greater the improvement in the child's health.

- *Family optimism and mastery.* The greater the family's efforts to maintain a sense of optimism and order, the greater the improvement in the child's health. Furthering one's understanding and mastery of the health regimen necessary to promote the child's health helps the adaptation process (McCubbin & McCubbin, 1996).

During any family crisis, disruption in the daily routine exacerbates the chaos and confusion. Within the context of divorce, for instance, it is important for the family to establish and maintain routines that provide continuity of family connections, such as Sunday brunch with Dad. Research on children's positive adjustment following their parents' divorce shows that predictability and reliability of contact with the non-custodial parent is as important as the amount of contact (Hetherington & Kelly, 2002; Walsh, 1991). It is also clear that authoritative parenting, which combines warmth and control, is a significant positive protection against family stress that children may encounter (Hetherington & Kelly, 2002).

Strategies to Strengthen Family Resilience

Effective communication, including problem solving and affirmation, is a critical variable for family success in facing routine and extraordinary challenges. Contemporary lifestyles may allow little time for really listening to children, discussing their problems, and affirming their value to the family. A growing number of parents and teachers realize that communication is not something that can be left to chance; they plan for it.

One family reported on the "talk" that took place each night at the dinner table (Feiler, 2004). First, dinner was designated as a sacred time and attendance was mandatory. No television was allowed. Instead, they played a game, "Bad and Good," which began with a moderator asking each person, "What happened to you today that was bad?" Everyone had to respond; respect for others was supported by not allowing anyone to criticize, interrupt, or refute another person's bad experience. It was important that parents participated, to demonstrate that bad things happen to all of us on a daily basis and how we cope is what matters. Next, the rotating moderator asked each person, "What happened to you today that was good?" As family members reported their good stories, others affirmed them and good news begot good news. Primary-grade children in the family learned to celebrate successes. Of course, some events had both good and bad elements; as the family discussed what happened, children learned that everything doesn't fit neatly into good or bad categories. Variations on the theme might be such questions as, "What are you most afraid will happen to you?" or "If you could have one wish, what would it be?" or "What makes you feel really special?"

Problem solving can be nurtured in this context by asking everyone for thoughts on solving family problems. Our daily lives are inundated by e-mail, voice mail, computers, video games, iPods, and other diversions that can replace face-to-face communication, and so we must take conscious steps to let children know we are listening and care about them and their ideas.

These strategies are easily adapted to the classroom. Teachers routinely listen to children during community time, at meals, and in small groups, and can pose questions for all to answer. Class meetings also can provide many venues for children to discuss issues related to their lives and the lives of their families. As part of a class meeting, carefully selected articles from the newspaper can be used to initiate conversation about issues that relate to the lives of the children in the class. For example, children can consider alternative ways of dealing with problems other than those exhibited by individuals acting unlawfully within the local community. As part of routine class meetings, children utilize problems that arise throughout the day in play situations in the classroom, coming up with appropriate resolutions. For example, if a problem has arisen on the playground between children, offering the opportunity for children to defend their position, as well as hear the positions of others, helps them to consider other people and become less egocentric in their reasoning. Hearing others' perspectives encourages the moral development of the child (Piaget, 1997) and encourages flexible thinking, which builds a child's resilience, both individually and within the family.

It is also important that parents and teachers teach children how to ask for help when they need it. One of the biggest predictors of resilience in the Kauai study mentioned earlier in this article was that children knew how to ask for help. We cannot assume that every child (or adult) will, or knows how to, ask for needed help. Today's society places a high value on independent action and neglects teaching collaboration. Parents and teachers can guide children in forming questions and in practicing their help-seeking skills (e.g., "Where would you go if no one was home when you came home after school?").

Within the classroom, teachers can use the writing workshop process to help children write about issues that trouble them. For instance, one teacher found it helpful to encourage a student, from a military family about to relocate, to draft a paper about her fears of moving to a new school. Through the writing and subsequent conferencing that preceded the final draft, the teacher and parent learned that the child's greatest fear was not having someone to sit with at lunch. The parent and teacher in the new school were able to find a "lunch mate" and thus eased the transition. A variation on the writing conference is to establish dialogue journals so that the student is writing to the teacher or parent and the adult responds in writing. Some children will write about fears that are difficult to verbalize.

Another important strategy is to strive to maintain an optimistic outlook, even when the going gets rough. The family that expects to prevail in times of crisis very often will prevail. An orientation toward such hardiness is reflected in the work of Steve and Sybil Wolin, who speak of "survivor's pride"—the deep self-respect that comes from knowing you were challenged and that you prevailed. Children who grew up in families that were *not* resilient and later compared notes reported very similar family experiences, as identified below:

- We rarely celebrated holidays.
- They [parents] hardly ever came to a soccer game, a school play, or a community picnic.
- There were no regular mealtimes.
- They forgot my birthday.
- The house was a pigsty.
- No one had a good word for me; nothing I ever did was right.
- They were always fighting with each other, tearing each other apart in front of us, as if we didn't exist. (Wolin & Wolin, 1993, p. 27)

If we turn this list around, we can see the practices of resilient families for primary-grade children. They *do* celebrate holidays and attend soccer games, school plays, and community picnics as a family. They make time for regular mealtimes and birthday celebrations. The house is clean enough to be functional and pleasant. Love and affirmation are given freely and parental conflict is minimized in front of children. Within the classroom, through conversations, parent meetings, and written communication, teachers can emphasize to parents the importance of participation in these activities as resilience-building strategies.

Importance of Family Traditions and Routines

A family that promotes its own resilience with these strategies takes deliberate steps in building the resilience of the family unit for all members, including the primary-grade child.

The family values traditions, saves mementos, and tells stories about family heroes. Conducting these activities within the family promotes pride in the family heritage and also can provide a link to the present. If the family reflects on the struggles immigrant parents faced in coming to a new country and the strategies they used to survive, the current move across town takes on a different perspective. Children in resilient families see themselves as part of the family unit and take pride in finding ways to contribute to the family's strength. Effective communication and family optimism work to create a resilient family that considers itself to be healthy and is reflected in such statements as:

- We are a good family.
- Home is a safe, welcoming place.
- We have a past that is a source of strength and we have good, sound values that guide our future.
- We are known and respected in the community.
- We like each other.
- Our blood runs thick; we will always be there for one another. (Wolin & Wolin, 1993, p. 40)

Without a doubt, a variety of challenges and crises can tax even the strongest family. Such situations call for all family members to pull together and use their collective strength (all of us are stronger than one of us) to weather the challenge. An attitude of family resilience gives the family a sense of its own competence and control over the outcome.

Deliberately structuring family time and rituals is another important strategy for strengthening resilience in families. Every family has a routine, even if it is one of chaos. Resilient families take control of the routine for the purpose of establishing predictability and stability—critical elements to family balance. Although sometimes difficult to establish, this strategy can make a difference in how the child copes with new events. For instance, a 7-year-old girl was confused by where she was to go each day after school and began crying every morning, saying, "I don't know where to go today." The mother and teacher combined forces to develop a routine in which the mother sent the teacher each Monday a list of where the child was to go every day of the week. She also tucked a note in the child's lunch box that said, "Today, you go to Brownies in the gym after school." The mother used a combination of words and picture symbols to be sure the child understood the message; thus, a stabilizing routine was established.

Family Communication with Children's Literature

Family mealtimes are important venues for communication, as mentioned earlier. They also serve the function of reinforcing family routine. Spending quality time together, including just "hanging out," is important for building family resilience. Family time together does not need to involve money or extensive time commitments. Playing board games or reading together can provide routine and meaning to family relationships.

Children's literature can be used at home or as part of classroom curricula to initiate caring and conversation related to issues that children and families face. When parents and teachers sit and read with children, caring for that child is reinforced and the child feels valued. Discussions of book characters and plots provide meaningful and relevant ways for children to consider the lives of others and begin to look at ways of dealing with problems they face. Resilience in children is promoted through time spent with a caring adult and their participation in retellings and creative dramatizations of story plots.

Table 1 lists examples of good books that promote resilience in primary-grade children. These books were selected because they address, either directly or indirectly, elements of resilience or strategies for strengthening the skills of resilience. For instance, in *Wemberly Worried* (2000), Henkes writes of Wemberly, the little mouse, who worries about everything, especially her first day of school. As Wemberly struggles not to worry, she taps into some basic resilience-building strategies (e.g., telling adults you're worried, finding a friend to share your worries, and building on your strengths by successfully navigating the first day of school and returning for another day). In Faith Ringgold's *Tar Beach* (1991), Cassie Louise Lightfoot, an African American 8-year-old growing up in Harlem in 1939, demonstrates how believing good things will happen and drawing on the love of friends and family can promote a feeling of pride. Critical elements in building resilience include a belief in a positive future and support from a loving community.

Another example of the power of these books is drawn from *Amazing Grace* (Hoffman, 1991). Grace is an African American girl who loves stories and regularly adopts the roles and identities of strong, problem-solving characters, such as Joan of Arc, Hiawatha, and Anansi the Spider, in the plays she writes herself. Grace's grandmother takes her to see a famous black ballerina to encourage her to do "anything she can imagine." That role model encourages Grace to work hard and ultimately achieve her dream of performing the role of Peter Pan in the class play. Grace demonstrates problem-solving skills, emulates successful positive role models, and maintains perseverance—all foundational traits in building resilience.

The literature on individual and family resilience underscores the importance of building strategies to secure a network of social support. Such support begins with a loving relationship between one child and one adult (generally, a parent). Family therapists have likened the resilient family to open systems with clear, yet permeable boundaries, similar to a living cell (Beavers & Hampson, 1993; Satir, 1988; Walsh, 1998a; Whitaker & Keith, 1981).

Boundaries are important for the child and an authoritative parent earns the respect that comes from predictability; "no" means no. Inconsistent reinforcement of family rules undermines trust within the family and is not healthy. In fact, Hetherington and Kelly (2002, p. 130), in their studies of divorcing families, reported that "children of authoritative parents emerged from divorce as the most socially responsible, least troubled and highest-achieving children." Parents building resilient families ask their children for help in maintaining the household.

Examples include setting the table, mowing the lawn, washing dishes, and caring for a younger sibling, all of which can contribute to the resilience, maturity, and competency of a child. Age-appropriate chores are an important aspect of building children's resilience and sense of self-worth.

Family and Community

Resilient families have strength and integrity in their interactions within the family and also know when to reach outside the family circle for satisfying relationships. In an ideal world, the family of a primary-grade child is actively engaged in the broader community and relates to the community and each other with hope and optimism. Family members go out into the community and bring strength and new learnings back into the family circle.

There is a practical element to having relationships outside the family. Other connections can provide information, concrete services, support, companionship, and even respite from difficult situations. A family's sense of security can be enhanced by meaningful relationships with others. Community activities, including involvement in school and extracurricular activities, foster family well-being. Regular participation in sports leagues, faith-based activities, and parent-teacher organizations can bolster protective and recovery processes for the family. Research suggests that there is a highly protective element in belonging to a group and having regular social activity. This is particularly true for those in isolation and depression (Walsh, 1998b).

Because extended family is too often far away or unavailable for other reasons, it is important that families establish connections to meet their life circumstances. In the armed forces, families regularly share meals and child care in support of each other. Some families turn to older people in the community to provide "family" contact and meaningful activities with children at home or school. Both children and elders benefit in these situations. Also, multifamily groups band together in other ways to support single parents or families coping with a chronic illness, and such support can be vital in managing chronic stress or crises.

Conclusion

In this article, we have presented guidelines for creating and sustaining resilient families for primary-grade children and offered strategies for developing effective communication and building an attitude of family hardiness or resilience. We suggested promoting the value of family time, authoritative parenting, routine, and the importance of social support. We offer this work with the caveat that family resilience is an emerging field and we have only touched the surface.

Yet, our research and conversations with teachers, parents, and other child care providers have convinced us that teachers can take particular steps to support children and their families. Work with school administrators to develop sessions for parents on building family resilience during the critical primary-grade years. Invite children to talk about their experiences and say

Table 1   Resilience-Building Books for Primary-Grade Children

Andreae, G. (1999). *Giraffes can't dance.* New York: Orchard Books.

Bottner, B. (1992). *Bootsie Barker bites.* New York: G. P. Putnam Sons.

Bradby, M. (1995). *More than anything else.* New York: Orchard Books.

Brimner, L. D. (2002). *The littlest wolf.* New York: HarperCollins.

Burningham, J. (1987). *John Patrick Norman McHennessy—The boy who was always late.* New York: The Trumpet Club.

Burton, V. L. (1943). *Katy and the big snow.* Boston: Houghton Mifflin.

Cannon, J. (1993). *Stellaluna.* Orlando, FL: Harcourt Brace & Company.

Cannon, J. (2000). *Crickwing.* San Diego, CA: Harcourt.

Carle, E. (1999). *The very clumsy click beetle.* New York: Philomel Books.

Clifton, L. (1983). *Everett Anderson's goodbye.* New York: Henry Holt and Company.

Couric, K. (2000). *The brand new kid.* New York: Doubleday.

Giovanni, N. (2005). *Rosa.* New York: Henry Holt & Co.

Havill, J. (1995). *Jamaica's blue marker.* New York: Houghton Mifflin.

Heard, G. (2002). *This place I know: Poems of comfort.* Cambridge, MA: Candlewick Press.

Henkes, K. (2000). *Wemberly worried.* Hong Kong: Greenwillow Books.

Hoffman, M. (1991). *Amazing Grace.* Boston: Houghton Mifflin.

Juster, N. (2005). *The hello, goodbye window.* New York: Hyperion Books for Children.

Kraus, R. (1971). *Leo, the late bloomer.* New York: Windmill Books.

Kroll, V. (1997). *Butterfly boy.* Honesdale, PA: Boyds Mills Press.

Lester, H. (1999). *Hooway for Wodney Wat.* New York: Scholastic Books.

Lithgow, J. (2000). *The remarkable Farkle McBride.* New York: Simon & Schuster.

McKissack, P. (1986). *Flossie and the fox.* New York: Scholastic Books.

Mora, P. (2005). *Doña Flor: A tall tale about a giant woman with a great big heart.* New York: Alfred A. Knopf.

Moss, S. (1995). *Peter's painting.* Greenvale, NY: MONDO Publishing.

Piper, W. (1986). *The little engine that could.* New York: Platt & Munk.

Puttock, S. (2001). *A story for hippo: A book about loss.* New York: Scholastic Press.

Ringgold, F. (1991). *Tar beach.* New York: Scholastic Books.

Salley, C. (2002). *Epossumondas.* San Diego, CA: Harcourt.

Seskin, S., & Shamblin, A. (2002). *Don't laugh at me.* Berkeley, CA: Tricycle Press.

Taback, S. (1999). *Joseph had a little overcoat.* New York: Scholastic.

Tafuri, N. (2000). *Will you be my friend?* New York: Scholastic.

Tompert, A. (1993). *Just a little bit.* Boston: Houghton Mifflin.

Wyeth, S. D. (1998). *Something beautiful.* New York: Dragonfly Books.

---

what they believe makes them "bounce back" when bad things happen. Get parents and others involved by creating informational programs and materials about the importance of family resilience. Together, we must do all we can to help families and their children develop and nourish their resilience.

References

Beavers, W. R., & Hampson, R. B. (1990). *Successful families: Assessment and intervention.* New York: Norton.

Children's Defense Fund. (2004). *The state of America's children 2004: A continuing portrait of inequality fifty years after Brown v. Board of Education.* Retrieved August 14, 2004, from www.childrensdefense.org/pressreleases/040713.asp

Cowan, P. A., Cowan, C. P., & Schulz, M. S. (1996). Thinking about risk and resilience in families. In M. Hetherington & E. A. Blechman (Eds.), *Stress, coping and resilience in children and families.* Mahwah, NJ: Erlbaum.

Feiler, B. (2004, August 15). A game that gets parents and kids talking. *Parade.*

Garmezy, N., & Rutter, M. (Eds.). (1983). *Stress, coping and development in children.* New York: McGraw-Hill.

Hawley, D. R., & DeHaan, L. (1996). Toward a definition of family resilience: Integrating life-span and family perspectives. *Family Process, 35,* 283–298.

Hetherington, E., & Kelly, J. (2002). *For better or for worse: Divorce reconsidered.* New York: W. W. Norton & Co.

McCubbin, H. I., & McCubbin, M. A. (1996). Resilient families, competencies, supports and coping over the life cycle. In L. Sawyers (Ed.), *Faith and families.* Philadelphia: Geneva Press.

McCubbin, H. I., Thompson, E. A., Thompson, A. I., & McCubbin, M. A. (1992). Family schema, paradigms, and paradigm shifts: Components and processes of appraisal in family adaptation to crises. In A. P. Turnbull, J. M. Patterson, S. K. Bahr, D. L. Murphy, J. Marquis, & M. Blue-Banning (Eds.), *Cognitive coping research in developmental disabilities.* Baltimore: Paul H. Brookes.

Patterson, J. L., Patterson, J. H., & Collins, L. (2002). *Bouncing back: How your school can succeed in the face of adversity.* Larchmont, NY: Eye on Education Press.

Piaget, J. (1997). *The moral judgment of the child.* New York: Simon & Schuster.

Satir, V. (1988). *Within our reach: Breaking the cycle of disadvantage.* New York: Anchor.

Stacey, J. (1990). *Brave new families: Stories of domestic upheaval in late twentieth century America.* New York: Basic Books.

Walsh, F. (1991). Promoting healthy functioning in divorced and remarried families. In A. Gurman & D. Kniskern (Eds.), *Handbook of family therapy.* New York: Brunner/Mazel.

Walsh, F. (1998a). *Strengthening family resilience.* New York: The Guilford Press.

Walsh, F. (1998b). Families in later life: Challenges and opportunities. In B. Carter & M. McGoldrick (Eds.), *The expanded family life cycle.* Needham Heights, MA: Allyn & Bacon.

Werner, E. (1984). Resilient children. *Young Children, 68*(72).

Werner, E. E., & Smith, R. S. (1982). *Vulnerable but invincible: A longitudinal study of resilient children and youth.* New York: Adams, Bannister, Cox.

Werner, E. E., & Smith, R. S. (1992). *Overcoming the odds: High risk children from birth to adulthood.* New York: Cornell University Press.

Whitaker, C., & Keith, D. (1981). Symbolic-experiential family therapy. In A. S. Gurman & D. Kniskern (Eds.), *Handbook of family therapy.* New York: Brunner/Mazel.

Wolin, S., & Wolin, S. (1993). *The resilient self: How survivors of troubled families rise above adversity.* New York: Villard.

JANICE PATTERSON is Associate Professor, Education Department, and **LYNN KIRKLAND** is Associate Professor, Education Department, University of Alabama-Birmingham.

From *Childhood Education,* Fall 2007, pp. 2–7. Copyright © 2007 by the Association for Childhood Education International. Reprinted by permission of Janice Patterson & Lynn Kirkland and the Association for Childhood Education International, 17904 Georgia Avenue, Suite 215, Olney, MD 20832.

The Consumer Crunch

Recession or not, American families will be forced to tighten their belts.

MICHAEL MANDEL

The long-awaited, long-feared consumer crunch may finally be here. That might not mean an economywide recession, but the pain for American households will be deep. In recent years the U.S. mostly has seen narrowly focused downturns, where a few sectors are hit hard while the rest of the economy and financial markets remain relatively unscathed. In the dot-com bust of 2001, for example, tech companies and stocks took it on the chin, while consumer spending and borrowing sailed through without a pause. This time the positions will be reversed, as consumers tank while much of the corporate sector stays on track. It's been a glorious run for the consumer. In the past 25 years, Americans have kept shopping through good times and bad. In every quarter except one since 1981, consumer spending rose over the previous year, adjusted for inflation. The exception was the first quarter of 1991, and even then the decrease was a mild 0.4% dip. The main fuel for the spending was easy access to credit. Banks and other financial institutions were willing to lend households ever increasing amounts of money. Any particular individual might default, but in the aggregate, loans to consumers were viewed as low-risk and profitable.

The subprime crisis, however, marks the beginning of the end for the long consumer borrow-and-buy boom. The financial sector, wrestling with hundreds of billions in losses, can no longer treat consumers as a safe bet. Already, standards for real estate lending have been raised, including those for jumbo mortgages for high-end houses. Credit cards are still widely available, but it may only be a matter of time before issuers get tougher.

What comes next could be scary—the largest pullback in consumer spending in decades, perhaps as much as $200 billion to $300 billion, or 2%–3% of personal income. Reduced access to credit will combine with falling real estate values to hit poor and rich alike. "We're in uncharted territory," says David Rosenberg, chief North American economist at Merrill Lynch, who's forecasting a mild drop in consumer spending in the first half of 2008. "It's pretty rare we go through such a pronounced tightening in credit standards."

Don't expect the spending to come to a screeching halt, however. Remember the stock market peak in early 2000? It wasn't until a year later that tech spending fell off the cliff and the sector didn't hit bottom until 2003. The same delayed impact holds true here. The latest retail sales numbers, which showed a soft 0.2% gain in October, suggest that spending may hold up through this holiday season.

Next year, though, will be much tougher. The consumer slump may be deep and long-lasting, and the political implications could be enormous. "There's growing evidence that the economy will become a dominant, if not the dominant issue of 2008," says independent pollster John Zogby. "It's even to the point where the numbers of people who say Iraq is the No. 1 issue are starting to decline."

Wide-Open Credit Window

Truth is, economists have been complaining about excessive borrowing and spending since the early 1980s. Journalists began writing about consumers being "tapped out," "profligate," and "spendthrift." Magazines and newspapers regularly ran stories about debt-ridden Americans not being able to buy holiday presents for their kids.

But no matter how many times economists predicted the demise of the consumer, the spending continued. The latest data from the Bureau of Economic Analysis show that the personal savings rate—the share of income left after consumption—fell from 12% in 1981 to just over zero today. And debt service, which is the share of income going to principal and interest on debt, kept rising. Those numbers aren't dead-on accurate: The data has been revised endlessly, and the BEA includes outlays on higher education as consumption rather than saving, which would seem odd to families who have socked away thousands of dollars for college.

But the story line is clear. Consumers' outlays have outpaced the growth of their income for a long time. Lenders learned how to judge risk and expand the pool of potential borrowers—and the party was on. "The most important factor has been that it is easier to borrow," says Christopher D. Carroll, a Johns Hopkins University economist.

The subprime crisis marks the beginning of the end for the long borrow-and-buy boom. Banks can no longer treat consumers as a safe bet.

While many companies struggled in the 2001 recession and afterward, American consumers just kept borrowing. "In 2001–02, the credit window was open for anyone who had a pulse," says Merrill's Rosenberg.

Fewer Trips to the Mall?

Not this time, though. "The consumer is retrenching, big-time," says Richard Hastings, economic adviser to the Federation of Credit & Financial Professionals. "It's starting to get to the point where people are achieving levels of debt that are getting uncomfortable."

The question, though, is just how much consumers will restrain their free-spending ways. Research by economist Carroll suggests that every $1 decline in house prices lops about 9¢ off of spending. The current value of residential housing is about $21 trillion, according to the Federal Reserve. So if home prices fall by 10%, as many people expect, that would lead to roughly a $200 billion hit to spending over the next couple of years. A 15% tumble in home prices would produce a $300 billion pullback in spending, or about 3% of personal income.

That accords well with calculations by BEA economists. They figure that households took out $340 billion in cash from mortgage and home-equity financing in 2006. That source of funding could largely disappear over the next couple of years.

Three percent—that doesn't sound like a lot. Look a little closer, though, and it's a bigger hit than it seems. The reason is that much of what the government counts as consumer spending is not directly controlled by households. For example, the $1.7 trillion in medical costs is counted as consumer spending, but 85% of that is spent by the government and health insurers, not individuals. And $1.5 trillion in "housing services" is listed as part of consumer spending, but for homeowners it really just represents the value of living in a home rather than any spending they can change. It's mainly a bookkeeping convention, not a real outlay.

A big pullback in spending may not lead to a recession. These days when Americans buy fewer clothes, the pain is felt overseas.

So that 2%–3% decline in income directly hits the wallet and the discretionary purchases that households actually control. One logical place for cutbacks is apparel. Autos will be hit. Another target could be luxury items, a surprisingly big part of discretionary spending. Pamela N. Danziger, president of Unity Marketing in Stevens, Pa., conducts a quarterly online survey of adults earning $75,000 a year and up. She found that people who make more than $150,000 have been unaffected, but the rest are cutting back on luxury goods such as fashion accessories. "They are taking a very cautious attitude," says Danziger.

A Lift from Exports

Will the consumer crunch spread to the rest of the economy? Conventional wisdom is that consumer spending makes up 70% of gross domestic product. While technically true, that figure is deceptive, because so much of what Americans buy these days is made overseas. Compared with the early 1980s, which was the last time consumers cut back, much more of what Americans buy is made abroad. Today, imports of consumer goods and autos run about $740 billion a year. That's fully one-third of consumer spending on goods outside of food and energy. As a result, most of the spending cutbacks won't cost Americans their factory jobs—those factory jobs have mostly fled offshore anyway. Workshop China, in contrast, will get hurt.

What's more, it's still a low-rate world for most nonfinancial corporations, which have access to relatively cheap funds for expansion and capital investment. Asia and Europe are continuing to expand, with German and French growth accelerating in the third quarter. Exports of aircraft and other big items are likely to rise, too, supplying the U.S. economy with an extra lift. In other words, globalization has made consumers less central to the American economy.

Still, the consumer recession will hit some parts of the economy harder than others. Particularly at risk are retailers, who have already seen sharp declines in their stock prices since the extent of the subprime crisis became clear. Nordstrom shares, for example, fell from 52 in September to as low as 32 before rebounding. On Nov. 14, Macy's cut its sales forecast for the fourth quarter, sending its stock down to $28 a share from $43 in July. "Retailers are looking to pare inventories," says Rosenberg.

Not everyone thinks American shoppers are tapped out. Consumers have about $4 trillion in unused borrowing capacity on their credit cards, enough to keep spending afloat, points out Stuart A. Feldstein, president of SMR Research in Hackettstown, N.J., which studies consumer loan markets.

But executives from Capital One Financial, Bank of America, Discover Card, Washington Mutual, and others have told investors in recent conference calls that they are using more caution in extending credit. Chief Financial Officer Gary L. Perlin of Capital One, the nation's No. 5 card issuer, says he believes last year's historically low defaults by credit-card holders were partly driven by the real estate boom, particularly in previously hot housing markets such as Arizona, California, and Florida. Those benefits also have seemed to run out. As a result, says Perlin, Capital One is tightening lending standards and limiting credit lines.

More rate cuts by the Fed can cushion the impact of the consumer cutbacks but not avert them altogether. It's best to think of this as the end of a long-term spending and borrowing bubble, where the role of policy is to keep the inevitable adjustment from turning into panic. "The Fed's job is to keep us all calm and reasoned," says Carroll.

Everyone now seems to be coming up with remedies. At a Nov. 8 congressional hearing, Fed Chairman Ben Bernanke suggested legislation that would temporarily add liquidity to the jumbo loan market. And the possibility of a consumer slump already has Presidential candidates and their staffs looking ahead. "Potentially, the next subprime crisis is the issue of credit-card debt," says Austan D. Goolsbee, economic adviser to Democratic hopeful Barack Obama and a professor at the University of Chicago Graduate School of Business. The Illinois senator's view, says Goolsbee, is that the U.S. needs to improve oversight in the credit-card market. Republican candidate Mitt Romney suggests eliminating taxes on savings and investment by low- and middle-class families, a move that could help make up for a tougher credit environment.

The politicians can say what they want. Recession or no, Americans had better get ready to tighten their belts.

With Peter Coy in New York and Dawn Kopecki and Jane Saseen in Washington.

Sparking Interest in Nature— Family Style

DONNA J. SATTERLEE AND GRACE D. CORMONS

"Daddy, come and look! There's a lizard on Tsara's jeans." Luís and his family are exploring the woods on a typical Family Learning/ Family Fun (FLFF) Day with the SPARK program. SPARK (Shore People Advancing Readiness for Knowledge) is a nature-based program designed to advance literacy and environmental knowledge in a rural Virginia county that has long been combating generational poverty and low literacy.

SPARK engages children between the ages of 3 and 7 and their families in nature learning. The program is a collaboration between the Adult Education Program at Eastern Shore Community College in Melfa, Virginia, and the Accomack County Schools, with support funds from Even Start and Title 1.

The SPARK program has grown from serving 25 families in 1998 to involving more than 200 today from a broad range of ethnic, economic, and educational backgrounds. Its purpose is to encourage and teach parents how to become involved in their children's education. To achieve this goal, we provide experiential learning activities by using nature as an outdoor classroom and the main learning theme.

How the Program Works

Principals at various schools encourage children and families to participate in the program. They invite SPARK staff to recruit at PTA and open house meetings and to set up SPARK bulletin boards. Teachers send home enrollment forms with pre-K and kindergarten students. Many teachers enroll their own children when they see that SPARK opens a whole new world for participating families. Parents and children spend more quality time together as they are introduced to new topics to learn about and new places to go, and to having fun.

Program participants receive weekly packets of reader-friendly, nature-oriented materials. Ideally, SPARK instructors explain the packets individually to participating parents (or grandparents, aunts, uncles), who pick up the materials at the elementary schools or, in some cases, their workplaces.

Typical packets may include live pussy willow branches and directions for rooting, a lesson on leaf identification and counting, or phonemic awareness activities using an alphabet series based on wildlife found on the Eastern Shore of Virginia. The program encourages parents to set aside time once a week to relax and enjoy doing SPARK activities with their children. The packet activities encourage the families to explore outdoors and document what they see.

The SPARK program is constantly evolving because of its focus on nature, which is ever changing.

The learning packets introduce families and children to new concepts and information relevant to the nature studies in upcoming outdoor trips, called FLFF Days. These outings are held two Saturdays and one Sunday per month. Families visit different ecosystems on Virginia's Eastern Shore. For some outings we use school buses, and for others families get there on their own.

SPARK Kids books are an important program resource. They feature photos of the families currently involved in the program during FLFF Day outings.

SPARK staff write one new book each year to record the nature field study trips. The books capture the story of families' discoveries and learning through easy-to-read captions and on-site photos. Eight different books exist to date and are enthusiastically used as learning tools by SPARK families, the Accomack County schools, and the general public.

Like the learning packets, the books are written in vocabulary-enhancing text that describes the photos in succinct, simple wording. Bilingual (Spanish and English) books and packets are used by speakers of Spanish to learn English and by speakers of English to learn Spanish.

Photo Books Are Preparatory Resources

The SPARK Kids photo books, along with the weekly packets, provide background information about the program's planned activities. For example, after reading "SPARK Kids in the Woods," we take the families on a hike through a local woodland, where they find many of the plants and animals described and illustrated in the book: daddy longlegs, lizards, squirrels, and woodpeckers, along with a variety of fall foliage, lichens on trees, or conical ant lion pits in sandy, sunny spots.

As part of the learning experience, the children and adults collect various natural items that we help them learn to identify before using in a follow-up art project. We often enhance the nature-based learning with relevant children's literature. For example, preceding a woods walk, the leader reads to the children *The Teddy Bears' Picnic,* by Jimmy Kennedy. During the walk the children miraculously discover teddy bears (thanks to our magical preplacement) having a picnic in the woods!

Another time we visit a marsh after an introductory reading of the "SPARK Kids in the Marsh" book and the families' preview of their resource packets. Together with the families we look for the fiddler crabs, periwinkles, marsh grass, mussels, and egrets that are shown in the book. The children catch killifish in small nets.

A favorite destination each spring is Sparky's farm. Families observe trees budding, geese nesting, and other spring events. The children can feed the chickens, hold a chick, pet a rabbit, milk a goat or cow, ride a horse, and get to know many of the other farm animals. In addition they may hunt for arthropods in the farm's fields, after seeing and reading about them in "SPARK Kids Find Arthropods." At the end of the day on the farm, families learn about echoes when they "meet" (hear) Echo in the woods.

Nature—An Ever-Evolving Program

The SPARK program is constantly evolving because of its focus on nature, which is ever changing. We continually adjust the materials according to what is happening at the time, often writing new text on the spot. For example, one fall there were many large, very hairy woolly bear caterpillars, and we wrote a woolly bear story and accompanying activity sheets. This is one way we keep the spark in SPARK.

We often enhance the nature-based learning with relevant children's literature.

Learning Skills and Having Fun

Another important facet of the program is exposing families to planning and organizational skills that they can use to be more effectively and efficiently involved in their children's education. To this end, we include date reminders in the packets and follow up with phone calls just before events. We provide a monthly events calendar as well as frequent newsletters for families. Our program planning emphasizes to the children and the adults that they need to prepare for trips by wearing suitable clothing, which usually means clothes they do not mind getting dirty.

Sparky the Blue Crab, our cartoon mascot, contributes to the success of the program. The blue crab is closely identified with Virginia's Eastern Shore. Sparky appears in the SPARK books and on stickers, T-shirts, flyers, materials packets, the events calendar, and the banner we use to welcome families to the program. The children love Sparky and often mimic him as he reads, asks questions, and investigates. Sparky helps to create a clublike atmosphere, giving a sense of belonging to all involved. As program incentives, participants receive Sparky stickers for completing activities in their packets and Sparky T-shirts for frequent attendance.

Trusting Staff and Program Quality

Another important program aspect is the trust and confidence families develop toward staff and the program activities. They count on us to interpret messages from the schools, lend a book, answer nature questions

Starting a Family Nature Program

Creating the Program

- Find an individual dedicated to child and adult learning, who is knowledgeable of natural history, enthusiastic about implementing a program, and prepared to try various ways to make it work.
- Locate a reliable assistant who shares a like passion for nature and learning.
- Have a mission/philosophy/goal and a name. Choose something that will identify the group and help create a club atmosphere. Identify an appropriate animal mascot for your area, such as a lizard for the desert, and find an artist who can draw it in a way that is appealing to children.
- Decide which is appropriate: to write your own curriculum or purchase a published nature-based curriculum.
- Get to know well the natural environment in your area, locating good places to explore with families. Remember, even small city parks offer many interesting plants and animals; children are fascinated with insects and tiny flowers; pigeons and sparrows can teach valuable lessons in natural history.
- Arrange for a place to meet families and distribute materials, for example, a preschool or Head Start center, public school, church, workplace, or library.
- Begin with program activities that take advantage of the best time of the year for doing things outdoors—in most areas, spring and fall.
- Find funding. Much can be done with volunteers, a copy machine, and an attitude that it is fun to "make do" with what is at hand. Local service clubs may donate funds, and individuals in the community may contribute to your program, especially if you ask for support for a particular trip or to put together a book. Check https://grants.gov for grants, or contact your local Community Foundation.

- Consider collaborative agreements with the school district for providing a parent-school connection. Check out adult education programs. Try the county Extension agency or other existing organizations in your community. Asking and networking often will solve a problem.
- Obtain transportation if needed by writing grants, connecting with the school for buses, car pooling, or using public or private transportation.

Leading the Sessions

- Get permission slips, release forms, and emergency contact numbers for everyone involved, including staff.
- Meet with adults in person to explain the weekly materials, which they then use with their children.
- Model healthful living. Include exercise as part of the program—taking a walk, for example, is essential for looking at things. Provide nutritious snacks.
- Take photos on Family Learning/Family Fun days to give to participants, use in a newsletter, send to the local paper, or put together to create resource books.

Working with Families

- Start small, ideally with 20 to 25 families you know well, who trust you and will bring others into the program.
- Involve parents, both physically and mentally, in all aspects of the program. Emphasize that it is a family program, not just for children. Require parents or other family adults to attend outings with the children.
- Communicate regularly with participants. Keep adults involved, interested, and connected through phone calls or e-mails that help all families stay in the loop.
- Respect parents and anticipate their possible reactions to materials (as "hard to read" and so on) or to field trips (like "Will we get dirty?" and so on).

thoroughly and carefully, or rescue a bird from a crab trap. To foster trust building, SPARK staff plan activities in advance. The result is that families are comfortable doing things they have never done before, such as wading through waist-deep water to reach an island or trudging through smelly mud to observe fiddler crabs. We are always amazed at how willingly and thoroughly our family participants immerse themselves (often literally!) in the activities.

One especially pleasing program outcome is the unusually high rate of participation by fathers. We believe that this is likely due to the outdoor focus of the program and having a male staff member who often leads FLFF Day events and makes fathers feel welcome.

> **Families are comfortable doing things they have never done before, such as wading through waist-deep water to reach an island or trudging through smelly mud to observe fiddler crabs.**

Conclusion

Children, adults, and families, from a variety of backgrounds, find nature fascinating. Because most people don't know very much about nature, everyone is on a level playing field. The exposure to something new and interesting serves as a common denominator that brings

Nature Activities for Families

Nature occurs almost anywhere. There are many ways families can explore nature. Start by sampling some of the following:

1. Find wildflowers and insects along roadsides, on lawns, and in local parks. Through car, bus, and train windows, watch for birds flying high in the sky or perching on telephone wires. On neighborhood walks, spy birds in trees, shrubs, and on lawns around houses. Playgrounds are good places for observing nature too.

2. Choose an object in nature that you regularly see (like a tree or a cactus) and start a back-and-forth family exchange of observations on its size, structure, movement, color, texture, and so on. Use all five senses to study natural objects. Don't forget to smell and touch, and if you know something is safe (like a wild blackberry), taste it. Draw and photograph your chosen subject at different seasons and as it grows. Compare photos to identify changes you notice. Study your subject in relation to other similar things in nature that you see, and discuss similarities and differences.

3. Visit a nature preserve. Find out (from friends or on the Internet) the names of nearby state parks or a national park or wildlife refuge you can visit as a family.

4. Learn about local organizations such as a bird club or find an active member of the community who can help you discover nature. Check your local library for publications from groups like the National Wildlife Federation and the National Audubon Society or visit the websites of The Nature Conservancy or other organizations.

5. Try some simple experiments like the following: fill up a large, clear plastic jar with rain or pond water and see how it changes each week. First, you may see green algae growing on the inside of the jar, and then you may discover tiny mosquito larvae wriggling around in the water. They will grow and change (you can cover the top of the jar with a piece of old panty hose to keep adult mosquitoes from exiting and biting anyone!).

6. Look around and use your imagination to find meaningful things to observe, learn from, and share with children. You might share what you did by writing about it in your local newspaper, neighborhood Listserv, or a school or nature organization newsletter.

7. Examine the weeds in a vacant lot, a small edge of woods, a yard with trees, a public park, a log or rock to look under, an overlooked corner of a school yard, a stream/creek/pond or somewhere where there is water occasionally and that is safe. Any places where small creatures and plants can live offer lessons waiting to be learned.

8. Grow things yourselves. For example, plant the seeds from apples and oranges in pots.

---

everyone together. Watching program participants easily establishing a cooperative and amiable network among themselves and with one another's children is rewarding.

Exposure to something new and interesting serves as a common denominator that brings everyone together.

We value our staff, who include individuals with knowledge and understanding of early childhood development. They model effective parenting behavior, including positive interactions and investigative behaviors, and they expertly use the natural environment. These aspects contribute to a successful program and support the SPARK philosophy that "learning is fun."

Last, there is a very positive, important corollary to the SPARK program that is part of the plan: families can learn to become good stewards of the environment, helping to assure the very survival of our planet in the future.

DONNA J. SATTERLEE, MED, is a full-time lecturer with the Department of Human Ecology at the University of Maryland Eastern Shore in Princess Anne, Maryland, and a child development specialist at the Eastern Shore Community College in Melfa, Virginia. She has 18 years experience as an educator focusing on experiential learning. djsatterlee@umes.edu **GRACE D. CORMONS,** BA, is the family learning instructor at Virginia's Eastern Shore Community College. Grace started teaching children and adults about nature at the American Museum of Natural History in New York City. She originated the SPARK program and gives presentations at national conferences. gcormons@es.vscc.edu

Test-Your-Knowledge Form

We encourage you to photocopy and use this page as a tool to assess how the articles in *Annual Editions* expand on the information in your textbook. By reflecting on the articles you will gain enhanced text information. You can also access this useful form on a product's book support website at *http://www.mhcls.com*.

NAME: DATE:
_____

TITLE AND NUMBER OF ARTICLE:
_____

BRIEFLY STATE THE MAIN IDEA OF THIS ARTICLE:

_____

LIST THREE IMPORTANT FACTS THAT THE AUTHOR USES TO SUPPORT THE MAIN IDEA:

_____

WHAT INFORMATION OR IDEAS DISCUSSED IN THIS ARTICLE ARE ALSO DISCUSSED IN YOUR TEXTBOOK OR OTHER READINGS THAT YOU HAVE DONE? LIST THE TEXTBOOK CHAPTERS AND PAGE NUMBERS:

_____

LIST ANY EXAMPLES OF BIAS OR FAULTY REASONING THAT YOU FOUND IN THE ARTICLE:

_____

LIST ANY NEW TERMS/CONCEPTS THAT WERE DISCUSSED IN THE ARTICLE, AND WRITE A SHORT DEFINITION:

We Want Your Advice

ANNUAL EDITIONS revisions depend on two major opinion sources: one is our Advisory Board, listed in the front of this volume, which works with us in scanning the thousands of articles published in the public press each year; the other is you—the person actually using the book. Please help us and the users of the next edition by completing the prepaid article rating form on this page and returning it to us. Thank you for your help!

ANNUAL EDITIONS: The Family 10/11

ARTICLE RATING FORM

Here is an opportunity for you to have direct input into the next revision of this volume.
We would like you to rate each of the articles listed below, using the following scale:

1. **Excellent: should definitely be retained**
2. **Above average: should probably be retained**
3. **Below average: should probably be deleted**
4. **Poor: should definitely be deleted**

Your ratings will play a vital part in the next revision.
Please mail this prepaid form to us as soon as possible.
Thanks for your help!

RATING	ARTICLE	RATING	ARTICLE
	1. Marriage and Family in the Scandinavian Experience		26. Children of Alcoholics
	2. Interracial Families		27. Impact of Family Recovery and Pre-Teens and Adolescents
	3. Children as a Public Good		28. My Cheatin' Heart
	4. Family Partnerships		29. Love but Don't Touch
	5. This Thing Called Love		30. Is This Man Cheating on His Wife?
	6. Pillow Talk		31. The Opt-Out Myth
	7. 24 Things Love and Sex Experts Are Dying to Tell You		32. Making Time for Family Time
	8. On-Again, Off-Again		33. Partners Face Cancer Together
	9. Fats, Carbs and the Science of Conception		34. Dealing Day-to-Day with Diabetes: A Whole Family Experience
	10. Starting the Good Life in the Womb		35. Navigating Practical Dilemmas in Terminal Care
	11. Not Always 'the Happiest Time'		36. Bereavement after Caregiving
	12. Adopting a New American Family		37. Love, Loss—and Love
	13. Free as a Bird and Loving It		38. Stressors Afflicting Families during Military Deployment
	14. Gay Marriage Lite		39. Children of the Wars
	15. Two Mommies and a Daddy		40. A Divided House
	16. Good Parents, Bad Results		41. Civil Wars
	17. Do We Need a Law to Prohibit Spanking?		42. Stepfamily Success Depends on Ingredients
	18. Children of Lesbian and Gay Parents		43. Get a Closer Look
	19. Prickly Père		44. The Joy of Rituals
	20. The Forgotten Siblings		45. Sustaining Resilient Families for Children in Primary Grades
	21. Being a Sibling		46. The Consumer Crunch
	22. Aunties and Uncles		47. Sparking Interest in Nature— Family Style
	23. Roles of American Indian Grandparents in Times of Cultural Crisis		
	24. Recognizing Domestic Partner Abuse		
	25. Domestic Abuse Myths		

BUSINESS REPLY MAIL
FIRST CLASS MAIL PERMIT NO. 551 DUBUQUE IA

POSTAGE WILL BE PAID BY ADDRESSEE

McGraw-Hill Contemporary Learning Series
501 BELL STREET
DUBUQUE, IA 52001

ABOUT YOU

Name

Date

Are you a teacher? ❑ A student? ❑
Your school's name

Department

Address   City   State   Zip

School telephone #

YOUR COMMENTS ARE IMPORTANT TO US!

Please fill in the following information:
For which course did you use this book?

Did you use a text with this ANNUAL EDITION? ❑ yes ❑ no
What was the title of the text?

What are your general reactions to the Annual Editions concept?

Have you read any pertinent articles recently that you think should be included in the next edition? Explain.

Are there any articles that you feel should be replaced in the next edition? Why?

Are there any World Wide Websites that you feel should be included in the next edition? Please annotate.

May we contact you for editorial input? ❑ yes ❑ no
May we quote your comments? ❑ yes ❑ no

NOTES

NOTES

NOTES

NOTES

NOTES

NOTES

NOTES

NOTES